The Derivatives Game

by Nigel Foster

Dedication

To my family, especially my daughters Victoria and Anna, and those who have guided and supported me along the way. Special thanks to Fischer Black for his inspiration who told me that derivatives were too important to be confined to the few and first encouraged me to write this book. My only regret is that I did not do so until after he was gone.

Contents

Introduction

"The race is not always to the swift, nor the battle to the strong, but that's the way to bet"

Damon Runyon (1880-1946)

I was drawn into the world of derivatives in 1980 whilst carrying out a project on options at London Business School. It led me from a career in engineering into the world of investment at a time when few were involved in options or any of the other instruments that have since collectively come to be known as derivatives. Although new derivative markets in futures and options were beginning to be established around the world, they were perceived as controversial in financial circles and not well understood outside a small group of enthusiasts and specialists. Most investors looked on derivatives with suspicion, pointing to their history as highly effective instruments for speculation. Those who engaged in derivative transactions were regarded as gamblers, and were treated as such by regulatory and tax authorities. In the early 1980s the financial world lived and breathed without derivatives.

But the effects of two catalysts that had been dropped into the financial market mix ten years earlier were starting to take hold, and an irreversible process began that, over the next thirty years, would transform the financial landscape and forever change the nature of investment itself. It is one of the reasons why any history of financial markets and investment since 1970 should give primacy to derivatives.

The catalysts could not have been more different. The first was financial futures, the creation of a determined Chicago trader and a Nobel Prize-winning economist. The second catalyst was more cerebral, the product of the brilliant minds who solved a problem that had eluded great thinkers for centuries; how to price risk. Another Nobel Prize marked this latter achievement, although formally awarded after the untimely death of its most remarkable architect, Fischer Black.

These catalysts were so potent that derivative markets have grown inexorably in size and scope ever since. Even when used by the perpetrators of financial excess and crimes, their deeds have served only to create greater awareness of derivatives.

These markets crossed the Atlantic water to Europe and then to Asia. In 1982, amid great scepticism and resistance, London International Financial Futures Exchange (LIFFE), Europe's first financial futures exchange, opened its doors. Within ten years it was to become the largest derivatives exchange in the world.

More than anything else, the capital, insurance and derivatives markets of today are a result of their place in history and the people who made them happen. An extraordinary combination of brilliant minds, visionary rulers, merchant adventurers, and canny traders played central parts. What drew them to the cause, and how they shaped its course, is as illuminating as the events of the market. Derivatives were never instruments or markets for the idle, dull or faint hearted.

There have been remarkable influences and coincidences running across many centuries. Crucial breakthroughs in thinking and mathematics were made by those whose principal interest was observation of the stars. It is to them that we owe the mystique and 'rocket scientist' badge that is often ascribed to derivative specialists. And then there was the rivalry between the Dutch and the British merchants that propelled the markets forward. The stakes could not have been higher; quite simply the means by which to dominate international trade.

I was lucky enough to be involved in the derivatives game as these instruments were transforming the investment landscape, and have also had the good fortune to be closely involved with many of those who charted its recent passage, of whom the most influential was Fischer Black. Being responsible for derivatives in the investment management business, it has been my good fortune to be close to the pulse of the derivatives story.

It remains a puzzle to me how, in spite of their growth in importance, derivatives still remain poorly understood and occupy an esoteric and mistrusted byway of finance. In part this can be attributed to the fact they were initially the domain of a small number of specialists who skillfully managed to use mathematics to shroud these simple instruments and their markets in intellectual smog. Their perceived central role in the 2008 financial crisis has served only to strengthen and further the suspicion that derivatives are complicated and dangerous.

That is why I have sought to tell the derivative story without the mathematics and technical jargon that overwhelm many textbooks on derivatives, with the aim of making the subject easily accessible to the lay reader. Many well-known events had derivatives at their heart, with the people involved ranging from those with the full spectrum of great technical knowledge to those with almost none at all.

My hope is that this book will bring out the colour, excitement and fun of the market place. Derivatives are the financial revolution of our time.

1. The heart of derivatives - futures and options

"I look to the future because that's where I'm going to spend the rest of my life"

George Burns (enduring entertainer 1896-1996)

With most financial transactions, whether personal when shopping or in business commerce, the exchange of money for goods takes place straight away. Derivative transactions also involve the exchange of money for goods but with one important difference; the exchange does not take place immediately but at a date in the future. It is this linkage to the future and not the present that is the common thread that holds all derivative contracts together, and distinguishes them from all other forms of transaction.

They became known as derivatives as, unsurprisingly, the price you pay for goods in the future is largely determined, or 'derived' from, the price you would pay for the same goods today. At their heart are two concepts, futures and options. Neither is new and there are only two.

A futures contract commits both buyer and seller to a price at which they must exchange goods for cash at a date in the future. All of the terms, from the nature of the product, quantity, price and date when the goods will be exchanged are agreed at the outset and recorded in the contract documentation. On the delivery day, cash and goods are exchanged in the same way as they would in any other transaction.

By contrast, the buyer has no commitment to exchange goods for cash under an options contract. Instead, there is a right or 'option' to buy or to sell goods in the future. As with futures contracts the terms on which these rights can be exercised are agreed at the outset, and set out in the contract documentation. There are two types of option. Those that give the right to buy are known as 'call' options and those that give the right to sell are known as 'put' options. Call options only have value if the price at which you can buy the goods, by exercising the option contract, is less than the price you would pay elsewhere. Conversely a put option only has value if you can sell the goods at a higher price by exercising the option contract than the price you could receive elsewhere.

Why would someone wish to enter into a derivative contract and what economic purpose do they serve? They create the means by which binding price transactions can be entered into even if the goods or money are not available for immediate exchange. This is particularly important to farmers wishing to agree a price for crops they are growing in advance of their harvest, or merchants seeking to agree upon the price of goods that have to be transported over long distances from where they are produced to where they are consumed. That is why it is perhaps unsurprising that the story of derivatives and their markets first unfolded on the farm and the ports on the sea routes of international trade.

Farming with futures

Farmers are in a risky business. The cost of nurturing their land, crops, livestock and equipment have to be funded upfront, often through borrowing, with the reward from their labours coming later when their produce is harvested. There is a perennial struggle with pestilence and weather that can render their efforts worthless and, even after safely navigating these risks, they can suffer the discomfort of being forced sellers of their produce, particularly if their crops are perishable. Under these circumstances they can be left at the mercy of the market, with no control over the price they receive.

When the market price is below the cost of production, farming skill or good fortune with the weather and pestilence cannot prevent them from losing money; indeed such circumstances are often associated with bumper harvests. To save the farmer from deploying money and effort in such a fruitless manner there has always been a need for guidance on the price that their produce will command at harvest time, as well as a mechanism for locking in a certain harvest price when the seeds of their crop are sown.

By selling futures contracts on the crop being planted, the farmer secures a known price at harvest time. The farmer may miss out on a possible extra profit if the harvest price is higher than the price locked in, but is protected against a lower price and the potential disaster should the harvest price turn out to be below the cost of production. Through futures the farmer can secure a known profit margin by passing the risk of lower prices onto someone else.

And it is not just the farmer who benefits from transactions struck in advance of the actual exchange of money for produce at harvest time. Purchasers of the crop are typically confronted with the opposite business risk to that of the farmer; that the price of the produce they need to buy will rise. A cereal manufacturer will gain from a fall in the price of grain but will suffer from higher raw material costs if the price rises. And these additional costs are unlikely to be recoverable from those who buy their cereals, which nowadays tend to be the big supermarket chains.

The futures transaction has protected the farmer by passing the price exposure at harvest time to the cereal manufacturer who, faced with the opposite price risk, has also reduced or 'hedged' price risk. This beneficial outcome for both parties could not be achieved without derivatives.

Options for dealing with uncertainty

Whilst futures work well for those goods you know you will produce or need to purchase, what do you do about goods which you may or may not produce or need to buy? The cereal manufacturer may be confident of a minimum level of demand but not wish to commit to buy more, lest ending up with an inventory of unsold grain. This conundrum can be dealt with by owning the right to buy or 'call' for more grain at a known price, as it removes the risk of having insufficient grain to satisfy customer demand, or having to obtain additional supplies at an uneconomic price. Buying a call option on the grain covers that risk by locking in a known price for the additional purchases if required.

On the other hand, the farmer may wish to lock in a selling price for additional produce if there is a bumper harvest. When unsure of the extra amount that might be produced, the purchase of a put option provides certainty on the selling price, without carrying the risk of having insufficient grain to meet a commitment made under a futures contract.

A parallel path with insurance

Options, in particular, look and feel like insurance in that both provide protection against uncertainty and adversity. As we shall see, markets in insurance and put options grew up alongside one another, put options providing protection against price risk, whilst insurance policies provided protection against other commercial risks, sometimes referred to as volume risk. For the farmer, insurance risks might be poor weather and pestilence causing damage to crops, whilst for those involved in international trade, the risk could be the loss of goods on the high seas.

The origins of both derivatives and insurance go back to ancient times with markets in both emerging later. In Europe, the driving force behind the creation of these markets came from the commercial risks of international trade whilst in Asia, it came from the cash flow needs of farmers.

2. Royal roots of protection against loss - Babylon 1760 BC

"If any one owes a debt for a loan, and a storm prostrates ("destroys") the grain, or the harvest fails, or the grain does not grow for lack of water; in that year he need not give his creditor any grain, he washes his debt-tablet in water and pays no rent for this year".

48th Law, Code of Hammurabi - LW King translation

The origins of both insurance and futures can be traced back to the Code of Hammurabi, the first written code of laws in human history. On this eight foot tablet of stone God is depicted handing Hammurabi, King of Babylon (1792-1750 BC), the laws by which he is to govern his people. The Code, comprising two hundred and eighty-two rules, established standards for commercial interaction and set fines and punishments to meet the requirements of justice, one of the best known being *"an eye for an eye"*. These laws were written down so that the same rules could be consistently applied to all of the cities that Hammurabi had united to form the Babylonian empire.

The statue on which the code is written was discovered in 1901 in Susa, Iran by the Egyptologist Gustav Jequier and is now on display at the Louvre Museum in Paris. It is the wording of the 48th law to which the origins of futures and insurance are ascribed which freed farmers from having to paying any interest or repay loans in years when their crops failed. This debt relief was important as it kept farmers solvent after a poor harvest. Furthermore, since failure to pay debts was punishable under the code by slavery, the law prevented a grain famine in one year being compounded by a dearth of farmers to till the land the following year on account of their consignment to slavery. A side effect of Hammurabi's law was that the modern propensity for the perpetrators of financial crimes to repeat their actions was rendered almost impossible as neither the dead nor slaves have access to money or credit.

It was this threat of slavery hanging over his citizens that is believed to have encouraged Hammurabi to use this law to ensure that lenders protected farmers from the effects of crop failures outside their control. For the lenders it was a better system than that of other kings who would periodically simply cancel all the debts of their subjects, thereby introducing arbitrary legal inconsistency into commercial transactions.

Hammurabi's law did not remove the risk of crop failure but, by transferring the risk to lenders, passed it on to those better equipped to carry the losses. The lenders lived with this enforced risk, not least as the penalty for breaking this law was typically to be put to death by one of the gruesome execution methods in common use at the time. As there was no process for appeal, or to take into account extenuating circumstances, there was little mileage for dissent.

The Hammurabi approach protected farmers against crop failure to an extent not matched by anything available today. Whilst lenders can no longer consign defaulters to slavery for failed business enterprises, the modern practice of banks to require a borrower's home to be pledged as security against their loans acts in a similar way, with those who fail to repay their debts suffering something akin to financial slavery. King Hammurabi had opened the door on the first recorded form of commercial protection.

Hammurabi also extended this protection to merchant shipping in a concept that became known as *"bottomry"*. Bottomry was a loan taken out by a merchant to fund a ship and its cargo. If the ship was lost at sea the loan did not have to be repaid and hence the concept was akin to free insurance.

After Hammurabi's death lenders were no longer governed by his laws and began to demand an additional sum in exchange for their guarantee that they would cancel the loan should the shipment be stolen or lost. Their introduction of paying a premium for protection is believed to be the first explicit form of insurance. They also demanded collateral to ensure repayment in a form that could be readily turned into cash if the loan could not be repaid. For those who lacked something valuable borrowers would have to pledge themselves as collateral, and if unable to repay the loan, would be consigning themselves to slavery. It was a form of protection that was later to become common practice in the ancient Middle East.

This early form of insurance was still in use nearly two thousand years later in Roman times although Emperor Claudius, keen to boost the corn trade, dropped the payment of premium, taking the risk of loss upon Rome itself. In effect he turned Rome into a one man premium-free insurance company with the state taking responsibility for all storm losses incurred by Roman merchants. Governments today act in a similar way in providing disaster aid to areas hit by earthquakes, hurricanes, or floods.

In Italy this trend was to continue many years later when farmers set up agricultural cooperatives to insure one another against the consequences of bad weather. Farmers in areas with a good growing season would agree to compensate those whose weather had been less favourable. Monte dei Paschi, which became one of the largest banks in Italy, was established in Siena in 1472 to serve as an intermediary for such arrangements and has continued in a local philanthropic vein ever since, and is believed to be the world's oldest bank. Similar arrangements exist today in less developed countries that are heavily dependent on agriculture.

Sadly the Monte dei Paschi's tradition of generosity was to contribute to their downfall in modern times when their support to Siena and Tuscany forced the Italian Government to step in to save them from bankruptcy in 2012.

3. Aristotle spots the economic potential of options - Greece 580 BC

Whilst agreements with the characteristics of insurance and futures date back to the 18th century BC, the first recorded option contract of financial consequence came later in the 6th century BC. It was arranged and entered into by the philosopher, Thales the Milesian (624-547 BC). The comments of Aristotle, who recorded the transaction, are as prescient as the transaction itself:

"There is an anecdote of Thales the Milesian and his financial device, which involves a principle of universal application, but is attributed to him on account of his reputation for wisdom. He was reproached for his poverty, which was supposed to show that philosophy was of no use. According to the story, he knew by his skill in the stars while it was yet winter that there would be a great harvest of olives in the coming year; so, having a little money, he gave deposits for the use of all the olive presses in Chios and Miletus, which he hired at a low price because no one bid against him. When the harvest time came, and many were wanted all at once and of a sudden, he let them out at any rate which he pleased, and made a quantity of money. Thus he showed the world that philosophers can easily be rich if they like but that their ambition is of another sort."

Aristotle - Politics (Jowett Translation: Book 1, Chapter 11)

In return for paying his deposit to the olive press owners in Chios and Miletus, Thales gained exclusive rights to their olive presses the following year at a rental price agreed in advance. He was not under any obligation to use the olive presses but had the right to 'call' on them at the agreed rental price if he so chose. Thales had purchased a call option to rent the olive presses.

Had the olive harvest the following year failed, Thales would not have exercised his call option and forfeited the deposit he had paid. His loss would only have been the deposit, not the much greater expense of renting all of the olive presses for the harvest period.

As it was, Thales profited to the value of the difference between the price at which he was able to hire out the olive presses to the olive growers and the lower rental price he had agreed with the olive press owners the previous winter, after deducting the cost of the deposit he had paid.

Thales was an extraordinary man. Bertrand Russell in *A History of Western Philosophy* describes him as no less than the father of science as well as philosophy. He was widely respected for his wisdom and the first of the 'Seven Sages of Greece.' He not only used his knowledge of the stars to make money by correctly forecasting the weather that gave rise to the bumper olive harvest, but also to predict an eclipse of the Sun in 585 BC.

A belief of his that was to endure and influence the development of derivatives was that, whilst the Earth rested on water, much of its surface was made of iron. Thales postulated that something akin to magnetism must hold objects to the ground and keep the heavenly bodies together. He ascribed the magnetic property of iron to the *"living spirits"* within the metal. His notion of magnetism holding the world together was to be reassessed over two thousand years later, when a student of Aristotle's writings and Thales' thinking, Sir Isaac Newton, postulated a subtle alternative, gravity. To provide a rigorous proof for his hypothesis Newton invented a new form of mathematics, calculus, which was to play a pivotal role in pricing derivatives.

Thales had a considerable influence on mathematics. He took the rudimentary form of geometry that the Egyptians had used to build the pyramids, and developed the subject to solve practical problems by deductive reasoning. The earliest and simplest case made his reputation. When asked by the King of Egypt to determine the height of a pyramid, Thales waited for the time of day when his shadow was as long as he was tall, and then measured the shadow of the pyramid. This shadow he rightly deduced to be equal to its height. Whilst in Egypt he also discovered how to calculate the distance of a ship at sea from observations taken from two points on land. It was Thales' introduction of deductive reasoning that led Russell to ascribe to him *"the invention of mathematics"*. Before him, practical solutions using arithmetic and geometry were founded on little more than arbitrary 'rules of thumb'.

Aristotle was remarkable in recognising the universal application of options, just as Thales was in identifying the characteristics and appropriate usage of a call option. Were Thales to return today he would find that the concept, which he first introduced, is unchanged. He would learn that his ideas had spawned market places bringing together buyers and sellers of options for almost every conceivable product, although sadly not as yet olive presses. In spite of the lack of a market place for trading options on olive presses he could still negotiate a private agreement, most likely with an investment bank acting as intermediary and counterparty. However, he might well be disappointed by the legal and financial measures that are now necessary to ensure people keep their word and stand by their agreements.

There would be one new development which he would enjoy turning his mind to, namely the mathematical models by which options are priced. He might be surprised that it took over two thousand years to achieve this, the next major breakthrough in options. But he would be pleased by the manner in which the riddle of option pricing, that had puzzled mathematicians since his time, was ultimately solved.

It was not until 1970 that another brilliant mind, tutored in studying the behaviour of the stars through astrophysics, deduced the solution. Like Thales he was a modest man with a philosophical disposition. His name was Fischer Black and once the paper describing this mathematical model had been published in 1973 the last cog was in place to enable Aristotle's *"financial device... of universal application"* to conquer the financial world.

4. The merchant adventurers and the advent of capitalism - Europe 1500s & 1600s

"Commerce defies every wind, outrides every tempest, and invades every zone"

George Bancroft (American Historian and Statesman 1800-1891, inscription on a plaque outside US Department of Commerce Building, Washington DC)

More than two thousand years after Thales, the first markets for trading derivatives contracts emerged in Europe during the 1500s and 1600s. They were established to meet the demands of international trade and developed alongside the first stock, bond, and insurance markets. The catalyst and driving force behind these, the first manifestations of modern capitalism, was a truly remarkable woman, England's Queen Elizabeth I. It was her brilliant solution to the grave political and economic difficulties that faced England during her reign that led to the creation of all of these markets. By her actions a seemingly irreversible economic decline was arrested and England, in her reign, became harnessed to the engine of global economic power, trade with the East. Her vision not only left an enduring legacy on financial markets; it was also to lay the foundations for a British Empire that would control over a quarter of the world less than two hundred years later.

England's untenable dependence on wool

When Elizabeth I came to the throne in 1558, England was in a parlous state. Her father Henry VIII had squandered the Crown's coffers through gross personal extravagance expended on his court and palaces, as well as through funding wars against France and Spain. Even his taking possession of Church land and property could not balance the books, with the Crown's annual expenditure running at around £2 million per annum against an income of just £100,000. Out of desperation to fund his increasing indebtedness, Henry had devalued the currency by issuing coinage that replaced gold and silver with much cheaper metals, earning himself the sobriquet *"The Great Debaser"*. Even with these measures he could still not balance the books and had to borrow money abroad from lenders in the capital of international banking, Antwerp.

Antwerp was also the international centre for the wool trade, which accounted for over 90% of England's national income. This Antwerp dependency was politically untenable as Spain controlled Antwerp whilst claiming sovereignty over England on the grounds that their King Philip II was now King of England by virtue of his marriage to England's recently deceased Queen Mary I. With their control over the wool trade and the national debt, the ambitions of the Spanish seemed unstoppable.

Spanish dominance also generated enormous fear across Europe on account of the brutal manner with which Philip had crushed the Protestant religion in all of the countries he ruled in favour of Catholicism. As a Protestant Queen surrounded by Catholic countries Elizabeth felt particularly vulnerable. Something had to be done to break England's reliance on the wool trade.

The obvious solution was to garner a share of the lucrative and fast growing trade in the myriad riches from the East. India and China were then the world's dominant economic powers, accounting for over 60% of global economic output. Goods from the Indies were diverse, ranging from silk and porcelain to spices, tobacco and coffee, all of which were prized more highly than gold in Europe.

But capturing that business would not be easy. Spain and Portugal had stolen a march on their European rivals and held a stranglehold on world trade. They were reaping untold wealth to further their economic edge from the goods that their galleons were bringing back from the East as well as those from the recently discovered New World of America.

The rise of Spain and Portugal as the superpowers of world trade

Spain and Portugal's dominance of world trade had come from

leading the exploration rush to find sea routes to the East some seventy years earlier. Italy had previously controlled the trade between east and west through Venice, when the main trading conduit was the tortuous overland 'Silk Route', made famous by the Venetian adventurer Marco Polo. From Constantinople (modern day Istanbul), all of the goods from China and India destined for the west were shipped through the Mediterranean Sea, which was controlled by Venice, a city ideally situated to command the maritime trade. Venetian merchants and money lenders made fortunes through their ruthless exploitation of this trading opportunity; their wealth and character being immortalised by the Elizabethan playwright William Shakespeare in *The Merchant of Venice*. To further their business ends, they even flouted a papal ban that prohibited any dealings with the Muslim world, one consequence of which was that they became the first to savour the Muslim drink of coffee that came to play a significant role in the development of financial markets.

This Venetian pre-eminence on trade with the East ended abruptly in 1453 when the Turks, under Osman Bey, captured Constantinople, and his Islamic Ottoman Empire closed off the overland route. Venice quickly declined in importance as the Mediterranean Sea turned from being the most important trading conduit into a constricting trap. Spain and Portugal stood between Venice and the Atlantic Ocean, the only route now open for reaching the East.

Spain was quick to spot and capitalise on the opportunity, after being persuaded by the Italian born navigator Christopher Columbus, that nothing but sea separated Europe from a direct westerly route to India and China. This perception harked back to the time of Claudius Ptolemy, the astronomer and geographer, who around 140 AD had attempted to map the shape and full extent of the world, a remarkable undertaking when little was known of what lay beyond the Roman Empire.

The Greeks had already established that the Earth was round. Their argument, the same as that used by Aristotle when tutoring

Alexander the Great, was that the shadow of Earth, which fell on the Moon in a lunar eclipse, was circular. However, in spite of his impressive predictions on the shapes of the land masses, Ptolemy had underestimated the circumference of the world, believing it to be around 29,000 kilometres rather than the 40,000 kilometres that it turned out to be.

It was a pity that Ptolemy went to considerable lengths to convince scholars that he was right as, by doing so, he overturned the correct answer that had been espoused much earlier in 240 BC by Eratosthenes, Chief Librarian of the Great Library of Alexandria and father of geography. Eratosthenes had noted that when the Sun was vertically overhead at midday in Syene (modern Aswan, Egypt) at the time of the summer solstice, the angle of the Sun in Alexandria 800 kilometres to the northwest was 1/50th of a circle (7.2 degrees) from the vertical. From these two simple observations he was able to measure the curvature of the earth, thereby calculating the circumference to be close to 40,000 kilometres.

By persuasively arguing and relying on his authority (some attest that he was the same Ptolemy who was King of Egypt of the time) that the world was not as big as Eratosthenes had calculated, Ptolemy was to muddle the search for trade routes to the East, a confusion that was to have significant repercussions, particularly for the Spanish.

When heading west across the Atlantic, Columbus ran into an unexpected obstacle on the route to the Indies, the *"New World"* of the American Continent. Anticipating the Indies to be much closer to Europe, Columbus wrongly surmised that the Caribbean islands, which he reached in 1492, lay close to or formed part of China and the Indies, even describing their inhabitants as *"Indians"*. However, once it became clear that this was a new continent, Spain sought to exploit its riches by ownership and control through colonisation.

The Catholic Church was anxious that the discovery of the New World did not give cause for Portugal and Spain, both Catholic countries, to compete with one another over the same territory, when there were plentiful spoils from colonising elsewhere. The Church's aim was to spread the creed of Catholicism around the world as speedily as possible. For this reason, the Spanish-born Pope Alexander VI issued a decree in 1494 that divided the world equally between Spain and Portugal, creating two Catholic zones of influence. In this '*Treaty of the Tordesillas*', the Pope deemed that the Catholic Church should have sole rights to the planet, Portugal owning the rights to all new discoveries in the half of the World to the east of a north-south meridian line drawn through America, and Spain the other half to the west. In 1500 they found that this line meant that the bulk of the New World belonged to Spain, giving Portugal a large mass of land on the eastern seaboard of South America that is now Brazil. The origin of Brazil's Portuguese speaking people in an otherwise Spanish speaking South American continent dates back to this decree. In exploration terms it led Spain to go west in quest of China and the Indies and Portugal towards the east.

Driven east by the papal decree, the Portuguese navigator Vasco da Gama proposed that Portugal seek a passage to India around the southern tip of Africa. In sharp contrast to Christopher Columbus, who crossed the Atlantic in thirty-six days and returned home empty-handed, in 1497 Vasco da Gama spent more than two years on his 40,000 kilometre return trip from Lisbon to India, then the longest journey in history. This first European expedition rounded the Cape of Good Hope in 1498, launching Portugal as a great trading nation ahead of England and Spain, giving them a head start on trade with India. Curiously, when his ships returned to Europe laden with valuable cargoes of silks, spices, and gold, that expedition was deemed to have disappointed in one vital respect. The primary objective of his royal sponsor King Manuel I had been to find the fabled Prester John, ruler of a legendary eastern Christian kingdom, in order to form an alliance that would "*outflank Islam and retake Jerusalem*". On this count they had at first been excited by the thought that the

Hindus were long-lost Christians, confusing Krishna with Christ. Nevertheless his mighty achievement was to give Portugal first mover advantage on trade with the east, in recognition of which Vasco da Gama was appointed Viceroy of what was then a Portuguese India. It was there that he died from malaria in Cochin in 1524.

New World riches delayed, but did not deter, the Spanish in their quest for a sea route to the East. With the realisation that America was a new continent, it was thought that the Spice Islands, which nowadays form part of Indonesia, lay just west of South America and within Spain's half of the world. The ocean to the west was discovered when the isthmus of Panama was crossed by the Spanish explorer Vasco Nunez de Balboa in 1513. Spain eventually succeeded in reaching the Spice Islands in 1520 when another Portuguese navigator, Ferdinand Magellan (1480-1521), persisted with the western route and found a passage around the southern tip of America through the straits that now bear his name. He then headed west for what he thought would be three day's sailing to the Indies. In fact he was crossing the 11,000 kilometres that Ptolemy had argued did not exist, a giant ocean that comprises nearly one third of the Earth's surface and contains over half of its water. His crossing was in such benign conditions that he named this ocean the 'peaceful' or *"Pacific"* Ocean. It took Magellan nearly five months to make landfall on a group of Indies islands, which he named the *"Philippines"* after his sponsoring monarch, King Philip II of Spain. His fleet of three ships arrived weak and close to starvation, never having expected the crossing to be so long. Magellan was killed there whilst leading a raiding party trying to subdue the islanders into acceptance of Catholicism. Afterwards the smallest ship of the fleet Victoria, now captained by Juan Sebastian El Cano, continued west for the homeward voyage to Spain, becoming the first ship to circumnavigate the globe.

Some measure of the value of trade with the East at that time was that the Victoria's cargo of twenty-six tons of cloves from the Spice Islands more than covered the entire cost of the three-year voyage.

It was an extraordinary journey, and the circumnavigation of the globe by Magellan's ship Victoria is still regarded by many as the greatest single achievement in maritime history, not least as it proved beyond doubt that the world was round.

Through feats like these Spain had become the world's superpower. Somehow England had to find a sustainable competitive edge to break into the lucrative trade with the East. The stranglehold by the Spanish and Portuguese on world trade could not be allowed to go unchallenged.

Searching for new trade routes on a shoestring

One alternative was to find a shorter sea route to the East. The southern routes pioneered by Spain and Portugal were long and arduous, with the shorter of the two round the southern tip of Africa taking over six months to reach India. If there was a shorter route from the north and they were to pioneer such a passage, England would have a clear competitive advantage over Spain and Portugal, without having to run the gauntlet of their naval fleets by passing south through their waters. In one stride England could become a competitive force, *"the new Venetians"*.

With this in mind King Edward VI tasked Hugh Willoughby in 1553 to seek out a North-East passage to Cathay ('China') via Russia that, if it could be found, would considerably shorten the route that Vasco da Gama had pioneered round the southern tip of Africa. The expedition was poorly organised and funded. Sick and just weeks before his death, the fifteen year old King waved the three ships that comprised Willoughby's fleet on their way. It was doomed to failure. Two of the three ships, including that of Willoughby, became stranded on the Arctic ice flows, and their crews were found frozen to death by Russian fishermen the following spring. The third ship found its way to Archangel from where its captain Richard Chancellor and his crew travelled 600 miles overland and wintered in luxury in Moscow with the Russian Tsar Ivan 'The Terrible' IV.

Chancellor's return to England, with news of the death of Willoughby and the two crews, was to be a turning point for the young Princess Elizabeth. She vowed then, in spite of the Crown's lack of money, that no poorly equipped expedition should ever again leave England's shores on such a hazardous mission. The search for a mechanism that would properly fund voyages of discovery was on.

But finding such a mechanism was not easy. Funding the great adventurers on their voyages of trade and discovery was costly and carried great risk. Frequently the flotillas of ships that left to seek out new territories or trade routes were never seen or heard from again. And those that returned were often much depleted.

The Crown had ended up paying for these voyages as no one else would finance them. Merchants were unwilling to fund such ventures, particularly those like Willoughby's that had been too ambitious. Whilst of great strategic importance to the Crown, the risks were deemed to be too high for the merchants to take on. Even with royal encouragement, typically through offers of land and titles, it was difficult to persuade the merchants to participate.

But as the Venetians had shown, the merchants were the main beneficiaries of the new trade routes opened up through voyages of discovery. Elizabeth was therefore determined to find a mechanism to compete with Spain and Portugal by convincing the merchants to share the risks of voyages of discovery with the Crown. It was to lead to the birth of first capital and then derivative markets; and be the catalyst for commercial insurance.

Queen Elizabeth I and the first joint stock company

Elizabeth's idea was to share the rewards from voyages of exploration exclusively with the merchants who had risked their own money by funding them. They should no longer profit by *"piggy backing"* off successes funded by the Crown. The mechanism she arrived at and actively encouraged was to be the foundation of modern capitalism, shifting much of the risk and reward from enterprise away from the state into private hands.

Before she became Queen in 1558 Elizabeth had pioneered this approach in 1551, by encouraging the merchant adventurer Sebastian Cabot to form the first joint stock company with Richard Chancellor and Sir Hugh Willoughby. It was to be the first of the publicly owned companies that we see listed on stock exchanges around the world today. The company was called the *Mystery and Company of Merchant Adventurers for the Discovery of Regions, Dominions, Islands and Places Unknown*" and Elizabeth herself was one of the 201 individuals who put up money and became shareholders in the enterprise. The name was a bit of a mouthful and would not sit comfortably with share listings in today's newspapers. It became shortened to the Muscovy Company in 1555 (it was re-chartered in that year by Queen Mary I of England) when, having retraced Willoughby's steps and confirmed that there was no north-east sea route from Europe to India and China, the company established an unexpected but nonetheless lucrative monopoly on trade with the Russians or 'Muscovites', initially to exchange wool for furs. This trading relationship through the Tsars continued for over 350 years until ended in 1917 by the Russian Revolution.

Whilst the idea of joint stock companies was beginning to gain traction in England, the wealth and economic prosperity that Portugal and Spain were garnering from the Indies and the New World was carrying them to greater and greater economic strength, leaving England and the other European kingdoms teetering on the brink, lurching from one economic crisis to another. All that the English, and later also the Dutch, could do in response was to resort to harassment and piracy, principally by attacking Spanish galleons and stealing or sinking their cargoes as they returned laden with gold and silver from America.

The most notorious of these pirate adventurers was Francis Drake. Initially, without financial support from joint stock companies, he funded his voyages to the New World by first stopping in West Africa and sending raiding parties to kidnap local inhabitants. He then held these unfortunate people, shackled and chained together in appalling conditions below deck, and set sail for the New World where they were sold into slavery to Spanish plantation owners in exchange for the gold, silver and pearls that would bring him riches in England.

Drake soon found that stealing from the Spanish was simpler and more lucrative than slave trading, and began to plunder Spanish ships and their trading ports on the Caribbean side of the Panama isthmus over which all the silver and gold coming from Peru had to be carried. The exploits of this original *"Pirate of the Caribbean"* was so fearsome that the Spanish named him *"El Draque"* ('The Dragon') and their King Philip II offered 20,000 ducats (around US$7 million in today's money) for his head. In one raid in Panama Drake and his companions attacked a Spanish mule train carrying over twenty tons of gold and silver. With the Spanish in hot pursuit, they buried the silver and made off with the gold back to their ships, a tale that is said to have given rise to the association between pirates and buried treasure.

Encouraged by Elizabeth and funded by joint stock company money, Francis Drake led an expedition to Peru, the main source of Spain's gold and silver riches. They followed Magellan's route round the southern tip of South America and then sailed up the west coast to Peru. For the homeward leg Drake continued west to circumnavigate the entire world on board his flagship the Golden Hind, a feat for which Drake was knighted on his return to England in 1580. His knighthood may have owed something to the value of the Queen's half share of his ship's cargo that was said to be worth more than the Crown's entire annual income from all other sources that year.

Capital markets dislodge the Spanish

As the Spanish Crown was funding voyages to America and claiming ownership of the Peruvian mines, these attacks on their galleons and colonies were regarded as acts of war. Faced with an increasingly bold challenge by the English and Dutch to their dominance of international trade, Spain declared war on England in 1585. But this act simply increased Drake's activity, culminating in a brazen attack on Spain itself when he attacked the ports of Cadiz and La Coruna in 1587. Thirty-seven naval and merchant ships were captured or destroyed in these raids, along with other goods stored on the quay. Some of the ships captured by Drake contained substantial cargoes of gold. The losses inflicted on the Spanish through this campaign postponed the then imminent Spanish invasion of England from taking place until the following year.

When the invasion was attempted in 1588, the Spanish Armada was defeated by the English fleet. The increasing traction of English joint stock companies had turned the tide against Spain, released England from economic dependence on Spain, and freed Holland from the shackles of colonisation.

Capitalising on the heroic outcome against the Spanish fleet, Sir Walter Raleigh turned to joint stock companies first to fund his attempt to colonise North Carolina in the United States for tobacco and again, in 1594, to find El Dorado, the fabled land alongside the Orinoco River in what is now Venezuela, that was said to be strewn with gold. Both ventures were to fail and, in part, explains why Raleigh was executed in the Tower of London after his second expedition to find El Dorado failed in 1618. It was a salutary reminder of the importance that the Crown attached to making money, but nevertheless a sad end for an explorer and military leader who had served the nation well, and been a favourite of Queen Elizabeth I.

Many of the early joint stock companies were set up to seek new enterprises, territories and sea routes along the north-east coast of America. This was in large part driven by a new exploration focus to find a north-west passage from Europe to the Indies, now that it was known that the shorter sea route from the north-east did not exist. The desire of other European nations to gain strategic advantage over Spain and Portugal by finding a shorter route was undiminished. France adopted a similar strategy to England, which is why their New World colonisation and discovery efforts were concentrated in what is now eastern Canada and the north-eastern United States.

The experience of these expeditions, and the companies that funded them, prepared England for an age of colonisation and trade expansion. As more and more companies were created over Elizabeth's forty-five year reign, new ideas were advanced for their governance and structure, many of which endure to this day. One was the idea of dividing up the profits of the voyage in the proportion of shares held by each investor, and paying out these *"divisions"* or *"dividends"* as they became known, in cash or goods. The central notion was to use wealth to create wealth, by sharing the risks and rewards of enterprise. It has remained the cornerstone of capitalism to this day and should capitalism to lay claim to a single founder, it must surely be Queen Elizabeth I.

With a funding mechanism that did not rely on the Crown's limited financial resources, and the capital constraint to exploration overcome, England was no longer dependent on wool and the Spanish hold on economic power began to wane. By the time Portugal came under the rule of Spain in 1578 following the death of King Sebastian, the seeds that England's Queen had sown for her country's recovery were beginning to sprout. Without that recovery it is likely that the combination of the two dominant powers in world trade might have led to all the other Crowns of Europe being subsumed into a Spanish superpower controlled by the Catholic Church.

Elizabeth's triumph had taken the keys to economic power away from Spain and Portugal. But she did not stop there. She then took this new mechanism a step further with a masterstroke at the end of her reign that was to be the cornerstone of an enduring British Empire that would grow and prosper long after she was gone.

Queen Elizabeth's masterstroke - The East India Company -1600

On 31st December 1600 Elizabeth granted a Royal Charter to a new company, the East India Company. The charter gave more freedom to that Company than had ever been given before or since, equivalent to no less than an outright monopoly on trade in the East Indies. The charter authorised the Company to acquire territory wherever it could and to exercise the various functions of Government, including legislation, issuance of currency, negotiation of treaties, waging of war and administration of justice. The only restriction placed on the Company was that it could not contest the prior trading rights of *"any Christian prince"*, citing the spread of Christianity as moral authority, in much the same way as the Catholic Church had justified colonisation by Spain and Portugal.

The Royal Charter effectively gave the Company the right to act as the Crown, but without any recourse to the Crown for money to finance the business. The company's purpose was capitalism in its purest form, to use money to make money. Its original fifteen year Royal Charter was extended to perpetuity in 1609 by James I, in recognition of the speed with which the Company had set about its task and the immediate commercial success from which the nation had prospered. The East India Company not only took the funding cost of colonisation away from the crown; it also placed the management and administration of these colonies into private hands. By 1611 the Company had established factories in India in the provinces of Madras and Bombay, whilst also forging trading businesses further east, even penetrating Japan.

The Company was to retain control of India for nearly 250 years until its increasingly raw form of capitalism precipitated the Indian Mutiny in 1857, forcing the Crown to revoke its charter and bring the lands and people colonised by the East India Company back under Crown control.

5. Rivalry born between the British and Dutch - East Indies 1600s

"If you ain't Dutch you ain't much"

Old saying (anon)

When Queen Elizabeth I died in 1603, the new King James I was able to unite the thrones of England and Ireland with Scotland into a Britain that was no longer dependent on the wool trade, nor shut off from trade with the East. It was a mighty legacy with which to leave the stage; the building of an empire well underway after inheriting a country close to economic collapse. Although Spain and Portugal were in retreat, Britain was not alone in picking up the spoils. The Dutch were also emerging as a strong and ambitious rival in international trade.

Famed for their seamanship, explorers from the Netherlands, principally from the region of Holland that lay below sea level, followed England in seeking the Northeast passage to China. They shared the view of many that there could not be a permanent Arctic ice cap, since the warmth of the Sun shone day and night during the summer months. Willem Barentsz had led three expeditions exploring this route in the 1590s. On the last voyage his ship had become trapped in the Arctic ice but, unlike the fateful voyage of England's Hugh Willoughby in 1553, Barentsz managed to survive the winter by building a wooden house for shelter and hunting for food.

Once the Dutch had effectively secured their independence from their weakened Spanish rulers by becoming ungovernable in the aftermath of the English defeat of the invading Spanish Armada; they were soon into their stride as fierce and able champions of international trade. By taking control of the port of Antwerp, which nowadays is part of Belgium, they were already at the *"centre of the entire international economy"* and the guardian of *"Europe's richest city"* according to the historian Fernand Braudel *(La Dynamique du Capitalisme, 1985)*.

Spain and Portugal had made Antwerp the central hub for their international trade with Northern Europe, just as Venice had been the trading centre when Italy had controlled trade with the East. Antwerp came to account for around forty per cent of world trade, with one measure of its importance to the Spanish crown being recorded by the historian Luc-Normand Tellier as: *"earning seven times more revenues from Antwerp than the Americas."*

Without a long-distance merchant fleet, and governed by an oligarchy of bankers and aristocrats who were forbidden by Spain to engage in trade, Antwerp had become a very cosmopolitan city with merchants, bankers and traders from all over Europe. As the prime centre for moneylenders and financiers in the mid-1500s, the city had built a significant banking business, including lending money to the English Government. This arrangement came to an end in 1574 as the relationship between England and Spain had become too hostile.

The Dutch, quick to spot the importance of the British East India Company, were encouraged by Thomas Hope to set up their own version in 1602, the United (Dutch) East India Company "VOC", with Hope as Head Regent.

Hope was a Scot who had established his reputation in the Netherlands by persuading the merchants of Amsterdam and Antwerp to form a legally binding monopoly for the international diamond trade. The benefits from this arrangement have been long lasting, with the Netherlands, through companies like De Beers, remaining at the centre of the diamond trade ever since.

Hope was also a close friend and adviser to King James VI of Scotland who would later become Britain's King James I when the thrones of England and Ireland were unified with Scotland. It is said that some of the shares in the VOC held in Hope's name actually belonged to King James. Had the dying Queen Elizabeth I been aware of this she would almost certainly have put a stop to Hope's advocacy, and to any British financial support for a rival Dutch enterprise.

Hope's influence, and that of his family successors in Dutch commercial life, was to come to the fore again a century later when opening the door into international trade for Baring Brothers, a British Bank, as it began its passage first to riches and royal connections, before coming to an ignominious end in 1995.

Through the grant by the Dutch Government of a twenty-one year monopoly over all territory east from Africa's Cape of Good Hope to the Straits of Magellan at the tip of South America, the Dutch East India Company quickly set about exploiting this massive opportunity to the full. Whilst other Western European nations were following suit with their own versions of East India companies, they were already too late. The British and Dutch had stolen a commercial march on other European colonisers, and were rapidly establishing new trading outposts in the East.

The Dutch wasted no time when taking over control of Portuguese and Spanish colonies. The progressive acquisition of the Netherlands as a fiefdom of the Holy Roman Empire by the Habsburgs, and thereafter by the Spanish Empire, had led to the aggressive enforcement of Catholicism. Along with a heavy taxation burden, the Spanish occupation had left the Dutch people with bitter scars. An indelible mark had been left by the severity with which the Spanish Army had put down the Protestant uprising in 1567, through the mass execution of their leaders. The Dutch meted vengeance on the Spanish wherever they found them with a ruthless urgency.

Britain was now the main competitor to the Dutch in international trade and a rivalry sprung up between the two countries which encompassed capital and derivative markets that was to run on for centuries, a rivalry that has continued to the present day. A pattern of behaviour was also to endure with the Dutch as the irrepressible buccaneers, flamboyant risk takers, and innovators whilst the British adopted a contrasting stance which, whilst cautious and less fleet of foot, was nonetheless determined and effective.

The ferocious determination of the Dutch to advance their cause in international trade was to reach its zenith in 1623, when representatives of the Dutch East India Company sought to suppress competition from the British East India Company at a trading station which the two companies shared in Amboyna, Indonesia. In an act of unbridled aggression the Dutch arrested, tried and then beheaded ten representatives of the British East India Company on the grounds of treason.

The Dutch also did something the Portuguese had not. They adopted the piracy tactics used by the English against the Spanish in America, systematically raiding foreign ships as they rounded Africa's Cape of Good Hope, laden with goods from the East. They maintained a fleet of ships in a natural harbour, which they had colonised in part for the purpose, and named Cape Town. It was to become a staging post whilst waiting for the monsoon winds that would carry them east, as well as a source of fruit and vegetables that they cultivated to reduce the scurvy that afflicted mariners on long voyages. It was from here that they were later to unearth treasures of a different kind, gold and diamonds, when they ventured into the South African hinterland. These finds in turn were to attract the British into Africa, eventually drawing them into conflict with the Dutch settlers in two Boer Wars towards the end of the 1800s. It served to reinforce the claim made by Herodotus, when writing in the fifth century BC and whom many view as the first historian, that commerce is the prime driver of history.

Wars with British cost the Dutch New York

When the Dutch followed the English lead and created their own joint stock companies, their efforts to find a Northwest passage to the Indies led to the establishment of a fur trading station in 1609 on a small island called Manhattan off the Northeast coast of the United States. The Dutch East India Company had hired the English sea explorer Henry Hudson to sail down the river that now bears his name, having been led to believe by the local inhabitants that this river flowed through the Great Lakes of the Midwest to the Pacific Ocean and the Indies, just as the Straits of Magellan did in the south. The burgeoning settlement established by the Dutch became the capital of the *"New Netherlands"* and was called *"New Amsterdam"*.

But the aftermath of the Amboyna massacre in Indonesia was to influence subsequent events in America, as the massacre was used as the pretext by the British to wage two Anglo-Dutch Wars. At the end of the second of these two wars in 1667, whilst the English were stalling the signing of a peace treaty, the innate daring of the Dutch came to the fore with spectacular effect when Michiel de Ruyter, Commander of the Dutch fleet, sailed up London's River Thames and attacked the English fleet at anchor on the Medway. Not content with sinking and setting alight thirteen warships, the Dutch captured and made off with the English flagship, HMS Royal Charles as well as the second in command, HMS Unity. To tow these large warships out to sea through the shallow water of the Medway, Ruyter decided to tip them almost onto their sides, thereby reducing the depth of water they needed to float. For the English crowd and military leaders watching from the shore, seeing their flagship taken so audaciously, was to add humiliation to one of the worst defeats ever suffered by the Royal Navy. Samuel Pepys, Secretary to the Admiralty and best known for the candid personal diary he kept as a young man between 1658 and 1669, paid tribute to the Dutch seamanship. In spite of the darkness of the moment when watching HMS Royal Charles being taken, his diary entry of 22nd June 1667 records: *"they did carry her down at a time, both for tides and wind, when the best pilot in Chatham would not have undertaken it, they heeling her on one side to make her draw little water: and so carried her away safe."*

The Treaty of Breda, which was signed shortly afterwards, ceded New Amsterdam to the British, which they renamed New York after the then Duke of York who would later become King James II. There in 1792, around a buttonwood tree situated outside 68 Wall Street, shares in joint stock companies were first traded in the United

States on what was called the New York Stock and Exchange Board. A year later they moved indoors and conducted their business at the Tontine coffee house. Later, in 1863, the name of the stock market was sensibly shortened to the New York Stock Exchange.

Energetically driven by the Dutch and the British, the latter half of the seventeenth century was to be marked as the era of burgeoning international trade. Ships arrived daily with cargoes from the colonies and suppliers around the globe, unloading a profusion of products that had hitherto been scarce or unknown. They were the luxury goods of the time and included sugar and spice, coffee and tea, raw cotton and fine porcelain. Their social effects were deep and wide ranging. Wealth was no longer something to be inherited from preceding generations. Instead it could be earned and accumulated through enterprise, which in turn provided the capital for investment in other new ventures. The world of modern capitalism had been born and the merchants of international trade took over the mantle of the rich and titled from landowners and those of noble birth.

The merchant drivers of this progress needed protection from loss and a search was on for a means to transfer the risk of loss from commerce. Markets in insurance and options were to emerge to cater for risk transference. Insurance sought to provide protection again loss in any form whilst put options were more confined, providing protection against falling prices. Thus started what was to be a long and parallel journey, insurance an opaque and encumbered alternative to the simpler and more free-spirited put option.

And it was not just protection against loss that the merchants needed help with; they needed guidance on which goods to buy from the East, and in what quantities. There was too much guesswork involved for their liking when chartering ships and deciding where to send them to, and with what cargo they should return with from their long voyages.

In tackling these issues the Dutch and British took different routes, to some extent reflecting their respective personalities and interests. It was therefore perhaps unsurprising that the Netherlands ran with put options whilst Britain developed the more conservative alternative of insurance to spread risk. The Dutch were first into the ring with tulips, an altogether more colourful starting point than the British, who began with insurance against fire and the loss of ship cargoes on the high seas.

6. Risk management and the emergence of options and insurance

Whilst Elizabeth I had created the mechanism for raising private capital through joint stock companies, there was little that these companies could do to protect themselves from the commercial risks they faced whilst conducting international trade. No one had paid much attention to these risks when Spain and Portugal had controlled international trade. Their Kings and Queens had borne these risks through the public purse, as they were accruing wealth and power so fast that such protection was rendered inconsequential. It had been a similar story for the Venetian merchants, although they had established some rudimentary form of insurance for protection. Venice had gained her pre-eminence by controlling the gateway between Constantinople and Europe, the trade route between producers and consumers for around ninety per cent of the goods from the East.

Dominance was a model for business success that the thirty-year-old John D. Rockefeller would replicate for the US oil industry in the 1870s. His Standard Oil Company bought up most of the oil pipelines and refineries across the country, exerting further control through negotiating almost exclusive rights from the railroad companies for transporting oil from where it was produced to where it was consumed. It left other oil producers having to choose between selling their oil to Standard Oil at a price of Rockefeller's choosing, or earning nothing at all as their oil would be left in the ground. By the age of forty Rockefeller had personally attained Venetian style dominance by controlling over ninety per cent of the US oil business, to become the world's richest man and first billionaire. If one adjusts money values for the effects of inflation, he was the richest person in history.

Rockefeller was later to devote the bulk of his fortune to philanthropy, one gift being $80 million to found the University of Chicago. Chicago was to become the hotbed of inspiration for creating markets in financial derivatives as well as for solving the mystery of derivative pricing.

At the time when the torch of international trade was passed from the Crown to merchants, the commercial risks were increasing. Trade was being conducted across much longer sea routes than before, and without naval support to provide safe passage. One in every five ships was being lost to the perils of storm and shipwreck, piracy, or seizure as prize of war. Poor navigation tools were the reason of many shipwrecks as, at that time, a ship at sea for over three weeks without sight of land could generally at best only gauge its position to within a hundred mile radius. Competition was also increasing as trade routes were becoming better established and the regular flow of goods more assured. On occasion, merchants were even finding that the supply of what had been rare goods was outstripping demand.

The two risks that particularly concerned the merchants were the selling price of the goods they were bringing home, and the costs they were bearing from cargoes that were damaged or lost at sea. The solution they came up with to deal with price risk was forward contracts, the forerunner to futures markets. For volume risk, particularly damage or loss of property as cargoes or from fire or other hazards, the solution was insurance.

Neither of these developments had gained much traction when a peculiar diversion took place in The Netherlands, through an unexpected commercial risk that came to grip the entire nation, the price of tulips.

Put Options emerge with Tulips - Holland 1634

Travellers in Turkey during the 1550s had been struck by the beauty of the 'dulban' flower, the name coming from the Turkish word for the turban that the flowers resembled. Brought to Vienna and called the 'tulip', the flower attracted considerable popularity and attention such that, within a few years, it was being cultivated in

Germany, Belgium, and Holland. When tulips reached England in the late 1570s, they became fashionable in court circles, and were soon the objects of speculative interest as the price of tulip bulbs rose rapidly. When the French joined the fray in the early 1600s, this excitement was to turn into frenzy.

Cultivated tulips occasionally produce striking mutations, caused by a virus, which enhanced their value. Growers would anxiously scan their crop for such rectified blooms which, if beautiful, attracted ready buyers. These buyers would use these bulbs for propagation purposes in much the same way as Derby winning racehorses today are valued as sires for the next generation of thoroughbreds.

By the early 1620s excitement over tulips and their mutations pervaded The Netherlands, with the rarest specimens selling for thousands of florins. As interest spread from a handful of enthusiasts to the nation as a whole, a speculative fever took hold. Avid trade in tulips and their bulbs took place in every local inn. Domestic gardens had a section cordoned off for cultivating tulips and fields, previously used for growing vegetables or grazing cattle, were turned over to growing tulips. As fever turned to frenzy, prices fluctuated wildly and the risks of participation increased sharply.

With prices hard to gauge and the normal auction process of steadily rising bids proving to be too slow, a new bidding process for perishable goods like flowers came into being. Still used today and known as a *"Dutch auction"*, the auctioneer begins by seeking an offer at a high asking price, and then lowers the price until a bid is forthcoming. The first bidder secures the goods and, as no other bidding is entertained, each lot is quickly sold. This process results in many more items to be sold in a single auction. It is a pity that the technique is not utilised more often today to avoid the slow and somewhat dull walk up in price from competing bidders at conventional auctions.

Put Options for price protection

Faced with high prices and rapid price movements, tulip growers had considerable capital at risk through their tulip crop. To contain this risk, growers were willing to pay cash in return for the certainty of a guaranteed minimum selling price for their tulips. That way they could secure a known minimum profit margin for their endeavours. Those on the other side of the bargain receiving the cash were willing to carry the risk that the price of tulips would be lower than the guaranteed minimum price, a form of price insurance. Thus, out of a desire in the marketplace for a mechanism that would provide a financial 'hedge' to protect them from adverse prices, a market in put options was born.

It is worth noting that put options came about as a means of protecting commercial growers from speculative excess. They were a response to volatile market conditions, not the cause of them. Fashion, not options, caused the speculative frenzy for tulips. However it would not be the first time that people were to confuse cause and effect with derivatives, believing them to cause or promote speculation. For this to be true, derivatives would need to have the ability to create risk. Popular attraction to the motivation of the risk taker draws attention away from the equal and opposite party at the table, the individual who hedges to reduce price risk.

As with any contract, the value of the various agreements in circulation on tulips was only as good as the guarantors behind them. There were no government bodies, exchanges, collateral or member firms with substantial financial backing standing behind the host of market relationships which came into being.

Contract specification and delivery proved to be a major source of dispute. The purchaser of a particular tulip bulb had no way of actually knowing that the bulb had the attributed characteristics until it bloomed. Another issue was that tulip bulbs do not look particularly rare or valuable, being easily confused with other plants. On more than one occasion onions were delivered instead of tulip bulbs. In one notorious case, the converse took place, where a consignment of rare tulip bulbs being shipped to merchants in

London, was mistaken by the ship's cook for onions and served to the ship's crew for dinner. In an attempt to contain such problems, new laws were passed and tulip notaries were appointed to supervise the trade.

At the giddy height of this speculative bubble, a single rare bulb was exchanged for a large French brewery and estates were mortgaged to finance tulip bulb purchase. Some owners of rare bulbs even resorted to hiring gangs to destroy similar bulbs found elsewhere, in order to preserve the rarity value of the line.

When tulip prices collapsed in 1636, the fabric of Dutch economic life was pulled down with them. Those who had sold price guarantees to growers by writing put option contracts were either wiped out or unwilling to honour their obligations, leaving the purchasers of protection holding the bag. Even worse, it turned out that put option contracts were unenforceable under Dutch law, as there was no legal basis for selling something you do not own. The lawsuits dealing with reneging on loans and transaction agreements were to choke the courts long afterwards.

Lessons on market structure from Tulips

Tulipwoerde ('Tulip Madness') not only exposed weaknesses in the legal framework surrounding derivative contracts; it also became evident that a better process and infrastructure was needed to uphold and honour such contracts. The ability to pay, or creditworthiness of counterparties, had to be assured; and the price needed to be clear and transparent to everyone.

As we shall see, the success of the modern marketplace has only been possible through overcoming these shortcomings and satisfying the requirements of governments, regulators and participants. Entities like exchanges and clearing houses came into being with their role and structures evolving to address these basic tenets. There is also a recognition that when these core aspects have been ignored, compromised or circumvented that failures, sometimes catastrophic, have come about.

Tulipwoerde was also the first of many occasions when options have been blamed for speculative excess, instead of being viewed as a symptom. However the Dutch, irrepressible as ever, were not daunted. After first tightening the legal framework around these contracts they, without further ado, listed options on shares in the Dutch East India Company shortly afterwards.

Meantime in England, watching from afar, pre-emptive action was taken to prevent a similar fate, by banning options altogether. Ever since then banning options has been used as a convenient device for dealing with any political fallout from financial scandals around the world; except in The Netherlands.

Plague and fire the catalysts for the London insurance market

Whilst the Dutch were dealing with the economic fallout from the tulip frenzy, another market was taking hold in England to deal with an unwanted Dutch import, plague. In 1665 a bubonic plague epidemic spread from Amsterdam to London. Carried by infected rats on merchant ships, it struck London and killed over a hundred thousand people, some twenty per cent of the city's population. Consternation was caused when King Charles II left London for the country to avoid the disease and, as the plague spread across England, there was a general exodus from cities to the countryside. One who took this course was Sir Isaac Newton, who left Cambridge for the safety of a country home in Lincolnshire. It was there that one of the great moments in science took place and a pivotal moment in the mathematical method by which risk and thereby option contracts are now priced. This is explored more fully later.

The plague was followed by another tragedy the following year, the Great Fire of London. The fire destroyed eighty per cent of the City of London, thirteen thousand homes and eighty-nine churches, including St. Paul's Cathedral. The fire was beneficial in one respect; it destroyed the streets, slums and open sewers that harboured the rats that carried the plague. The Monument, which stands just across the street from the building where I worked for many years, commemorates the Great Fire, which began in a nearby baker's shop.

In response to these tragedies, and with encouragement from the Crown, two new forms of protection emerged alongside that for international trade, life and fire insurance.

Insurance the constrained put option to handle volume risk

The contrasting responses of the Dutch and British to tulips, plague and fire were to colour their respective thinking on markets for dealing with commercial risk far into the future. As the Dutch had suffered from a pricing shortcoming, they were to become the strongest advocates of options whereas the British, who had suffered from loss of life and property, their focus turned towards insurance.

Perhaps it was because the Dutch knew options were a symptom, and not the cause of the tulip madness, that they were not diverted from their path. In any event it was to be the beginning of a long running conceptual rivalry between put options and insurance. Although there are similarities in that both provide protection against loss, their commercial roles and mode of action are very different.

Put options provide protection against price risk. In the case of Tulipwoerde, the growers who bought put options were seeking insulation against a fall in the price of tulip bulbs. For the contracts to pay out the tulip bulbs had simply to fall in price, not physically be lost or stolen. By contrast with insurance, there is always an event giving rise to a physical loss; a death, a cargo lost at sea, the burning down of property, or stolen goods. The principle behind insurance is one of indemnity; that the insurer will put the injured party back into the same condition as prevailed before the loss took place. As a consequence the payment the policy holder will receive is unknown until the loss occurs, with the amount paid out determined by the contract wording. Those with home or car insurance today will be familiar with the uncertainty as to amount and the timing of payments after suffering losses.

Because of the principle of indemnity, insurance policies carry a heavier legal framework. The burden of proof and the requirement for *"uberrimae fidei"* (utmost good faith on the part of the insured), can slow the payment of claims or lead to claims being sidestepped altogether by the insurer. In many commercial contexts indemnity has been a weakness, as there has to be evidence that a physical loss has been suffered, and the payment amount is not known until after investigation. Even though this principle has come about for good reasons some aspects of its workings have in recent times come to be seen as arcane. Later this weakness was to lead to some big companies shunning insurance altogether in favour of more transparent and less onerous protection structures, built around put options to achieve certainty.

7. Coffee Houses and the advent of public markets

"What on earth could be more luxurious than a sofa, a book, and a cup of coffee...Was ever anything so civil?"

Anthony Trollope, The Warden

One afternoon in 1637, whilst the Dutch were toiling to resolve the economic fallout from the tulip frenzy, a classics scholar called Nathaniel Canopius brewed himself a cup of coffee in his chambers at Oxford University. This energising drink, made from roasted coffee beans, had been introduced to England from Holland, taking its name from the Dutch word *"koffie"*. When Canopius recorded the renewed energy and vigour that this enjoyable drink brought to his readings of literature from ancient Crete, he could not have expected that the same pleasure would become so common amongst the students that would follow, nor that he would come to be regarded as the first person to drink coffee in England.

The origin and spread of coffee

There are a number of legends about the origin of coffee, the favourite of which concerns Kaldi's 'dancing goats'. Kaldi was a young goatherd in Abyssinia (now Ethiopia) who, accustomed to his goats having a docile disposition, noticed with amazement that after chewing certain tree berries, they began to prance about excitedly. He tried the berries himself, forgot his troubles, lost his heavy heart and felt himself to be the happiest person in Africa. A monk from a nearby monastery found Kaldi in this state and decided to try the coffee berries himself. He felt so much more alert that night during prayers that he told his brother monks. Word soon spread and monks all over the country were soon found to be chewing the berries and praying, without feeling drowsy.

The earliest recorded evidence of coffee as a drink appears around 1450 in the Sufi monasteries of Yemen in southern Arabia, where coffee beans were first roasted and brewed as they are today. Knowledge of the drink then spread further afield through the Yemeni port of

Mocha, its initial popularity enhanced by the medicinal qualities some ascribed to the drink. The hills above Mocha on which the coffee beans were grown soon became the main centre for Arabia's coffee exports, giving its name to the popular Mocha style of coffee that we drink today.

From Yemen, coffee spread to Egypt and North Africa. By the 1500s it was drunk throughout the Middle East, Persia and Turkey. The ability of coffee to drive away sleep made it popular amongst Sufi monks. But it was this same stimulatory effect that led conservative orthodox imams to declare coffee a form of drug, and to have the drink forbidden in 1511 by the theological court in Mecca. However such was the popularity of the drink that this ban was lifted in 1524 by order of the Ottoman Turkish Sultan Selim I and the Grand Mufti Mehmet Ebussuud el-Imadi, who issued a celebrated fatwa which permitted the consumption of coffee. As with bans of alcohol, the prohibition of coffee had simply driven the business underground and into unsavoury hands. The drink has suffered from many bans over the years, including a ban imposed in Egypt in 1532, which was enforced by burning to the ground every coffee house and warehouse storing coffee beans in Cairo. This heritage of being subject to bans and frequently blamed for the actions of their users is a feature that coffee was to share with options. By some strange parallel that is hard to explain, tea and futures have always been able to summon powerful allies to rescue them from adverse sanctions, whereas coffee and options have languished without support and suffered.

Coffee first travelled outside the Muslim world into Italy through Venice, despite a papal ban forbidding all trade with the Muslim world. The success of the Venetian merchants had been built through a ruthless focus on making money rather than obeying rules. Coffee then spread to the rest of Europe, principally through the Dutch trading companies, which imported coffee beans and plants from the East. The Dutch had won the race to commercialise coffee over their European competitors by joining forces with the natives of

Kerala in Southern India against the Portuguese. They made off with some live coffee trees and beans, which they then cultivated in the East Indies. They also cultivated coffee in The Netherlands, some in greenhouses originally built for tulips. Within a few years the Dutch had become the main suppliers of coffee to Europe through their colonies, Java in Asia and Surinam in the Americas.

Brazil, the only major producer today not introduced to coffee growing by the Dutch, had acquired the plant from Cayenne in the neighbouring French Guiana in 1727 (Guiana is now an overseas department of France and part of the European Union). Legend has it that Francisco de Melo Palheta, an emissary for the Emperor of Brazil, attracted the attentions of the French Governor's wife, and was given a coffee plant hidden inside a bouquet of flowers as a token of her affection. The full circle was completed when coffee from Brazil was introduced into Kenya and Tanzania in 1893, not far from where Kaldi's goats had first danced in Ethiopia six hundred years before.

It was through the British and Dutch East Indies companies that coffee became available in England. The first coffee house in Europe was opened in 1650, at the Angel Inn in Oxford, by a Turk called Jacob, probably to serve the needs of Canopius' successors. London followed suit two years later when Pasqua Rosee, believed to be of Armenian origin, opened a coffee house in St. Michael's Alley in Cornhill. By 1675 there were more than three thousand coffee houses throughout England and the popularity of coffee houses spread rapidly across Europe, and thence to America.

Within a short period much of England's business was being conducted in these congenial establishments, where merchants would gather to exchange information and conduct business over a cup of this fashionable drink. In Europe women were not allowed to frequent coffee houses, as there was concern that the stimulatory effect of the drink might have adverse behavioural consequences on the conduct of their male business clientele. A major benefit from conducting business in a coffee house, as opposed to an ale house, was that you came out *"more sprightly than when you went in, stimulated not intoxicated".*

The coffee houses, rather like clubs, acquired their own identity and clientele. By bringing together people with common business interests, they became the market place for the goods or services being discussed and transacted. Unlike today, where information passes quickly, widely and cheaply by electronic means, in those days it was passed by word of mouth. Knowledge of prices and data concerning commercial activity was the key to business success, and closely guarded by those who possessed price sensitive information. Unlike today there was no desire or legal requirement to disseminate widely, and the notion that it was wrong or unfair to trade on privileged information ('insider trading') was unknown. Quite the contrary; unless you could evidence that you possessed inside information and acted upon it for profit, you were unlikely to be employed for long.

It is a far cry from today where the main role and revenue source for exchanges is selling data and information on trading activity and prices. The loss of floor trading to electronic trading through computers is perhaps unsurprising, as a physical presence is no longer necessary, not least as the sharing of private information is now discouraged, even outlawed. Exchanges now police their customers to prevent insider trading instead of acting as the forum and facilitator of the process. Their role today, much less fun, is simply to disseminate data and to ensure through credit control and other measures that contracts entered into under their auspices are honoured.

Lloyd's Coffee House and the birth of insurance markets

The most prominent coffee house to emerge as a central market around this time was that opened by Edward Lloyd, on Tower Street near the River Thames, in 1687. It quickly became a favourite haunt of those associated with the ships moored at London's docks, moving to much larger and more luxurious premises on Lombard

Street in 1691, where tea and sherbet was served alongside coffee. Lloyd's was the principal meeting place where ship owners, sea captains and merchants involved in maritime business congregated. International trade on the high seas was now a thriving business, thanks to the success of Queen Elizabeth I's brilliant endeavours a century earlier. They came to Lloyd's to discuss how to mitigate the commercial risks they were taking and to agree terms with those offering insurance against disaster.

Edward Lloyd was much more than a skilled coffee house host. Recognising the value of his customer base, and responding to their demand for more and more information, he launched 'Lloyds List' in 1696, a journal that carried information on the arrivals and departures of ships, as well as intelligence on conditions abroad and at sea. Information from abroad was provided by a network of correspondents in the major ports around the world and on the Continent. Ship auctions also took place on his premises, with Lloyd obligingly furnishing paper and ink to record the transactions. One corner was reserved for ships' captains where they could compare notes on the hazards of the new sea routes that were opening up; voyages that led them further afield than ever before. Lloyd's establishment was open almost around the clock and was always crowded.

Samuel Pepys, best known for the candid personal diary he kept as a young man between 1658 and 1669, a period that included the Great Plague (1665), the Great Fire of London (1666) and the Second Anglo Dutch War (1665-1667), frequented coffee houses for news of the arrival of ships he was interested in. Pepys regarded the news he received from coffee houses as more reliable than that from the official naval channels which he accessed, first as Clerk of the Acts to the Navy Board and later as Chief Secretary for the Admiralty.

This flow of information was less popular in other circles. In the absence of mass media, coffee houses became the primary source of news and rumour. In 1675, concerned that too much information was being disseminated amongst the public, and that this was weakening the Crown's control and potentially lead to dissent, Charles II shut down all the coffee houses. However the uproar was so great that he had to reverse that edict sixteen days later.

Lloyd's coffee house served from the outset as the headquarters for marine underwriters, in large part because of its excellent mercantile and shipping connections. Lloyd's List was eventually enlarged beyond the usual notices of ship arrivals, departures and reports of accidents and shipwrecks, to include daily news on stock prices, foreign markets, and high water times at London Bridge. This publication became so well known that its correspondents sent their messages to the office addressed simply 'Lloyd's'. The government even used Lloyd's List as the official channel for publishing news of battles at sea.

Lloyd's formal claim to be the market for insurance came in 1771, when 79 underwriters subscribed one hundred pounds each and formed the Society of Lloyd's. They were known as *"Lloyd's underwriters"* as they recorded their names underneath a description of the risk they were assuming on Lloyds headed paper. They were a group of entrepreneurs operating under a self-regulated code of behaviour. These original Members of Lloyd's were later to become known as *"Names"*, each committing all their worldly possessions and financial capital to meet their insurance promises to customers. It was this commitment that was one of the principal reasons why Lloyd's business grew rapidly, and evolved into the insurance giant Lloyd's of London is today.

Forward markets to determine goods and remove price risk

For merchants chartering ships, where to send them to and what mix of goods to bring back were decisions of critical importance. It was not much help knowing what was currently selling best. What they needed to ascertain was what goods would be most profitable a year hence, when the ships that they were about to dispatch returned with their cargoes.

As business links to overseas traders and suppliers became better established, merchants began to enter into firm commitments with one another on quantity and prices for goods on future voyages. Wholesalers and retailers were also willing to make similar commitments to purchase the cargoes that arrived at London's docks. As the practice grew, the merchants were able to obtain more certainty around their costs, revenues and likely profit margin on the full range of goods that came from the East.

These forward agreements were the forerunners of futures contracts, and performed exactly the same function for the merchants. The only difference between these forward agreements and futures contracts is that forward agreements are privately negotiated between the two parties, whereas trading in futures takes place in the more open and regulated setting of an exchange. Nowadays these early forward agreements would be called 'over the counter' or OTC agreements.

Forward markets followed the pattern of insurance and other businesses, with individual coffee houses becoming the meeting place and market for particular goods. Over time these coffee houses would become futures exchanges for the same products. In London as recently as the 1990s, one could still find over twenty futures markets for commerce ranging from shipping to hops, most of which owed their origins, and in many cases their location as well, to that period.

The ramifications of forward markets were far reaching as they gave suppliers and buyers more confidence in their budget forecasting, and greater certainty to plan ahead. By encouraging forward thinking, the pattern of plenty or shortages was mitigated. It also helped the fledgling insurance market to assess the value of claims on cargoes lost at sea. In short the establishment of forward markets markedly reduced the commercial risks associated with international trade and placed this critical component of economic activity on a much sounder business footing.

Stock Markets for companies

The clientele which Jonathan Miles attracted to his coffee house in Change Alley (now called Exchange Alley), assumed risk in a very different form from those of Edward Lloyd. Those who frequented Jonathan's bought shares in trading ventures, using the funding mechanism that Elizabeth I had pioneered, profiting from success in return for carrying the risk of failure. Shares in the East India Company were traded at Jonathan's along with those for the companies of Hudson's Bay (1670), Africa (1672) and the South Sea (1711), each receiving monopoly rights to territory under Royal Charter. Their shares were bought and sold at Jonathan's by brokers acting as intermediaries for investors.

Bond Markets to fund governments

Debt markets followed in 1694, the last of the core capital markets to be established, when the British Parliament announced the *"Million Adventure"* to raise one million pounds from the public by offering ten pound 'tickets' to participate in the Adventure, a form of lottery. £40,000 was to be given away in prize money each year and, irrespective of this bounty, the Adventure paid 10% in interest each year for sixteen years. Unlike modern day bonds, no capital was returned when the bond matured. In the same year a group of London merchants formed The Bank of England, a joint stock company to lend money to the state and act a national bank. The Bank was granted a Royal Charter and continued as a private company until 1946, when brought into public ownership. It is the world's second oldest central bank after Sveriges Riksbank, the Central Bank of Sweden, which was founded in 1688.

The British Government needed to borrow money in order to finance a series of costly wars against the French that had begun with Louis XIV's abortive invasion of England in May 1692, and ended with the British victory at Blenheim and the subsequent signing of the Treaty of Utrecht in 1713.

The founding of the Bank of England finally resolved the unholy muddle over the nation's debts. Historically this debt had been the personal obligation of the monarchy, but relied on Parliament to levy taxes to pay them off. With the monarchy's penchant for waging wars and a refusal by bankers in 1672 to lend Charles II any more money, the nation's debts had remained unpaid. The Bank of England was clever in making sure that lenders viewed them as an institution that was of commercial relevance which could be trusted. The Bank demonstrated its commercial relevance by spending half of the proceeds from its first loan on rebuilding the Royal Navy. As the Navy safeguarded the trade routes which brought in the goods on which taxes were levied, a virtuous circle for securing repayment to those funding government borrowing came into being, allowing the obligations of the crown to pass to the people with the Bank of England acting as intermediary. In recent times the narrative around the value of lending money to government has become lost; a pity, perhaps, as accountability falls away too.

And thus Canopius' cup of coffee led to the establishment of the major financial, derivative, commodity and insurance markets around the world.

Towards the end of the 1700s coffee houses died out abruptly in England with tea, a relatively unknown drink until the late 1600s (the diarist Samuel Pepys first mentions trying the drink in 1660), replacing coffee as the national drink (alongside gin and ale). The Dutch and French controlled the coffee industry and the British East India Company could make no inroads into that market. However, through colonising India and Ceylon, Britain controlled the tea trade and, supported by the Royal Family and through the Court switching to tea, persuaded the home market to become and remain known as a nation of tea drinkers.

Encouraged by the Crown, the connection between trading associations and coffee houses fell away. Jonathan's dropped its coffee connection in 1773 and renamed itself the Stock Exchange whilst Lloyd's followed suit the following year, becoming the Society of Lloyd's. Even without this royal dictum, the link between coffee and markets would probably have been broken, as exchange floors became more and more crowded. With standing room only, the habit of sitting down to conduct trading business over a cup of tea or coffee was falling into disuse.

Coffee houses have made something of a comeback in recent times as stock markets have increasingly turned electronic, and the crowd of people on the floor of exchanges has declined or disappeared altogether, supplanted by computers. There may be no greater symbol of this change than that when the New York Stock Exchange, the world's largest stock exchange, gave a concession on its trading floor to Starbucks, a coffee shop chain whose shares are publicly listed there.

8. Maths breakthrough from betting on the stars - London and Cambridge 1684

"If I have seen further it is by standing on the shoulders of giants"

Sir Isaac Newton (1643-1727) in letter to Robert Hooke

The stars that had led the Greeks to the concept of a call option, were once again to play a pivotal role in the development of derivatives. In the search for better navigation tools to guide the merchant adventurers on their long voyages of discovery a new form of mathematics, calculus, was developed to track the movements of the stars and planets. When later fused with probability and statistics, another new arm of mathematics developed alongside calculus to solve gambling puzzles, the resulting stochastic calculus was to provide Fischer Black and others with the analytical firepower with which to finally price risk.

Three polymaths and a coffee house

In 1684 two of Britain's leading astronomers, Edmund Halley and Sir Christopher Wren, met with the scientist Robert Hooke at the Grecian coffee house in Devereux Court off London's Strand. By then the fashion for coffee houses as meeting places extended well beyond the world of commerce and finance.

In common with many of the intellectual giants of the Renaissance period, Wren, Halley and Hooke were all true polymaths in the Ancient Greek sense where poly means 'many', and manthanein 'to learn'. Their skills and knowledge transcended more than one discipline, such that a single label could not adequately convey the diversity and richness of their knowledge. The mighty achievements of such individuals are often cited in support of the view that increased specialisation in education and the work place of modern times has been a hindrance to innovation. Too few individuals have sufficient breadth of knowledge and experience to *see the wood for the trees*. This was certainly the view of the American economist Jack Treynor when explaining how it was that an astrophysicist, rather than an expert in either finance or economics, who made the crucial breakthrough in the field which transcended the two disciplines, financial economics.

Wren, although Savilian professor of Astronomy at Oxford University, was knighted as an architect for building the current St. Paul's Cathedral, which stands on the site of its predecessor that was burnt down in the Great Fire of London.

Halley is best known for his belief that the comet sightings of 1456, 1531, 1607 and 1682 were of the same comet whose orbit brought it within view of the earth every seventy-six years. He was not alive to witness the next sighting that he predicted would occur in 1758 and was named Halley's Comet in his honour. Halley also made significant contributions to geophysics, mathematics, physics and meteorology. In the latter field he identified that it was heat energy from the Sun in conjunction with the rotation of the Earth which gave rise to the atmospheric weather motions. Halley was also to establish the relationship between barometric pressure and height above sea level. His influence was to permeate into actuarial science, where his paper on life annuities provided the British Government with the necessary analysis to calculate the appropriate price to charge people according to their age.

Although Robert Hooke tends to be remembered for his law of elasticity, Hooke's Law, which states that an elastic body stretches in proportion to the force that acts upon it, the range of his achievements is astonishing by any measure. The noted historian Allan Chapman described him as *"England's Leonardo da Vinci"* as he had that rare combination of experimental and theoretical brilliance which was the source of the crucial breakthroughs of the scientific revolution.

As an assistant to Robert Boyle, Hooke built the vacuum pumps which Boyle used for his gas law experiments. Much of Hooke's scientific work was conducted in his capacity as first curator of experiments, and then secretary of the Royal Society, a post he held from 1662 until 1691. He also built some of the earliest Gregorian telescopes, through which he observed the rotations of Mars and Jupiter. In addition, based on his observations of fossils, Hooke was an early proponent of biological evolution. He also investigated the phenomenon of refraction, deducing the wave theory of light, and was first to suggest that matter expands when heated and that air is made of small particles separated by relatively large distances.

Hooke also performed pioneering work in the field of surveying and map-making and was involved in the work that led to the first modern plan-form map. However, he was disappointed that his plan after the Great Fire in 1666, to rebuild London on a grid system as New York is today, was rejected in favour of restoration of its former conformation of muddled street routes and alley ways.

Hooke was also the father of microscopy. He invented the compound microscope and coined the term 'cell' to describe the basic unit of life when using this instrument to study plants. In short he was truly remarkable as a natural philosopher, architect and scientist.

Wren was very different but no less remarkable than the other two men. A natural leader who had studied Latin and Aristotelian physics at Oxford, he was one of the founders in 1660 of what was to become England's premier scientific body, the Royal Society, which was created for *"the promotion of physico-mathematical experimental learning"*. It was his great breadth of expertise in so many different subjects that helped to create the exchange of ideas between scientists, and led to his appointment as President of the Royal Society in 1680.

At the time of Wren's involvement with St. Pauls Cathedral, a project completed in 1710 after a thirty-five year construction period, the profession of architect as we know it today did not exist. Architecture was then regarded as a branch of applied mathematics and it was not unusual for well-educated gentlemen, or *"virtuosi"* as they were known, to carry out such endeavours. Wren's engagement to rebuild St. Pauls Cathedral came about as King Charles II was impressed by the ideas Wren had expressed to the Royal Society on light and optics, insights gained through his study of Italian architecture.

Wren had arranged the meeting at the Grecian coffee house with Hooke and Halley, fellow members of the Royal Society, to discuss the empirical observations made by German mathematician and astronomer Johannes Kepler in 1605. Kepler's measurements suggested that an inverse square law explained the movements of the planets, with the force attracting two planets towards one another being inversely proportional to the square of the distance between them. This meant that if you doubled the distance between two objects their force of attraction to one another becomes four times weaker (the square of two being four).

Copernican Revolution challenges the Church

Kepler's findings had built on the work of Nicolaus Copernicus, the Polish astronomer, who first postulated that the Sun, not the Earth, was the centre of the universe. This heliocentric 'Sun-centred' cosmology challenged the core geocentric 'Earth-centred' foundations of astronomy, based on the premise that the Earth was the stationary centre of the universe and that all of the planets and stars, including the Sun, rotated in perfect circles around the Earth. This geocentric cosmology had been articulated by Claudius Ptolemy in 150 AD and recorded in the Almagest or *"Great Treatise"*. Ptolemy's thesis on the universe had stood as the authoritative treatise on the motions of the stars and planets for over fifteen hundred years, just as his estimate of the circumference of the world was assumed to be correct, until found otherwise when Magellan's search for the Indies was confused by the unexpected size of the Pacific Ocean.

Kepler's work had been funded by the Holy Roman Emperor, Rudolph II. The church's view that the Earth was the stationary centre of the universe was not founded simply on dogma. There were many who plausibly argued that a moving earth would be an unstable planet to walk upon, as well as being very windy. But Kepler's observations that the planetary motions were ellipses and not circles gave further credence to the theory that all of the planets, including Earth, were orbiting around the Sun.

Kepler was an astrologer, physicist and a mathematician, a combination that provided the breadth of knowledge to make this mathematical linkage. His view on astrology, expressed in *Harmonics Mundi* (Chapter 7), was that *"The soul of a new born baby is marked for life by the pattern of the stars at the moment it comes into the world, unconsciously remembers it, and remains sensitive to the return of configurations of a similar kind"*. Such thinking remains at the heart of the prognostications of the many astrologers who ply their trade in newspapers and magazines today.

Copernicus was perhaps the greatest polymath of the Renaissance period, his thoughtful and varied learning providing him with the skills to be a notable mathematician, astronomer, physician, artist, economist, governor, military leader, diplomat and Catholic cleric. Just as remarkable was his mastery of five languages, a polyglot talent that enabled him to be a classical scholar and translator. Drawing on these skills he translated Latin and Greek literary, historical, and oratorical texts into Italian and German. These books had been carried by the Roman and Greek refugees who had fled westward when Constantinople fell to the Islamic Ottoman Empire in 1453. It was this event that closed off the land route from Europe to China and the Indies and was to trigger the merchant adventurers to explore sea routes instead. It was the bringing and translation of these ancient texts that sparked the rebirth or *"Renaissance"* of interest in the classics and a re-examination of ancient philosophy, mathematics and science. For Copernicus astronomy figured as little more than an avocation, yet it was in that field that he made his mark upon the world.

In his book *"De revolutionibus orbium coelestium"* (On the Revolutions of the Celestial Spheres), Copernicus demonstrated that the observed motions of celestial objects could be explained by placing the Sun at the centre of the universe instead of the Earth. His views challenged far more than just the foundations of astronomy. To the church these beliefs were tantamount to heresy, as they undermined the notion that mankind was the central and crowning achievement of God's creation. Copernicus appears to have been well aware of this sensitivity, describing the Sun as a symbol of God and by dedicating his masterpiece to Pope Paul III. He also avoided the wrath of the church by delaying publication until shortly before his death in 1543.

Anxious for proof that Copernicus was wrong, Pope Urban VIII encouraged and funded fellow Italian Galileo Galilei to use a telescope, the device Galileo had invented to give the Venetian fleet military advantage in sea warfare. The Pope wanted Galileo to make observations of the stars and confirm the church's stance. As a respected national hero who was equally adept at making as theorising, he epitomised the difference between the scholarly Greeks and the Renaissance brilliance that combined craftsmanship with academic talent. However, by turning his telescope from the high seas to the stars, Galileo's reputation was swiftly brought down to earth. Unfortunately for the Church, what Galileo saw and described in his book *'Dialogue (Concerning the Two Chief World Systems)'* supported the heliocentric view and Copernicus' theory. His comparison of the two alternatives left the Catholic Church with little option other than to enforce the status quo through the bullying strategy of having their Holy Office of the Inquisition in Rome decree in 1616: *"that the proposition that the Sun is the centre of the universe is absurd in philosophy and formally heretical and that the proposition that the Earth has an annual motion is absurd in philosophy and at least erroneous in theology"*. For his unacceptable conclusions the Inquisition found Galileo guilty of heresy and forced him to recant, before condemning him to house arrest for the remainder of his life.

Such was the controversy surrounding Copernicus' theory that those who were convinced of its veracity concluded that it could never be accepted without unequivocal proof. In what was to become a landmark in the history of science, and referred to as the Copernican Revolution, a variety of scientific investigations were stimulated, of which Kepler's was the most significant. The period has come to be regarded as the starting point of modern astronomy and the defining epiphany that began the scientific revolution.

Sir Isaac Newton and the discovery of Calculus

The only way to prove beyond doubt that the Earth revolved around the Sun and was not the centre of the universe was by coming up with a mathematical theorem that explained Kepler's observed laws. Aristotle and Pythagoras were the first to use mathematics to describe the physical world, with Galileo describing mathematics as *"the language of science"*. Hooke's hypothesis was that the planets were moving in space or in a vacuum, describing orbits around the Sun on account of the combined effects of inertia and attraction towards the Sun. Wren's challenge to Halley and Hooke was to provide an absolute and undeniable mathematical proof of Kepler's laws.

Wren offered thirty shillings to the one who was able to provide this proof. Hooke suggested there and then that he could achieve this proof. However, nothing subsequently materialised and, in any case, Halley was not convinced that Hooke would do so. It was this challenge that triggered what some contend to be the most remarkable meeting in the history of science, one that not only established a rigorous proof that the Earth was not the centre of the Universe, but also unearthed the laws of gravitation and the mathematics of calculus.

Halley was imbued with the spirit of the Reformation. As a committed atheist and strong advocate for freedom of thought, he had little time for the control that the Roman Catholic Church sought to exercise over its membership. His disdain for religion had been further strengthened by accounts that were then circulating of abuse by the clergy, heightening his motivation to use scientific methods to debunk one of the central planks of religious doctrine.

But being an atheist did not endear Halley to the establishment, particularly as he was also an opium user, writing openly of its pleasurable effects. This may explain why, in spite of his towering achievements, Halley was never knighted.

As he knew he could not come up with the answer to Wren's challenge himself, Halley travelled to Cambridge in 1684 to put the problem to the University's Lucasian Professor of Mathematics, Isaac Newton. Halley was delighted and astonished when Newton immediately said that he already had a mathematical proof which conclusively demonstrated that the force between the sun and planets resulted in elliptical orbits, and that the gravitational force between them acted in accordance with an inverse square law. Halley asked to see the document concerned but Newton could not find it amongst his papers, instead promising to send the proof to Halley as soon as he had found it. Newton said he had established this proof some twenty-four years earlier in 1665 whilst staying at Woolsthorpe Manor, his family home in the Lincolnshire countryside, to escape the ravages of the Great Plague. Folklore has it that the laws of gravitation came to him when he saw an apple fall whilst walking in the orchard, Newton questioning why it had fallen vertically downwards. That same tree has been preserved to this day.

Halley was not to know that Newton was familiar with Aristotle's writings and that Thales was one of his intellectual *"giants"*. Thales' idea of magnetism derived from *"living spirits"* within iron holding objects to the ground was not far removed from Newton's notion of gravitation.

Three months later Halley received from Newton *"De Motu Corporum Gyrum"* (On the Motion of Bodies in an Orbit), a document which proved Kepler's laws in terms of an inverse square law of gravitation along with Newton's three laws of motion. Newton's work on gravitation would probably never have come to light but for Halley's visit.

Halley suggested publication, but Newton was reluctant and

initially refused. With perseverance Newton relented and, at Halley's expense, a revised and expanded version was published in 1687. This *"Philosophiæ Naturalis Principia Mathematica"* treatise held that gravity binds the universe together and that the laws of motion hold true throughout the universe.

Newton's interest in gravitation and planetary motion had stemmed from a desire to help ships at sea to navigate more accurately from reliance on the positions of stars and planets. To this end he invented a form of mathematics to understand motion and force in terms of infinitesimal changes with respect to time that he termed *"fluxions and fluents"*. This mathematics described how moving objects change their positions over time and could be used to predict how they would move in the future.

At more or less the same time a German mathematician Gottfried Liebniz came up with the same mathematical concept whilst working on a very different problem, which was how to calculate the area of unusual shapes not easily worked out by geometry. Liebniz coined the term 'Calculus' after the Latin word for a small stone used in counting, as his approach was to add together tiny quantities to calculate the area of a larger whole.

Once Newton was able to explain Kepler's relationships from his own laws of motion and law of universal gravitation, using classical Euclidian geometry, the relationships came to be known as Kepler's laws. Together with Newton's mathematical theories, they form part of the foundation of modern astronomy and physics.

The importance of Newton's achievement cannot be over-estimated. For mathematicians, calculus is the study of change, in the same way that geometry is the study of shape and algebra a method of qualitative reasoning about numbers. Through calculus, a more precise understanding of the nature of space, time, and motion was gained and expressed in mathematical terms. Using his three laws of motion and the law of universal gravitation, Newton explained how such diverse phenomena as the motion of planets, moons and comets within the solar system, the movement of water around earth in the form of tides, the precession of the equinoxes and the irregularities in the moon's orbit. This was the final stage in the demolition of the Aristotelian world view, begun by Copernicus, and developed by Kepler. It also removed the last vestige of argument emanating from the church that the Earth was at the centre of the Universe and was the triumph Halley had hoped for. It was the moment that science emerged from the obfuscation of religious prejudice and folklore.

Robert Hooke never recovered from losing Wren's bet. His later life was tragically dogged by ill-health, and dominated by an intellectual dispute over the credit which he felt had been wrongly given to Newton for his own work on gravitation. There was also jealousy at Newton's elevation to the higher echelons. It is claimed that Newton, as President of the Royal Society, did much to obscure Hooke's work, some even suggesting that he had Hooke's only known portrait destroyed.

Up until 2015 there was a small statue in memory of Robert Hooke outside St. Paul's Cathedral. I used to walk past this statue every day on the way to work, its tiny scale relative to Sir Christopher Wren's architectural monument a reminder of the fickle dividing line between great achievement and the recognition of greatness. The statue has been replaced by a water fountain and, when I enquired as to the whereabouts of Hooke's statue, was told it had been lost.

Gamblers add their flavour to the mathematics mix

Another new form of mathematics, probability, was also being developed around that time but for a different purpose; to solve gambling problems. Probability theory introduced the notion of uncertainty into mathematics, something the Greeks had never accepted on philosophical grounds. In their view there was always certainty. Even if they, as mere mortals, were unsure of things, their Gods had no doubts at all. Hence to them a form of mathematics that recognised uncertainty was fundamentally flawed.

In *"Principia"* Newton laid down a system that was not seriously challenged until the twentieth century, through Albert Einstein's theories of general and special relativity and the quantum theory of light. By fusing these two components of mathematics together into what became known as stochastic calculus, Einstein provided Fischer Black and others with the mathematical toolkit with which finally to solve the puzzle of how to price risk.

9. Rice and the first futures exchange - Japan 1730

"The rice was crammed to the tops of the warehouses. People bought and sold by speculating based on the condition of the sky, the evening winds, and the morning rains. They argued over a mere one or two bu of silver, the market was full of people, and people who had never met before would trade thousands or even ten thousands of koku of rice, and once they had clapped hands over it, neither party would breach the contract".

Ihara Saikaku, Novelist and son of Osaka
merchant (1642-1693)

Whilst markets in finance and insurance were developing in Britain and Holland to manage the risks associated with international trade, an altogether different development was taking place on the other side of the world; the establishment of the first futures exchange in Japan. Its purpose was to meet the needs of farmers and the staple product that fed that nation, rice.

Although the main purpose of futures markets today is to manage price risk, that was not why the futures exchange came into being at the Kitahama Rice Market in Osaka. Instead, it was the regular and substantial cash needs of the feudal landowners, who were the main producers of the rice crop, which led to the exchange being established.

At the time Japan was a society largely cut off from outside influence, with the Shogunate ruling de facto on behalf of the Emperor. The feudal Samurai lords were required by decree to spend at least half of the year in the capital Edo (Tokyo) where the central government was located, a ruling in part designed to prevent them from organising any form of uprising against Shogun rule.

For these absentee landlords, lack of cash was not a problem at the point of production as those who tilled their farmland were paid in kind, principally in rice. Where these landlords ran into difficulty was in the urban centres of Edo and Osaka, where a monetary economy had evolved, and they needed cash in the form of silver coins to pay for their lifestyle. For this reason rice and other agricultural products grown on their manors were hauled into Edo and Osaka to be sold for cash. As the rice crop is seasonal, shipments were not evenly spread over the year. Making their budgeting task harder was another Shogunate decree that they maintain households throughout the year in both the country and city. Everything was expensive, even the travelling to and from their country homes. The Shogun prescribed that, as his ambassadors, they were to be accompanied by an elaborate entourage which included a large number of Samurai soldiers and also, any such journey should be conducted with much formality and dignity.

To add to their financial woes the Shogun frequently required his nobles to contribute liberally to public works such as the building and repair of castles, construction of roads, reclamation of land, and provision for the maintenance of armed forces. Unsurprisingly these expenses often left the nobles short of cash.

At first the landlords issued tickets in the form of warehouse receipts as proof that they had stored rice in the country, or in warehouses within the city. These rice tickets were bought by merchants to ensure supply for much the same reason as cereal manufacturers do today. Rice tickets soon were negotiable and became the standard currency for trading rice.

When trading in rice tickets was initially supervised by public officials, the process and administration was probably well balanced and fair to all concerned. However this was to change when merchants favoured by the Shogunate took over this role. This new system was to give overwhelming market power to these merchants, as it was decreed that all rice trading had to be conducted under their auspices. By setting the rules and the spread between purchase and selling prices, the merchants were able to secure a substantial profit margin for themselves, a recipe which made the favoured merchants very wealthy indeed at the expense of the landowners.

The most important merchant was Saburaemon Yodoya, whose home in the Kitahama district of Osaka became the central location for trading rice tickets. He came to dominate the Osaka rice trade. Merchants met at his home to exchange information and negotiate transactions with one another, in much the same way that business in insurance and shares was conducted in particular London coffee houses. The rice price at Yodoya's came to be regarded as the prevailing market price in the city of Osaka, and Yodayas became formalised as a commodity futures exchange in 1650. When the first British East India Company delegation arrived in Japan in 1660 to establish trading links, that market had already been in existence for a decade. Official recognition of the exchange and its code of dealing was given by the Shogunate in 1730 and served to protect the market and the sanctity of its contracts with formal backing from the highest authority of the realm.

A remarkable feature of this market was its sophistication. The rice warehouse receipts traded were standardised in terms of rice quality, contract life and settlement. Contracts were not between the two parties to a trade but with a central counterparty, who guaranteed performance and monitored the creditworthiness of participants, an entity we would today describe as a clearing house.

By only allowing trading in rice futures to be carried out *"cho ai mai kaisho"* ('in the market place') of Yodoya's house, and giving him complete control over the rules and membership of his exchange, the merchants ruled the roost. There were few speculators to counter their influence and, as a result, the exchange was more about wealth transference from the feudal landowners to the merchants than risk transference.

The benevolent King Hammurabi of Babylon would have disapproved of such an outcome. His laws were designed to protect farmers against crop failures, forcing the merchants who funded them to shoulder the burden of loss. By favouring the merchants over the farmers, the Shogunate had created a system that worked the other way round.

It was actions such as these that were to lead to the rise of the mercantile class at the expense of the feudal landowners, as a similar approach was adopted by the Shogunate for trading other commodities. In the copper market the merchant granted similar status by the Shogunate to that of Sauraemon Yodoya in the rice market, was Masatomo Sumitomo. A former Buddhist priest, he was to make a fortune from that role and from smelting copper ore to extract silver for coinage. His family successors were later to open Japan's largest copper mine and dominate trading in copper around the world. Their presence in copper was still in evidence some three hundred years later when derivatives markets were rocked by the actions of their chief copper trader.

One hundred and eighteen years were to elapse before the next organised futures exchange came into being. This one was in the Western world in Chicago, with its rationale and story very different from that of Japan.

10. 'Old Hutch' corners all the wheat in America - Chicago 1860s

"Where troops are gathered, prices go up"

Sun Tzu "The Art of War" (China 400 B.C.)

When the great prairies of the American Midwest were first ploughed up and planted with wheat and corn, the merchants of Chicago, by virtue of their location by the Great Lakes, became the principal intermediaries between the Midwestern farmers and the hungry masses of the east coast. As the scale of the business increased, financing the grain trade became increasingly difficult, not least as the Chicago merchants wanted to keep their dealings with east coast bankers to a minimum. They had little fondness for the east coast business style, which seemed to them to place too much emphasis on legal documentation and take too little on trust. So the citizens of Chicago elected to build a trading culture and infrastructure that better suited their character and beliefs, and to control it themselves. As a result the group of businessmen who founded America's first futures and options exchange in 1848, Chicago Board of Trade (CBOT), adopted the antithesis of the prescriptive commercial laws, first set out on tablets of stone three thousand years before by King Hammurabi of Babylon. Out of sight of Washington DC and the Federal government, they incorporated themselves under local state law, with the clear intention of governing themselves without east coast interference.

This approach by the CBOT founders was not new. They were upholding a mercantile self-governance tradition that, whilst not as old as Babylon, could be traced back to the Middle Ages, when agricultural fairs in southern France held *"courts of the fair"* to arbitrate disputes between farmers and merchants. Then as now, the idea was the same; to keep the law of the land out of business.

Speculators on Chicago's grain futures market help to feed the Unionist Army

By the time the American Civil War began in 1861, Chicago had become the most important agricultural trading centre in the United States. Geography and industrial technology played their part, with the Chicago merchants pioneering the giant grain elevators which stored, protected and facilitated the speedy and secure transfer of grain from train wagons to ships.

The CBOT futures market played a critical role in developing this trade through Chicago, with their quality definitions and delivery requirements quickly becoming established as the industry standard. With so many grain dealers and storage facilities gathered in one place, the CBOT price became the trusted benchmark, as it was reached through free competition between many buyers and sellers. The open pits, where all trading took place, were the epitome of transparency, even a popular spectacle; with a crowd of traders calling out prices and gesticulating their orders through a language of hand signals.

Towards the end of the Civil War the Chicago futures markets came into public and political prominence by providing much needed certainty of food supply to the fighting troops. In its wake had come a deep rooted respect for market forces and the trading freedom of speculators that has been ingrained into American culture ever since.

The Unionist Army had found it hard to secure enough grain for their troops as they could only buy the harvested stock held in local silos and warehouses. Futures contracts were attractive as they augmented these physical purchases with the promise of future supplies from grain growing on the prairies.

Few farmers participated in the grain futures markets but speculators did, of which one, Benjamin Hutchinson, became a market legend nicknamed *"Old Hutch"*. It was he and others like him who changed the dynamics of future grain supply, even though he was neither farmer nor merchant. Old Hutch achieved this by committing to sell grain that he did not own to, amongst others, the quartermaster for the Unionist Army. By 'short selling' grain futures contracts, he increased the contractual supply of grain that the army could buy.

He was able to do this short selling, as the seller was not obliged to own any grain when entering into the futures contract. Provided the grain the short seller had committed to provide was delivered on the maturity date of the futures contract, he had kept his side of the bargain. The approach of speculators like Old Hutch was not an altruistic desire to help the Unionist Army. His aim was simply to sell grain futures contracts at a high price and profit from buying the contracts back more cheaply before the delivery date.

In 1863, the price of wheat and oat prices had been driven up by heavy demand from both armies. Making the situation even worse was the fear that the land of the northern farmers would be confiscated should the Confederates win. Old Hutch was convinced that the Unionist army would prevail and wheat prices would drop afterwards, so he sold as many wheat futures contracts as he could. When the Union army won the Battle of Gettysburg that summer, the fear that had gripped the markets subsided, and the wheat price plummeted. Old Hutch was then able to reap a fortune, by buying back the wheat futures contracts he had sold at a much lower price.

By increasing the committed supply of grain to the Unionist cause through futures contracts, the CBOT exchange had played a vital role in the northern military campaign. Futures contract commitments had sucked food in from the prairies, pumping grain to the Unionists, leaving the blockaded Confederates to slowly starve. Futures had become a weapon of war no less potent than the rifle and gunboat. Shortly after the Confederates surrendered in May 1865, Generals Grant and Sherman visited the CBOT trading floor to express their thanks. When they shook hands with Old Hutch it was hard to say who was more grateful. His actions in futures market had helped the Unionists win the war but it had also made him a *"hero from zero"* as he had gone from having almost nothing to making a fortune.

Over the next thirty years, Old Hutch was to become a legendary figure in Chicago, spawning many imitators. The lesson of 1863 was that speculators like Old Hutch, and thrifty users of the market like the Army, needed one another. Speculators had provided 'liquidity' in return for the market paying them a profit margin in the form of a trading bid/offer spread. It was very different from the controlled model of the Japanese rice futures market, where the raw speculator had played a subsidiary role.

Speculators lose their popularity through market corners

The heroic reputation of speculators did not last long. After the war their peacetime exploits soon had them cast as villains who ruined farmers and merchants through manipulation of commodity prices, by a technique known as 'cornering'.

The latter half of the 1800s is now regarded as the golden age for commodity futures manipulators. The internal rules of exchanges did not place any limits on individual position size or their disclosure, and their boards showed little interest in interfering with the freedom of the market. As for regulatory constraints, they were virtually non-existent.

With a market framework built around knowledge and trust amongst participants, there was no perceived need for an impersonal and heavily legalistic approach. This light touch extended beyond contract documentation and into creditworthiness. Buyers and sellers were confidently expected to meet their obligations through reputation and physical presence on the trading floor. Much less emphasis was placed on the more impersonal models of modern times, where collateral, or margin, have to be posted to maintain positions.

In the 1860s, so long as you were a member of the exchange, you could buy a million dollars' worth of grain futures and be charged only a small broker commission. For farmers growing corn and wheat and the merchants buying grain for cereal manufacture, this latitude on credit helped them to buy, sell and to hedge the price on delivery cheaply and effectively. Speculators were also trusted to be able to borrow money to fulfil their obligations to deliver if they held the contracts to maturity. This trust allowed them to control assets of much greater value than they could possibly afford without having to borrow money from a bank. It was this leverage from futures contracts that gave them the firepower to launch corners.

How 'Corners' are used to manipulate prices

The corner was first defined by the CBOT in the 1800s as the practice: *"making contracts for the purchase of a commodity, and then taking measures to render it impossible for the seller to fill the contract, for the purpose of extorting money"*.

It is a strategy by which the perpetrators use the force of their buying power and scale of their market positions to overwhelm those on the other side. In an extreme case a speculator might buy all of the available supply of certain goods and force those who need them to pay an extortionate price.

Speculators attempting to corner a market frequently take such large positions that the market price is driven by their weight of their money to move in their direction. In the Chicago corners of the 1800s, speculators bought virtually all the wheat due to be delivered at a certain time, and then could dictate the price at which they sold because no one else had any wheat left to sell at a lower price.

For those who had sold futures that were due in the same month and who needed to buy to fulfil their obligations, the results could be devastating. It was also often humiliating, as defeated `shorts' would be forced to plead in person for lenient terms from their victorious opponent.

Notorious corners in the 1800s

Old Hutch was involved in many attempts to manipulate the Chicago commodity futures markets and establish corners. In 1866, believing that there would be a poor wheat harvest, he built up a considerable long position in both physical wheat and in wheat futures contracts during May and June for less than $1 per bushel. Over the summer months, as reports came in of weak harvests in Illinois, Iowa and other states that sold their grain through Chicago, the wheat price rose steadily. Midway through August Old Hutch drove the wheat price up to $1.85, by demanding delivery from those who had shorted August futures contracts to him. Many of these were farmers who had hedged their wheat crop, suffering huge losses when the harvest failed to produce the amount of wheat they had confidently contracted to sell.

Not all corners were successful. Some failed, and in spectacular fashion, as John Lyon, one of Chicago's biggest wheat merchants, was to find out in 1872. The previous October a huge fire had destroyed much of Chicago, including six of the seventeen largest grain elevators. Grain storage capacity was reduced from 8 million bushels to 5.5 million bushels. Lyon felt he could profit from a potential supply shortage by buying as much wheat as possible. With this in mind Lyon joined forces with Hugh Maher, another grain dealer, and PJ Diamond, a CBOT broker.

In the spring of 1872, they started buying physical wheat and wheat futures contracts for less than $1 a bushel. Over the summer the wheat price rose steadily, reaching $1.35 per bushel at the beginning of August. All seemed to be going to Lyon's plan, to create a situation where there would be insufficient wheat to meet deliveries under the August futures contract.

Lyon was a little concerned when observing that wheat deliveries from the prairie into Chicago during July were higher than normal. But his cause was helped when another elevator was destroyed by fire at the beginning of August, and the 300,000 bushels of wheat stored inside were lost. There was suspicion of foul play and even the suggestion that Lyon himself might have been behind the fire. With bad weather reports reinforcing rumours that the new crop would mature too late for delivery against the August futures contracts, it seemed to Lyons that victory was at hand. This belief appeared to be substantiated when the price of the August wheat futures contract jumped to $1.61 on 15th August.

But news of the price hike in Chicago provoked an unprecedented response from the farmers. They brought forward and accelerated their harvesting, even buying lanterns so they could work at night. Instead of the 30,000-40,000 bushels per day usually delivered to Chicago at the peak of the harvest, trains were returning from the prairies every day with between 175,000 and 200,000 bushels. Making it worse for Lyon was that the normal trade routes went into reverse. Instead of wheat from Chicago being shipped to Buffalo and thence to the east coast cities, wheat that had already been shipped to Buffalo was brought back to Chicago and delivered to Lyon.

To keep the price up and his corner intact, Lyon was forced to buy more and more wheat. However, on the afternoon of Monday 19th August, the consortium had run out of money and, with the banks unwilling to lend more, the buying ceased. With no other buyers, the price of wheat plummeted. Unable to pay his debts Lyon was ruined whilst P.J. Diamond, who had orchestrated the futures operation, destroyed his trading books and fled.

Old Hutch and the most successful corner

The most successful corner of this period, and one considered by some to be one of the most successful ever attempted, was launched by Old Hutch in 1888. In the spring of that year he began to accumulate physical wheat and futures contracts for September delivery. Over the next few months, he acquired most of the 15 million bushels of wheat stored in Chicago for around 88 cents per bushel. His purchase price was kept down by a group of professional traders who systematically sold a proportion of the wheat crop each year. They had noted that the price of physical wheat tended to decline at harvest time and used short positions in the futures markets to cover their losses in physical wheat. In 1888 the September wheat futures contract turned into a heavyweight fight between Hutchinson and the short sellers.

Up until August, the two sides were well-matched and the wheat price held steady around 90 cents per bushel. But then reports came in of a heavy frost that had destroyed a big part of the harvest in the northwest, just as estimates of European demand were increasing radically to around 140 million bushels. On 22nd September, the price of wheat reached the psychologically important level of $1. Nevertheless, the shorts kept selling in the belief that Old Hutch would not be able to absorb all of the wheat coming to market. But they were wrong and Old Hutch kept buying all the physical grain and futures contracts that came to market.

On 27th September, three days before the contract delivery date, the September wheat futures contract opened at $1.05 and kept rising throughout the day, reaching $1.28 before the market close. The shorts were now in a state of panic and had no alternative, other than to capitulate. They went to Old Hutch and begged him to sell them some of the contracts he owned to enable them to close off their short positions.

Old Hutch now knew he had complete control of the market. Instructing the broker John Brine *"Let them have what they want at $1.25"* Old Hutch left the floor of the exchange, leaving the shorts to stand meekly in line and buy back their positions. Old Hutch had won the game.

Regulators turn on the speculators

As corners became a regular occurrence, the goodwill generated towards speculators after the Civil War evaporated. After Old Hutch's success in 1888, Chicago newspapers began to blame the suicides of those who had lost money on the perpetrators of the corner. Their aggressive speculation was also increasing volatility, leaving the farmers and consumers, who were the reason the market existed, to suffer from wild price swings. For the first time politicians took notice.

The final straw had come in 1898, when another speculator, Joseph Leiter, attempted another wheat corner. His plan failed when one of his intended victims, Philip Armour, who had sold wheat futures to Leiter, shipped in millions of bushels of wheat to Chicago using a privately chartered fleet of boats on the Great Lakes. With such chicanery at work, the activities of futures speculators transfixed the popular imagination and news wires.

Leiter was assailed as little better than a thief. He was vilified as an oppressor of the people, a man who ground the faces of the poor, and a man who bathed in luxury wrung from the toiling millions.

At the same time another type of contract had made an appearance. Called 'privileges' these contracts resembled futures except for one key difference. While the seller of a grain future has to deliver regardless of whether the price has gone up or down, privileges permitted the seller to refuse the delivery if the price had gone up; in other words when facing a loss. Because of the `privilege' of not delivering, the seller paid a premium up front. Nowadays these 'privilege' rights are known as options.

However, the national mood was changing. As an emerging global power with millions of mouths to feed, and an increasingly sophisticated electorate, America could no longer leave its food supply in the hands of a few businessmen and financiers. By the First World War, regulators were paying close attention to Chicago futures markets. As speculators like Hutchinson openly boasted that they were betting on prices, lawmakers and their supporters began accusing the CBOT of being a glorified gambling den. They were of the opinion that futures and privilege (options) contracts should be banned.

The speculators' only line of defence was that futures ultimately resulted in a physical grain delivery, even if they changed hands dozens of times beforehand. To emphasise their case, the CBOT decided to sacrifice privileges, which were considered even more suspect, because delivery was not always necessary. Reluctantly buying into the argument in 1934, Congress banned all privileges on commodities while permitting futures to remain.

The government did not stop there. In the Great Depression the writing was on the wall for futures speculators like Hutchinson and Leiter. After setting up a commission to monitor the futures markets, Congress made corners illegal under the Commodity Exchange Act in 1936. From then on all large futures positions had to be reported. Never again, in the United States at least, would a single speculator be allowed to control trading on an exchange.

Under the harsh spotlight of government regulation, options became a furtive species of contract, with the only type of options still legal after 1934 being options on stocks. This was the second time options had been banned. Just as with tulips in the 1600s, options were sacrificed on account of speculation, whilst futures survived. It was to happen time and time again in the years to come right up to the present day. It is a ritual that comes after periods of speculative excess; so predictable that it has almost become a tradition.

As evidence that the perpetrators of corners are not necessarily unscrupulous, one has only to look across New York harbour at the Statue of Liberty. This planned gift by the people of France to the United States was in danger of foundering in the 1870s due to a lack of funds. Completion was only made possible when the French copper industrialist, Eugène Secrétan, donated 60,000 kilos of copper, over half the copper plate needed for its construction. He was later to lose his entire wealth in the copper crash of 1889 when his 'Société Industriel et Commerciale des Métaux' went bankrupt after a failed attempt to corner the copper market in London.

To this day the speculator has yet to make a popular comeback, not least because the money that can be made by manipulating markets remains an irresistible temptation. And, just as was the case in that golden era of the late 1880s, those attempting corners have met with triumph and disaster in equal measure.

11. Sparks of freedom ignite a financial revolution - Chicago 1970

"There is nothing so strong as an idea whose time has come"

Victor Hugo (1802-1885)

When derivatives finally reached the financial world, the leaders of change were not to emerge from the bankers or investors whose markets they were to revolutionise; nor did they come from the efforts of the citizens of New York, London, nor any of the other cities that are home to the world's major financial markets. Instead they came from champions of freedom, particularly those who had suffered most from its absence. That is why Chicago, a city with little historical influence on financial markets, but one whose citizens' passion for free markets is matched only by their abhorrence of regulation by east coast politicians, was to take centre stage.

Building from a tried and tested framework for derivatives markets in food and agricultural products, two sparks ignited this financial market revolution in Chicago. The first was the free market credo behind the creation of markets to trade financial derivatives; the second a mathematical solution for pricing risk. It was largely a coincidence that both happened at the same time and in the same place, not least as the people who initiated and drove these innovations, could not have been more different.

The inspiration and backbone that drove the push for free market capitalism came from someone who had been and gone from Chicago, Friedrich Hayek. He was safely ensconced back in his European home when the sparks really began to fly.

Friedrich Hayek - Capitalism's free market inspiration

Friedrich Hayek was born in Vienna in 1899, to a family of academics and civil servants. Like others who played a significant role in the development of derivatives he was much taken with the writings of Aristotle, in particular his treatise on ethics. Conscripted into the army during the First World War, he was decorated for his bravery whilst a spotter in the flying corps, a role which left him with severe hearing difficulties for the rest of his life.

After the war Hayek earned two doctorates in law and economics, coming to public attention in the 1920s by causing a big stir in economic circles, through a provocative series of lectures on the causes of economic booms and busts. When offered a lecturing post at the London School of Economics just before the depression in 1929, he came into immediate conflict with his contemporary British rival John Maynard Keynes after a blistering review of *A Treatise on Money* that Keynes had just published. Afterwards he raised the temperature still further, through a public exchange of letters published in The Times newspaper in which he tore into the entire edifice of Keynesian thinking.

Hayek found himself championing the cause of capitalism and free markets at an unfashionable time, arguing that government attempts at intervention in the economy were misguided. He was particularly critical of those who, like Keynes, advocated the loose monetary policies of printing money and running up public debt in a vain attempt to spend their way out of recession and into economic growth. To Hayek such policies did nothing other than to devalue the currency and stoke the fires of inflation, which he regarded as the greatest economic evil of all.

In the midst of economic depression and the high unemployment of the 1930s, the politics were stacked against Hayek's philosophy. Nations elected governments who were willing to take action, rather than those who were content to stand by benignly. But Hayek stuck tenaciously to his guns and became a lonely voice speaking in opposition to public spending and government intervention in the economy.

Hayek was not just an ardent critic of Keynes. He was also a passionate opponent of the other fashionable economic icon of the time, Karl Marx. Although Marx had died some time before in 1883, his views were now gaining credence and popularity, particularly in the East. Marx advocated that capitalism and the profit motive should be abandoned altogether, on the grounds that such systems created a wealthy few who exploit a poor majority. But, to Hayek, state control of the economy simply created a different elite, and communism was no better in principle than capitalism, whilst economically much less effective. As the economic historian John Kenneth Galbraith put it: *"In capitalism man exploits man; in communism it's the other way round"*.

With the direction of travel against him, the debate in Western Europe finally settled against Hayek after Keynes published his *General Theory of Employment, Interest and Money* in 1936. Keynesianism became the dominant intellectual force in Western Europe as their social democracies boomed, whilst in the Soviet Union and other centrally planned economies, the Marxist ideology flourished as they scored impressive feats of industrialisation. Hayek's reputation went into eclipse and, although respected for his early contributions to monetary theory, he was to be ignored by other economists for the next thirty years.

Hayek continued lecturing at the LSE throughout the 1930s and 1940s, publishing his most famous work *The Road to Serfdom* in 1944. In this he predicted that the Marxist creed of collectivism would fail, whilst warning Western Europe and the United States of the dangers of socialism and big government. The book provided a rallying cry for free market intellectuals during what was, for them, a very bleak period. In 1950 Hayek moved to the United States to take up a professorship at the University of Chicago where he wrote the book that many consider to be his second masterpiece, *The Constitution of Liberty*. After its publication in 1960 he left the United States, returning to Europe in 1962.

But just as the wheel of fortune had been against him in the 1930s, so it turned in his favour in the 1960s and 1970s. In the West, economic growth began to stall, and the notion that currency exchange rates could be managed and controlled was falling into disrepute. But above all, inflation was beginning to erode the advances made in post war living standards. In the East dissatisfaction with the notion of state managed economies had been growing for some time, and it was one of those ironies that Hayek was being widely read in state controlled Eastern Europe at a time when his ideas were being ignored in the free democracies of the West.

By the mid-1970s Keynesian thinking was in retreat and Hayek's monetarist creed began to be advanced. His views now resonated and were even becoming fashionable with economists and politicians in both East and West. Confirmation that the tide had truly turned in his favour came in 1974 when he was awarded the Nobel Prize for his work in the 1920s and 1930s on money, prices and the causes of the business cycle. As recognition of his views became more widespread, his disciples now took up the reins and promoted his cause.

In February 1975, Margaret Thatcher was elected leader of the British Conservative Party. Soon afterwards the Institute of Economic Affairs arranged a meeting between Hayek and Thatcher in London and she was much taken by his humility and the simple clarity of his thinking. As she put it: *"Hayek's powerful Road to Serfdom, left a permanent mark on my own political character, making me a long-term optimist for free enterprise and liberty"*. Shortly afterwards, and at the only meeting of the Conservative Research Department she ever attended, a paper advocating that the party should steer a *"middle course"* in economics was presented. Thatcher interrupted the speaker part way through by reaching into her handbag and holding Hayek's *The Road to Serfdom* aloft for everyone to see. With the remark *"This is what we believe"*, she placed the book down next to the presenter and left.

One belief that Thatcher took from Hayek was that it was just as important for individual freedom that free choice be exercised in the market place as at the ballot box. US President Ronald Reagan was also an enthusiastic disciple of Hayek, describing him as one the handful of people who most influenced his philosophy. Reagan welcomed him to the White House as a special guest on many occasions during his tenure as President between 1981 and 1989.

Further honours were to follow his Nobel Prize. British Queen Elizabeth II, on Thatcher's recommendation, appointed Hayek to the Order of the Companions of Honour in 1984 for his *"services to the study of economics"* and he received the US Presidential Medal of Freedom from George W. Bush in 1991. His writings were also a major influence on many of the leaders of the 'velvet' revolution in Central Europe. Amongst his most ardent admirers was Vaclav Klaus, who was to become the first prime minister of post-communist Czechoslovakia in 1992.

But for Hayek, his greatest moment of triumph came when the Berlin Wall was taken down in 1989, and with it the collapse of the old Soviet Empire and its communist regimes. For him it was proof that his free market creed was right and Karl Marx had been wrong. His views on the economic inadequacies and political ills of central planning were now accepted, as was the recognition of the role he had played in highlighting the dangers of loose monetary policy and inflation.

As Milton Friedman, his greatest disciple amongst economists, was to put it: *"There is no figure who had more of an influence ...... on the intellectuals behind the Iron Curtain than Friedrich Hayek. His books were translated and published by the underground and black market editions, read widely, had undoubtedly influenced the climate of opinion that ultimately brought about the collapse of the Soviet Union".*

When Hayek died in 1992, three years after the fall of the Berlin Wall, his reputation and creed were at their peak. He was mourned by political leaders around the globe, some being woken specially to be told the sad news. A great man, who had championed the cause of free capital markets all his life and influenced so many prominent people inside and outside economics, had left the stage.

Milton Friedman unravels Keynesianism

Hayek's following in the United States, even after he won the Nobel Prize, mostly comprised a small band of monetary economists, of which Milton Friedman from the University of Chicago was the most notable. Like Hayek, he too held that rapid growth of the money supply was at the root of all outbreaks of inflation.

Born in Brooklyn in 1912, Milton Friedman was one of four children born to Jewish immigrants. He studied at Rutgers, Chicago and Columbia Universities, focusing on mathematics and economics. After the Second World War he began to display his free market colours at a time of Keynesian domination. Profoundly influenced by Hayek, he set about the task of unravelling all that Keynes had advocated.

Keynesians were supporting the deployment of short-term stimuli to spur consumer spending and the economy. Their belief was that giving temporary tax breaks through stimulus payments and the like would have the effect of increasing spending in the economy, which would be more than repaid through future tax revenues. In this way the government could have its cake of economic recovery and eat it too. Friedman took on this *"win win"* idea and analysed its efficacy against actual empirical evidence. This was in contrast to Keynes and his followers who rarely tested their hypotheses against such evidence.

Friedman and the other economists at the Chicago school led attack after attack on concepts like the Keynesian 'multiplier', which suggested that a government could stimulate new economic activity for a relatively modest cash outlay, by directing the money towards the people who spend most on the consumption of goods. Keynes argued that their extra spending would encourage businesses to hire more people, and their income would in turn then trigger further consumer spending. In this way each unit of public expenditure would multiply economic activity. Friedman's opposition to the Keynesian multiplier was on the grounds that the more the government borrows to spend, the greater the incentive it has to encourage inflation in order to lessen the real cost of future repayments. In Friedman's view such an approach was damaging, a form of tax on long term saving.

Friedman showed that people adjusted their annual spending habits in response to real changes in their lifetime income, not temporary artificial changes to their current income. Something substantive like a salary rise might prompt a family to spend more but a short-lived boost from a stimulus payment would not. This was the first crack in the Keynesian framework and was soon followed by attacks on other questionable assumptions underlying the theory.

Instead of trying to boost the economy by trying to fool consumers, Friedman believed the same objective could be met by minimising government involvement through lower taxes and non-inflationary policies. Friedman regarded inflation as just an attempt to fool consumers into thinking they were earning more, when the corresponding rise in the cost of living was actually cancelling out any gains in wages.

In his speeches and writings Friedman made the case that it was monetary policy not a failure of free market capitalism that had led to the Great Depression. Friedman surveyed almost a century of monetary policy during crashes, booms, recessions and depressions and came to the conclusion that the US Federal Reserve, created in response to the Panic of 1907, was the culprit for the depression. By shrinking the money supply by over a third between 1929 and 1933, Friedman argued that the Fed had turned a crash, something the U.S. had bounced back from many times before, into an extended depression.

Friedman began to focus more and more on the role of money in the economy. He had originally supported a gold standard to check inflation and prevent bank runs, but had subsequently shifted toward a hard money policy, where the amount of money in circulation should only be allowed to increase at the same pace as the nation's economic growth. He believed this would be a sufficient check to keep governments from printing as much money as they pleased, without causing the supply of money to constrain growth.

He was one of the few defenders of free market capitalism and became its global champion when his book *Free to Choose* and the accompanying television series, broadcast in 1980, made him the most famous economist alive.

The end of fixed exchange rates

In keeping with his opposition to Keynesian thinking Friedman took an active dislike to the Bretton Woods Agreement, which was an attempt to fix currencies rather than leaving them free to 'float' with market forces.

In 1967, convinced that the British pound was overvalued and about to be devalued by the British Government, Friedman attempted to sell pounds short in favour of US Dollars at the prevailing exchange rate of $2.80 for each £1, and then to secure a profit by buying the pound back afterwards at a lower exchange rate. When he approached his bank to carry out this transaction they refused, as did every other bank he contacted, pointing to a longstanding prohibition amongst US banks that prevented their retail customers from speculating in foreign currencies.

When the British Prime Minister Harold Wilson announced three weeks later that the pound was to be devalued by 14% so that £1 could now be exchanged for only $2.40, Friedman was furious that he had been unable to place his bet, venting his indignation in a regular column he wrote for the magazine Newsweek. It was there that he also made the case for floating exchange rates and freely tradable currencies.

Like Hayek, he accepted that free market capitalism might not be the perfect solution, but asserted that it was by far the best of all the alternatives being espoused. When the Keynesian system buckled in the 1970s under stagnant growth and rising inflation known as 'stagflation', economists began to take Friedman's anti-inflation, hard money policies much more seriously. Monetarism began to eclipse Keynesian solutions and, as Friedman and other Chicago School economists were appointed as economic advisors to many governments, they urged their political masters to adopt policies of hard money and small government.

Friedman himself became something of a Svengali to British Prime Minister Margaret Thatcher, encouraging her to open up London's capital markets to international competition, a policy which she adopted with her 'Big Bang' strategy.

Friedman and the Chicago School garnered several Nobel Memorial Prizes in Economic Sciences for their work in dismantling the most damaging Keynesian concepts, even though their 'hands off' approach never sat comfortably with governments and their treasury departments. It was only natural for civil servants to resist as this approach took away much of their decision making, even their raison d'etre. As Friedman opined in a 1998 speech: *We have gained on the level of rhetoric, lost on the level of practice.*" By this he meant that academic circles had accepted free market principles as superior to Keynesian thinking, but governments and their treasury civil servants preferred the power vested in them through Keynesian thinking. Friedman had introduced an alternative to big government trying to control economic activity, but few governments were willing to give up the reins.

Leo Melamed and the birth of financial futures

It needed something more than the intellectual thinking and influence of Hayek or Friedman to bring markets in financial derivatives into being. So many great ideas founder in delivery and practical implementation. This did not happen with financial futures and the credit for this achievement goes principally to the energy and persistence of a determined Chicago trader called Leo Melamed. Without him, Hayek and Friedman's vision might not have come into being.

Leo Melamed was born in Bialystok, Poland in 1932. He was only seven when captured with his family by the Nazis at the outbreak of the Second World War. Escaping to Lithuania, they still faced almost certain death as Germany took control, but were very fortunate in coming into contact with Chiune Sugihara, Consul for Japan in Lithuania. Against the orders of his superiors, Sugihara issued over 4,500 transit visas to Jews during the one month period in 1940 that he was stationed in Lithuania. Leo was one of just 300 children covered by those visas, through which he and his family were able to cross Russia on the Trans-Siberian Railway, and reach Japan. From there they crossed the Pacific Ocean to the United States on one of the last ships to do so, before the Japanese attack on the US naval fleet at Hawaii's Pearl Harbour in 1941 placed the two countries at war. Leo was nine years old when he and his family arrived in Chicago.

Melamed became involved in futures trading completely by accident. As he described it: *"I was (a twenty year old) in law school looking for a law clerk job and answered a want ad. The firm in question, Merrill, Lynch, Pierce, Fenner & Bean, was looking for a 'runner' to work between the hours of 9am and 1pm which was perfect for my class schedule. With that many names, how could this firm be anything but an established law firm looking for a clerk to run to court?"* In fact it was Wall Street's biggest securities house and Melamed found himself working as a runner in the agricultural commodity futures markets of the Chicago Mercantile Exchange (CME), where he learned the commodities futures business. He practised law initially but over time was drawn into the CME futures pits where he was successfully to trade eggs, butter, onions, pigs and poultry even being referred to as the *"Big Bacon and Egg Man"* by the Chicago Sun-Times. Joining the CME Board aged just 36, Melamed became Chairman in 1969.

Melamed realised that the most fertile source of new customers and products for the CME would be found by servicing the needs of the financial sector, and therefore set about transforming a moribund exchange for trading storable commodities into a thriving global exchange with a diverse product base.

Currency futures lead the way

Friedman's articles on currency trading restrictions encouraged Melamed to push for the creation of a currency futures market. He consulted with Friedman about the probability of the Bretton Woods System of fixed exchange rates falling apart as, without freely traded floating exchange rates, there could be no viable currency futures market. Friedman assured Melamed that Bretton Woods would collapse and that one currency after another would become free to float. In Friedman's view trading in currencies would become the most active financial market in the world and, once free from arbitrary exchange rate pegging, there would be many healthy benefits for international trade and consumers.

Friedman gave Melamed the confidence to plan for a currency futures market. As he put it: *"The IMM would not have been conceived were it not for the help and inspiration provided by Professor Friedman. It was he who gave us the courage to believe we were onto something big and worthwhile. It was his unquestionable prestige and authority that not only opened doors for us in Washington but enabled us to pronounce with credibility that a futures exchange in currency was a necessity and that its time had come. I seriously doubt if we would have proceeded without his full embracement of this project."* Friedman and Melamed both needed one another and they knew it.

Nailing the growth plan for the CME firmly to the financial futures mast, the exchange was ready to launch currency futures on its International Monetary Market (IMM) in 1972, shortly after the Bretton Woods agreement collapsed. Melamed had worked tirelessly to convince regulators, governments, and a new customer base of the efficacy and importance of financial futures in currencies.

Bretton Woods and the collapse of fixed exchange rates

The Bretton Woods system was agreed and came into force after a conference that forty-four World War II allied nations held in 1944 at Bretton Woods in the United States. The system laid the framework and rules for commercial and financial relations between the world's major industrial countries.

Bretton Woods set up the system of rules, institutions, and procedures that was to regulate the international monetary system including the establishment of the International Monetary Fund (IMF) and International Bank for Reconstruction and Development (IBRD).

The main feature of the Bretton Woods system was an obligation for each country to adopt a monetary policy that maintained the exchange rate by tying its currency to gold, with temporary imbalances of payment bridged by the IMF. The system also provided protocols to address lack of cooperation between countries, in particular to prevent competitive devaluation of currencies for economic advantage.

On 15 August 1971, the United States unilaterally terminated convertibility of the US Dollar to gold, effectively bringing the Bretton Woods system to an end, and rendering the dollar a 'fiat currency'; in other words one that has no medium for exchange into physical goods (from the Latin fiat 'it shall be') This action, referred to as the "*Nixon shock*" after the President who introduced the measure, Richard Nixon, created the situation in which the United States dollar became a reserve currency used by many countries. At the same time, a number of currencies, like the pound sterling, that had previously had their exchange rates fixed, became free-floating.

But the launch of the world's first financial futures exchange by commodity traders in Chicago was neither popular nor respected in New York financial circles; indeed it was even jeered at. One

New York foreign exchange trader commented on the eve of IMM opening: *"I'm amazed that a bunch of crap shooters in pork bellies have the temerity to think that they can beat some of the world's most sophisticated traders at their own game"*. There can be few who were happier than Melamed to prove those of that ilk wrong. As Merton Miller, another of Chicago's Nobel Prize winners (1990), was to say: *"In my view, financial futures represent the most important and far-reaching financial innovation of the last 20 years. They have changed forever, and for the better, the way business firms here and throughout the world manage and control the exchange-rate risks, interest rate risks, and portfolio risks they face. The times were indeed right for just such an innovation as foreign currency futures in the early 1970s."*

Early adopter of electronic trading

I first met Leo Melamed some fifteen years later at a conference in 1987. He had lost none of his creative resourcefulness and drive. The Chicago exchanges had followed up currency futures with interest rate and stock index futures. Melamed's determination to build an unimpeachable reputation for their financial futures market had been demonstrated on many occasions, not least in how he had dealt with the billionaire scions of HL Hunt over their dealings in currency futures. He was also to watch them fall when they made their assault on the silver market in 1980, which is discussed later.

When our paths crossed Melamed's entire focus had shifted to building a global franchise through pioneering electronic trading of financial futures. It was a very controversial topic, particularly in Chicago, where the champions of 'open outcry' pit trading met and traded in the flesh. His exchange members would lose out if such a style of trading became outmoded. But Melamed could already see that advances in computer and telecommunication technology would facilitate global electronic trading anyway, and was determined that the CME should lead the way. At another conference, which we both attended, he energetically sought out international investors, keen to test ideas and plans on international products and trading methods. These came together later that year when their international offering 'Globex' was launched. This leap of faith into electronic trading, initially to extend the trading hours beyond those of the Chicago floor, required vision, perseverance, capital investment, and an unbending faith and a willingness to change how customers and the exchange interacted with one other. He also never lost sight of the importance of educating the regulators and carrying the exchange membership with his vision.

Friedrich Hayek died in 1992, aged 92. He should have been content that his thoughts originating in the 1920s were finally taking good effect, and were bringing the West and East to a better place. He had also watched his torchbearers in Milton Friedman and Leo Melamed advocate and implement his creed around the world. The many honours heaped on him were of secondary importance to seeing his vision for free markets taking hold around the world.

Milton Friedman left the stage in 2006, a timely departure before the global financial crisis in 2008 called the free markets philosophy into question, and led to a re-emergence of Keynesian thinking amongst Western political leaders.

To this day Leo Melamed continues on his financial mission for the CME. He may take great pride in recent developments like the 2007 CME merger with the CBOT, the exchange that had been the industry giant when he joined the CME. He never met Hayek, but his closeness to Friedman is reflected in the 'Rose and Milton Friedman Suite' at his home in Scottsdale, Arizona. But I doubt if anything can ever eclipse his creation of financial futures in his home town of Chicago, far from the madding crowds of New York.

Unsurprisingly Melamed has never lost sight of his roots, and the memory of the dangerous journey he and his family were forced to make from Poland to America. Nor has he forgotten the debt he owes to Chiune Sugihara, the Japanese Consul in Lithuania, who issued Leo with the transit visa that saved him and his family from almost certain death.

Just outside the Holocaust Exposition in Vilnius, Lithuania's capital, there is a modest but lovely plaque to Sugihara. I visited this monument in 2013 and sent photographs to Leo of this and another monument situated just outside the Radisson Blu hotel. The latter is set amongst cherry trees, which were planted by alumni from Sugihara's University to mark the centenary of his birth.

Leo was delighted that Sugihara had been recognised in this way, even visiting Japan in 2014 at the age of 82 to attend a ceremony to honour Sugihara. For Leo: *"Any time anybody asks me to do anything that relates to Sugihara, I do, ... I've never said 'no' to anything."*

He was also amused to learn that the reason for my visit to Vilnius was when Lithuania held the European Union (EU) Presidency, and was hosting an EU Financial Forum to discuss how to make sure the financial market infrastructure around derivatives remained safe long after he has gone.

12. Fischer Black and the mathematical model that revolutionised finance

"Ye can lade a man up to th' university, but ye can't make him think."

Finley Peter Dunne 1867-1936 (Mr. Dooley's Opinions)

In 1997, the Nobel Memorial Prize for Economic Science was awarded jointly to Robert Merton and Myron Scholes. Unusually the citation referred to someone who had died two years before, Fischer Black. The press release that announced the prize stated simply:

"Robert C. Merton and Myron S. Scholes have, in collaboration with the late Fischer Black, developed a pioneering formula for the valuation of stock options. Their methodology has paved the way for economic valuations in many areas. It has also generated new types of financial instruments and facilitated more efficient risk management in society."

The *"pioneering formula"* which the Nobel Prize Committee referred to came to be known as the Black-Scholes option valuation model. Risk and time were the problems that defined the modern field of finance and had perplexed great minds for centuries. Black-Scholes was the mathematical solution that addressed this central issue.

The article setting out Black and Scholes ideas was written in 1970, but not published until May 1973. Entitled *The Pricing of Options and Corporate Liabilities* the article turned out to be one of the most influential pieces of research ever published in the field of economics and finance, even though it was rejected by the research journals of both disciplines. Fischer Black suspected that his *"lack of tribal war paint"* in part explained their reticence. Fischer had neither a degree in economics nor in finance but, as Jack Treynor was to say in his address to the International Association of Financial Engineers (IAFE) after his death in 1995:

"Fischer never took a course in either economics or finance, so he never learned the way you were supposed to do things. But that lack

of training proved to be an advantage since the traditional methods in those fields were better at producing academic careers than new knowledge. Fischer's intellectual formation was instead in physics and mathematics, and his success in finance came from applying the methods of astrophysics".

The Greek philosopher Thales had pioneered this way of thinking over two thousand years before. As Treynor explained: *"the astrophysicist relies on careful observation and then imagination to find the simplicity underlying apparent complexity. In Fischer's hands, the same habits of research turned out to be effective for producing new knowledge in finance".*

The challenge of option valuation

Determining the value of an option necessitates an assessment of the price of risk over the life of the option contract. The holder has the right to buy ('call option') or sell ('put option') an asset at a known price for a certain period of time and its value essentially fuses together two constituent parts. The first, the option value if exercised straight away, is called 'intrinsic value' whilst the second, the chance of a higher value in the future, is known as 'time value'.

Intrinsic value, the economic value of the option if exercised right away, is simple to calculate and certain in value. A call option to buy an asset for $100 has no value if the asset price is below $100 as you can purchase the asset elsewhere for less. However if the market price of the same asset is $120 the option has real worth, an intrinsic value of $20. This intrinsic value can be secured by purchasing the asset for $100 by exercising the option contract and then selling the asset straight away for $120. An option with intrinsic value is said to be 'in-the money' whilst one without is 'out-of-the-money'.

Time value is the amount by which an option price exceeds its intrinsic value. It is an assessment of how likely the option is to have intrinsic value during its life, and how great that value might be. Time value is more complicated to determine and the outcome less clear cut than intrinsic value. That is because intrinsic value can be calculated with simple arithmetic whilst time value is assessed through the mathematics of risk, probability and statistics.

The Black-Scholes Model

Black-Scholes, in their formula for a call option, concluded that five variables determined the option value:

- Current price of the underlying share
- Exercise price of the option
- Life of the option
- Cost of money (risk-free interest rate)
- Volatility

Black-Scholes Call Option Formula

$$C = SN(d_1) - N(d_2)Ke^{-rt}$$

$$d1 = \frac{\ln(S/K) + (r + s^2/2)t}{s \cdot \sqrt{t}}$$

$$d2 = d1 - s \cdot \sqrt{t}$$

C = Call option value	S = Current share price
t = Time until option exercise	K = Option exercise price
r = Risk-free interest rate	N = Cumulative standard
e = Exponential term	normal distribution
s = Standard deviation	ln = Natural logarithm

Certain assumptions are built into the model:

- The option can only be exercised at expiration ('European Style)
- No dividends are paid on the shares during the life of the option

---

- Stockmarkets are efficient (i.e. their movements cannot be predicted)
- There are no transaction costs
- Trading is frictionless, continuous, without any liquidity constraint
- The cost of money and volatility of the underlying are known and constant.
- Returns on the underlying are normally distributed.

As we shall see later these assumptions are of considerable importance. When they were ignored, particularly those concerning trading and liquidity, catastrophe was never far away, as those behind the stockmarket crash of 1987 and the collapse of the LTCM hedge fund in 1998 were to discover to their cost.

Although the formula appears complicated, even intimidating, the mathematics in essence express that:

- An option that has intrinsic value is worth more than one that has not.

- One with a long life is worth more than one with a short life as there is more time, and hence opportunity, to profit from intrinsic value.

- Interest rates matter as there is a cost saving from not having money tied up from owning the asset. When interest rates are high this benefit can be considerable and reflected in greater time value.

Whilst the above four variables into the formula are known and can be input with certainty, there is considerable difficulty determining what number to input for the final variable, volatility. This measure of price movement seeks to quantify the extent to which the price of the asset is likely to move up and down during the remaining life of the option contract. The more the price moves, the greater the chance of profiting from intrinsic value.

Options on assets with high volatility have greater time value than those whose price moves less.

Academics and practitioners have spent a great deal of time and effort trying to improve the estimation of future volatility. In truth it is a fruitless task, as you are trying to predict the future armed only with current observations and data from the past. It is akin to weather forecasting. If you wake up on a summer morning and are deciding what clothes to wear, history might suggest a coat will be unnecessary. If the weather forecast that morning is predicting sunshine and warmth you might elect for light clothes, and to leave your coat at home. But were you to looking out the window and note that others people were wearing coats and carrying umbrellas, their conduct would appear to imply wet and windy conditions were anticipated. From this mix of historic, forecast and implied information you will decide what to wear, but will only know if you were right at the end of the day.

Numerous academics who claim refinements to the BlackScholes model have really only made a different assumption on the distribution of asset returns, or their guess at future volatility. One experienced trader who had been subjected to the full gamut of valuation models put it thus: *There are four volatility assessments. An historical value, which tells you where it used to be; a forecast value which draws on lots of clever models, observations and theories drawn from past data to suggest what it ought to be; an implied volatility, which is the market's best guess. Then there is the number you're striving for, the actual outcome, which is usually completely different to the other three!"*

The British comedian Peter Cook, in one of his sketches with Dudley Moore, claimed his Uncle Bert could foresee the future. One proof Uncle Bert gave as evidence was: *"The weather is going to be unpredictable; he predicted that."* For all the intellectual and computational power that has been deployed on estimating volatility in financial markets, we have not advanced much further with volatility than Uncle Bert did with the weather.

Elegance of the Black-Scholes solution

Those who had sought to come up with a mathematical solution to option pricing had laboured with complex notions of how asset prices, and shares in particular, moved over time. The elegance of Black-Scholes was to consider an option as simply a dynamic mixture of cash and the asset to which it related. As Emmanuel Derman a colleague of Black's at Goldman Sachs explained: "*Black and Scholes showed that you can manufacture an IBM option by mixing together some shares of IBM and cash, much as you can create a fruit salad by mixing together apples and oranges.... Whereas a fruit salad's proportions stay fixed over time (50% oranges and 50% apples, for example) an option's proportions must continually change as the share price rises or falls. The exact recipe you need to follow is generated by the Black-Scholes equation and its solution tells you the cost of following the recipe. Before Black and Scholes, no one guessed that you could manufacture an option out of simpler ingredients...*"

The brilliance in the thinking behind the Black-Scholes solution was in observing a parallel with the mathematics of the 'heat equation', a differential equation for calculating the time it takes for heat to diffuse from one end of an object, typically a metal bar, to the other.

It was this insight and evaluation that allowed those offering options to hedge the risk they were taking on. Black-Scholes provided the mix of cash and assets to be held for a particular share price, the 'hedge ratio' as well as a cost estimate for running the strategy.

Before Black-Scholes, risk had been priced by intuition and the experience of past outcomes. The most common form of risk pricing was insurance policies where the main determinant in pricing new insurance business was past claims. Pioneered by Edmund Halley in the 1600s, this approach made the past more important than perhaps it should have been in determining the future. It was a tradition initially carried on with option pricing and why historical volatility was initially overemphasised, and the notion of implied volatility largely ignored.

What keeps the academics going is the same thing that keeps weather forecasters going, the link between historic patterns of movement and subsequent ones. There is no shortage of evidence to demonstrate that assets that have moved up and down in price in the past tend to carry on doing so in the future. Equally those that have not moved much in the past tend to maintain their dullness. It is intuitive too as the earnings and future prospects of some companies are much more predictable than others.

Impact of Black-Scholes option valuation model

In one of those strange coincidences where important linked events occur independently at the same moment in time, the Chicago Board Options Exchange (CBOE) opened for business in April 1973, one month before the Black-Scholes paper appeared in print. The CBOE offered standardised contracts in stock options, initially operating on the floor of the smoking lounge in the Chicago Board of Trade (CBOT). Market makers quoted option prices and provided liquidity with the CBOE regulating trading practices and publicly reporting transactions.

The second coincidence was that, at the very time the Black-Scholes article appeared in The Journal of Political Economy and the CBOE started trading stock options, the hand-held electronic calculator first appeared on the scene. Within six months, Texas Instruments, then the dominant player in the calculator market, included the Black-Scholes option valuation computation on its most advanced financial calculator, taking out a half-page advertisement in The Wall Street Journal to announce this feature. Within a very short period of time the Texas Instruments calculator was being used to price options on the floor of the exchange and for the first time the language and mathematical expressions of the Black-Scholes article, such as hedge ratios and Greek symbols, entered the financial lexicon. The world of risk management had vaulted into a new era.

Revolutionary thinking expressed with humility

Fischer Black's influence on finance went well beyond the Black-Scholes option model, particularly after he joined the investment bank Goldman Sachs in 1983. It was then that his orbit expanded beyond the academic gods of modern finance and came to include practitioners in financial markets.

I first met Fischer when he came over to London, shortly after joining Goldman. I was president of The Options and Futures Society (TOFS), an organisation founded to educate and promote financial derivatives in Europe a small group of traders and investors had founded. Fischer was interested to learn how we were progressing and the hurdles we were confronting. He was very supportive, offering a great deal of advice on how to convey the derivatives message, having learned much from writing regular news sheets himself to inform and encourage US market practitioners in the late 1970s.

I interviewed Fischer for the TOFS quarterly journal on what was then a very sensitive topic: Should companies be concerned when options were listed on their shares? This was an important issue as options were being listed for the first time on the shares of more and more companies and there was concern about their effects on the underlying share price. A common view that was held then was that the volatility of the shares would increase. Furthermore some were advocating that companies should try to prevent put options being listed on their shares since they would facilitate betting on share price decline through 'shorting'. Then, as is still the case with many today, profiting from rising prices is seen as *"good investment"* whereas benefiting from falling prices by shorting was undesirable, even immoral.

After quietly considering the issue Fischer expressed the view that: *"Listing options on a company's shares is like a public relations campaign; more people will consider the shares so the price will probably go up."* Several months later, and unprompted, he sent through some analysis he had subsequently carried out, with data supporting his initial thoughts.

On another occasion I joined him and Harry Markowitz for a meeting at the Institute of Actuaries in London. Markowitz was another who would receive the Nobel Memorial Prize for Economic Science, in his case for his pioneering work on the influence of risk, correlation and diversification on portfolio returns, the very foundations of modern portfolio theory. When asked to comment on the option pricing paper being presented, one that described how historical experience alone could be used to value options, Fischer, whilst courteous, was typically honest and succinct: *"Has the world of financial economics been completely ignored?"*

Over the years I turned to Fischer for his thoughts and advice on many occasions, the most important of which concerned an investment strategy known as *"Portfolio Insurance"* which is discussed later. He was always interested in hearing the issues facing practitioners and was willing to help. Solving problems was his reason for living.

As an individual he was unfailingly thoughtful, modest and patient. Jack Treynor marvelled at the large number and wide range of people who regard knowing Fischer as one of the most important things in their lives. That is certainly how I feel. Even Myron Scholes, his co-author on Black-Scholes, found himself asking *"What would Fischer say?"* when confronted with a new intellectual problem after Fischer's death.

Fischer Black was in so many ways the modern embodiment of Thales the Milesian. Like Thales, his study of the stars provided earthly insights of extraordinary consequence. As one of his partners at Goldman Sachs remarked: *"Fischer was the only genius I have ever met"*. Like many others I know of no one more worthy of that badge.

13. Changing the rules to deny the victor - the Hunts and silver - London and New York 1980

"Invest in silver and you can never go wrong"

Nelson Bunker Hunt (1926-2014)

How much money is enough? The response of John D. Rockefeller, the richest person who ever lived, was: *"just a little bit more."* Perhaps that view helps explain why he kept pushing until his Standard Oil Company had a virtual monopoly in the US oil business. After suffering a massive fine for violating the Sherman Anti-Trust Act the company was forcibly broken up in 1911 by the US Government. The company was divided into five separate regional companies, including what became Exxon, Mobil, Chevron and Amoco. As often seems to be the case with enforced break up of businesses, this action only served to make Rockefeller even richer. Until recently overtaken by Apple, one of these companies, Standard Oil of New Jersey, better known as Exxon, was America's most valuable company. When at this pinnacle, Exxon was even able to cement its position by joining forces with one of the original band members, Mobil, formerly Standard Oil of New York.

Bunker, Herbert, and Lamar Hunt clearly subscribed to a similar view. Left with trust funds in 1974 approaching US$2 billion each by their father, H.L. Hunt, the brothers came to personify the adage that: *"the best way to make a small fortune in commodities is start with a large one."*

The story of the Hunts and silver is not simply a tale of a rich man's offspring squandering their inheritance. It is one of using supreme money power to first corner a market and then overwhelm every other player in the game. Well planned and executed, it turned into a battle between the financial muscle of formidable moneyed outsiders and a market establishment whose most potent weapon was control over the rules of the game.

Why the Hunts pursued silver in the brazen way that they did, and how their long running controversy with authority and the US Government goaded the establishment into breaking them, goes to the very heart of Texas and the oil business. There is a sense of pride mingled with confidence and self worth amongst Texans encapsulated in the expression: *"Never ask a man where he's from; if he's from Texas he'll tell you; if not there's no need to embarrass him."*

Playing poker for oil leases - HL Hunt makes a fortune

"Money is just a way of keeping score"

HL Hunt (1889-1974)

Their father Haroldson Lafayette (HL) Hunt was a man who had been many things from cowboy to farmer; but at heart he was a gambler. Poker was his game and early in 1921, following oil discoveries at El Dorado, Arkansas, HL took his poker skills to the oil patch, using gambling winnings to buy oil leases. After failing to find oil in Arkansas, HL moved to Texas in 1930 where he ran into a wily but broke old wildcatter, Columbus Joiner, who had persisted in drilling for oil on a farm near Kilgore in East Texas that belonged to a genial widow called Daisy Bradford. It was bleak territory and the geologists from the big oil companies had written it off as an area unlikely to contain oil.

Joiner had struggled to raise money to drill exploration wells and had ended up 'over promoting' the property to fund a second well which, like the first, came in 'dry'. The over promotion had come from selling stakes in the property that in total added up to over 100% of the lease, leaving Joiner with no interest left for himself and embroiled in a legal mess arising from the fraud. Joiner remained optimistic that there was oil under the Bradford Ranch but was no longer able to fund or initiate any further drilling.

Hunt took Joiner to a hotel in Dallas and kept him there ostensibly to negotiate a way out of his predicament. Meanwhile Hunt was secretly keeping tabs on a crucial well being drilled adjacent to the Bradford Ranch. When Hunt heard news that this nearby well had struck oil, he offered to extricate Joiner from his debts and fund another well by paying Joiner $30,000 in cash for the Bradford oil lease, with more if they struck oil. At the time HL only had $109 in the bank, but raised the $30,000 cash needed to buy out Joiner by selling on a 20% interest in the Bradford lease. Joiner chose the site and, with little cash at his disposal, drilled Hunt's first well using a drilling rig consisting of rusty pipes powered by a sawmill boiler with old tyres and wood for fuel. Joiner's crew comprised one experienced driller and some out-of-work farm hands.

In a matter of days oil had spurted out, stabilising at an extraordinarily high rate of 7,000 barrels a day. They had found what turned out to be the huge six billion barrel East Texas oilfield, the largest in the world. Forty-five miles long and five miles across, the field was to spark the most aggressive oil rush in the industry's history, and to set HL Hunt on the way to his fortune. He was eventually to vie with another oilman, Jean Paul Getty, for the title of the *"richest man in the world"*. Sadly Joiner, now known as *"Dad"* for fathering of the East Texas oilfield, suffered the fate of many pioneers, retiring in penury to a small house in Dallas where he died in 1947. His only legacy was that the town that grew up around the oilfield he had discovered was renamed Joinerville in his honour.

Washington politics and Texas

Some of HL's gambling instinct was to rub off on his offspring. After HL handed over the reins of Hunt Oil to his sons, the business prospered until 1973 when their biggest oilfield, the Bunker Hunt field in Libya, was nationalised by Colonel Gaddafi to punish the United States for supporting Israel in that year's Arab-Israeli war. Gaddafi described the nationalisation as *"a good hard slap on their (American) cool and insolent face."*

The Hunts were furious. Hunt Oil had lost its biggest asset because Washington was pursuing a foreign policy which the family vehemently opposed. And no one in Washington seemed to care about their predicament. As Nelson Bunker Hunt put it: *"Up North they never liked rich Texans, and we were the richest."*

The episode served only to reinforce the Hunts' support for Texas to become independent from the rest of the United States. Profligate spending domestically, a foreign war in Vietnam, and support for Israel in their view was undermining the nation's economic strength. Furthermore the Hunts' fortune was being eroded by inflation and the loss of confidence in the US Dollar. President Richard Nixon had made the unilateral decision to *"close the gold window"* in 1971, by ending convertibility between the US dollar and gold. Amongst economists it was called the *"Nixon Shock"* as there was no consultation with any other country in the international monetary system, in spite of the immediate and global effect. A floating exchange rate system, without convertibility of paper currency into gold, has been in place ever since.

By removing the constraint on printing money, this measure weakened the currency as a store of value and fuelled further inflation. John Maynard Keynes had described inflation as the means by which: *"Government can confiscate, secretly and unobserved, an important part of the wealth of their citizens;"* Nelson Bunker Hunt expressed it rather more succinctly: *"a billion dollars ain't what it used to be."*

The Silver Game

By the time HL died in October 1974 the family had had their first foray into the silver futures market. They regarded precious metals as the best hedge against inflation, in part because strong currencies historically were backed by gold and silver. They could not buy gold as it was illegal for any citizen of the United States to hold more than $100 worth of gold. This 1933 law had been brought into force during the Great Depression by President Franklin D. Roosevelt to stem the tide of people exchanging paper money for gold, as US gold reserves had become dangerously low from gold hoarding. Passing this law had been the only way to maintain a gold underpinning for paper money without threatening the national monetary system.

In addition to the protection which silver afforded against inflation, the economic case for a higher silver price was also strong. Demand for silver was well ahead of supply, and reserves were low. The silver $price also looked attractive relative to gold as international investors with similar inflation worries had driven up the gold price by concentrating their financial firepower on the metal.

Preparing for the Silver Corner - Hunt Brothers hone their skills and test the water

Against this background, the Hunts opted to purchase enormous quantities of silver at around $2 an ounce. They bought everything with the word silver in it; mines, coins, ingots, and alongside these physical purchases, futures too. Their aggressive buying helped run the silver price up from $3 to $6. The higher price attracted new supply out of hiding and the price retreated, leaving the brothers nursing what for them was an inconsequential loss of around $25 million. This whole foray was however to prove to be a useful pilot run and prepare them for what was to come.

After this initial experience the Hunts worked assiduously to develop their investment and trading skills as the means for protecting their wealth from being eroded by the vagaries of inflation.

They became large and experienced users of derivative markets, principally foreign currency and silver futures. They also formed alliances with Saudi investors who, like them, were earning their revenues in a weakening US dollar, and suffering erosion of their wealth through inflation.

In October 1979, the Hunt brothers, in conjunction with prominent Saudi Arabian investors, made another move, a second assault on the silver market. The price was rising, fuelled by inflationary fears, and those who had sold silver futures short were forced to pay substantial amounts of cash to the purchasers each day in variation margin to cover their unrealised losses. Silver soon moved up to $16 an ounce and the squeeze was on.

Their opponents were known as *"The Silver Bears."* These short sellers of silver futures were mainly commercial producers of silver who sold futures contracts to lock in the price at which they could sell the silver they produced. A handful of professional bullion dealers, who made their living buying and selling silver bullion, hedged the price they had paid for their inventory by selling futures. With the price rising so quickly the silver bears were paying out a great deal of cash in mark-to-market variation margin and had to find a way to stop the bulls; otherwise their own liquidity position would worsen.

Rapidly running out of cash, their choices were to 'close out' their short futures positions and take the price risk of 'riding the bull', to default on the contracts, or to change the rules of the game. The Silver Bears opted for the latter and went to the regulators.

Their first port of call was the Commodity Futures Trading Commission (CFTC), which had been created in 1975 to regulate futures trading. The CFTC's main purpose was to detect and correct market disturbances. In October 1979, the commissioners were alerted about the Hunts, in particular to the fact that they were taking delivery of enormous quantities of silver when the futures contracts matured. Although perfectly legal, this was rarely done as the silver futures market was principally used for hedging. Those seeking to acquire silver generally did so by buying physical silver in the 'cash market' and not by taking delivery from derivative contracts. However, after looking into the Hunts activities, the CFTC took no action after concluding that there was no direct manipulation of the silver market.

This outcome was not accepted by the directors of the two US exchanges where silver futures were traded, New York's Commodities Exchange (Comex) and Chicago's Board of Trade (CBOT), not least because their best customers and biggest users were 'short' and being hurt by the bear squeeze.

It did not help that the Hunts were not well liked by both the exchanges and those with the power to change the rules of the game, in spite of the business the Hunts were generating. Lamar Hunt had rubbed up Leo Melamed the wrong way in the mid-1970s in an aggressive meeting over a precautionary margin increase in Mexican Peso foreign currency futures that the CME had introduced. Lamar had claimed that the Hunts' wealth was such that the credit checks imposed on their trading need not be as stringent for them as on other participants, making clear that the margin increase was not to his liking. Melamed was unmoved, but that incident was typical of the bullying manner adopted by the Hunts who were accustomed to having their own way.

By the beginning of January 1980 the Hunts and their allies controlled over 192 million ounces of silver, the equivalent of half of the world's deliverable supply, and had driven its price to over $37 an ounce. As the silver price rose they had the nice problem of deciding what to do with all the cash they were accumulating in variation margin on their unrealised gains. They decided to invest in Bache Halsey Stuart Shields (later part of Prudential), the brokerage firm which was acting for them in the silver market, who were profiting considerably from the commissions generated by the Hunts' trading.

Such investment was not unusual in the oil business. JD Rockefeller, Standard Oil's founder, bought and merged two banks, Chase and Manhattan, to form Chase Manhattan Bank (which later bought JP Morgan and adopted their name) ensuring their success through handling all of the money Standard Oil was generating from the oil business. But in the case of the Hunts their investment in Bache was to be their undoing.

Changing the rules of the game - Hunts in trouble

On 8th January 1980, after silver had closed above $40 the previous evening, the Comex board met and adopted Silver Rule 7, limiting an individual to no more than 2,000 contracts or 10 million ounces of silver. The rule was to take effect on 18th February and this meant that the Hunts could not buy any more silver futures on New York's Comex, prompting them and the Saudis to transfer their business to the London Metal Exchange (LME) where there were no such restrictions. With their sales on Comex more than matched by their purchases on the LME and the silver price resumed its upward climb, peaking at $49.48 per ounce on Friday 18th January.

Comex appeared to have been outflanked. The Silver Rule 7 was progressively shifting business from New York to London, without relieving any pressure on their main customers who continued to be squeezed. From watching the pattern of trading and size of outstanding contracts, known as 'open interest', on Comex and the LME, it became clear that reducing the Hunts' positions on Comex to below 2,000 contracts by 18th February would not undermine their control of the silver market at all. Something had to be done, and quickly, as the Hunts' silver squeeze was not just hurting their customers; Silver Rule 7 was in danger of marginalising Comex's competitive position in the silver futures market.

On Monday 21st January 1980 Comex declared an emergency. They cited the political crisis resulting from 53 US citizens who had been taken hostage the previous November in Tehran by the new fundamentalist Iranian Government of Ayatollah Khomeini, (which would later lead to a disastrous rescue mission), to opine that the silver market had been destabilised by unforeseen events, creating speculative demand for precious metals.

Two new measures were introduced to deal with the emergency. First they raised 'initial margins', the capital that had to be deposited to back futures positions. Second they ruled that trading in silver futures would be limited to 'liquidation only'. This latter measure meant that no one could buy silver futures except for those with an existing short position that they wished to close out through an offsetting purchase. For those like the Hunts who only held long positions in silver futures, it meant that the only people they could now sell to were those who had already sold futures contracts.

Surrender to the defeated

The Hunts were now trapped. The 2,000 contract restriction under Silver Rule 7 was forcing only one player, the Hunts, to cut their positions by 18th February. And the emergency provisions meant they could only sell to the shorts. Comex had effectively delivered the Hunts into the hands of those they had just vanquished on the battlefield.

The shorts needed no encouragement and marked the price they were willing to pay the Hunts to close out their futures positions sharply lower. The next day the silver price closed at $41.45, a 16% decline; the following day it fell to $35.76, a 28% decline. The shorts knew they had a forced seller and they were the only buyers. The squeeze had been turned around and it was the Hunts, not the sellers who were being put to the torch.

For the Hunts leverage now worked in reverse. They were the ones needing cash to meet their variation margin requirements. But much of the cash they had gained in variation margin on the way up was now tied up in a share stake of more than 5% of Bache. This made them insiders, and they could only sell a small proportion of their stake in Bache each month on account of Securities and Exchange Commission (SEC) rules. Moreover, when trading in Bache shares became suspended, the value of their Bache stake could no longer be used as collateral in a margin account.

On 27th March, silver plummeted over 50% in a single day, falling from $21.62 to $10.80, forcing the Hunts into default as they were unable to meet a $135 million margin call. Within a matter of weeks they had run up around $1 billion of losses on their silver positions. A consortium of banks, worried by the panic that had seized the market, bailed the brothers out by lending $1.1 billion to their Placid Oil Company. Burdened by this debt and in a climate of falling oil prices, Placid was to collapse as well, filing for bankruptcy in 1986.

The story of the Hunts, both business and personal, was so extraordinary that a highly successful TV series was based on them in the 1980s and revived in 2012. Called *"Dallas"* it followed the fictional Ewing family in their oil and personal adventures. Extraordinary as the Ewing characters seemed, there are many who view the real life of the Hunts as even more colourful and extreme.

The Hunts were beaten but had enjoyed many victories and had come close to winning the game. The family was far from broke but no longer the financial force they once were. Their personal assets, including racehorses and coin collections, were kept safe from creditors but, through the silver debacle, they had managed to give the entire HL Hunt fortune back in less than half the time taken to accumulate it.

Having studied the game, learnt the rules, tested whether or not they could be bent and, after concluding that any attempt to stop them was unlikely to succeed, they had played an aggressive game to win by the rules. But they were not club members and had made no attempt to be popular. Their strategy put them on a collision course with the stalwarts and they only lost because the rules were deliberately changed to stop them. Moreover they were only just beaten and took the whole club to the wire.

One is left to ponder what would have happened if the Hunts had been more secretive and less abrasive in their approach, executing a less aggressive pricing strategy over years, rather than a few months. When Nelson Bunker Hunt was asked this question, his view was that they had made one error in execution, which was to tie up too much capital in the Bache shareholding. But that alone would not have unravelled them. Where the Hunts and their consortium of backers went wrong was in underestimating the antipathy of their establishment enemies towards them, and the speed and aggression with which they would muster their friends with regulatory influence to change the rules of the game against them.

But perhaps we have since received a clue as to the outcome of a less abrasive campaign. There was someone who was trading in another metal on Comex and the LME at the same time who was watching carefully as the Hunts' strategy to take control of the silver market was overturned. He may have reckoned that a slower, more secretive and less confrontational approach would have succeeded. How such a 'slow burn' alternative approach might fare was put to the test some sixteen years later, when the person who had watched the Hunts rose to become the chief copper trader for Sumitomo.

14. Exchanges proliferate and boom - 1980s onwards

The Hunts episode with silver gave succour to those who believed derivatives were instruments for speculation, but did nothing to slow their advance. The clearest evidence of their increasing adoption and acceptance came in the early 1980s when derivative exchanges opened up all over the world, thereby broadening the range of assets and financial instruments on offer. Exchanges have been opening up ever since.

Profitable symbols of financial modernity

The story of international derivatives exchanges in the 1970s and 1980s has parallels with the airline industry, in that they were as much symbols of national pride and maturity as a response to an economic imperative. Opening a local financial futures exchange carried with it the messaging of free markets and financial modernity.

Other factors that led to their establishment were local competition between exchanges and rivalry between neighbouring countries. If you had a stock exchange trading local company shares but no derivative exchange sitting alongside, there was a danger that someone else would offer derivative trading in your domestic shares as a platform to seize the share trading as well.

Those that built derivative exchanges well, with genuine purpose and decent management, quickly became profitable. Unlike national airlines, they were not expensive to set up. Warren Buffett had highlighted the weakness in the airline business model in a 2008 letter to his Berkshire Hathaway shareholders, when describing an investment in US Airways in the early 1990s as one of his biggest mistakes: *"The worst sort of business is one that grows rapidly, requires significant capital to engender the growth, and then earns little or no money. A durable competitive advantage has proven elusive ever since the days of the Wright Brothers. Indeed, if a farsighted capitalist had been present at Kitty Hawk (scene of the first manned flight) he would have done his successors a huge favour by shooting Orville down."*

United States sets the pace

Thanks to Leo Melamed, it was Chicago which led the way into financial derivatives through the launch of currency futures contracts on the Chicago Mercantile Exchange (CME) in 1972. As home to both free market philosophy and a derivatives expertise stemming from their commodity futures heritage, Chicago proved to be a strong and effective champion.

The East Coast bankers held them at bay in currencies through forward contracts. Unlike futures contracts, forwards were operationally much simpler to process. Margin did not have to be posted every day to ensure credit worthiness, as it was a banking market at a time when there was little fear of a bank counterparty defaulting. Even when exchange controls were abandoned in 1979, a decision which freed up currency trading in countries like the UK and sent cumbersome currency hedging alternatives like back-to-back loans into retirement, currency futures did not flourish as the balance had already been tipped in favour of forwards.

The breakthrough for financial futures came from interest rate contracts when Richard Sandor, a young professor from University of California in Berkeley, when on sabbatical as Chief Economist at the Chicago Board of Trade (CBOT), designed the US Treasury Bond futures contract. It was an immediate success and to this day remains the most widely traded and imitated interest rate futures contract in the world. It is one reason why in some quarters Sandor is regarded as the *"father of financial futures"*, an epithet he is more than happy to share with Leo Melamed.

Sandor had started out believing that insurance contracts would be the most important futures contracts, advocating their early launch. It is only recently that these contracts have been developed and taken to market with him, unsurprisingly, as its champion through the Chicago Climate Exchange which he founded. Sandor was also to coin the term *"derivative"* to describe a futures or options contract traded on the Chicago exchanges, on the grounds that their prices were derived from the price of underlying cash settled contracts.

The success of Chicago in financial futures, and the development of the Black-Scholes model for pricing share options, brought US regional stock exchanges into the derivatives game through their listing traded options on local company shares. The Chicago Board of Trade (CBOT) was first to do so by establishing an options exchange in one corner of their futures floor, which they called the Chicago Board Options Exchange (CBOE). New York and Philadelphia were not far behind through the American Stock Exchange (AMEX) and the Philadelphia Stock Exchange (Philly) respectively. A fourth exchange on the West Coast, the Pacific Stock Exchange (PSE), with trading floors in Los Angeles and San Francisco, started trading options on local shares in 1976. The PSE was particularly fortunate when one of their local enterprises, Microsoft, rose to become the most traded share in the world.

The regional exchanges were able to flourish as the technological difficulties of order routing to multiple destinations made it hard for rival exchanges like Chicago to list competitor products. In any event there was a form of gentleman's agreement for allocating option listing of companies between the exchanges, so as not to fragment liquidity by competing with one another. This practical but somewhat cosy arrangement fell away when competition had become easier through innovations like electronic trading and simplification of pricing by quoting in decimal points instead of fractions. First their trading floors disappeared and then their regional face too, including even the Pacific Stock Exchange, which through a series of mergers, eventually became part of the New York Stock Exchange in 2006.

Once Chicago had set the ball rolling it was the Philly, founded in 1790 and America's oldest stock exchange, that was to prove the most innovative and fleet of foot. They knew they had to be different and work harder to compete with their powerful cousins in Chicago and New York, and were to toil tirelessly, literally day and night, to do so.

The Philly first launched currency options in 1982 with the support of the banks, and were able to build a successful business, whilst Chicago floundered with the option contracts they listed on their currency futures contracts instead of the underlying cash currency. As the currencies on which the Philly listed options on were mainly traded outside US trading hours, they progressed towards twenty-four hour trading by first introducing a trading session beginning at 2.30am to coincide with European markets, and subsequently a late evening session for Asian currencies. .

Visiting this beacon of light at 3am one morning in 1985 from the dark and empty streets of Philadelphia, I tried to imagine the bold advocate of the scheme presenting the idea of trading currency options to the Board of the Philadelphia Stock Exchange. *"So we're going to trade currencies when all we do now is trade a limited range of US shares and their option contracts. And we're going to do this round the clock. And the rest of the world, most of whom don't even know where Philadelphia is, will come and trade on the floor of our exchange. And at 3am there will be a Chicago-like buzz of energy and presence from smart option traders taking orders by telephone from all over the world."* The extraordinary achievement of that small domestic US exchange is because that Board approved the proposal and the answer to all of those questions was a resounding *"Yes!"*

Trading volumes were now booming and the tide moving overwhelmingly in favour of derivatives over the securities to which they related, as their trading costs were a fraction of those for securities and, to the surprise of the doubting 'Jeremiahs', large orders were easier to execute.

American threat forces the rest of the world to respond

The meteoric success of US derivatives exchanges was initially confined to contracts on US securities and products. When they turned their heads towards Europe, and started to unleash international ambitions, they acted as the catalyst that broke the long history of derivative market rivalry between the Dutch and the

British, leading to a cessation of hostilities as they teamed up with one another to face their transatlantic foe.

When the stock exchanges of London and Amsterdam proposed a joint venture to offer a share options market to rival the US quartet led by Chicago's CBOE, their fear was that US exchanges would start trading options on European shares and then go after the share trading business of their stock exchanges. However, once again the worried scepticism born in the 1600s held Britain back and the London Stock Exchange (LSE) got cold feet, withdrawing their consent to join forces with the Amsterdam Stock Exchange. Amsterdam, as ever bold and taking pride from being the oldest stock exchange in the world (they were founded in 1602 to provide a market for the stocks and bonds of the Dutch East India Company), recruited the LSE's Technical Director Michael Jenkins in 1978 to help set up the European Options Exchange (EOE) in Amsterdam. The market makers or 'jobbers' on the LSE were furious at this decision, and took steps to launch their own options market in London.

Goaded by the jobbers and worried that Amsterdam would take the next step and list UK shares in Amsterdam elicited a half hearted response from the LSE, who listed a handful of option contracts on UK shares in one corner of the Exchange floor. The notion of financial futures had an equally 'unclean' feel and, as with put options in the 1600s, most in London thought and hoped that the derivatives fad would pass; and the sooner the better.

LIFFE leads the European response

But not everyone agreed, John Barkshire in particular, the feisty head of a financial conglomerate called Mercantile House. Behaving as though he was Dutch, Barkshire pointedly took out a lease on the Royal Exchange, just across the road from the London Stock Exchange and the Bank of England. Opened by Queen Elizabeth I in 1571 and Britain's first specialist commercial building, the Royal Exchange symbolised the determination of London to rival Antwerp which then, according to the historian Fernand Braudel, was the *"centre of the entire international economy"* and *"Europe's richest city"*. The Royal Exchange had initially been the central market for most commercial goods coming into London until, running short of space, some markets moved away to ply their trade in nearby coffee houses. Some, like the insurance market that had moved to Edward Lloyd's coffee house, were to return to the Royal Exchange when space became available, before finally moving out in 1928. Barkshire then recruited Michael Jenkins from Amsterdam's European Options Exchange as Chief Executive in 1981 and boldly announced that the London International Financial Futures Exchange 'LIFFE' would launch the following year. The gauntlet had been thrown down.

Everything that LIFFE was proposing to do felt uncomfortable to the establishment. Their great innovation was to bring members of London's hitherto discreet and fiercely independent markets together, not just jobbers and brokers from the stock market, but also those from the discount and commodity markets as well as money brokers and banks. In this way they created an environment where everyone in the chain could participate and compete with one another on the floor of the exchange. Such practices, the norm in New York and Chicago, were unknown in London. LIFFE also deliberately adopted the Chicago market structure of open pits with traders wearing coloured jackets, rather than the more sober London precedents.

LIFFE was breaking down barriers in a way that first upset and shocked, but later led to the LSE changing its own rules in 1986 through what was called the *"Big Bang"*, an event driven by the free market instincts that Hayek and Friedman had convinced British Prime Minister Margaret Thatcher to adopt. It was an event that was to change the financial landscape of London forever as well as to sow the seeds for the demise of the old City firms who were unprepared and lacked the necessary skills to succeed. Many names simply disappeared altogether whilst others like Barings, Britain's oldest bank, which tried to take on the US investment banks in the new world of finance, collapsed from ineptitude. When the Bank of England brokered a merger between LIFFE and the LSE's London Traded Option Market (LTOM), in 1991 it symbolised capitulation by the old guard of the LSE who had viewed derivatives as simply a dangerous short-term fad to be resisted. LIFFE's massive business volumes and worldwide reputation had made the LSE look pedestrian and out of touch.

With such radical change afoot, it was a time of opportunity, energy and excitement to be involved in these market developments. With a great effort underway to educate and win over investors and regulators, a group of us launched The Options and Futures Society (TOFS) in 1982, to build awareness and educate investors on derivative instruments and their markets. We benefitted greatly from the support of the exchanges and major market participants. As the society's first President, I was fortunate to come to know many of the leaders of the derivative revolution, of whom Fischer Black was the most influential. Through TOFS I also came to know and form an enduring friendship with LIFFE's first Chief Executive Sir Michael Jenkins, who would later become Chairman of an electronic trading network where I was Chief Executive.

Europe responds with electronic trading

On the Continent, the French launched their own financial futures market in 1986, the Marché à Terme International de France (MATIF), which has since been absorbed into NYSE Euronext. Next came the Swiss in 1988 with the launch of Swiss Options & Financial Futures Exchange (Soffex) who, embracing Melamed's vision of electronic trading, opened the first exchange with no trading floor and no people. The Germans copied the Swiss electronic model and quickly followed suit by launching the Deutsche Terminbörse (DTB) in 1990, primarily to win back trading in their government bond market contract, the 'Bund', from London's LIFFE exchange. Both of these new exchanges were built by Andersen, the leading accountancy firm that was to collapse following the Enron scandal in 2001, just when the two exchanges they had spawned were merging with one another to form today's Eurex exchange.

Unlike in London and Amsterdam, where the exchange launches were driven by a belief in these markets and a perceived need for derivatives, the force elsewhere in Europe came more from a desire to bring their antiquated financial centres up to date. The financial world was polarising around New York, London and Tokyo; France in particular was actively seeking to gain a foothold. In Switzerland, Soffex was a Zurich led initiative set against the high cost and inefficient practices of Switzerland's six regional stock exchanges. Their decision to go wholly electronic was not simply a vision that they could *"dematerialise"* security trading by holding orders, confirmations and trade instructions electronically, thereby eradicating much of the mountain of paper associated with securities trading. Just as important was killing off local competition in share trading, removing the rationale for multiple stock exchanges and congregating the trading business around the initiating city, Zurich.

Easy money holds back product innovation

With the leaders of most of the European exchanges more interested in modernising their local markets than being evangelists for the new financial world, market practitioners were somewhat underwhelmed by the disappointingly unimaginative contracts that the new exchanges offered. Most simply mirrored the products offered by Chicago and London with a domestic focus. France, Germany and Switzerland all offered interest rate futures contracts on their local government debt, alongside stock index futures contracts on their local shares. They also listed traded option contracts on these futures contracts as well as on their most actively traded local shares. By now exchanges had dispensed with the old habit of listing call options before put options, offering both types together from the outset.

With regulatory protection around their local markets and an attractive business model of low set-up and running costs, the polar opposite of airlines, these new derivative exchanges quickly flourished and became profitable. Further encouragement came from the growing tide of politicians and regulators supporting more sensible regulatory and tax treatment for derivative usage. Up until then market regulators and lawmakers had sought to apply existing securities laws to instruments that were not used, traded or behaved like securities. For those managing the new exchanges, the top priority was to establish the core local contracts. As an investment manager I was invited to participate at meetings or to join exchange boards that advised on new products. The pace of progress was frequently more akin to patient international diplomacy than business urgency. Key decisions were taken with an eye as much on politics as economics and, with conservatism offering a profitable and safe strategy, most exchanges opted to stick to the basics.

With the exchanges making good money, yet no great differentiation beyond offering their local contracts, the big push then was in marketing to encourage investors to use their products, and to win their loyalty. Those charged with the task of developing derivative capabilities in even the biggest investment management firms were predominately young and relatively junior. To attract their business, exchanges competed to outdo one another in the entertainment, conference venues and activities on offer. Market share was built and maintained as much through lavish entertainment as by price competition. As ever, liquidity was the key to winning the game and anything that increased the possibility of choosing one exchange to trade on versus another was considered. The exchanges themselves, awash with cash and given generous marketing budgets, held their main industry gathering in Burgenstock with its stunning view of Switzerland's Lake Lucerne. It made for a fun, exciting and stimulating environment to be a part of a business success that was now global in reach.

In Asia, a new dynamic was afoot. Their first financial futures exchange, the Singapore International Monetary Exchange (Simex), was launched in 1984. By successfully listing a futures contract in

1986 for Japan's main stock market barometer, the Nikkei 225 Index, they threw down the gauntlet to the Japanese who, until then, had been reluctant to enter the derivatives fray. Japan's strong response came two years later in 1988 when the Osaka Securities Exchange (OSE) introduced their own Nikkei 225 futures contract. It was this contract which, buoyed by the Japanese stock market overtaking the United States to become the biggest in the world, and a thriving Japanese government bond (JGB) futures contract, that led in the early 1990s, to their becoming the biggest futures market in the world.

Meanwhile Hong Kong Futures Exchange (HKFE), which was launched in 1976 and had its roots in commodity contracts, had also listed an array of futures and options contracts. They were unfortunate in suffering a major setback when the global stock market crash in October 1987 caused the exchange to cease trading. A powerful local individual who had lost HK$1 billion speculating in futures had refused to pay, claiming that he was protected by the limited liability of two Panamanian-registered companies through which he had traded. The exchange was only kept alive by a government bailout, funded by Hong Kong taxpayers.

But everyone knew that the cosy local franchises could not last. Europeans in particular were conscious of the threat from across the Atlantic posed by Melamed's drive to extend the CME's trading hours into European and Asian time zones through their Globex initiative. It was a first step towards a global electronic derivatives market controlled by Chicago. Everyone knew that first mover advantage in the derivatives business was critical, as business would ultimately gravitate to where the greatest liquidity and the lowest trading costs were to be found.

From people in pits to computers

But the biggest threat of all was the change in culture and ethics underway in financial markets, as voice and physical communication between people became supplanted by computers and electronic communication. Today, with trading electronically from computer terminals the norm, it is hard to imagine how the trading world and its hierarchy operated before information and communication travelled so quickly and comprehensively by electronic means. Nowadays the idea of physical floor trading seems almost arcane, but in truth it worked really well. That is why it was such a surprise when Leo Melamed, a man coming from an environment of people and the pits, championed electronic trading long before the technology to bring it about had been developed.

To the people in the trading pits, the advent of fast electronic communication, allied to computing power, was initially seen as an improvement to their working environment, rather than the precursor to their demise. On New York's Comex traders used telephones rather than emplying 'runners', covering the exchange floor with thousands ofphone leads often over 200 metres long. They saw price data flow through their system faster and more cheaply. In Chicago they adopted modest enhancements to their offering, including a facility to trade outside normal trading hours, introducing 'round-the-clock' trading in small amounts. However they still expected that the greatest liquidity would only be in evidence during US trading hours, when the lords of the jungle locked horns on behalf of the market giants in the trading pit.

Continental Europe had none of the history and culture of Chicago, which is why the Swiss were the first to launch an electronic exchange. They were largely ignored as peripheral, with the inevitable early technology glitches being rounded on by critics as proof of failure.

Life and culture on the exchange floor

The shift from physical trading on the floor of an exchange to anonymous electronic trading from a computer terminal has not been a wholly good thing. The pride and culture of the floor has been lost, along with safeguards developed over time to react when weaknesses emerged.

The floor of an 'open outcry' exchange was capitalism and meritocracy at its most raw. There were no privileges to be had from birth or money. The best found their way to the top on talent alone. The barriers to entry in Chicago were almost nil and the process of progression open and transparent.

In the trading pits life was tough and physical, with the hierarchy of the floor determining all behaviour. A newcomer would start as a runner taking messages and information to the phone lines and out to the financial world at large. Running back and forth all day and paid little, they nevertheless saw and learned about the people and trading patterns from the grass roots up. In the bars around town at the end of the day, relationships and knowledge were shared in ways little different from those of the coffee and ale houses of London in the 1600s.

Advancement was to progress from runner to manning the phone lines connecting the trading floor to the broker offices, where the interaction took place by phone direct with investment clients who were the ultimate owners of the buy or sell decisions. Enhancing the learning process in the trading arena were those with pit badges who might lend their badge to a runner over quiet periods, generally over lunchtime. With strict limits on the amount they could trade, they could watch, learn and modestly participate in the market action. The wise novices noted the market stars, the lords of the jungle, and simply copied their trades in smaller amounts. Often the market stars would nurture those starting out by offering them a small piece, a contract or two, from a much bigger position they had taken, in much the same way as lions dispense morsels to their cubs. Amongst all the trading ferocity the floor retained the flavour and affection of family. From these small beginnings ambitious young lions would be spotted and emerge to be given access to more money to trade with. Some would rise and become the supreme creature, the position taker. For these mighty traders, the game of taking modest positions and trading them quickly throughout the day and then retiring to the bar with flat positions at the market close was not enough. For them big was good and for the market it was their presence that made the exchanges powerful. So important were the big position takers that the major banks and brokers would offer them large trading credit lines so that their customers could find the liquidity they needed when they wanted it. Security for the loan was the track record of being smart, and the visibility of a market floor to watch how they were doing. The system worked well and would have continued unaltered had it not been for the advent of the game changing innovation of fast and cheap communication technology.

Electronic trading did more than take away the open trading methods that were central to the Chicago way of life. The removal of people from the floor also took away the open training culture through which knowledge was passed on and talented individuals were identified and progressed up the trading ladder. A new electronic culture for cubs to grow into lords of the jungle was called for, but none was there. Human beings have no past experience or particular empathy with relationship building by electronic means. Even today, in an age where social networking is the norm, it is doubtful that electronic interaction can ever completely replace the physical alternative and, to the traders in Chicago's pits in the 1980s, the idea was unthinkable. Trading culture, etiquette and controls are now built less around people but around computer systems instead. Laudable and thorough as these systems are, they are only as good as the people operating them.

No one realised it then, but found later and sometimes at tragic cost, that once electronic systems for risk management and accounting replaced people, new weaknesses, not seen before, would spring up. Little did the Swiss realise when they launched Soffex, the first electronic derivatives exchange, that they were also sowing the seeds for rogue trading, a modern form of financial terrorism. The combining of transactions that do not involve any exchange of cash for goods with a trading environment where learning, knowledge and trust is difficult to gauge, has opened the door for massive fraud by individuals often completely unknown to senior management within their own firms. The ultimate irony is perhaps that the bank which pressed for and led the Soffex initiative was UBS, Switzerland's biggest bank, the very same that was almost taken down by this cultural weakness many years later in 2011 by the rogue trading of Kweku Adoboli.

Expansion and consolidation a pattern that has endured

Whilst unsurprising that derivative exchanges grew quickly in the 1980s and 1990s as their usage spread more widely and covered greater geography and range of asset classes and instruments; the surprise to me is that, even to this day, the appetite for opening new exchanges continues unabated. As with airlines, exchanges have merged and consolidated, led by Melamed's CME, with another giant Intercontinental Exchange (ICE) operating twenty-three exchanges and clearing houses around the world including NYSE of which LIFFE is now a part. But the habit of proliferation dies hard and this urge is so well ingrained that more exchanges have been opening up in recent times than at any time in the past. Whilst the gold rush feeling that pervaded the introduction of new markets and products in the 1980s is no longer so strong, excitement remains high. In particular the Chinese, whose appetite for innovation appeared modest, and were very cautious when opening their financial markets to foreigners, have begun trading stock options and set up a financial futures exchange. With such an important new economic power entering the derivatives game, new opportunities are plentiful.

The culture of trading on exchanges has become more ingrained and encouraged by regulators as a consequence of financial scandals and crises. As time has passed more and more products have become exchange traded, including those steeped in mystique and tradition. Even London's gold market appears to be headed that way as they are already losing the business of some of their biggest customers who are more comfortable with the exchange environment. Watching business gravitate to other countries from customers seeking the environment of an open exchange is a sure fire way of forcing the *"fuddy duddies"* at home to mend their ways.

Trading floors with people milling about have become a rarity. Some of the space they once occupied is now taken by coffee shops where conversation and ideas are exchanged. The centre of LIFFE's original trading floor in the Royal Exchange is now a bar surrounded by chic shops and a restaurant. Where once the need for trading space had driven coffee off the floor now it is flowing back to where it all started in the 1600s.

15. Financial engineers chase a quick buck

"I asked one of my four grandchildren what he wanted to be when he grew up. When he responded 'a financial engineer' my heart sank"

Paul Volcker (born in 1927 in New Jersey),
Chairman of US Federal Reserve 1979-1987

Although futures and options markets were springing up everywhere, the financial world was not ready for them. Their market structure, tax laws, rules and regulations were all built to handle physical securities and not designed to cope with derivatives. The bright and swift spotted this, seeking to exploit the loopholes that these shortcomings opened up. There seemed to be plenty of easy pickings from what management consultants would describe as *"low hanging fruit"*. But making money was not as easy as some had thought, particularly amongst the academics and mathematicians who believed that insights from pricing models alone were enough to bring them riches. Their thrill at cracking the risk pricing code had led to an almost religious zeal for their methods. With this came a belief that a new financial order was about to emerge, with academics and mathematicians at the helm.

No free money for the mathematicians

In their enthusiasm to capitalise on the new pricing models, some left the careful rigour that normally accompanied academic research behind in the rush for money. Many saw the Black-Scholes option pricing model as a panacea in itself, rather than a door that was ajar providing a first glimpse into a new world of financial engineering. In their hurry to be the *"early bird that catches the worm"*, new investment strategies were introduced without proper thought or rigorous testing.

An early idea was to buy options that looked cheap on a pricing model, and to sell those that appeared expensive. It seemed such a simple way to profit from pricing anomalies, and ideally suited for exploitation by quick minded mathematicians. But the judgement that an option was cheap or expensive relied heavily on correctly estimating one particular input to the model, volatility, a measure of how much a share price moves up and down. There was plenty of good academic evidence to show that shares that had moved a great deal in the past continued to do so. And it made intuitive economic sense too that the share price of an exploration company drilling for oil should be more volatile than the share price of a utility company distributing water to people's homes. After all, the value of a small oil company could be radically transformed by drilling a successful well as was evidenced by the fortune made by HL Hunt following the *"gusher"* on Daisy Bradford's ranch in East Texas.

The problem was that the shares with the biggest option price anomalies, instead of being the source of the greatest profits, turned out to be the biggest losers. Those options that pricing models highlighted as very expensive, were more likely to indicate that the company's business outlook and share risk had altered, than a golden opportunity to make money from mispricing. Options on the shares of companies about to be bid for would almost always be accorded an 'expensive' rating on an option pricing model, when in truth this mispricing was really an early warning that circumstances had changed. After losing a lot of money in pursuit of what had been thought of as clever mispricing trades, the *"penny dropped"* and investors started to compare the volatility that was implied by market prices with their historic volatility, viewing big differences as a market signal that something unusual was going on. This notion sat uncomfortably with the purists, who believed there was little or nothing to be gained from *"reading tea leaves"*, as markets were supposed to be efficient and all information on the company already embedded in the share price.

The explanation for these differences became obvious as news about the companies emerged. Someone contemplating a bid for a company would regard their call options as cheap, even though they looked expensive on pricing models. The problem for many of the mathematical smarts was that few of them knew much about the companies, or the trading characteristics of the shares they were trading in. They thought they could make money from the numbers without the hard graft of understanding the businesses, their trading outlook and share price characteristics. At times, their focus on the numbers was accentuated by an even more dangerous vice, an intellectual disdain for traders. It was a mistake that was to be repeated time and again, costing the investors in academic driven strategies a great deal of money. There were even bankruptcies, some going close to undermining the entire financial system.

It was a shame they did not heed the dictum of Clarence Day, the American author and one time stockbroker: *"Information is pretty thin stuff unless mixed with experience"*.

For the pure mathematical investor, the historical price data determined the volatility number to be plugged into the Black-Scholes formula. The difference between the model and market price was the noise of simple people; and therefore an opportunity to make money. Another observation they noted was that out-of-the money options tended to be overpriced relative to at-the-money options, so were deemed attractive to sell even though they received little cash in return as option premium.

In the early days, there were banks whose trading books were run by academics who priced options with the same volatility number for all exercise prices whether 'in', 'at', or 'out-of-the-money'. Only through losing a great deal of money did they discover that the market prices volatility differently across exercise prices, a characteristic that nowadays we call 'skew'. Another observation was that options of different maturity appeared to present arbitrage opportunities, as their prices implied different values for volatility. They too were caught out, as what they had really discovered was that, just as the yield on fixed income securities have a term structure, so do options. It is instructive to note that the concepts of implied volatility, skew and the term structure did not come from new academic thinking, but from a practical realisation that the losing bets were arising from false assumptions.

Thinking street traders make a killing

During the 1970s, the locals on the Chicago Board Options Exchange (CBOE) made good profits by gently picking off the first wave of mathematicians who were trading share options. The locals may not have properly understood the mathematics, but they were adept at interpreting and profiting from the information that came from their presence on the trading floor. This was to change dramatically in the early 1980s when a new breed of street savvy traders used option pricing models to give them the edge to make real money from their calculations. In the vanguard were two firms founded in 1977, Chicago Research & Trading (CRT) and O'Connor & Associates.

CRT's founder was Joseph Ritchie, a very smart options trader who regarded the Black-Scholes pricing model as *"incomplete"*. One aspect was his distrust of the notion that academics priced into their option models, that the distribution of future share price movements followed the statistical pattern called the 'normal distribution'. In this bell-shaped distribution, the vast majority of outcomes lie around a middle value, with only a tiny number at the extremes or 'tails' of the distribution. Often taught in school using people's heights for illustration, people in the lower tail are referred to as *"jockeys"*, those at the upper end *"basketball players"*, with the vast majority in between the *"fans"*. In financial markets as in many other facets of life, extreme events occur much more frequently than the normal distribution would predict, and are described as 'fat tails'. As Paul Volcker was to put it: *"I've seen more fat tails in finance than on animals"*.

Ritchie had briefly traded share options on the CBOE in 1976, using a Texas Instruments calculator programmed with the Black-Scholes model which gave him competitive edge as he *"instantly became a one-eyed man in the land of the blind."* Before leaving the CBOE floor he gave his calculator to Steve Fossett, a serial adventurer, who attributed his success in trading options and financial fortune to Ritchie. Both Ritchie and Fossett were adventurers on and off the trading floor. Ritchie was an aviator who broke a transcontinental speed record in his private plane, whilst Fossett was best known for hot air ballooning, particularly his collaboration with the British entrepreneur, Sir Richard Branson.

After his brief stint on the CBOE, Ritchie returned to the CBOT, where he pioneered computer driven strategies for trading options on futures contracts using his own bespoke valuation models. CRT were soon trading more option contracts than any other firm, typically executing over $2.5 billion by value every day. Their use of computers to track their positions was novel, and the system they developed was far ahead of the curve, enabling them to monitor millions of positions at once. They won the lion's share of business by quoting narrow bid-offer spreads, making their money in small increments on many positions, as well as by spotting and exploiting weaknesses in the models that their rivals relied upon. Ritchie described these opportunities as: *"like card counting before the casinos knew card counting existed."*

O'Connor & Associates, although similar to CRT in taking advantage of option pricing models and developments in computer hardware and software, had a very different genesis and philosophy. Their champion was a mathematician, Michael Greenbaum, who had run the risk management for the options clearing business of two influential and highly successful Chicago derivative traders, Ed and Bill O'Connor. The O'Connor brothers were smart enough to know that new skills were needed to succeed with financial options, and backed Greenbaum to do the job.

From his risk management experience, Greenbaum knew that the best hedge for an option position was another option position. It was much less risky and easier to manage than the conventional alternative 'dynamic delta hedging', which called for regular and timely trading of shares or futures contracts as prices moved up and down. O'Connor also took the portfolio approach of aggregating share and options positions into a single book, which enabled them to hedge their overall risk with a handful of option positions. By using recent advances in computing power and programming architecture, they were able to turn academia's mathematical models of derivatives into trading and risk engines. O'Connor worked closely with Steve Jobs, the co-founder of Apple, in the period after 1985 when Jobs had left Apple and started NeXT. Both had spotted the value that could be extracted from building a technology that offered solutions across hardware and software. Later on, after his return to Apple, Jobs was to develop these ideas further by purchasing NeXT.

Both CRT and O'Connor proved to be innovators ahead of their time, although perhaps their greatest strength was to avoid the pitfalls of so many others who had brought 'rocket science' to financial markets. Like Ritchie, they never lost sight of the fact that a mathematical model can only be applied to the real world after simplifying or ignoring some of the model assumptions. By similar dint a model should not be followed in circumstances where the simplified assumptions do not make practical sense.

It is ironic that the financial academic icons, Robert Merton and Myron Scholes, were each to take home a Nobel Prize for their equity options pricing model, whilst Joe Ritchie and his firm, CRT, took home more than $1 billion by figuring out that those same famous financial engineers and their option pricing models, were *"off the mark"*. In an interview in the mid-1980s Ritchie, when asked what he would say to the academics who claim markets are efficient, had answered: *"Well, I don't want to talk them out of it. Let them keep thinking it. They'll teach, I'll trade."*

The low hanging fruit proved to be much less tasty than the financial engineers expected. But rather than retreat after their early losses, they progressed quickly from small mistakes to bigger ones, the largest of which came to threaten the global financial system. The first was a flawed form of portfolio insurance that acted as the trigger for a global stock market crash in 1987. Other mistakes were to follow, with the collapse in 1998 of a hedge fund called Long Term Capital Management (LTCM) the most prominent.

In the new millennium the biggest mistakes have come from ascribing too much trust to 'correlation', a statistical term which describes the price and risk relationship of a mixed bag of different assets. The mistake made with correlation was always the same; trusting that a price and risk relationship was more stable than was really the case, and not worrying enough about the extremes and their "fat tails".

16. Portfolio Insurance and the Wall Street Crash - New York and Chicago 1987

"Everything should be made as simple as it can be, but not simpler"

Albert Einstein (1879-1955)

When insurance first appeared in the world of investment management, it was a shadowy impostor of the real thing and a strange case of an academic experiment played out in public markets. And it was undertaken with the savings of the most vulnerable, pensioners who could ill afford to lose money. It was the first of a number of forays by academics through which they demonstrated an alarming lack of grounding in their knowledge of the real world of markets.

The 1987 Wall Street Crash

After the trading bell had brought business to a close at 4pm on Monday 19th October 1987, a day that came to be known as *"Black Monday"*, stunned officials at the New York Stock Exchange met with leading market participants in an attempt to understand why the US stock market's record 108 point fall in the Dow Jones Industrial Average the previous Friday had been trumped by the 508 point rout that they had just witnessed.

There was little doubt that pressure to sell shares had been relentless all day, but what most alarmed the officials was the final hour of trading when the weight of sellers, seemingly with no regard for price, had completely overwhelmed any buying. As the findings of the Brady Commission which was set up by the US Government afterwards to investigate the cause of the stock market collapse, made clear: *"From the close of trading Tuesday, October 13, 1987 to the close of trading Monday, October 19, the Dow Jones Industrial Average declined by almost one third, representing a loss in value of all outstanding United States stocks of approximately $1.0 trillion. What made this market break extraordinary was the speed with which prices fell, the unprecedented volume of trading and the consequent threat to* *the financial system."*

Friday's record fall had sent shock waves around the world and prompted substantial falls on the stock markets in London, Hong Kong, and Tokyo the following Monday. There had therefore been considerable nervousness in advance of the opening of the US stock market.

The scale of Black Monday's stock market collapse had disturbing implications for financial theory. Many investment practitioners had built their models around a 'random walk' hypothesis, which suggested that share price returns followed a statistical pattern known as the normal distribution. This distribution implied that the chance of the 20.5 per cent one day fall in the broader US stock market S&P 500 Index that had just taken place was well-nigh impossible, as a move of this magnitude was not expected to occur more than once in the life of the Universe. Even a 6 per cent fall in a single day was an extreme event, expected only once every four million years.

'Super DOT' system drives the Wall Street collapse

The meeting at the New York Stock Exchange on Monday evening had a single purpose; to identify where the indiscriminate selling had come from and why the sellers appeared to have had a complete disregard for price. Those present spent little time discussing the economic background, even though there was serious concern that the recent decline in the US Dollar against all of the major currencies meant that the Louvre Accord, an agreement reached by G7 nations to stabilise international currency markets at a meeting in Paris earlier that year, had already failed.

It was quickly evident that systematic selling had not come from frantic trading by brokers on the floor of the exchange in response to heavy selling pressure from investors. The principal source had been the exchange's high speed 'Super DOT' automated execution system. This computer trading system provided a fast and efficient mechanism for selling packages of shares, a device that had been introduced to replace the wheelbarrows carrying baskets of individual share tickets, that had previously facilitated trading in portfolios of shares rather than individual shares. Super DOT bypassed the floor broker and went straight from the trading rooms of the major Wall Street investment banks to the 'specialist' market makers who provide price quotes for each of the shares listed on the Exchange.

With this indiscriminate selling coming from investment banks accessing Super Dot, the next question posed was why the banks were selling so aggressively. This they found to be in direct response to sales of stock index futures in Chicago, and specifically those on the S&P 500, an index of the 500 companies listed on US stock exchanges that were judged by the ratings company Standard & Poors to best represent the US economy. Who was selling these futures contracts in Chicago and why was this selling prompting share selling in New York?

The arbitrage link between New York and Chicago

The second question was easy to answer. The linkage between the share market in New York and the stock index futures market in Chicago was well understood, and came about through a process known as index arbitrage. Stock index future prices in Chicago were tied to stock market prices in New York through their 'fair value' relative to one another. A much more powerful force binding this relationship is a form of financial gravitational pull known as 'convergence' which drags the price of a stock index futures contract closer and closer to the share prices that comprise the index, until the price of both are one and the same on the day the futures contract matures.

Because of these two effects, arbitrageurs carry out offsetting transactions in the intervening period which keep the two markets in line with one another. When the price of futures on shares is cheap relative to the purchase of the underlying shares, they buy futures contracts and sell the related shares. The investment return from index arbitrage has nothing to do with the return on the stock market, as they have bought and sold exposure in equal amounts, leaving them with a 'synthesised' investment exposure analogous to holding cash on deposit.

Index arbitrage between shares and stock index futures

The fair value of a stock index futures contract is the value of the shares as calculated within the index with two adjustments; one to take account of dividend payments, the second interest earned on cash. The owner of the share portfolio receives dividends on the shares within the index whereas the owner of the futures contract does not. By contrast the owner of the futures contract earns interest on cash as no money is tied up owning shares. The fair value of a stock index futures contract is therefore:

Stock index futures contract = Stock index value - dividends + interest

Index arbitrageurs keep the index and futures prices close to fair value without making any bet on the direction of the market. If the futures are cheap relative to fair value they buy futures contracts and sell the same value of shares in the proportion as represented by the index. Conversely when the futures price is expensive they sell futures contacts and buy shares to the same value. In both cases the gains manifest themselves as a higher rate of interest on cash, usually small, although on Black Monday the rate of interest that index arbitrageurs could synthesise in this manner was 18% higher than cash deposits.

The selling pressure from the stock index futures pit at the Chicago Mercantile Exchange (CME) that Monday kept driving the price of the S&P 500 stock index future to a discount relative to its 'fair' value, prompting arbitrageurs to move in and buy futures in Chicago whilst selling shares short in New York through the Super DOT system. At one point they were synthesising the equivalent of a 25%

per annum cash return when the interest rate paid on cash deposits was less than 7% per annum. Whilst index arbitrage explained why shares on Wall Street were being sold, it did not explain why the stock index futures were being sold relentlessly in Chicago.

It was when they turned their attention to the sellers of the stock index futures contracts that the focus of attention fell onto an investment technique called 'portfolio insurance' and in particular an investment firm, LOR.

LOR and Portfolio Insurance

Portfolio insurance was an investment technique developed by two academics, Professors Hayne Leland and Mark Rubinstein. Their idea was to draw on the rapidly growing markets in futures and options to provide capital protection on stock market investments. To bring their concept to market they had joined forces with a brilliant salesman called John O'Brien and launched LOR in 1980, a new company that took its name from one initial from the surnames of each of the three founders.

At the time, the US pension fund industry was crying out for a capital protection solution. Pension fund portfolios were heavily weighted towards shares, typically holding over 70% of their assets in the stock market. Their investments had grown rapidly in value from a 'bull' stock market of unprecedented length and magnitude, that had begun in August 1982. As a consequence, the desire to maintain this winning formula was strong, as was pension trustee enthusiasm to protect their considerable gains. Less visible, but very influential, was a new accounting standard for pension funds introduced by the Federal Accounting Standards Board known as FAS 87, which was forcing actuaries to pay attention to market prices when measuring pension scheme solvency. Prior to this accounting standard, actuaries would smooth the vagaries of stock market movements through calculations that ignored short-term swings and applied much longer term investment return assumptions. The desire to protect the capital value of stock market investments, rather than resort to selling shares, was becoming enormous.

The approach that LOR came up with was a form of the 'stop loss' strategy that is familiar to most investors. Investors often tell their broker to retain their shares in a company providing that the share price stays above a certain value. If the share price falls below that level the broker has instructions to sell the shares to 'stop' any further loss in value. Portfolio insurance is very similar except that the stop is applied to the value of a portfolio, not a single share, and the liquidation process is gradual as the minimum portfolio value comes closer, rather than an abrupt sale of all shares at a moment in time.

A more obvious method to achieve this capital protection was to purchase put options on portfolio holdings so that any fall in the share price below the exercise price would be covered by the contract. LOR had tried to promote this idea to investors with little success as the cost of put option protection was unattractively high. Moreover the number of shares on which traded options were then listed was limited.

For LOR the big breakthrough came in 1983, when the Chicago Mercantile Exchange (CME) launched futures contracts on the S&P 500 stock market index. Most US pension fund portfolios imitated this index or used it as the yardstick for measuring the performance of their US stock market investments. Instead of painstakingly buying and selling dozens of individual stocks to replicate a put option on the stock market as a whole, LOR could achieve the same result through a single instrument, the S&P 500 stock index future contract. For LOR the replication of a put option by 'delta hedging' through the S&P 500 futures contract had simplified their task immeasurably.

A 'delta hedge' calculation carried out each day on LOR's computers and a single call to a futures broker in Chicago to buy or sell the requisite number of stock index futures contracts, was all that was needed to replicate the put options their customers were seeking.

> **How portfolio insurance was supposed to work**
>
> The trustees of a pension fund holding $120 million in stock market investments might set a minimum portfolio value of $100 million. This objective could be met without any use of derivatives, simply by systematically selling shares into a falling market until, when the portfolio value has reached $100 million, the pension fund would be holding only cash.
>
> The high transaction costs of buying and selling shares made the futures approach attractive, because buying and selling stock index futures could be carried for a fraction of the cost, typically 5-10% of share dealing costs. What made the futures proposition even more compelling was that futures markets had become more liquid than the stock market itself, with volumes in the S&P 500 stock index future three to five times those of the underlying shares. So, instead of meeting their objective by a mix of cash and shares, the LOR approach was to retain all of the stock market holdings and reduce market exposure through sale of stock index futures, until the portfolio at the minimum level would comprise physical shares matched by an equal and opposite offsetting exposure through stock index futures. By so doing LOR had synthesised a cash exposure instead of holding physical cash.

The illusory magic of portfolio insurance

The way portfolio insurance worked was to leave stock market investments intact whilst the market was strong, but to reduce exposure when the stock market fell. Investors in this strategy set a minimum 'floor' value below which their portfolio should not fall. The LOR technique was simply a systematic strategy to liquidate the stock market exposure of a portfolio until, at the agreed minimum value, the portfolio held 100% cash exposure and could lose no more.

Whilst the idea of progressivley liquidating a portfolio until effectively it comprised cash to represent the minimum capital value made sense, it was far from being insurance, as the protection was not guaranteed. Protection relied on carrying out the transactions the LOR formula prescribed in the right amounts at the right price, at the right moment in time. There was also a worry that implementation costs might prove excessive if markets bobbed up and down a lot, causing a lot of buying and selling, but ending up in the same place, known as 'whipsaws'. There was also an uncomfortable intellectual difficulty in yielding to a technique that bought shares after they had just gone up, and sold them after they had just gone down.

Although reading the small print of LOR's investment management contract made it clear that there was no guarantee that the promised minimum value would be achieved, the branding of their strategy as portfolio insurance made LOR's offering very 'hot' in marketing terms. It was dressed up as the product everyone wanted, and seen as a brilliant practical breakthrough achieved by the new academic gods of financial economics. Soon their strategy was being adopted by some of the largest and most prestigious pension funds in the United States. Whilst their approach was simple, LOR gained a form of exclusivity and cachet by covering up their simple trading algorithm in a secret mathematical sauce that only their clients could access.

But something was wrong. The goods which customers were buying were not insured at all. There was no promise of payment against loss if the portfolio value fell below the agreed minimum, and no guarantees from a provider with the wherewithal to pay out if things went wrong. It was simply 'best efforts' assurance that LOR would try to manage the portfolio in such a way as to provide the capital protection being sought.

Warning signs that went unheeded

By 1986, with portfolio insurance winning over more and more adopters, concern was also growing that portfolio insurance was fatally flawed and would not work when most needed. In Europe,

LOR was making slower progress as providers were unable to use the word 'insurance' since it carried the connotation of a guarantee which was not on offer. Amongst investment managers a fierce debate erupted on the merits of the LOR approach.

As a hot topic on both sides of the Atlantic it was decided to hold a public debate on the pros and cons of portfolio insurance. The venue chosen was the financial industry's biannual derivatives investment conference, which was to be held in January 1987 at the Hotel Coronado in San Diego, a hotel made famous as the central location for one of Marilyn Monroe's most popular movies *Some like it hot*. Sponsored by Chicago's derivatives exchanges, Leo Melamed was the keynote conference speaker and he used the occasion to promote Globex, CME's pioneering initiative to extend its international user base through the facilitation of electronic trading.

When asked by the conference organisers to speak against the LOR approach, I telephoned Fischer Black for advice. He had just published a research paper for Goldman Sachs entitled *Simplifying Portfolio Insurance* in which he had introduced a simple equation e = mc as an alternative to LOR's mysterious secret formula. As a play on Einstein's $e = mc^2$ equation for relativity, it was Fischer's tongue in cheek way of conveying that LOR were implying brilliance for something little different from a stop-loss strategy.

For Fischer the crucial question was 'Does it work?' rather than 'Is it a good idea?' He worried about the notion of futures being dressed up as options and pondered the concerns of the strategy's detractors. In his view a *"dynamically replicated put option is cheaper than the real thing for a good reason; a genuine put option is exercisable against the writer whether or not there is liquidity in the market."*

He suggested an analogy I should use at the conference to make the point, which was to treat the LOR strategy as an untested drug launched on the market by a pharmaceutical company. Without tests or trials and being given to elderly pensioners, in effect LOR was a drug that was being sold to the most vulnerable. No one knew if the drug worked or had adverse side effects. In Fischer's view, a dangerous real life test was underway without any proper controls.

We also discussed a form of warning sign from the market's solar system, 'sunshine trading'. Whenever portfolio insurers had very large trades, they informed the market in advance of the direction, size and timing of the orders they would be placing. LOR argued that sunshine trades reduced confusion and speculation by investors, by making the large transactions more transparent and attracting participation by all interested parties. To Fischer sunshine trading was simply an admission that there was insufficient liquidity for their strategy to work properly.

The Black Monday Collapse

Just eight months later he was proved right. By that time LOR was directly managing their portfolio insurance strategy for over around $30 billion of shares with a further $50 billion 'protected' by other investors mirroring their approach. In the week before Black Monday, the US equity market had fallen by 10% which, for LOR clients, required approximately $12 billion worth of stock index futures to be sold. With not enough buyers to provide this liquidity and, in spite of being the aggressive seller in the CME S&P 500 stock index future pit on Friday, the portfolio insurers had only managed to sell $4 billion worth of futures. They now had an $8 billion backlog of stock index futures which they were hoping they could sell the following Monday. And they were anxious that the market did not fall any further, as they would then have more futures to sell, leaving their clients even less protected than they already were.

But Friday's record fall on Wall Street had not drawn in buyers; instead it had had the opposite effect. Over the weekend investors in the US and abroad had become nervous and sent orders to their brokers to sell shares when the US market opened. Furthermore the desperation with which the portfolio insurers had been selling stock index futures during Friday had not gone unnoticed by the traders in Chicago's futures pit.

On Monday, 19th October 1987, the US Dow Jones index dropped 200 points almost as soon as the opening bell rang on the New York Stock Exchange. Over the day 600 million shares with a value of $21 billion were traded. So great was the volume that the exchange computers were overwhelmed.

It was even worse in Chicago. The $8 billion backlog of S&P 500 futures to be sold resulted in an immediate 7% drop, which in turn triggered additional sell orders from LOR and others who had adopted similar strategies. These sale orders completely overwhelmed the Chicago futures market and LOR gave up attempting to trade. Their portfolio insurance strategy had failed. One trader who was attempting to sell futures for one of the biggest portfolio insurers said: *"The fund manager just froze; he hardly carried out a trade all morning and then panicked and dumped everything in the last hour".*

By the end of Black Monday, $20 billion of stock index futures had traded. The selling pressure on the futures market had been so intense that the S&P 500 futures contract price had fallen by 29 per cent, a full 9 per cent more than the 20 per cent that the S&P 500 index itself had dropped. In theory this should not have happened as arbitrageurs should have stepped in to match the bargains, earning themselves free money by bringing them back in line. In practice they simply could not keep up with the pace of the selling.

The effect was disastrous for the clients of LOR and its competitors. They needed to sell futures to cover against the index going down but, because of the discrepancy, it meant that any portfolio insurance transaction carried out that day cost an extra 9 per cent. That meant the choices were either to withdraw altogether from the market and be uninsured, or to pay 9 per cent of a portfolio away for short term protection.

Martians land on LOR

For the academic creators of the technique, what had happened in the real world made no sense. Stock market moves of this magnitude were almost unthinkable. Nothing like this had happened since the Wall Street Crash of October 1929, when the Dow fell by 23 per cent over two days. In the past, Mark Rubinstein of LOR had joked to his colleagues that only a Martian landing could trigger off the kind of fall in the market that would undermine their strategy. As he put it afterwards: *"When we did our simulations all the way back to the Great Depression, there was never a situation that could have posed a really serious problem. We weren't expecting a move like that. We used to wonder what could cause such an event. It would either be World War III, a Martian landing or something else really incredible. We didn't think it could be anything that was not clearly fundamental or, even worse, our own self-defeating strategy".*

On Black Monday Rubinstein thought that his computer program had crashed the global financial system and he went into a deep depression. It is said that he was unable to rise from his bed for weeks afterwards. Later he was to admit that: *"The portfolios that were being 'insured' in 1987 were so large that it was impossible to sell enough futures in such a short period of time to keep the portfolio insurance strategy on track. The ironic thing … was that our very strategy may have been the vehicle that helped create a new situation in which an extreme event could occur. For me, as a simple professor at the University of California at Berkeley, it was difficult to believe that I could have been involved in a small company that had such an incredible effect on the markets".*

Liquidity lessons from Black Monday

The 1988 Brady Report, commissioned by the US Government, blamed the portfolio insurers for exacerbating the Crash and recommended 'circuit breakers' to halt trading on both the stock and futures exchanges if the index fell too far over the course of a day. When Fischer Black visited London afterwards he told clients that *"Much more academic research time and effort goes into modelling option pricing than into understanding the way the market works. We don't think enough about liquidity. We just assume it's there. Maybe the influence of calculus has us thinking in small pieces, so the big picture has become obscured".* It was another reason why he respected traders with their rudimentary pricing methods that he and I dubbed the *"Black & Decker"* pricing approach.

The Great Storm of 1987

One group of investors survived the Crash particularly well, not by anticipating the Crash, but instead by their response to a different storm, the violent extra-tropical cyclone that struck the UK on the night of 15th October 1987. Fears that insurance claims might severely damage the share prices of insurance companies prompted purchases of put options on Friday 16th October on the limited range of insurance shares for which exchange traded contracts were then available. Whilst a proportion of their substantial profits came from Friday's market reaction to the Great Storm, the bulk came after the storm had gone, just before Black Monday. Such are the vicissitudes of markets.

A further irony was that LOR had begun to pilot a put option strategy as an alternative to futures just before the Crash, but only a handful of their clients were then signed up.

With the attendant bad publicity, the aftermath for LOR and its competitors was a story of rapid decline as disappointed clients quickly dropping away. Portfolio Insurance disappeared within six months, and has not reappeared since. From then on investors would demand contracts and securities to protect their portfolios, not strategies.

But the failure of the academic Gods of finance to grasp the importance of liquidity was to return to haunt markets eleven years later in 1998, with the collapse of a giant hedge fund Long Term Capital Management (LTCM) for, as Rubinstein himself was to put it, *"much the same reason".*

17. Corporate raider masterclass from Robert Holmes à Court

"A good decision is based on knowledge and not on numbers"

Socrates as recorded by Plato (428-348 BC)

If the low hanging fruit that the academics identified from their option pricing formulae proved to be illusory as a profit making machine, the simpler commercially driven strategies were much more successful. Corporate raiders saw an altogether different opportunity with derivatives, arising from the rules and legal requirements around stake building and takeovers. They spotted that, whilst ownership of physical assets was subject to myriad stakeholder rules and carefully policed, exposure to the same assets through derivatives was not. It was therefore perhaps unsurprising that Robert Holmes à Court, a lawyer turned businessman, was to point the way through the adroit usage of simple option strategies. There were many who were to learn from him and successfully exploit the corporate raiding methods he pioneered, but none with his panache and skill.

Robert Holmes à Court was born in South Africa in 1937 and spent much of his early life in what is now Zimbabwe. From there he moved to Perth, Australia where he studied and initially practised law. It was through his legal work that he came into business in 1970, when turning round a small company from bankruptcy for which he had been appointed receiver. Holmes à Court swiftly rose to prominence and built a reputation for daring takeover raids, first in Australia and then in the UK. Most of his acquisitions were media companies where he found himself going head to head with an Australian rival six years his senior, Rupert Murdoch, from whom he bought several Australian newspapers. Although on the losing end to Murdoch when they both bid for the London based Times Newspapers in 1980, he was to eclipse Murdoch in personal wealth by becoming Australia's first billionaire.

Through his public company, Bell Resources, his name came to international prominence in the early 1980s when he stalked Australia's biggest company, the resource rich Broken Hill Proprietary (BHP). Over a three year period he cleverly took share and option positions to build a stake of just below 30 per cent, through which he gained a seat on the company's board of directors. A close friend who acted for Holmes à Court on his first two BHP share swoops was much impressed by Robert's ability to remain detached and unfazed by the market turbulence that his actions caused, calmly refining his tactics as circumstances changed.

Around this time he also developed a London based operation called Carisbrook Property in the City of London, a square mile that then pretty much comprised the entire UK financial district. The bulk of his income now came from trading in company shares, a task he executed with stunning simplicity and clarity. Holmes à Court's approach was always practical, with a clear focus on market conditions and anticipation of the likely stance and tactics of key players. Liquidity in the target company would influence how quickly or slowly he proceeded and his approach was driven more by gut feel and market instinct than the maths of financial economics. With option pricing he preferred a rudimentary and intuitive approach, although he kept tabs on prices derived from the Black-Scholes option pricing model so that he could gain insight into the motivation and likely decision making of market players whose investment strategy was determined by model pricing.

I first met him in 1984 around the time when the shares in Jaguar Cars were first listed on the London Stock Exchange. A tall, unassuming man with a quiet voice and manner, he was courteous and exhibited no sign of the commercial ruthlessness for which he was renowned. In his understated style, he formed strong views that he stuck by. Jaguar had just been demerged from the state owned British Leyland and was a poster child for British Prime Minister Margaret Thatcher's privatisation plans. As one of the hundred most valuable UK companies, Jaguar shares had immediately become a constituent of the stock market FTSE-100 Index, and traded option contracts had been introduced alongside the shares. I had visited Jaguar's manufacturing plant and met with management prior to its flotation as part of an investor road show. Holmes à Court was keen to understand how the stock was perceived by the large institutional shareholders who now owned the shares.

What struck me as unusual was that he was just as interested in the likely share price volatility as he was in Jaguar's earnings and takeover prospects. He harboured no takeover ambition for Jaguar himself, but realised that, given his reputation in media and natural resource companies, some in the market might view his investment activity in that way. He was also conscious that the major motor manufacturers would be keen to buy Jaguar for both strategic offensive and defensive competitive reasons once the UK Government's restriction preventing anyone from holding over 15% of the company expired in 1990. This proved correct when car manufacturers from BMW, Fiat, Peugeot, Audi, Nissan, Toyota to the world's two biggest, General Motors and Ford, expressed interest. The latter two eventually fought the final takeover duel, with Ford ultimately prevailing and becoming the owner of the Jaguar marque.

Trademark pattern of option trading to wrong foot the market

Holmes à Court had grasped straight away the advantages of gaining an exposure interest in a company through derivatives, as opposed to the ownership interest that came with shares, with all the baggage of regulatory reporting and stake declaration. His trademark pattern for corporate stake building with options was simple and repeated often. He would buy cheap call options in a target company to initiate a stake. No one knew he had established a position because stock market rules did not require market exposure to be declared. His idea of a cheap call option would usually appear to be expensive on a Black-Scholes option valuation model but an attractive purchase price when set in the context of the company's takeover prospects and his own market intentions. He would build as large a call option exposure as he could without attracting attention and then, after exercising his options into the shares, would sit back to observe how the market reacted to the news of his stake. Usually the share price would rise sharply as the stake building would be interpreted as a first step towards a takeover bid.

If the share price rose he would cannily return to the options market, this time selling call options at a higher exercise price to reap the benefits from the higher option premium available, as the shares would now be expected to be much more volatile. The option premium he received from this call option writing provided him with more than enough money to pay the interest on any borrowings he had taken out to purchase the shares. In effect the call option writing acted as a very cheap source of funding for his stake, allowing him to become an unhurried predator who could stalk large prey at leisure.

By simply sitting on a share stake, Holmes à Court would sometimes lead the market to believe a bid was not imminent. Often the 'hot money' that had followed him in, having driven up the share price with their purchases, would face their own funding difficulties, and come under pressure to sell their shares. If the price fell enough, Holmes à Court would purchase more shares or buy back the call options he had initially sold for much less than he had been paid.

Another tactic he particularly enjoyed was to sell put options which, if exercised, would result in his purchasing shares below the prevailing market price. If the stock price remained high the put options would not be exercised and he would keep the premium, thereby augmenting his financial firepower. He viewed his willingness to buy a stake in a company at the option exercise price as being philosophically analogous to an underwriting commitment. His view was that: *"If I'm willing to commit to buy the shares if the price falls I should be paid a fee for providing that service".* And paid handsomely he was. His brilliance was to combine a deep fundamental knowledge of the company he was investing in with the different aims and objectives of its shareholder base, including the modellers who on occasions he tortured with their own mathematics. To watch Holmes à Court at work was to see a master financial puppeteer toying with the marionettes of the market.

He confessed that his questioning was always to identify any shortcomings or weaknesses in his trading approach that might undermine his strategy. He launched brilliant hostile takeover assaults on countless companies and his motivation for doing so was as much fascination with the options game as it was corporate stake building.

The stock market crash in October 1987 hurt Holmes à Court badly as he was heavily leveraged through his stakes in many companies, holdings that were funded by bank borrowing. He was forced to cede control of his interest in Bell Group to Alan Bond, another mercurial Western Australian businessman. Bond had become something of an Australian hero after wresting the America's Cup yacht challenge from the United States in 1983, the first time the New York Yacht Club had ever lost the trophy in its 132 year history.

Sadly Holmes à Court died of a heart attack in 1990, aged just fifty-three whilst at the height of his powers, leaving behind a legacy that would serve almost as an instruction manual on the use of options for merger and acquisition purposes. His methods have lived on and been followed by others to good effect, although no one has come close to his brilliance. A similar approach, with more sophisticated options not available in Holmes à Court's day, was used by Porsche in 2008 for its audacious attempt to buy Volkswagen. Over time those making the rules of the market have learned from Holmes à Court and the disciples that followed his creed, making his stake building methods much trickier to accomplish.

Also, through him, business builders like James Hanson in the UK and corporate raiders in the US who set the stage for the Enron story we discuss later were to find the low hanging fruit in the early days of financial derivatives markets. But, as for Robert Holmes à Court, we shall not see his like again.

18. Put options keep Robert Maxwell afloat

"You are as safe with me as you would be in the Bank of England"

Robert Maxwell (1923-1991)

Whereas Robert Holmes à Court used options to build stakes in companies he did not own, Robert Maxwell used them for an altogether different purpose; to prop up the share price of the publicly traded company that bore his name and that he treated as his own, Maxwell Communications Company (MCC).

Ján Hoch was born in Czechoslovakia in 1923. He came to the UK after serving with the British Army during the Second World War, changing his name to Robert Maxwell. Other than a six-year stint as a Member of Parliament (MP) for the Labour Party in the 1960s, he devoted all his energy to building an international newspaper and publication empire. This he grew principally through acquisitions, the most significant of which took place in the 1980s. As with Robert Holmes à Court his main business rival was the Australian, Rupert Murdoch.

He acquired the British Printing Corporation (BPC) in 1981 and later renamed the company Maxwell Communications Corporation (MCC). In 1984 he bought Mirror Group Newspapers (MGN), publisher of the Daily Mirror, a pro-Labour Party UK tabloid newspaper, before making his biggest acquisition in 1988, the $2.6 billion purchase of the US publisher, Macmillan.

Maxwell borrowed heavily to fund these acquisitions, with the lending banks holding MCC shares as security for these loans, in much the same way that banks hold legal title to property when providing mortgages to home buyers. To seal the Macmillan acquisition, Maxwell had pushed his borrowings to the limit, leaving him with an uphill struggle to generate the necessary cash flow to meet interest payments on these loans. This pressure was to force him to sell Pergamon Press and Maxwell Directories businesses, shortly after the MacMillan purchase, to the Dutch publisher

Elsevier for £440 million. After these sales, the key plank supporting the borrowing of MCC and Maxwell's private companies became the market value of MCC shares.

A colourful character with a flamboyant lifestyle, Maxwell lived in a mansion near Oxford, commuting to his London headquarters on Fleet Street each day by helicopter. Amongst his many outside interests were football clubs. He bought his local club, Oxford United, as well as becoming a major shareholder in another, Derby County. Later Maxwell attempted to go further still and purchase Manchester United, but was rebuffed.

The MCC share support operation

Maxwell sought to support the MCC share price in three ways. First he drew on the public relations machine of his media empire and his own formidable personality to express confidence in the prospects for MCC's business. He sought to bolster this argument by claiming he was *"putting money where his mouth was"* when spending £75 million to increase his stake in MCC shares from 56% to 62%, just before poor interim results in September 1990. But, as we shall see, these purchases were forced on him by the share support mechanism he had put in place, not through optimism about the company's prospects. Indeed, it was against his own interests to be building his stake at this time, as it served to undermine the acceptability of MCC shares as loan collateral. Large personal stakes in public companies were viewed in a negative light by the banks, not least because, were Maxwell to own a 75% stake, the company would lose its public listing and be reclassified as a private company, rendering MCC shares ineligible as loan collateral.

His second approach was illegal, using money that was not his but over which he could exert control, to buy MCC shares and to relieve other cash pressures. The main source of these funds was the Mirror Group Newspapers (MGN) Pension Fund, from which he was ultimately to plunder around £450 million, to the detriment of the scheme's thirty thousand pensioners. He was also to rob MCC itself by taking some of its assets and businesses into his own private companies.

Maxwell's third strategy was to persuade others to buy MCC shares with their own money. With the company's business outlook weak, the only way he could achieve this was by indemnifying purchasers against loss. However such practice was illegal for a publicly traded company and a recent scandal had brought the risk of this approach into stark relief. In 1986 Guinness had acquired Distillers, Scotland's largest company, through a $4 billion hostile takeover bid. Distillers was one of the largest whisky and spirits producers in the world, with myriad brands ranging from Johnnie Walker scotch whisky to Gordons and Tanqueray gins. In the course of the bid a group of investors had bought Guinness shares to support the share price, so that a high value was maintained for their cash and shares offer for Distillers. Once it was discovered that a concert party to provide share price support had been orchestrated, and the investors putting up the money had been indemnified against loss, Guinness's Chief Executive and others who had participated in the share support scheme were sent to jail leaving the blue-blooded British merchant banks who had advised on the deal badly scarred.

The Guinness scandal made corporate raiders much more wary over crossing the line into illegality. Their activities were already under close public scrutiny, particularly in the United States, where movies like *Wall Street* and *Pretty Woman* had drawn attention to their ruthless self-serving tactics and unsavoury practitioners. One prominent US corporate raider called Ivan Boesky, who had participated in the Guinness share support operation, was later to be convicted of insider trading on another corporate raiding venture.

The Guinness prosecution was to change the style of corporate raiding, and led to considerable interest in option strategies. In the UK, Lords Hanson and White, serial acquisitors through Hanson Trust, the company they ran, took particular interest in options shortly after completing the £2.5 billion purchase of Imperial

Tobacco in 1986. When making Hanson Trust's next big move, the £3.5 billion purchase of Consolidated Goldfields in 1988, their share purchase and acquisition tactics were very different from those they had employed in the past. Instead their approach bore all the hallmarks of the methods championed by Robert Holmes à Court.

Against this background Maxwell took a great deal of interest in share support and acquisition methods that did not infringe either stock exchange rules or the law of the land. It was in this light that his interest turned towards using put options as a disguised form of share price guarantee. I personally became aware of this interest in options in 1989 when approached to become chief investment officer (CIO) for London & Bishopsgate International (LBI), the investment management firm he owned. LBI managed the assets of all of Maxwell pension funds outside the US, including those of Mirror Group Newspapers (MGN) that he was to plunder. Introduced to his son Kevin by a derivative specialist I knew well, who ran Maxwell's US pension arm, I was told that the incumbent CIO would shortly be leaving and that they were seeking someone with derivative expertise for the role, an unusual requirement for a pension fund CIO at the time.

The attraction of put options was that they allowed Maxwell to offer a third party purchaser of MCC shares a legal form of indemnity against loss, without being deemed a connected party. The argument used to support this stance was that the owner of the put option does not know, when entering into the transaction, whether or not the put option contract will be used for any sale of shares and, even under those circumstances, whether or not it will be to a connected party. A further advantage of the put option approach was that it provided the holder of the put option with a real incentive to go out and buy MCC shares. With no shareholding the put option derived no benefit if MCC shares rose in value, whilst as a shareholder they would reap all the gain. By contrast were the shares to fall in price, they would lose nothing as shareholders, since they could exercise their put option contracts, passing their share losses to Maxwell. For a third party to buy shares when handed a put option contract in the same shares was in effect an unmissable *"win with no risk of loss"* investment opportunity.

The share support strategy and its execution

Maxwell most needed third party support for MCC shares during what are known as 'closed periods'. These occur shortly before a company publicly announces its financial results and is the period when directors and other connected parties are prohibited from dealing in the company's shares. Maxwell could not personally buy MCC shares over the closed period, rendering him powerless to defend their value against share price weakness. Unless someone unconnected to him was willing to buy MCC shares during these closed periods, there was a risk that the loans he could ill afford to repay might be recalled on the grounds that the value of the MCC shares used as collateral for the loans had become insufficient. With Goldman Sachs as their corporate adviser and the main market maker in MCC shares, they were the most obvious third party for him to turn to. And so he did; carrying out a series of put option transactions over closed periods.

The first put option contract he struck was in August 1990, with expiry set two days after the MCC closed period ended in November. The contract covered almost all of the 16.7 million shares Goldman then owned, thus ensuring that they had no incentive to sell over the closed period. A second transaction in January 1991 covering the 30 million shares Goldman now held, had its expiry set shortly after the next closed period in mid-February 1991. This contract had an exercise price struck above the prevailing share price at 152p. These put options took away any incentive for Goldman to do anything other than hold onto the shares, even if news and the share price outlook were poor. Were the MCC share price to fall, Goldman's loss on the shares would be exactly matched by their gain on the put options. As before, were the MCC share price to rise, Goldman would scoop all of the profit.

Whilst very attractive to Goldman, the put options did little to help Maxwell beyond stalling the inevitable. In mid-February 1991, when the share price was below the exercise price, Goldman exercised their option contracts and put their stake to Maxwell, forcing him to find £46 million in cash and to increase his MCC stake from 64% to 68.5%.

To outsiders the share price performance of MCC shares was puzzling, seeming to defy gravity. They were one of the best performing shares in the UK stock market during the first quarter of 1991, yet their trading results were so poor that they were obliged to issue a profits warning in April. As stock market interest in the option transactions MCC were having to declare grew, I was asked to investigate, writing an internal research note in September 1991 entitled *"Maxwell Communications Corporation - Is the share price being manipulated by option transactions?"* Its concluding remark was: *"He (Maxwell) seems to be committed to spending more and more of his cash trying to support less and less valuable MCC shares. On the day Robert Maxwell inadvertently takes MCC private (over 75% stake) he will also be bankrupt".*

Maxwell's hunger for cash became reflected in his urgency to sell the companies he had acquired, either privately or publicly through stock market flotation. The public flotation of Mirror Group Newspapers (MGM) was seen by many as a symptom of mounting panic. Sinking deeper into debt as the value of his MCC share collateral slumped, the banks he had borrowed from demanded repayment of their loans. The funds raised from the flotation of Mirror Group Newspapers in May 1991 was far from being sufficient and on 31st October 1991, with no tricks or cards left to play, he boarded the Lady Ghislaine in the Canary Islands, the yacht named after his daughter. On that same day Goldman began to liquidate the MCC shares it held as collateral for the money they had lent him.

Robert Maxwell's Death

On 5 November 1991 Maxwell was declared missing, and was

presumed to have fallen overboard. His body was subsequently found floating in the Atlantic Ocean. Although the official verdict was death by accidental drowning, doubts still remain. They were said to be reflected in the James Bond film 'Tomorrow Never Dies' when, in response to a press release announcing the death of newspaper baron and lead villain, Elliot Carver, that he had fallen overboard from his luxury yacht and drowned in the ocean, M informs Bond *"at present there is speculation of suicide"*.

Rupert Murdoch, Maxwell's long time media rival, appeared to share this view when he invited David Cornwell, a former British Intelligence Officer who writes spy novels under the pseudonym John le Carre, to lunch at London's Savoy Grill where he asked: *"Who killed Robert Maxwell?"* Following what amounted to an Israeli state funeral, Maxwell was buried on the Mount of Olives in Jerusalem.

After his death it was found that Maxwell controlled 82% of MCC shares, in breach of a stock exchange rule that limited private ownership of publicly listed shares to 75%. Many of these shares were held in secret through *'sub rosa'* deals, an expression whose literal meaning is *"under the rose"*, reflecting an ancient practice where a rose was hung over a meeting table as a token of secrecy. According to John Talbot of Arthur Andersen, the joint administrator appointed to the myriad private companies, Maxwell had paid overseas entities some £153m to buy MCC shares between April and July 1991.

Maxwell's death triggered the collapse of his publishing empire as the banks called in loans. His sons briefly struggled to keep the business together, but failed once it emerged that Maxwell had stolen hundreds of millions of pounds from his own companies' pension funds to keep his business empire afloat, in addition to the £450 million taken from the MGN Pension Scheme.

The Maxwell private companies filed for bankruptcy protection in Chapter 11 in the US and for administration orders in the UK in December 1991. Maxwell's son Kevin was personally declared bankrupt with debts of £400 million in 1992. In 1995 Kevin and his brother Ian, along with two other former directors, went on trial for conspiracy to defraud but were to be unanimously acquitted by the jury in 1996. The lasting legacy came from the public outcry at the ease with which their father had plundered the retirement assets of MGN pensioners. New legislation was introduced by the UK Government on the stewardship of pension funds intended to prevent interference from corporate influence. A pensions compensation board funded from levies raised by a new regulatory authority was also set up, now called the Pensions Regulator.

19. Clearing Houses - Clark Kent or Superman?

"What happens if they (clearing houses) go bust? I can tell you the simple answer: mayhem. As bad as, conceivably worse than, the failure of large and complex banks."

**Sir Paul Tucker, Deputy Governor,
Bank of England (2002-2014)**

To those who saw him every day in the office, Clark Kent appeared to be a quietly spoken clerk, in an uninteresting job, with a dull life. But when a crisis struck he would don his signature combat clothing and be transformed into the all action hero, Superman. In the world of derivatives there is an entity that generally sits quietly at the heart of derivatives markets and goes by the innocuous name of 'clearing house'. Like Superman they only emerge into public view and prominence during crises, quietly returning to their desks after restoring order and calm.

This derivative Superman is the antithesis of the brash highly charged trader whose image is so etched into the public mind when thinking about financial markets. Yet it is these foot soldiers in the financial trenches who patrol all trading activity, ensure integrity, and have consistently proved their worth in battle.

The business of clearing houses has nothing to do with emptying or demolishing properties. The term clearing house reflects its role in sweeping up transactions from a host of participants; a tidy and well organised home that takes charge of all activities from the time a transaction is entered into until it is finally settled. A key part of their job is to make sure that transactions are settled in accordance with market rules, even if either buyer or seller become insolvent prior to settlement, and cannot honour their side of the bargain.

Clearing houses do everything in their power to keep everyone who enters into derivative contracts on their watch safe. For all their flexibility and efficiency, derivative contracts are simply words written on paper or recorded electronically that set out the rights and obligations of the two parties to the transaction. Great reliance and monetary value can be vested in these contracts being honoured, even though no cash or assets may change hands when they are agreed. With clearing houses it is the quiet things that matter; documentation correctly recording the details, checking everyone abides by the rules of the market, collateral to ensure credit worthiness is of the right quality and value, and that this collateral is held in the right place. In short they are the glue that makes derivative contracts hold fast in practice or, as some have described in more physical terms: *"the heart and lungs of markets.... the most important organs, which reside inside the body and cannot be seen on the surface"*.

The concept of clearing derivatives first emerged in Japan in 1730 to safeguard the trading of rice futures, and came later to London in 1888 to provide sanctity for forward contracts in coffee and sugar. Then, as now, the role of the clearing house was to act as a credit intermediary between buyer and seller, guaranteeing performance of derivatives contracts.

In London the idea came from German merchants. They had lost money when forward contracts which they held failed to be honoured by their English counterparties, and could find no legal or financial means for redress. It is thanks to these German merchants that London has remained at the forefront of the derivative clearing business in Europe ever since. London Clearing House (LCH), the entity Germany spawned and which, over time, subsumed many of the clearing houses situated along London's river Thames, is today the dominant player amongst many European commodity and financial derivative exchanges.

The difference between a forward and futures contract

A forward contract is very similar to a futures contract. The purchaser is committed to buying the product in the amount specified on a date in the future at an agreed price. Where they

---

differ is that a forward contract is privately negotiated between two parties who trust one another to perform on the contract, generally holding the contract until maturity. A futures contract is tradable on an exchange with performance guaranteed by a central counterparty that stands between the buyer and seller. The clearing house, by acting as the central counterparty, demonstrates financial security by demanding money in the form of a deposit known as initial margin. Creditworthiness is then maintained throughout the life of the contract by posting cash, called variation margin, every day from loser to winner to cover the change in market value.

In recent times, LCH has garnered more and more business as private OTC contracts in interest rate swaps and other derivative instruments have been forced into clearing by regulations drafted to counter the weaknesses in the OTC market infrastructure exposed during the financial crisis of 2008. In Europe, the Germans have been the standard bearers behind this regulatory drive and Frankfurt's derivative exchange and clearing house, Eurex, has found it particularly galling to be regarded as *"the new kids on the block"* when struggling to gain traction against LCH, the well-established competitor which their forebears spawned in London.

What clearing houses do

A clearing house stands between the buyer and seller and acts as a central counterparty to guarantee contract performance. As such the clearing house is the buyer to every seller and the seller to every buyer.

Collateral, also called margin, is secured from both parties to ensure that any value embedded in the contract is *"money good"* in the event that an adverse price movement results in a loss of such magnitude that one party becomes unable to meet their obligations to the other.

By standing as a robust and well capitalised counterparty, the clearing house gives both parties to the transaction confidence that the contract will not fail and they will continue to be *"position good"* even if the other party fails to meet its obligations. This is because the clearing house has assumed the obligations of both parties under the contract.

The main task of the clearing house is to act as the risk manager to the market. It is they who monitor agents and participants in the market to ensure that their solvency, record keeping and administrative processes are up to scratch. A further defence is to increase or reduce the amount of margin payable, depending on market conditions of volatility and perceived risk. Clearing houses must also be ready to step in to maintain an orderly market and position sanctity should a clearing member or any other third party default.

The presence of a clearing house between buyer and seller has other side effects, mostly beneficial. For example, by standing in the middle, they also act as a wall of anonymity between buyer and seller, so neither can see who is on the other side of the market trade

Not all clearing houses are the same

The quality of construction of a clearing house is critical to its safety and longevity. Some are structurally solid with robust risk management, capital and legal frameworks and strong regulatory oversight. Others are less transparent about how they operate, and less careful about ensuring the safety the money entrusted to them by investors. Participants in the products held in less secure clearing houses never feel confident about the safety of their money and positions. From time to time there have been occasions where clearing houses have been built on the financial equivalent of sand.

In the 1980s and early 1990s, regulators in Europe required

investment managers to check and certify that the derivative clearing houses where they placed their clients' money were safe and properly run. To meet this requirement, I used to visit clearing houses with derivative specialists from rival firms. In determining which houses to place on the *"approved clearing house"* list, what really counted was not their financial statements, for which we relied on the opinion of their auditors, but their risk management capabilities and the structure of their business model. Partly on account of this regulatory requirement, a comprehensive analysis of all clearing houses, *The World's Clearing Houses*, was published every year setting out their capital structures, as well as business and risk management processes. Exchanges like France's MATIF were easy to approve as the French Government through the Bank of France formally stood behind them, guaranteeing the sanctity of their contracts and the solvency of the clearing house. Having the taxpayer guarantee the market was not difficult to justify, when the first and most important futures contract MATIF listed was in their own national debt, French Government bonds. Nowadays checks on clearing houses are part of general counterparty credit procedure and assessed in much the same way as banks are evaluated as OTC derivative counterparties.

The monitoring of clearing houses brought to light some fascinating cultural differences. The early American exchanges in Chicago were founded on commodity trading where the atmosphere and structure was akin to that of a family or club. Participants knew and socialised with one another with trading conducted in the close proximity of small pits on the floor of the exchange. Many futures trading businesses passed within families from one generation to the next. Fiercely independent and far removed from the bankers in New York, whom they viewed as faceless and unnecessarily legalistic, their approach to policing users was through intimate knowledge of market participants and observing at close hand their trading activities on the floor of the exchange. Light on rules but heavy on knowing what was going on, the Chicago exchanges forged a mutual risk structure that kept costs low whilst giving their exchanges the power and flexibility to speedily adapt to changing market practices and product needs.

Ebb and flow of American and European business models

When the Chicago exchanges offered financial contracts, they saw no reason to change their culture or their tried and tested approach to clearing. However their model of deep knowledge and mutually shared risk did not travel well around the world, as new derivative exchanges had neither the experience nor personal relationships to provide the level of trust needed to run with what became known as the 'American Model'.

In Europe, the financial derivatives revolution was not led by the well-established London commodity futures markets following in the footsteps of Melamed and the other Chicago commodity futures exchanges. Europe's derivative markets were set up alongside stock markets in the major financial centres. The banks were leading the charge, and elected to adopt a different model for ensuring sanctity of financial derivative contracts formulated around the construct of the banking system. Avoiding what they saw as a 'cowboy' commodity market structure, they sought to avoid reliance on relationships and trust. They built a clearing model that was tight on legal documentation, heavy on rules and capital, and laced up with formal guarantees where possible.

This 'European Model' had the local banks owning, operating, and guaranteeing the credit standing of the market. In London the clearing house was owned by the major retail banks at the behest of the Bank of England, who provided what was described as an *"informal guarantee"*. By going a step further, with a full guarantee for the MATIF, the French Government had much greater control over their derivative markets as well as gaining competitive advantage over London in terms of the safety of the money that investors had entrusted. At that time Government bailouts of financial institutions in times of crisis were not of political concern. Furthermore, the notion of the major banks running and controlling the system was seen as a good thing, not least as it was then almost unthinkable for a major bank to default or even run into difficulty. This sanguine perception was to change radically following the financial crisis of 2008.

Whilst the inclusion of the MATIF on the approved clearing house roster was relatively straightforward, others were just as easy to reject. Several start-up exchanges, often in far flung locations, gave little confidence that there were any mechanisms in place to safeguard money posted as margin on behalf of clients. It was also hard to uncover much about the financial strength or risk management processes within the clearing house. Such exchanges were excluded from investor 'approved' lists on the grounds that no clearing house is better than a weak or opaque one.

The American and European models sat comfortably side by side, with proponents for each extolling the virtues of their particular approach. Most of the new derivative exchanges opted for the European model for their clearing houses, principally because there was no family or club infrastructure to build from, unlike that in Chicago. Over time, as confidence and trust were built in these markets and better knowledge gained of the players, the necessity for some form of guarantee from central banks fell away, allowing guarantees to be quietly withdrawn, moving clearing houses established on the European model closer to the American model. But the idea was to return to prominence in the aftermath of the financial crisis of 2008, when confidence in the credit standing of banks cast doubt on a European model without central bank support, as well as questioning the effectiveness of self-policing. Later, in 2011, when a major clearing agent MF Global collapsed and money posted by their clients as margin was put at risk, the strength of the American model was also called into question.

Paradoxically it was Melamed's visionary efforts in developing electronic trading that were ultimately to undermine the American clearing model that Chicago had nurtured. Electronic trading killed off once and for all that light touch and robust family policing of the 'open outcry' physical markets. After 2008 the case for reverting back to the more impersonal structure of the European clearing model could not have been stronger. But equally there was no political will to offer central bank guarantees to derivative exchanges in distress, through taxpayer funded bailouts of their clearing houses. At that time such guarantees could not have been less acceptable. With no tenable solution to marry investor protection without any call on the public purse, agreement on the optimal clearing model remains unfinished business to this day.

Failures and near misses

Debate around clearing houses and their business models has always been muted and of little public interest, except when coloured by events that bring their relative strengths and weaknesses to the fore. Whilst there is no doubt that having an entity that stands between buyer and seller as a central counterparty and polices credit standing is much safer than having no credit intermediary, there has to be confidence that the clearing house is robust and safe, and that this structure comes at a tolerable cost. However, unlike Superman, clearing houses have not always proved to be of superhuman strength.

In the 1970s and 1980s, when financial futures markets were gaining traction, the safety of clearing houses and their business models became the subject of fierce debate, as difficulties experienced by their commodity market cousins shone a spotlight on their weaknesses.

An early example came in 1974 when the Paris based Caisse de Liquidation failed. A sharp drop in sugar prices had left a major participant facing huge losses and unable to meet margin calls on his futures contracts. Weaknesses in risk management had exacerbated the crisis, as margin was not called for quickly enough in response to the price shocks. The default management process afterwards was also found wanting and a number of participants took the clearing house to court with accusations of favouritism and lack of transparency in their distributing the losses. The participants won their case and the clearing house was subsequently declared insolvent. This failure of an American model clearing house was to have a marked influence on those planning the launch of France's first financial futures market, the Paris based Marché à Terme International de France ("MATIF"). Launched in 1986 investor protection for MATIF participants was secured by a cast iron fashion by a formal central bank guarantee from the Bank of France.

Tin in crisis after producing countries refuse to meet margin calls

Perhaps the most vivid example of clearing house frailty came from an exchange that some would argue did not have a clearing house at all. In October 1985 the London Metal Exchange ('LME'), the world's premier metals market, was brought to its knees after having to suspend trading in tin. At the time I was managing a commodity futures fund, where the bulk of the metals exposure came through LME futures contracts. The International Tin Council (ITC), a group principally comprising tin producing countries that acted rather like the Organisation of Petroleum Exporting Countries (OPEC) in the oil industry to regulate the price and supply of tin, announced that it had run out of cash and was leaving the losses it had run up to be met by LME clearing members.

The ITC had been supporting the tin price at $12,000 per ton and the LME suspended trading at this level on 24th October 1985. But this suspension price had no validity as tin was soon being traded outside the LME for under $10,000 per ton. Investors and traders, used to seeing the ITC support the tin price at this level, irrespective of supply and demand conditions, were left hanging with no real feel for where economic fundamentals might take the price of tin. As a consequence more reliance than usual was placed on the dark arts of an investment process called technical analysis. Investors adopting this approach eschew decision making based on economic fundamentals, in favour of chart patterns of historical prices. There are some who regard technical analysis as akin to witchcraft with fundamental analysis as the proper investment science. However, in a climate of fear where technical analysis soothsayers were claiming that the tin price would fall without buying any support to $6,000 per ton, the market was braced with the daunting prospect of shouldering losses in excess of $300 million.

Founded in 1877 by a group of metals merchants over a hat shop in the City of London to provide a market for the growing trade in Chilean copper and Malaysian tin, the LME later added lead, zinc, nickel and aluminium to its roster of contracts, and became the world's main trading venue for industrial metals. The exchange also became involved in precious metal trading through clearing and other linkages with the London Bullion Market, which to this day conducts the trade in gold and silver.

Their members had faced crises before, one of which took place shortly after the exchange was founded. The French copper industrialist, Eugène Secrétan, who is best known for donating over half of the copper plate used to construct New York's Statue of Liberty, caused a stir in 1889 by attempting to corner the copper market through LME positions. He was to be bankrupted when the corner failed.

At the request of the ITC, the LME board agreed to halt tin trading on 24th October 1985, while discussions were held with banks, dealers and ITC members. Their aim was to reopen tin trading without triggering a sharp price fall as a collapse in the tin price would render several large LME member firms bankrupt. Unlike most other commodity and futures exchanges, the LME then had no independent clearing system and its dealing members traded as principals. This meant that if a client defaulted, their unmet obligations became those of the dealing members. There was also no buffer of clearing house capital or the concept of sharing losses amongst clearing members. If a client owed money to the exchange, it was the dealing member that was on the hook to pay up.

But the suspension of LME trading in tin did not bring tin trading to a halt. The bulk of metal trading had always been carried out off the exchange, at prices set with reference to one of the two 'fixing' auctions which the LME held each day. With the price at which the LME had suspended tin more than double the true market price, it was no longer a valid benchmark for agreeing commercial transactions between industrial producers and consumers.

Weakness in LME crisis management infects other metal prices

The tin crisis infected activity in every other metal traded on the LME with volumes slowing to a trickle. The price of all of the metals traded on the LME fell, as dealers sold other metals to cover their tin losses, because no one was sure if their money was safe, nor if the positions in any LME futures contracts would be honoured. Without a clearing house and with client margin at risk, there was a complete loss of confidence in the LME. Like many other investors, we took the decision to liquidate all of our LME positions for the commodity fund which I managed. On an altogether different scale, Inco of Canada, the world's largest nickel producer with 30% of the non-Communist world's nickel production, asked the LME to stop trading nickel, as the nickel price had been pushed down nearly five per cent. Inco observed that *the current tin crisis is unduly influencing the LME price of nickel*" and added that: *"for the duration of the tin crisis Inco will not be considering the LME nickel price as a meaningful indicator."* Other major metal producers followed suit with external trading of lead and copper based on LME prices suspended.

Pursuit for payment from the countries in the ITC, in spite of a series of legally binding international agreements established over 30 years, proved impossible even though none of the countries involved were bankrupt. The commercial contracts drawn up between ITC members and the LME were rendered unenforceable as politics took precedence and there was no appetite in government circles to press for repayment.

The LME managed to survive, but the credibility of their business model without a formal clearing house was lost. The crisis also called into question the lighter regulatory and credit touch of the LME over its New York rival Comex, an approach that had paid dividends in attracting business away from New York, especially from the big players as the Hunts had shown with silver. Tin changed that regime for LME members and the UK regulatory authorities, although the exchange provided greater latitude in off exchange or 'curb' trading than Comex, an activity that we shall see later helped Sumitomo with their copper market operations.

Afterwards clearing responsibility was outsourced to what is now the LCH and only recently, after a thirty-year absence, did the LME re-establish sufficient credibility again to run the clearing for the metals it trades.

How to keep a clearing house safe

The worry about clearing house solvency was not new to one of the principal members of the ITC, Malaysia. In 1983, less than two years before the tin crisis broke, the Kuala Lumpur Commodity Clearing House was closed down after a collapse in the price of palm oil futures had left six of their clearing brokers unable to meet variation margin calls.

Whenever clearing houses are in difficulty, the subsequent post mortem generally identifies two causes, often both working in conjunction with one another. Inadequate risk management systems are almost always in evidence, and generally found to be woefully weak. The second cause is the sense of panic, rather than a robust management crisis process, that often takes hold of those dealing with the crisis. They are sometimes likened to *"rabbits in the headlights"* as they see the scale of the losses and the prospect of default. Too often the desire to keep the clearing house afloat is allowed to outweigh the protection of participants who have kept their word and honoured their contractual obligations to the market. The participants' interests are always best served by keeping them *"money good"* by repaying their margin deposits and voiding their market positions and attendant exposure. The trouble is that the people in the hot seat are the club members, those who stand to lose by having to pay for their failure. Sometimes those facing failure put survival of the clearing house ahead of fulfilling its central purpose, the protection of participant money and positions. Instead of worrying about their good creditworthy customers in a crisis, their attention can wander by trying to save their clearing member from being hurt by a defaulting customer.

In a subtle, and some might say devious, sleight of hand, clearing members brought about a nuance which passed the risk of losses from a client in difficulty from themselves to their other clients under the somewhat innocuous term 'omnibus account'. With an omnibus account all client money is kept separate from the clearing member. However, in the event of one of their clients defaulting, it is their other clients, and not the clearing member who pick up the tab. It was one of many occasions where the risks in the market were passed on to the investors instead of residing with those really culpable. The omnibus account still survives to this day, although few professional investors allow their customers to be exposed to such risk.

Clearing house performance during financial crises

The stockmarket crash of 1987 provided perhaps the ultimate stress test of the processes and systems that had been developed to keep financial derivative markets safe. The 25% fall in the S&P 500 Index was thought to be a once in the lifetime of the universe event; furthermore the volume of derivative trading throughout the stock market collapse had been substantial. This event was therefore viewed as a live test of clearing house processes and systems under financial Armageddon conditions.

For such an extreme event, the outcome looked surprisingly good. In the United States, clearing members who were about to default on their margin calls, were saved by a $400 million emergency bank loan.

Many exchanges had had to call for margin more than once during the trading day and investors were very worried that their money and positions might be lost. Overseas, the Hong Kong Futures Exchange had to close for four days before reopening, after the government stepped in and made good on unmet margin calls. But no investor lost any money through a defaulting counterparty and all the market positions remained intact. For Chicago and Hong Kong there were difficulties and rapid decision making had been critical but, under the circumstances, it was unsurprising that there were some creaks. Compared with what the 'naysayers' had been predicting would happen from much smaller swings, it was a major triumph for the exchanges and their clearing houses.

As a consequence the review of the 1987 experience by the industry was very positive. In identifying how important the expertise and professionalism of the major clearing agents had been in maintaining market confidence, a test exercise was set up the following year to ensure that the market was able to withstand the default of a major clearing agent. The most important part of this test was to determine the effectiveness of the process by which money and positions could be transferred in large scale from a defaulting clearer to solvent ones. The transfers worked well enough in the test environment, although some harboured the view that the process would not proceed as smoothly in the real world. They did not have to wait long to find out as, early the following year, the event they had prepared actually took place.

Drexel Burnham Lambert was the fourth largest clearing agent in the world when the firm collapsed from losses in its junk bond business on 14th February 1990. In Chicago there were many who expected that their derivatives exchanges would suffer the financial equivalent of the massacre Bugs Moran's gang suffered on St. Valentine's Day in 1929, when Al Capone's mobsters' machine gunned seven of their members to death. In the event the transfer of Drexel's massive book of exchange traded derivative contracts passed without incident, whilst their customers who held private

OTC derivative positions outside the clearing house regime, lost everything.

The clearing house emerged from the crash of 1987 and the 1990 Drexel bankruptcy as an unlikely hero, with a transformed image far removed from that held before of a mere administrator of the murky detail. It was to give investors and regulators great confidence in the clearing system for financial derivatives. It seemed that the lessons from clearing house difficulties before 1985 had been learned, with further confirmation coming in 2005 when Refco, the biggest independent clearer in the world, collapsed with scarcely a ripple of concern that client money or derivative positions would be lost or compromised.

It was not until the Lehman collapse in 2008, and that of MF Global in 2011, that those regulating the market faced scrutiny over how safe cash posted by investors as margin really was. It seemed that, when in crisis, banks had found it easier than they should to raid client money to prop up their own failing businesses. Lehman was to afford another example of how successful clearing systems can be, when LCH Clearnet took over its positions and was able to liquidate them through a default manager without loss either to their clients or to the market.

No backup for Superman

The security that clearing houses provide does not come for free. Their risk management systems and processes incur costs that have to be borne by those whose money and positions are kept safe by their services. Capital is also needed to give participants confidence that unexpected shocks and defaults can be absorbed.

Their success in modern financial markets may now be becoming their Achilles heel, as the clearing house model is seen as the answer to every question on financial market security. It is almost as though Superman is being asked to deal with all the world's emergencies whilst those who were responsible contemplate disbanding their armies and police forces. This idea was most in evidence after the 2008 Financial Crisis, when much of the blame was laid at the door of OTC derivatives, the wilder freewheeling cousins of exchange traded derivatives.

The low cost and cheap administration of OTC derivatives became lost in the noise of the crowd clamouring for OTC derivatives to be forced into mandatory clearing. As the call for transparency of positions, pricing, and knowledge of the players reached fever pitch a new model, which cloned the exchange traded market as closely as practicable, emerged. Branded 'Central Counterparties' or 'CCPs' these super clearing houses are much bigger and more costly than those catering for exchange traded derivatives. Their structures, rules and new operational processes are so convoluted that they introduce what some call *"4x4 off-road vehicle risk"*. Bigger and more sophisticated than conventional cars a 4x4 can take you to places that were previously inaccessible. However, once in trouble, the risk is much greater, as the places where 4x4s become stuck present much greater challenges when attempting to pull them out of their difficulty.

Meanwhile the most robust model, the European style clearing house, has fallen away as the idea of taxpayer bailouts has been deemed politically unacceptable and the issue of who steps in to rescue a clearing house in difficulty has become a dangerous game of 'pass the parcel' with no one wishing to carry the risk. In desperation, some have even mooted the idea that the investors whom the clearing house is designed to protect should themselves rescue clearing houses from the misdeeds of the banks and clearing house managers. The only virtue in such an approach is that it reduces the amount of capital that banks and clearing houses have to put up.

The clearing house model is being inexorably morphed away from the modest, quiet and thorough risk manager in the Clark Kent mould into that of a stand-alone giant with extraordinary powers.

It brings to mind a story concerning Muhammad Ali, the former World Heavyweight Boxing Champion and voted the greatest sportsman of the 20th Century. When asked by an air stewardess to fasten his seatbelt Ali quipped: *"Superman don't need no seatbelt."* Her quick riposte: *"Superman don't need no plane"* elicited a smile and quiet acquiescence.

The structure and model for the clearing houses of the future that are robust and safe is far from resolved. There is a fear that we may simply be replacing giant banks as the 'too big to fail' systemic risk in financial markets with giant derivative clearing houses. Regulators and those charged with mandates for financial stability have rooted an assumption into their thinking that clearing houses must not fail under any circumstances. They have also taken to heart the political imperative that taxpayer money should play no part in keeping a struggling clearing house alive. They forget that clearing houses fail when they lose the trust of their customers. Having massive amounts of capital behind them is of little comfort when their risk management processes are seen to have failed. You know something is not right when mechanisms are proposed that involve taking money from customers in order to keep a clearing house on life support, while the first responsibility of clearing houses is to protect their customers' money. We still need Superman to keep us safe but he cannot do it on his own.

20. Swaps - Freedom fighters for financial markets

After financial futures, the next and most potent financial weapon for realising the free market vision of Hayek and Friedman were swaps.

This new derivative instrument came to prominence in the 1980s and had an immediate impact on financial markets, its subsequent growth quickly dwarfing that of its predecessors, futures and options. However, swap trading did not initially take place in public on the exchanges that Leo Melamed had created in Chicago, but instead were privately negotiated between the two parties to the transaction.

The roots of swap transactions could not be simpler, an agreement to exchange one thing for another, the presumption being that they are of equivalent value. Most children are familiar with the concept, swapping toys or other goods with one another. And the practice is not new to business. Bartering or swapping one set of goods for another was the norm, long before money became the principal means of exchange. In a sense the real puzzle is not why the financial swap market grew so quickly, but why it did not emerge sooner.

With the most successful instrument, the interest rate swap, a regular stream of payments based on cash deposit rates is exchanged for a corresponding series of fixed payments. The cash deposit rate moves or 'floats' with short-term interest rates, whilst the fixed payment is set at the start and does not change throughout the life of the swap contract.

The floating interest rate is generally calculated with reference to the interest rate that banks borrow from one another, known as London Inter Bank Offer Rate, or 'LIBOR'. No one in the early days of swaps would have thought that this calculation would ever become controversial, let alone become associated with a major financial scandal that would shake many major banks, give rise to enormous regulatory fines, and send people to jail. But that was when the amount of money being paid at the LIBOR reference price was small, and the rate at which banks lent to one other varied little. Later on, in a very different world that would lead to the financial crisis of 2008, the prospect of major bank defaults became a real worry, and LIBOR came to vary a great deal from one bank to another. Strong banks borrowed from other banks at much lower rates than their weaker brethren, and the money paid through swap contracts against the LIBOR reference price was so great, that small changes in its value had a marked influence on the money that banks made from their swap business.

IBM and World Bank open the door

The transaction that paved the way for a financial market in swaps took place in 1981, when IBM and the World Bank agreed to enter into a $210 million currency swap with one another over a ten year period. The contract committed the World Bank to paying the interest coupons on bonds that IBM had issued in Europe denominated in Deutsche Marks and Swiss Francs, in return for which IBM paid the interest coupons denominated in US Dollars on a bond the World Bank issued in the United States.

What differentiated this swap agreement from the commitments associated with forward or futures contracts was that the swapping of currencies was not a single *"one off"* event on a particular day in the future but an agreement to exchange a series of currency payments on several future dates. The payments dates under the swap contract were designed to match those of the coupon payments on the IBM and World Bank bonds.

It was a natural extension of the futures contract where, instead of a single occasion when cash is exchanged for goods, the swap contract agrees a series of exchanges of cash for goods. In a sense a swap contract is a group of forward contracts bolted together. The transaction between IBM and the World Bank set the precedent for all subsequent swaps. Nowadays virtually all swap contracts take the form of agreements to exchange a series of financial payments in the future. No money tends to change hands at the outset, as the value of the stream of future payments to each party is typically assessed to be the same. Furthermore, as with all derivatives contracts, they are tradable and can be bought, sold, or cancelled before their final maturity date.

Why did IBM and the World Bank do this? In IBM's case, they wanted to remove their foreign currency exposure arising from their European bond issues as their businesses in Germany and Switzerland no longer generated local currency revenues of this magnitude. For the World Bank it was a way of matching the money they were borrowing to the currencies of the overseas projects they were funding. At the time the World Bank was unable to issue either Deutsche Mark or Swiss Franc bonds on account of borrowing limits that had been imposed on them by West Germany (before the reunification with East Germany in 1990) and Switzerland.

For IBM and the World Bank the swap idea, which was proposed and brokered by Salomon Brothers (now part of Citigroup), was simpler, faster, and much less costly than those of the traditional capital market channels. IBM avoided the costly and protracted exercise of redeeming their European bonds early, whilst the World Bank was obviated from having to renegotiate their borrowing limits with European central banks.

The transaction also demonstrated something far more significant than just an efficient means of insulating both parties from unwanted currency risk. Here was a mechanism that had skirted simply and freely around local regulatory constraints. The parentage of the transaction, involving two of the most respected entities in the market, appeared to signal tacit acceptance, even approval, by the regulatory authorities they were circumventing.

This point was not lost on companies and banks all over the world. The swap transaction between IBM and the World Bank was seen as establishing an important precedent; that it was now acceptable for swaps and other derivative instruments to be used to bypass local rules, regulations, even tax regimes. A market solution had been found that would do more for free trade than any global accord between nations.

Corporates and banks now sought the lowest cost provider of market exposure, even forming new purpose built entities that were structured and located to capture tax, regulatory and capital cost savings and efficiencies in the most effective manner. These entities passed on these benefits to their clients whilst also extracting a good profit margin for the banks for their intermediation.

They soon found there was considerable power from combining bonds with swaps. A bank could issue a bond in the jurisdiction, currency and maturity that best met the appetite of investors and then, through swaps, transform the risk to suit the maturity and currency preference of the corporate issuer. It made bond issuance easier as the needs of borrower and investor no longer needed to be matched. For example a Swiss Franc bond of a particular maturity could be transformed into a Sterling bond of a different maturity, simply by conducting the appropriate interest rate and currency swaps alongside the Swiss Franc bond issuance.

For investors, swaps have in many ways become preferred for investment over bonds. Bonds are less flexible compared with swaps, with their high frictional costs associated with issuance and maturity. Bonds are also harder and more expensive to trade, as their liquidity can be very poor.

The swaps market has thrived ever since the IBM and World Bank transaction, with the range of swaps on offer expanding to include interest rates, credit, and all manner of other asset exposures. More than any other derivative instrument, swaps have become the means by which unwanted risk exposure coming from asset ownership has been transferred elsewhere.

21. The OTC world of private bets

"If you can't explain it simply you don't understand it well enough"

Albert Einstein (1879-1955)

When derivative transactions take place privately between two people or businesses, and outside the auspices and rules of public exchanges, they are known as 'over-the-counter' or 'OTC' transactions. The term owes something to the way the transaction is negotiated and agreed; in much the same way as a shopkeeper and customer negotiate price and exchange goods over the store counter.

As exchange traded markets developed and trading volumes increased, their customers struggled to cope with the administrative and operational demands of exchanges and their clearing houses. This was not a time of speedy electronic communication and the efficiency of computer spreadsheets, but a time of manually intense processing involving people, hand written notes, typewriters and telephones. Electronic messaging by telex and fax was regarded as technologically advanced. It was therefore hard work to trade derivatives in any significant volume, and few organisations had the operational infrastructure to cope.

It was unpopular for a portfolio manager to trade after lunch, since it meant that those engaged in the post trade activities of confirmation and settlement had to stay late into the evening. Shares were much simpler to process than derivatives as, once bought and paid for, ownership becomes conferred through paper certificates that were stored in a safe until sold.

By contrast exchange traded derivatives have a lifecycle of events, which had to be monitored and acted upon every day of their life. After paying a deposit, known as initial margin, on the day after the opening transaction, a derivative position was then marked-to-market each day with the unrealised gain or loss, known as variation margin, paid in cash by loser to winner. As these positions tended to have short lives, with maturity or expiry typically no more than a month or two ahead, further transactions to 'roll' the position forward had then to be carried out to maintain the market exposure. With options there were additional actions related to their exercise that have to be monitored and then dealt with at very short notice. Something was needed that reduced the administrative hassle and associated operational risk.

The answer was to bypass exchanges and clearing houses altogether and to trade directly with the banks. Many companies and investors were more comfortable with this approach, preferring to conduct their financial dealings in private with the banks, away from the public eye. It also suited the banks to encourage this thinking, as their competitors were kept in the dark on their derivatives dealings, and regulatory scrutiny was minimal. Better still, no one could see the prices the banks were making; even their own customers could not compare the price a particular bank was charging them relative to that for their other customers. This allowed the banks to segment their customers and to set prices according to their importance and sophistication. Customers that were weak and lacked pricing expertise could be charged more than those who were more knowledgeable and experienced. This lack of openness or transparency with OTC transactions provided yet another way for the banks to extract exceptional profits from their derivatives business.

The partnership between OTC and exchange traded derivatives

Within the world of exchanges some viewed OTC derivatives as a deadly rival. One prominent management consultant even suggested that exchanges should treat OTC volumes as transactions they had lost, a measure of their own business failure. But the truth was that the two markets were complementary, more akin to allies than competitors, particularly in the early days when education of customers and product innovation were critical ingredients for success.

OTC derivatives brought business to exchanges, as a bank entering into an OTC contract with one of their customers would typically offset the market risk they had taken on their books by trading an exchange listed contract with similar characteristics. Exchanges also learned a lot from observing new ideas and products developed in the OTC environment. The OTC market often conceived, incubated and refined new derivative products so that, when they became listed in a standardised form on exchanges, there was confidence and a reasonable certainty of commercial success. In a sense the OTC market acted as a research and development facility for exchanges, garnering interest in ideas and creating the initial liquidity and customer base for successful new products.

In the absence of OTC activity to guide them, exchanges had to adopt a more 'hit and miss' approach to new product development, often described as the *"spaghetti"* strategy of *"throwing lots of ideas against the wall to see which stick"*. Sometimes a great idea for a new contract would wither on the vine of poor liquidity by failing to attract enough early trading interest. It was also much quicker and cheaper to offer a new OTC contract and helpful for exchanges in gauging their likely liquidity, as well as offering a useful pricing reference for traders. It seemed that exchange traded innovation and the OTC markets were natural bedfellows.

For the banks the OTC derivatives market quickly became a huge money spinner, a business so lucrative that several major banks gleaned the bulk of their profits from this source. Their symbiotic relationship with exchange traded derivatives and the other benefits they brought, particularly access to cheap capital from the margin deposits of customers they held as clearing members, encouraged the banks to give derivative exchanges their wholehearted support across a wide range of products all over the world.

OTC customers facing losses call in the lawyers

The OTC derivatives market first came into public prominence in 1989 when the legality of transactions, entered into by the London

Borough of Hammersmith & Fulham, a UK local authority, was challenged in court. The success of legal action in releasing customers from their losing bets was to bring into being a form of 'coin tossing' game strategy that corporates and public authorities came to play against the banks all over the world, known as the *"heads we win; tails we call in the lawyers."* It was to culminate in 1994, when cases concerning OTC derivative losses, particularly those involving Procter & Gamble, the world's largest consumer goods company, attracted the most attention, and lead to no less than four legislative bills proposing regulations for OTC derivatives being tabled in the US Congress.

The central argument that the lawyers brought to bear was that derivatives were complicated, opaque and easily misunderstood. Furthermore their contract documentation was turgid, and laced with strange language and nomenclature that rendered the terms almost incomprehensible. As a result the customers of banks who carried out these contracts could be misled or, in the case of Hammersmith and Fulham, judged to have been persuaded to enter into transactions that their officers were not legally empowered to do.

Going to court turned out to be an effective approach as the banks, whilst not as unpopular as they were to become after the financial crisis of 2008, were eager to sell ever more complex derivatives which were difficult to value, telling simple but misleading story lines on their risks and potential outcomes. What became lost in the legal wrangling was that often this oversimplification came about at the behest of customers who wanted prospective transactions to be presented in this way to ease their internal approval processes.

Hammersmith & Fulham play dumb - London 1989

The foray of Hammersmith & Fulham, a London local authority district of some 150,000 residents, into OTC derivatives had nothing to do with prudent financial management; it was pure speculation to replace money lost to them from spending cuts enforced by central government. A Conservative UK Government, led by Margaret Thatcher, had imposed spending restrictions on all local authorities, through 'capping' the amount of local taxes they could levy on local residents in the teeth of fierce resistance from the Labour Party opposition. For the Labour controlled council of Hammersmith & Fulham, interest rate swap contracts were just one of a series of measures that the council introduced to circumvent cuts to their spending budgets.

It was the view of the Hammersmith & Fulham investment committee that short-term UK interest rates, then fluctuating in a 7-8% range, would not exceed 11% for the foreseeable future. The investment committee therefore regarded an interest rate swap, where they received interest fixed at 11% or more, as being very attractive since they were confident they would always be paying a much lower rate of interest on the floating rate to their bank counterparty. The Council also entered into interest rate option contracts predicated on the same interest rate view. Over a period of time Hammersmith & Fulham built up almost $10 billion (£6 billion) of payment commitments through their swap market transactions, far in excess of their £300 million annual revenues. In the process, they had become the largest customer participating in the interest rate swap market for the British pound representing, by some estimates, over 50% of the entire market.

The accounting trick they played that circumvented the spending restrictions of central government was to deem the difference between the 11% that they were receiving in interest each quarter from the swap counterparty, and the lower amount they were paying out based on short term interest rates, as current income that the council could spend immediately.

However, the Council's investment committee had misjudged the determination of the government to shadow other European currencies as part of the experiment known as the Exchange Rate Mechanism (ERM) that would in time lead to a new European currency called the Euro. Already struggling to keep the British Pound from falling outside the ERM currency range which they were trying to shadow, the government kept raising short-term interest rates from 8% in 1988 to just under 15% in 1989, leaving the council facing losses of £1.3 billion to close off their liabilities under the swap contracts.

Once these losses became known, panic set in and the positions were 'frozen' for over seven months with no one allowed to take any action to 'manage' the positions down. When clearance was finally given to close their positions they received *"forced seller"* prices from the banks according to the findings of the independent 'Veeder Inquiry' that was subsequently set up by the UK Government.

The Council refused to pay the banks the losses that they had run up, choosing instead to default on their obligations. Rather than saddle each resident of Hammersmith & Fulham with thousands of pounds of additional tax to pay off the banks, the local authority's leaders went to the courts and claimed that the swap transactions were illegal or, to use the Latin term, *"ultra vires".* The court upheld the Council's position in a decision that many believed had been subject to political interference. The banks appealed this judgment and, in 1991, fought their case all the way to Britain's then highest court, the House of Lords. However the Law Lords ruled that not only had all of Hammersmith & Fulham's swaps been illegal, but all swaps with all other local authorities had also been illegal, even where entered into for sound, conservative, non-speculative reasons.

It proved impossible for the banks to claim back any money from local authorities who had profited from swap contracts, just as the court decision had rendered them unable to claim from those that had lost. It was a costly lesson for the banks and one that left them bruised and feeling they had been victims of political interference. Many years later Lord Justice Woolf, the lead judge on the case, who by then had become Lord Chief Justice and Master of the Rolls, suggested that their judgment had been mistaken as their decision had been *"ignorant of the market implications"* and largely determined through derivatives *"appearing to the untutored eye... as a form of gambling".* To this day UK local authorities have been kept out of the market by this judgment and forced to use more expensive and less effective risk management tools.

Procter & Gamble (P&G) plays local card

When William Procter, a British candle maker, formed a partnership in 1837 with his wife's Irish born brother-in-law James Gamble, a soap manufacturer, they could not have been more removed from the world of finance. The setting for the Procter & Gamble enterprise was Cincinnati, Ohio in the Western United States, known colloquially as *"Porkopolis"* on account of its association with the pig business, pig fat being the raw material for both candles and soap.

They added lard to their product line, selling direct to customers by pioneering product recognition and loyalty through branding. Their initial success came from winning a government contract to supply candles and soap to the US Army. When the soldiers returned to their homes across the United States, comfortable and familiar with their products, local retailers began to stock P&G branded products to retain the custom of the soldiers and their families. Once through the store door, P&G were then able to launch new products like *"Ivory it floats soap"* into local retailers, backed by what was then unprecedented advertising and promotion spend. From these roots P&G flourished and grew into the branded consumer giant it is today, with soap and margarine still at the heart of their business.

Just as UK local authorities had suffered heavy losses in 1989 from swap contracts after being caught out by an unexpected rise in short-term UK interest rates, so US local authorities companies like P&G ran into the same difficulty in 1994 when the US Federal Reserve unexpectedly raised short-term US interest rates. The Fed had become worried that the US economy was starting to overheat after several years of loose monetary policy, and signalled this concern to the market by changing direction in February with a modest rise in short-term interest rates from 3% to 3 ¼%. This policy was reinforced by tightening the screw five more times during the course of the year, taking six month LIBOR (LIBOR is the London Interbank Offered Rate, the interest rate at which banks lend to one another) from 3.6% to 6.8%. As the initial rise had also been accompanied by disappointing economic data that had caught markets by surprise, a surge in bond sales ensued.

With so many of the OTC derivatives transactions that had been sold by banks to investors during 1992 and 1993 premised on rates continuing to fall, the abrupt hike in interest rates wrong footed many investors. Even George Soros was caught out, conceding later in Congressional testimony on derivatives, *"The risks involved are not always fully understood even by sophisticated investors, and I am one of them."* The surprise to the US Federal Reserve and other economic authorities was the nature of the victims and the magnitude of their losses. It was to reveal the extent of the leverage some investors had taken on through borrowing and derivative instruments, often unwittingly, and throw one particular bank into the limelight, Bankers Trust.

Bankers Trust (BT) and the secret world of OTC derivatives

Bankers Trust was originally set up in 1903 to provide trust services to banks throughout the United States. Although owned by numerous banks, effective control was in the hands of John Pierpont Morgan, with Bankers Trust generally viewed as a JP Morgan offshoot. As the company name implied, Bankers Trust acted as the banker for banks, entrusted with holding the reserves of other US banks and trust companies. Another purpose of the bank was to provide stability to the banking system by lending money to banks in difficulty when public confidence was faltering, thereby preventing a 'run' by nervous retail depositors. During the Panic of 1907, Bankers Trust took on the role of a central bank by working closely with JP Morgan and steering a course to prevent a general financial collapse by lending money to soundly run banks to keep them afloat. In the wake of that crisis the US Government established its own central banking system, passing the Federal Reserve Act in 1913, and appointing the President of Bankers Trust, Benjamin Strong Jr., as first Governor of the Federal Reserve Bank of New York.

Discouraged from competing with their shareholder banks in the lending business, Bankers Trust focussed on trust related activities, one of which was investment management when US companies first established pension funds in the late 1950s. In the 1980s they saw a new opportunity in providing risk management and trading advice for the nascent derivatives markets, an area of endeavour in which their commercial bank customers had little presence and were showing little interest.

The business quickly turned into a gold mine. Providing corporate treasurers with advice on interest rate products was the mainstay of their activity, owing to the increasing funding rate uncertainty companies were suffering from wildly fluctuating interest rates. These same customers were also struggling to manage the currency volatility that had come with floating exchange rates. With the risk management needs of most companies very bespoke in terms of coverage and time span, the tailoring of OTC derivatives offered by Bankers Trust appeared to be a much more attractive proposition than the *"off the peg"* offering of exchange traded futures and options.

By convincing corporate treasurers that a better fit could be tailored from OTC derivatives, Bankers Trust was able to persuade them to invest in more exotic instruments. Bankers Trust now held the role of adviser to their corporate customers on the products they should buy as well as being the arbiter of the price they should pay for them, a lucrative profit model. They sold complex derivatives to clients who could not value them, at whatever price they saw fit, and would then manage the subsequent valuation process to suit the client's temperament and needs.

Bankers Trust business approach to structured products and derivatives

Bankers Trust built their derivatives business around innovation, making exceptional profits through 'first mover advantage' on investment ideas and concepts. They targeted less sophisticated institutions with complex products, neutralising much of the risk of these deals by breaking the products into component risks, which they would then hedge in the wholesale markets. The alternative would have been to warehouse the risk but, whilst derivative pricing tools can be built quickly, the associated risk management tools are much more complex. In this way Bankers Trust did not have to develop books of offsetting risk in exotic products. Instead they could take handsome profits from a single *"juicy"* deal. This approach was quite unlike that of many of their competitors, who sought to build a strong client franchise in derivatives, proceeding with caution when entering exotic territory.

Their corporate customers had initially carried out OTC transactions to protect their business against financial risk. Over time their clients were to morph towards investment bets, typically in an attempt to lower funding costs. Success would also make the corporate treasurer look smart. The OTC providers facilitated these transactions by working out the hedges required and charging the cost to the client, with a hefty profit margin loaded on top.

With customers, the only basis for their entry into the more complex transactions, was their complete trust in the integrity of Bankers Trust. It was Bankers Trust who had invented the product and could value these instruments. There was no market from which to obtain a reference price, no one from whom one could obtain a competitor price, and no one else to sell the instrument to when the customer wished to exit the position. For the vast majority of their customers it was Bankers Trust who sold them the idea, provided the explanation of the benefits and risks, and persuaded them pay the price that their proprietary models said it was worth. You had to take the 'Trust' in the Bankers Trust name as an article of faith to go down this path.

Bankers Trust ran a brilliant advertising campaign, with illustrations to runs with the strapline: *"Risk isn't what you think it is"*. One I still have shows a man fishing on a desert island, his bait dangling in front of the mouth of an enormous fish. What the fisherman perceives to be the security of the island he is sitting on is, in fact, the back of the fish he is tempting with his bait.

Digging deeper and more elaborate holes to recover losses

In 1993, P&G entered into a $200 million leveraged five-year interest rate swap with Bankers Trust. It was a transaction linked to the price of US Treasury bonds that, provided interest rates held steady or fell, would reduce the firm's overall financing costs over the period by 0.4% per annum. Under the terms of the swap Bankers Trust paid P&G a fixed 5.3% rate of interest, receiving a floating rate payment from P&G in return. Leverage was introduced by embedding a put option on the price of US Treasury bonds into the swap structure. P&G was paid $7.5 million in premium to write this put option, which served to reduce the floating rate payment they made to Bankers Trust by 0.75% per annum. The risk P&G took was that they would suffer a much greater loss were the price of US Treasury bonds to fall. Rising interest rates during 1994 had just that effect on US Treasury bonds, generating a loss for P&G of over $100 million on this transaction alone, an extraordinary amount to lose on a swap with a $200 million notional value.

Making matters far worse, and compounding P&G's losses, was a vain attempt to stem their losses that were emerging from their initial leveraged swap. Shortly after US interest rates began to rise, P&G rolled the option dice once again and entered into another five-year leveraged swap. Once again they took the view that interest rates would not rise, but this time bet that German, not US, interest rates would hold steady. This leveraged swap position, known as a *"wedding band"* was even more aggressive than the first as two options were written on the $93 million notional amount, not one as on the earlier swap position. With a wedding band both a put and a call option are written, creating a bet for P&G that German interest rates will stay within a certain range. In P&G's case they would not lose money unless the German interest rate referenced in the swap contract, then 5.35%, fell below 4.05% or rose above 6.10% at any time during the first year of the swap contract. Quite apart from the leverage risk of two options on the same notional amount, the very nature of this form of 'barrier option' is much more risky than a conventional option. With the barrier option the interest rate has only to touch one of the exercise prices for an instant to become live and generate a loss, unlike a conventional option that has to possess value at expiry to do so. We will see just how powerful these 'knock in' features of barrier options can be later, when discussing the way in which how they turbo charged a takeover bid for VW by Porsche in 2008.

The wedding band P&G took out generated just under $1 million of option premium from writing the two options at each end of the range; if rates moved outside the range or 'band' they would lose money. For a company to be 'married' to such a risk has no economic purpose in hedging their interest rate risk; it was simply a bet to reduce their existing losses on their US Treasury swap contract. However the transaction served only to compound their difficulties as it took just 16 days for the upper exercise of 6.10% to be struck, 'knocking' the option into life. After abortive attempts to cap their potential losses from a strange formula that calculated P&G's interest payments for the remaining life of the swap contract, the company was left to book $157 million in losses from derivative trades with Bankers Trust that year.

Procter & Gamble was Bankers Trust's most high profile victim. When the press became aware of how complex and risky their OTC derivatives bets had been, and how they had exacerbated an initial loss with more complicated bets, the firm became dubbed with the unflattering sobriquet of *"Gamble & Gamble"*. As a director in another company, which had entered into a similar wedding band transaction for much the same reason as P&G, remarked: *"It's a lot like gambling. You get in deep. And you think, I'll get out of it with this one last trade."*

Meanwhile, in P&G's home town of Cincinnati, a more modest company called Gibson Greetings, whose business was selling greetings cards, announced that they too had been caught out by OTC derivative trades with Bankers' Trust, reporting what was for them, the huge loss of $23 million. Soon many other companies and municipalities around the United States came out of the woodwork, announcing shockingly large losses relative to the scale of their businesses, some to the point of bankruptcy. Amongst the losers were professional investors and asset management companies who should have known better.

Selling methods attacked in court

It was when P&G and Gibson Greetings took Bankers Trust to court that a Pandora's Box was opened into the bank's behaviour. Gibson Greetings was the case that lawyers chose to showcase how unsophisticated customers had been duped. As a conservative regional company new to derivatives, Gibson Greetings had told Bankers Trust that they did not want their trading activity to incur losses greater than $3 million. Early profits had made Gibson Greetings comfortable with their derivative activity, encouraging them to progress into deeper waters. They were soon immersed in the exotic world of complex derivatives, swimming with much more dangerous derivatives fish with strange names that included ratio swaps, periodic floors, spread locks, knockout call options and Libor linked swaps. Through such instruments they soon racked up $17.5 million of losses. In their hurry to escape they copied their corporate neighbour P&G into a wedding band transaction, hoping to quickly bring down their loss to within their original $3 million limit. However, as their wedding band also went wrong and their losses reached $20.7 million, Gibson Greetings followed P&G and called in the lawyers, suing Bankers' Trust.

Some measure of the risk of these positions can be gleaned from an interest rate contract Gibson Greetings entered into called the LIBOR-squared swap. Amongst derivative aficionados such a transaction falls into the 'turbo powered' category and was said to have alone cost Gibson Greetings US$23 million. Under the terms of the swap contract Gibson Greetings was paid interest at a fixed rate of 5.5% in return for which they paid Bankers Trust a variable 'floating rate' benchmarked on LIBOR, the interest rate at which highly creditworthy banks then lent money to one another. The rate paid was not simply LIBOR, as would normally be the case with interest rate swaps, but a mathematical formula where LIBOR is raised to the power 2 ('squared') and then divided by 6. With LIBOR at 3% Gibson Greetings would pay Bankers Trust (3x3)/6 = 1.5%, which would result in an attractive net interest payment to Gibson Greetings of (5.5 - 1.5) = 4%. Were interest rates to rise to 7% the tables would be turned the other way round and Gibson Greetings would pay interest of (7x7)/6 - 5.5 = 2.7% to the bank. Gibson Greetings stood to profit if interest rates fell but suffer losses in an exponential fashion if interest rates rose. By way of example should reference interest rate rise to 12% their net interest payment to Bankers Trust would become (12x12)/6 - 5.5 =18.5%.

P&G took a different tack from Gibson Greetings in court, filing racketeering charges against Bankers Trust over their selling methods. As P&G's Chairman, Edwin Artzt, put it: *"The issue here is Bankers Trust's selling practices. There is a notion that end users of derivatives must be held accountable for what they buy. We agree completely, but only if the terms and risks are fully and accurately disclosed."*

The most compelling source of evidence for P&G's case came from tape recordings, a new weapon in financial litigation that was to become more and more potent in the future. At that time, recording of internal conversations and trading terms agreed over the telephone was in its infancy. Bankers Trust was innovative with their extensive usage, seeing them as a powerful legally binding tool for confirming trading terms. P&G however, by obtaining over 6,500 tape recordings of conversations between Bankers Trust employees, was instead to evidence the dangers of such records.

In the tapes Bankers Trust executives describe the extra charge they levied on their more unsophisticated customers as the *"ROF or rip-off factor"*. They also laud their internal valuation models as: *"the beauty of Bankers Trust"* since customers are: *"bound by a pricing model we do not disclose so they will never know how much money was taken out by us"*. The tapes concerning Gibson Greetings talked of managing the differential between the value they told their customer their position was worth and the true value Bankers Trust ascribed to the position. In one conversation between Bankers Trust executives the tapes record: *"We should just call [the Gibson contact] and maybe chip away at the differential a little more. I mean, we told him $8.1 million when the real number was 14. So now if the real number is 16, we'll tell him that it is 11. You know, just slowly chip away at that differential between what it really is and what we're telling him."*

There was no regulatory oversight of their activities, even though noises had been made by both the CFTC and SEC in the United States that they should be monitoring their activities. The fear of an SEC probe had one employee comment on the tapes: *"as soon as we quit selling dynamite maybe we'll have a good business"*.

Bankers Trust was sued by four of its major clients; Federal Paper Board Company, Gibson Greetings, Air Products and Chemical, and Procter & Gamble. The first three cases were settled out of court for a total of $93 million. The $195 million Procter & Gamble suit was settled at a net gain to P&G of $78 million. The most lasting damage, however, was to the reputation of Bankers Trust.

When the nature of these transactions first came to light, I was a member of the Bank of England's Derivatives Joint Standing Committee, representing the investment management industry. Considerable concern was expressed as many of these transactions had been entered into under UK regulatory jurisdiction. When we investigated what other exotic contracts were *"out there"*, other worrying instruments were identified, including interest rate contracts that were even more 'turbo charged' than the LIBOR-squared swap contract Gibson Greetings had bought. One such contract was a 'LIBOR-cubed' swap where the floating interest rate was raised to the power 3 ('cubed') instead of 2 ('squared'). Were short term interest rates to rise to 12%, a transaction such as that entered into by Gibson Greetings would have pushed their interest payment from 18.5% for their LIBOR-squared swap to a catastrophic $(12 \times 12 \times 12)/6 - 5.5 = 282\%$ for a LIBOR-cubed swap.

There were stories of even more risky OTC contracts in existence. When the banks were probed about these, perhaps embarrassed by their existence and the public outcry, there was anecdotal evidence of such contracts being quietly closed off in private, generally on terms that favoured the customer. There appeared to be little appetite amongst the banks for further forays into courts of law or exposure to the limelight of public opinion.

P&G were not alone in the public eye. Orange County, a US municipality in California, suffered much heavier losses and together they were to spark an acrimonious public rage against OTC derivatives and the banks that had sold them. A welter of legal claims as well as new legislation was to follow in the aftermath.

Investment genius of Orange County turns out to be leverage

Orange County suffered from the same interest rate bet going wrong as P&G. In the early 1990s, their county treasurer Robert Citron had sought to boost the municipality's investment returns through leverage and a bet that US short-term interest rates would fall or at worst remain low. To do this he invested heavily in inverse floating rate notes, *'inverse floaters'*.

Inverse floaters are a type of debt instrument where the interest coupon paid is not fixed at the outset but determined by the difference between a fixed reference rate and prevailing short-term interest rates, usually LIBOR. Unlike normal floating rate notes where the interest coupon paid rises or falls with short-term interest rates, inverse floaters move in the opposite direction, rising when interest rates fall and falling when interest rates rise; the inverse of a floating rate note.

Inverse floaters are much more risky than their floating rate cousins as, not only is the interest coupon uncertain, but also their capital value is at risk. When short-term interest rates fall, both the price of the note and the yield of the inverse floater increase in value. Conversely, when short-term interest rates rise, the capital value of the note can drop significantly as interest coupons fall. These effects magnify the interest rate risk and make the price of inverse floaters highly volatile.

Initially, the tactic was successful. In 1993 Orange County's investment pool returned 8.5% against the state average of 4.7%, encouraging nearby municipalities to increase the size of their deposits with Orange County from around $3 billion in 1991 to $7.6 billion in 1994. Through borrowings of $12.5 billion the size of Orange County's portfolio was over $20 billion, of which roughly $8 billion was invested in structured notes, with inverse floaters the dominant structure.

When interest rates began to rise, Citron stuck with his conviction that they would soon head down again and increased Orange County's bet by piling on further borrowings. The Federal Reserve Chairman Alan Greenspan was later to describe this action as *"Citron leveraging up to his chin"*. As the losses continued to mount the banks that had lent money to Orange County, demanded additional collateral. When the losses reached $1.7 billion there were no assets left to post and the municipality was forced to file for bankruptcy.

Politicians vent public anger through fierce derivative legislation

It was Orange County that most struck a political cord as the municipality struggled with their budgets and were forced to cut back the services they provided to the local community. And with Orange County operating an investment pool into which the county and its cities, school districts, and special districts deposited their tax receipts, there was also infighting over how the losses should be distributed.

The sense of public outrage was not simply confined to the US but it was there that the indignation felt was at its strongest. America's General Accounting Office (GAO) issued a highly critical 196-page study on the state of the derivatives world, with conclusions diametrically opposed to those of the G30 report. *"Derivatives trading"*, it declared, *"was marked by significant gaps and weaknesses in risk management that created a wider systemic risk".* Indeed, so great were the dangers, the GAO even argued that derivatives might even end up causing a debacle as bad as the (recent) Savings and Loans shock. The report concluded that there was an *"immediate need"* for Congress to step in.

The media also joined the fray, unleashing a torrent of criticism. Adam Smith's Money World declared that derivatives might be the financial equivalent of the next space shuttle disaster. Fortune published a cover with the word 'derivatives' on the jaws of a giant alligator with the ominous warning: *"Financial derivatives are tightening their grip on the global economy....and nobody knows how to control them".*

Warren Buffett proposed a solution that I thought would work much better than any legislation, suggesting every CEO be required to affirm in the annual report that they understood each of the derivatives contracts the company had entered into. *"Put that in, and I suspect you'll fix up just about every problem that exists."*

Such an affirmation might have saved the banks themselves ten years later when the habit of designing complex derivatives that senior management did not understand was to emerge in an even more toxic form in the US housing market.

22. George Soros' assault on the Pound - London 1992

"Markets are constantly in a state of uncertainty and flux, and money is made by discounting the obvious and betting on the unexpected."

George Soros (born in Budapest in 1930)

Whilst Governments were welcoming derivatives as powerful tools in their policy armoury for freeing up financial markets from all manner of inefficiency and protectionism, it came as something of a surprise when this same freedom was turned against them. It took a bold investor to use the torch of free markets to change the economic policy of a sovereign government but in 1992 George Soros, through his Quantum Group of hedge funds, did just that. He took on the British Government and drove a coach and horses through their foreign exchange policy by forcing them to breach the artificial currency range within which they were trying to maintain the Pound. And for his trouble Soros notched up a £1 billion profit.

Intent and operation of the ERM

In 1979, France and Germany set up the European Monetary System (EMS) as the means to stabilise exchange rates and bring about monetary stability within Europe. It was a first step towards economic and monetary union and, in 1999, culminated in the consolidation of myriad national currencies into a single pan European currency, the Euro. To progress towards this goal the Exchange Rate Mechanism (ERM) set a central exchange rate against which each participating country was to manage its own currency relative to a basket of European currencies known as the European Currency Unit (ECU).

Participants in the ERM were required to maintain their exchange rates within a 2.25 percentage band above or below the central rate. This task proved to be a struggle from the start, with the project only kept alive by realigning the central exchange rate nine times between 1979 and 1985. These realignments only served to paper over the cracks of the many fault lines that were already evident. Britain did not participate initially, only joining in 1990. In light of the struggles other countries had had, the pound was given the extra leeway of a 6 percentage exchange rate range relative to Germany's Deutsche Mark (DM) with a central target of 2.95 Deutsche Mark to one British Pound.

In spite of many of the participating countries failing to stay within their agreed bands, the ERM was claimed to be a success until mid-1992 on the grounds that the disciplinary effect of leadership by Germany's central bank, the Bundesbank, had reduced inflation throughout Europe. However it was already clear that relative stability of European currencies could not last, as significant political and economic events had rendered the exchange rate that several countries were seeking to maintain unsustainable.

The most important of these was Germany itself. The reunification of East and West Germany in 1989 had led to a surge in government spending, forcing the Bundesbank to print more money. This had led to higher inflation, leaving the German central bank with little alternative other than to increase interest rates. But raising German rates had repercussions on everyone else in the ERM as it placed upward pressure on the Deutsche Mark, forcing the central banks of every other country in the ERM to follow suit, raising their interest rates to stay within their exchange rate band.

With the UK suffering from a weak economy and high unemployment, Soros took the view that the British government could not sustain high interest rates for very long and would have to make a choice between one of two options, either to devalue the currency within the ERM or to leave the ERM altogether. In his view whichever course they elected to take, the British Pound would fall against the Deutsche Mark and that was the bet he decided to make.

British Pound is forced to exit the ERM

As part of the move toward European monetary union, capital

controls on the movement of funds around Europe had progressively been relaxed. International investors now had much more freedom to take advantage of perceived disequilibrium, so Soros and others were now able to sell Pounds and buy Deutsche Marks in large amounts by borrowing Pounds, which they then sold to buy Deutsche Mark denominated assets. He was also able to make the same bet using derivatives through forward foreign exchange contracts. The Quantum Fund rapidly built up its position against the Pound until on 16th September 1992, a day that was to be dubbed *"Black Wednesday"*, the position had reached $10 billion. And Soros was not alone; many other investors had followed suit and were selling the British Pound.

Forward foreign exchange contracts

A forward foreign exchange contract commits two parties to exchange currencies at an agreed price and date in the future. In the case of contracts entered into by Soros and the Bank of England, Soros committed to deliver British Pounds to the Bank of England one or three months after entering into these transactions in exchange for the Bank of England delivering Deutsche marks, each in the amount set out in the contract. As the value of the Pound fell relative to the Deutsche Mark, Soros was able to buy back the Pounds for fewer Deutsche Marks than they had been sold for, the difference realising a profit of circa $1 billion.

With tremendous downward pressure on the currency the Bank of England sought to defend their ERM straitjacket by drawing on their reserve funds to buy £15 billion. But these purchases were met by more selling and the Pound continued to trade dangerously close to the bottom of its ERM range. The Bank of England then attempted to apply pressure on those who had sold Pounds by announcing a 2% rise in interest rates from 10% to 12%. When this increase in borrowing costs had no effect panic set in and, little more than an hour later, a further interest rate rise to 15% was announced.

This move also had no effect on the exchange rate so, smelling blood Soros and other sellers ratcheted up their positions a notch or two higher. By now the Bank of England was the only buyer and was rapidly depleting its now meagre reserves. Finally at 7 pm the Chancellor, Norman Lamont, threw in the towel and announced that Britain would leave the ERM, also determining that interest rates would revert to the 10% they had stood at that morning.

In the weeks that followed, the pound depreciated by almost 15% against the Deutsche Mark and 25% against the US Dollar, reaping huge gains for Soros and others who had bet against the British Government. The Quantum Fund alone was said to have made over £1 billion, earning Soros the epithet *"The man who broke the Bank of England"*.

The cost to the UK Treasury of their attempted support on Black Wednesday was put at £3.4 billion and, although then regarded as a disaster and a national humiliation, a much kinder view was taken afterwards. The weakening of the pound is credited with providing much of the impetus for the UK's subsequent strong economic performance, some commentators even referring to Britain's final day in the ERM as *"White Wednesday"*. Many were delighted to see Britain leaving the European currency experiment, not least Norman Tebbit, a former senior cabinet minister in the UK Government, who had taken to referring to the ERM as the *"Eternal Recession Mechanism"* as the UK had fallen into recession *"from the moment we joined"*.

There is no doubt that the embarrassing ejection from the ERM by free market forces played a big part in making UK politicians very cautious about joining the Euro. Other European nations who did join the Euro were to suffer greatly some twenty years later from losing the lever of weakening their national currency to counter those periods when their goods and services were not competitive internationally. The real test of central control of European monetary policy under the Euro was always going to be when the tide went out and a recession exposed those who had been *"swimming naked".* Perhaps the British people should thank George Soros and free markets for saving them from a flawed financial experiment.

Since then Governments have tried on many occasions to support their exchange rate through the old tricks of capital controls and sharply increased borrowing costs, in the vain hope that they will hurt those selling their currency. Whilst these actions are intended to create fear amongst those betting against the wishes of a sovereign government, all they do in practice is to signal that the authorities are in a state of fear. It is another manifestation of a dictum by the American philosopher Eric Hoffer: *"You can discover what your enemy fears most by observing the means he uses to frighten you."*

Governments still try to intervene with these ineffective tricks. As recently as 2014, the Russian Government acted in a similar fashion to Britain, by raising short term interest rates in the course of a single day by 6.6% to 17% in a vain attempt to reverse a precipitous decline by over 60% of the Rouble relative to the currencies of their major trading partners. Often such action is taken because Governments feel they have to do something. In Russia's case they feared a re-run of the August 1998 financial crisis when a market belief that the Rouble was about to be devalued led to the collapse of Russia's stock, bond and currency markets, plunging the country into a deep and painful recession. On that occasion, even the extreme measure of hiking their short-term interest rates to 100% could not stem the tide. In the chaos that ensued, Russia defaulted on its debt, and the Rouble lost 75% of its value in just three weeks. The political scars, from inflation spiking to over 85% the following year and picture of starving people demonstrating in the streets over empty shelves and high food prices, are still in evidence.

23. Not sure if they were hedging or gambling - Metallgesellschaft 1994

"If you can't understand it, don't do it"

Sir Dennis Weatherstone (1930-2008)
Chairman & Chief Executive, JP Morgan

Losses from derivatives have always been much more embarrassing for companies than those suffered within their mainstream commercial activities. It is not simply on account of the rotten public reputation that derivatives have acquired. More telling is the palpable sense of confusion and discomfort that the facial expression of the chief executive betrays when attempting to explain how the losses occurred. My own favourite of this genre goes back to 1973 when Rowntree, a confectionery manufacturer that is now part of Nestle and best known for its Kit Kat chocolate wafer biscuits, lost £32 million trading cocoa futures. With the headlines reading *"Rowntree loses millions in cocoa"* one puzzled shareholder wrote in to ask *"Why couldn't you fish it out with a spoon?"*

In December 1993, one of Germany's largest industrial conglomerates, Metallgesellschaft, came close to collapse from $1.5 billion in derivative losses run up by a New York subsidiary company employing a handful of their 20,000 employees. Only a massive rescue operation by a consortium of banks kept the company afloat. It was a huge shock to discover that just one of their 250 subsidiaries could bring such a large and well diversified conglomerate to its knees, with no protective shield from revenues in excess of $10 billion diversified across businesses spanning mining, specialty chemicals, commodity trading, financial services and engineering. The same incredulity was to resonate again in 2008 when the world's largest insurer, AIG, had to be rescued by the US taxpayer on an altogether grander scale as a result of losses suffered by a London subsidiary employing a tiny fraction of their 160,000 employees.

The initial management effort by Metallgesellschaft to bring the matter quickly and quietly to a close, claiming that *"unauthorised gambling"* had led to the loss, backfired when their chief trader brought a court case against the company, demanding compensatory as well as punitive damages. Having brought the company close to bankruptcy through his trading, the claim seemed absurd. What the case did, however, was to provide a legal test of whether derivative transactions, intended to reduce business exposure to price risk, constituted hedging or gambling.

The business MGRM was facilitating

Metallgesellschaft Refining and Marketing (MGRM) was set up to service the needs of customers for whom oil products were a significant component of their business costs. In the main these customers comprised independent petrol retailers, manufacturing companies and public sector entities, all of which shared the common difficulty of struggling to cope with the vagaries of short-term fluctuations in energy prices.

What hurt these businesses most was when the spot price of oil rose, and they were unable to pass on the extra cost they were bearing quickly enough to their customers. Too often they were left having to shoulder the extra cost themselves, with their business margins suffering as a consequence. Protecting themselves was tricky as there were no easily accessible forward markets in oil products to insulate them from short-term price fluctuations.

MGRM's idea was to plug this gap by offering forward contracts to supply these businesses with gasoline, diesel fuel and heating oil at fixed prices for periods of up to ten years. With no long term forward market of any consequence, MGRM chose to hedge these contracts by buying short term futures contracts for the same amount of oil or other oil products that their customers had contracted to buy from them. They believed there was an arbitrage opportunity that could profitably be exploited between the spot oil market and the long-term contract market through skilled use of the futures contracts in oil products, and that this would become MGRM's stock in trade.

The contracts offered and their terms

In 1991 MGRM started to market three types of long-term oil product contracts. Their *"firm-fixed"* programme offered customers monthly delivery of an agreed amount of oil products at a fixed price. Their *"firm-flexible"* contracts gave customers the latitude to change the delivery date for up to 20% of their annual commitment to energy supplies, but not the total amount they bought each year; a useful flexibility for customers who found it difficult to predict seasonal demand. The third category, the *"guaranteed margin"* contract, was very different from the first two in that the price was not fixed in absolute terms, but by reference to the retail price that their local competitors were offering. This contract was particularly attractive to independent petrol retailers as it secured profitable business margins whilst keeping their pump prices competitive.

MGRM's business developed well over the initial two years, then accelerated rapidly during the first nine months of 1993, when their contracts swelled from 43 million barrels of oil equivalent to 208 million barrels, a monetary value of $4 billion. Driving demand for these long-term contracts was a decline in the price of crude oil, which had fallen from $18 to under $15 a barrel. This price drop made retailers fret over the damage a sharp spot price turnaround would have on their profitability. MGRM now had contractual commitments to supply 102 million barrels of oil products under their 'firm-fixed' programme, 52 million barrels under the 'firm-flexible' programme, and 54 million barrels under their 'guaranteed margin' offering.

To cover their hedging costs, they set their fixed delivery prices $3 to $5 above the prevailing spot price when entering into these contracts. This price margin was also to cover the cost of additional 'bells and whistles' that they offered their customers, one of which was a 'blow out option' which could be activated if the futures price of the oil product rose above a certain level. Under these circumstances customers who had opted for this facility could make a single cash payment that cancelled all their future purchase obligations to MGRM.

'Stack and roll' hedging strategy

Since long term contracts to offset their contracts with customers were not available in the market, MGRM opted to use short-term energy futures and swap contracts to hedge their exposure. These positions were typically for the same number of barrels that they had committed to deliver to their customers in the future, a 'barrel for barrel' hedge. By rolling these transactions forward at maturity MGRM created what is known as a 'stack' hedge, in that deliveries for all future dates were stacked up into a single short term hedge.

The strategy was regarded as consistent with the risk management policy of MGRM which specified that *"the firm may not engage in speculative trading and therefore may not hold any outright long or short position".*

Risks of their hedge strategy

Because of the maturity mismatch between the hedge and the delivery contracts and made worse by the extra features MGRM offered their clients, their hedging strategy exposed the business to four significant financial risks; rollover, funding, credit and basis.

The rollover risk arose from the short-term nature of their derivatives contracts. They were selling maturing positions and 'rolling' them into new positions with longer maturity almost every month, in order to maintain the price exposure they had taken on through their oil product contracts. The stack made profits when the price of the longer dated futures and swap contracts they were buying was cheap relative to the short dated contracts they were selling. This condition occurred when the 'spot price' of the oil products they were hedging was higher than the future price, a condition known as 'backwardation'. By contrast when long dated futures prices were more expensive than the short dated contracts they owned, a condition known as 'contango', the roll gave rise to losses. As the market dynamics for backwardation or contango conditions were outside MGRM's control, gaining or losing money from rollover risk was not a matter of skill or judgement, but simply luck.

Funding risk came from the requirement to post or receive margin on unrealised losses. When energy prices were rising MGRM had the benefit of receiving cash for the mark-to-market value of their unrealised gain. By contrast when energy prices were falling, MGRM had to find cash to post as margin.

Credit risk arose when customers defaulted or refused to pay for their oil products at the agreed price. This risk was the most prevalent issue when energy prices were falling as their customers could buy oil products cheaper elsewhere on the spot market. Of particular concern was that this kind of behaviour was most likely to occur when MGRM were already suffering from cash outflows to fund margin calls from mark-to-market price losses on their futures contracts.

A considerable additional risk to MGRM's hedging strategy was basis risk, the difference between the price of the contracts agreed with customers and the price movement of the instruments they were using to hedge. When the prices of the contract offered to customers move together the basis risk is said to be nil. Where there is a difference of, say, 1% between the price movement of the customer and hedging contracts, the basis risk is said to be 1% (the term 'basis' is typically expressed as 1/100 of a percentage point, 100 basis points being 1%).

The fundamental worry was that a barrel of oil for delivery in one month's time is simply not one and the same as a barrel of oil delivered in ten years' time. The value of the two different dated obligations does not move in lock step. A rolling stack of short dated futures is also more risky as cash flow movements are more volatile and unrealised losses on the entire stack of contracts have to be settled at least monthly; and daily in the case of futures contracts.

By contrast the compensating cash flow gains from oil product deliveries to customers flow through gradually over the ten-year contract life. When the oil price was falling, the cash flow effect could turn a hedge based on the rolling stack strategy into a more dangerous beast than having no hedge at all.

Cash flow difficulties from margin payments

During the latter part of 1993, with new business pouring in, everything that could go wrong for MGRM's strategy did. The oil price fell sharply from $19 a barrel in June to $15 a barrel in December, giving rise to over $900 million in margin calls to cover unrealised losses. Making things worse was that the futures market was in contango for almost the whole year, so they were losing money every time they rolled maturing futures contracts. Had energy prices been rising the contango would not have been so worrying as they would have been generating cash from the receipt of margin from their unrealised gains.

MGRM were now in a similar cash squeeze to the one that had brought down the Hunt brothers when the silver price began to fall. In December 1993 MGRM were forced to reduce their hedge as their swap counterparties refused to allow them to roll positions, citing credit concerns. In addition New York's Nymex Exchange, where they held the bulk of their oil futures positions, reduced the size of the positions they were allowed to hold, for the same reason.

Collapse and liquidation

When the oil price fell further towards the year end, MGRM ran out of cash. Unable to roll over its stack of oil futures contracts and with no assets to post as collateral, they also could not fulfil their swap contract obligations. Facing losses of nearly $1.3 billion and the prospect of the entire company being declared bankrupt, a $1.9 billion emergency line of credit was speedily arranged with the banks. Metallgesellschaft's Supervisory Board fired the parent company's top management and took urgent steps to liquidate MGRM's derivative positions, cancelling the forward supply contracts they had entered into with customers. These actions brought the firm's involvement in the oil market to an end, along with several other businesses they were forced to sell to repay their debts.

It is still something of a puzzle as to how the loss became so large. Some commentators have suggested that much of the loss came from the panic of the supervisory board in the face of the huge margin calls, and that they hurt themselves with a rushed liquidation. Closing off their contracts with customers may have been a huge mistake, as the losses from their futures contracts would have been substantially recouped from the fixed price contracts set at much higher oil product prices. With hindsight the stacked roll strategy created more risk than it hedged, inflicting real damage through a mismatched maturity structure and a stack position that was far too big for the potential basis risk.

Trying to ascribe rogue trader status to their chief trader proved to be elusive, as implementation of a flawed strategy is viewed very differently by the courts than the perpetration of a secret fraud. The same questions were to be asked when the Sumitomo $1.6 billion loss from copper trading emerged two years later, and again in 2012, when a JP Morgan trader known as the *"London Whale"* changed tack from hedging credit risk to taking an outright market bet on credit.

24. Breath-taking incompetence - the collapse of Barings - Singapore & London 1995

"Mr Leeson pulled the trigger, but the bank gave him the gun, the bank gave him the ammunition, cash. When he wanted more ammunition they gave him as much as they could give him… until they ran out; and then the bank was bust."

Christopher Sharples, former Chairman of Securities and Futures Authority (SFA)

There was nothing clever in the downfall of Barings; no price manipulation, no attempt to corner a market, no seemingly intelligent new trading strategy that worked in theory but proved flawed in practice. In fact there was nothing heroic at all, just an individual lost in a world of his own who was left unfettered to bet the bank. And bet it he did, consistently losing money until there was none left. If the Barings collapse had not occurred one might reasonably assert that it was fanciful to suggest it could. The most remarkable aspect of the Barings bankruptcy is that it happened at all.

It is a story of rotten bets, trading ignorance, unsophisticated fraud but, above all, breath-taking incompetence. The starting point was a lack of understanding and control by the bank's management of their derivatives business, the denouement an astonishing sequence of warning signs that were ignored or missed. But it created a financial folk hero in Nick Leeson. There have been many who have *"bet the bank"* but few who have done so in such spectacular fashion without the bank realising it.

'Big Bang' and the transformation of Barings

When Leeson joined Barings in 1989 the bank had already embarked on a new and more aggressive business strategy. They were moving away from being a merchant bank that earned fees for providing financial advice and raising capital for companies and governments. They were turning into a bank that actively traded in financial markets not only for their clients, but also for themselves.

This latter activity, known as proprietary or 'prop' trading, meant that they were not just taking risks with their clients' money, but also putting the bank's own money on the line as well. This radical shift from acting as an agent carrying out business on behalf of their clients to principal where they were risk takers was driven by a new management team. They were trying to gain a share of the spoils that the US investment banks were capturing, particularly from derivatives trading, in the aftermath of London's 'Big Bang'.

Outside the financial world, Big Bang is a hypothesis to explain the origin of the Universe; created at a moment in time in an explosive fashion and why the universe has been expanding ever since. For London's financial markets Big Bang was also a significant event, albeit not of cosmic importance. It was a moment in time, the 27th October 1986, when the London Stock Exchange (LSE) enacted fundamental changes to the rules that governed trading in securities. The members of the stock exchange that had once resided in Jonathan's Coffee House did not want these changes. However they had little choice in the matter after being pressed to do so by Britain's determined first female Prime Minister, Margaret Thatcher. It was her threat to refer the LSE to the competition authorities unless they reformed their restrictive clubby market practices that had goaded the exchange into action.

Thatcher's concern was that, whilst London was still a major financial centre, it had been overtaken by New York on her watch and was no longer the biggest in the world. London was in danger of falling still further behind, as others marched to a tune more in keeping with the free market times. Much influenced by Hayek and Friedman, her instincts were at one with the view that the main reasons for the decline of London's financial markets came from too much regulation and the dominance of elitist 'old boy' networks. She saw the latter as protecting the comfortable status quo that prevented competition from outsiders, foreigners in particular. Thatcher's solution was to release the free market doctrine of unfettered competition and meritocracy.

Big Bang did away with the cosy but antiquated business model which separated stockbrokers, who acted as agents for investors, from risk taking market traders known as stockjobbers, and merchant banks who raised money and provided financial advice to companies and governments. Stockbrokers were acting as the exclusive dealing agent for investors and were paid generous commissions for their services. Their high reward was unsurprising as their own club, the LSE, set a fee schedule that was consistent with providing their members with a comfortable lifestyle.

Keeping these three roles separate had made sense and been enforced, as it avoided the conflicts of interest that had wreaked havoc in the early days of share trading, particularly in the South Sea Bubble of 1720. From these scandals it had become clear that combining trading in shares with sales distribution had left investors unprotected. It was well encapsulated by Sir Isaac Newton who, in response to his own £20,000 South Sea Bubble loss (over $3 million in today's money) had remarked: *"I can calculate the motions of heavenly bodies, but not the madness of people."* Years later that doyen of investors Warren Buffett had added his own Newton epitaph: *"Had he not been traumatized by this loss, Sir Isaac might well have gone on to discover the Fourth Law of Motion: For investors as a whole, returns decrease as motion increases."*

Before Big Bang stockbrokers acted only for investor clients and therefore had their best interests at heart. Those that traded with their own money, the market makers, had no involvement or responsibility towards investors, only themselves. Through face to face interaction between stockbrokers and market makers on the floor of the exchange, trading activity took place under the watchful eye of stock exchange officials.

The model made sense in principle and might have continued if the LSE had allowed competition between brokers to bring down commission charges, a practice that the New York Stock Exchange had introduced in the United States a few years earlier. It was odd to watch the manner in which LSE members resisted competition in commissions. Their negotiating stance with government was more akin to that of the labour trade unions that they found abhorrent, and far from that of the champions of enterprise and free markets that they claimed to be.

Their reason for defence of practices that appeared indefensible to outsiders was not simply to protect a comfortable status quo. It was raw fear that they would suffer the same fate as stockbrokers on the other side of the Atlantic when 'negotiated' commissions sent most of the small brokerage firms to the wall as commissions were cut to the bone in a race for market share. In the rapid consolidation that followed, a handful of giant investment banks, who were built more around proprietary trading than client business, was to emerge. These banks came to dominate financial markets in the years that followed before reaching their own demise in the financial crisis of 2008 that they had done much to stoke.

The most profitable banks were those who used information they gleaned from their client business to make money for themselves. One particularly aggressive investment bank described their client flow business internally as *"camouflage"* to reflect its usefulness in gleaning market information for their own trading as well as making it hard for outsiders to spot the bets the firm was making for itself. The business model of Big Bang was beginning to look more like a return to the free for all that led to the savage exploitation of investors in the South Sea Bubble, not a laudable opening up of the stock market to free competition. However a semblance of confidence and belief was maintained as the banks claimed to manage conflicts of interest internally by placing information barriers known as *"Chinese Walls"* between their own interests and those of their clients. Few really believed this as, if there was no benefit from information flow, there was little purpose served by joining all of the banking pieces together. As one banker described it: *"We've put up these Chinese Walls but have no plans to hire any Chinese to police them."*

In the period leading up to Big Bang there was a flurry of consolidation amongst small stock broking firms, bulking themselves up for the onslaught ahead. Meanwhile the banks, brokers and market makers combined to prepare for the bridging of the divide that had hitherto separated them from one another.

But something else was coming into the mix that was making these changes much easier to facilitate and was to have major consequences in the years to come. Computer technology was becoming more sophisticated, whilst telecommunication connectivity was increasing the speed and amount of data that could be transferred electronically. As the cost of data storage and transfer fell, a new age of electronic trading processing began. Soon the rule that all trading should physically take place on the exchange floor by 'open outcry' between stock exchange members was revoked, opening the door to the often frenzied activity we now see taking place on trading floors within banks instead. It also allowed foreigners in who could pursue the new business model, acting as agent and principal in issuing, distributing and making markets in securities.

Just as the creation of the first capital markets by Elizabeth I had turned the tide on England's economic decline four hundred years earlier, so in the reign of Elizabeth II her Prime Minister Margaret Thatcher was to return London to first place amongst the world's financial centres.

Big Bang was also good for London's derivatives markets, helping to propel the LIFFE exchange to overtake Chicago, becoming the world's biggest derivatives exchange less than ten years after its inception.

Barings the oldest and most blue-blooded British bank

Barings Bank was amongst the old guard that Big Bang was seeking to reform. They came from the merchant banking camp which provided advice to businesses and facilitated the financing for international trade. But they had not always been such and neither risk nor near bankruptcy were new to them. Barings had been rescued before. Founded in 1762 by John and Francis Baring the bank had remained in family ownership ever since. Peter Baring was the incumbent chairman and much of the family fortune was still invested in the business. Originally in the wool trade, Barings were to diversify into other commodities before growing rapidly when a route into the lucrative business of international trade opened up in 1793, through a tie up with Hope & Co., the Amsterdam based bank. Through the enduring relationship with the Dutch East India Company that Thomas Hope had helped bring about, the firm had built up a formidable franchise in international trade. In keeping with the family tradition, the commercial relationship between the two banks was cemented by one of Francis Baring's daughters marrying into the Hope family.

Progression into the heart of government and nobility also came through the Hope connection when Barings and Hope were called on to facilitate the Louisiana Purchase in 1802, a transaction involving the United States and France, the largest land purchase in history. This purchase by the US Government of over two million square kilometres encompassed far more than simply the State of Louisiana. The purchase included all or substantially all of fifteen US States and the two Canadian provinces Alberta and Saskatchewan, thereby more than doubling the size of the United States. The $15 million purchase price was cheap by any measure. Less than 3 cents per acre then, in today's money it would be less than $250 million or 50 cents per acre.

Remarkably this transaction for the French Government was accomplished whilst Britain was at war with France, with the proceeds being deployed to fund Napoleon's war effort. Barings and Hope acted as principals and not intermediaries on the transaction, which meant that the United States purchased Louisiana from Barings and Hope, not France. After receiving a $3 million down payment in gold, the remainder of the purchase was made in U.S. Government bonds, which Napoleon subsequently sold back to Barings at a 12 ½% discount to their $100 par value, reaping the banks an additional $1.5 million on top of their advisory fees.

Even with hindsight, it is extraordinary that a bank, which claimed to be British to the core, would wish or could be permitted to provide the financial firepower to arm a foreign enemy to kill its own people. Napoleon Bonaparte was not slow to make political capital, commenting when signing the agreement that: *"This accession of territory affirms forever the power of the United States, and I have given England a maritime rival who sooner or later will humble her pride."*

Lord Byron immortalised the power, influence and morality of the bank over politics and world events at that time in the poem *Don Juan*:

> *"Who keep the World, both old and new, in pain*
> *Or pleasure? Who make politics run glibber all?*
> *The shade of Buonaparte's noble daring?*
> *Jew Rothschild and his fellow-Christian, Baring."*

Perhaps there has never been a golden age of banking morality.

A reminder that dealing with sovereign states is far from riskless, arose when Barings went to Paris to negotiate the Louisiana Purchase, as they nearly found themselves dealing with the wrong country. Little did they know that Louisiana was actually owned by Spain and had been since 1762. The treaty transferring Louisiana from France to Spain had been kept secret, and this vast tract of land was only legally transferred back to France on 30th November 1803, just three weeks before its sale to the United States. Had that transfer not taken place, Barings could have become the unwitting victim of a massive sovereign fraud when passing the sale proceeds to France instead of the real owner, Spain.

A century later the legendary con man Victor Lustig, had successfully sold Paris' Eiffel Tower to a French scrap metal dealer. Afterwards he immigrated to the United States where he had the brass neck and guile to persuade none other than the Chicago gangster Al

Capone to invest $50,000 in a stock deal. Sensibly he kept Capone's money in a safe deposit box for two months and, having second thoughts, returned the money to Capone claiming the deal had fallen through. Impressed by what Capone read as Lustig's integrity, Capone gave him $5,000, which a relieved Lustig happily took. In a curious twist of fate, Capone and Lustig were both incarcerated in the island prison of Alcatraz in San Francisco Bay, Lustig joining Capone for printing counterfeit money. They died within six weeks of one another in 1947.

Money power to match great nations

Barings moved to 8 Bishopsgate in 1806, the site for their headquarters for the remaining life of the bank. By now their influence was much more than that of a mere merchant bank with the Duc de Richelieu in 1817 famously listing the six great powers in Europe as *"England, France, Prussia, Austria, Russia - and Baring Brothers".*

In 1832, they established an office in Liverpool specifically to capitalise on new North American opportunities. By facilitating the Louisiana Purchase, Barings had become well established in US political and commercial circles and were appointed exclusive agent to the US Government in 1843, a position they were to hold until 1871.

Barings cautiously and successfully ventured into the North American railroad boom following the American Civil War. A new railroad town in British Columbia was renamed Revelstoke in honour of the first Lord Revelstoke, the Barings partner running the bank which, with Glyn, Mills & Co., saw the funding of the Canadian-Pacific Railway through to completion.

Later in the 1880s, it was through underwriting South America debt that they deemed to be *"daring"* but nowadays would be described risky, that Barings got into serious trouble through overexposure to Argentine and Uruguayan debt. When the Argentine president Miguel Juárez Celman was forced to resign in 1890, following the

"Revolución del Parque", and the country was close to defaulting on its debt payments, the vulnerability of Barings was exposed. Lacking sufficient reserves to support the Argentine bonds until they got their house in order, the bank had to be rescued by a consortium that included French and Russian banks which was organised by the Governor of the Bank of England, William Lidderdale. The associated turmoil in financial markets became known as the Panic of 1890 and was the 'Lehman' of its day.

Although the rescue averted what could have been a worldwide financial collapse, Barings never regained its dominant position. They nevertheless continued to maintain the close relationship with the monarchy and aristocracy until Barings' collapse in 1995. Diana, Princess of Wales, was a great-granddaughter of a Baring.

With such pedigree and influence around the world it therefore came as a humiliating surprise that a bank of such stature, history and pedigree was brought down by a plasterer's son.

Barings looks East

In the run up to Big Bang, Barings was not the most fleet footed of banks; missing out on acquiring the blue bloods of the stockbroking world as well as the small band of market makers that might have been more natural bedfellows. Late to the party, they alighted on a firm located almost next door to them in the City that, whilst not top tier, presented an opportunity of a different kind. Henderson Crosthwaite was a stockbroker that covered most major stock markets but their principal attraction was a strong Asian franchise built by an enterprising individual called Christopher Heath. Heath regularly featured in the financial press as Britain's highest paid stockbroker whilst also covered on the sporting pages as an enthusiastic race horse owner.

With no trading heritage, Barings hired people from other trading banks with trading skills. Derivatives were seen as a critical component in the mix and Asia their territory of competitive advantage. Establishing a strong derivatives presence in Asia became a key priority. When building their team, they hired a derivatives settlement clerk called Nick Leeson in London from Morgan Stanley in 1989, transferring him to Singapore in 1992. It was a time when cautious expansion was seen as dithering, and Barings set about speedily growing their Asian derivatives business. Enthusiastic and short staffed, Leeson quickly established himself as the senior derivatives manager covering the things he knew about; the bookkeeping, cash margining, settlement and risk controls of derivative trading. But to these responsibilities, and ultimately fatally, he was also given responsibility for an activity he was supposed to support and police but had never been directly engaged in before, trading. The poacher and gamekeeper was one and the same person. It was the recipe for the disaster that was to come.

The competitive buzz of Asian derivatives

These were heady times for Asian derivatives markets. New contracts were springing up in abundance and there was fierce competition between exchanges in the region. Asian markets had become the battleground for the rival electronic and open outcry trading models. It was a spicy brew full of opportunity. Hong Kong and Singapore had locked horns trying to gain the ascendancy over one another, seeking to become the dominant exchange for Asian business. The Asia prize had gained particular prominence internationally in 1987, when the Japanese stock market overtook the United States to become the world's largest by market capitalisation.

Singapore strategy to win Japanese derivative business

Singapore had launched stock index futures on Japan's Nikkei 225 index the year before, Japan's equivalent of New York's Dow Jones stock market index. Subsequently in 1988 the Japanese also listed the Nikkei-225 contract in Osaka, an appropriate home since the first futures exchange had been born there three hundred years earlier.

Being the most important Asian equity contract, Singapore saw competing with Japan in the Nikkei-225 contract as central to their strategy. Noting that Osaka was seeking to maximise profitability and to use licensing and differential pricing to protect Japanese securities firms from the full force of foreign competition, Singapore made sure that their market was better equipped for international participation with floor trading, like Chicago and London, conducted by open outcry. Their model was less onerous and more favourable in terms of charging structure, margin requirement and interest paid on deposits and led international participants to back Singapore. Not wishing to be seen supporting a rival foreign market, none of the big Japanese brokers in Osaka participated in Singapore, leaving just a handful of international players to compete with one another in both trading venues.

There was real opportunity too. International investors were finding Osaka an unfriendly trading venue. Quite apart from levying high charges, they had also imposed circuit breakers that confined permissible daily price movements to a narrow range. Their purpose was to prevent the market from experiencing short term price shocks from order imbalances between buyers and sellers, in much the same way that an electrical circuit breaker prevents a voltage surge in one part of the circuit from causing damage elsewhere. This was a laudable aim, designed in the aftermath of the 1987 portfolio insurance debacle, to give the market time to adjust to order imbalances. However the price range set by Osaka was too narrow, and a circuit breaker mechanism intended to cater for extremes was often triggered by the normal 'to and fro' of daily market movements. As a consequence trading in stock index futures on Osaka was suspended on many occasions for no good reason and the contract proved to be of limited use for those who wished to use the contract to hedge their exposure to Japanese shares.

These shortcomings were not lost on those running the Singapore International Monetary Exchange (Simex). They could see an opportunity to win the international investors and gain a share of Japan's lucrative stock index futures market by offering the same Nikkei 225 contract not just with lower charges band but also without confining circuit breakers.

Leeson progresses from arbitrage to position taking

For Barings and a handful of major foreign investment banks, participation in both markets had big advantages and gave them real competitive 'edge' over their rivals. The only source of information for Singapore locals on Nikkei futures trading came from watching the price tape from Japan. The frequent delay in the transmission of this price information meant that those with a direct phone link into the Osaka floor and the ability to trade on both markets had a head start. Osaka was an electronic market so the Singapore locals could also examine the price and size at which bids and offers were made in the Osaka market and make trading judgements accordingly. Without actually trading, those operating in both markets could place or remove bids and offers in ways that would influence the behaviour of Singapore locals. For example, if a large electronic order to buy the Nikkei 225 had been placed on Osaka's order book just below the prevailing market price, locals in Singapore could be led to believe that there was strong buying support. They might therefore be willing to accept large selling orders on the grounds that there was little downside risk. However if it was Barings that had placed the large buy order in Osaka, the Singapore locals could be duped into making an attractive bid for a Barings sell order. As soon as they had filled their order in Singapore, Barings could pull their electronic buy order in Osaka, leaving the Singapore locals finding themselves abruptly exposed to a market fall without the buying support they had anticipated.

This practice of *"spoofing"* through the judicious placement of electronic trading orders was new to stock markets. It was particularly effective as the Singapore locals were initially unaware of this smart trickery by investment banks. In the modern era of the internet and very fast electronic trading this kind of behaviour was to become so simple that individuals could act in the same manner on a computer from the comfort of their home. There have been some extraordinary cases of market manipulation from home, of which the *"Flash Crash"* of the US stock market in 2010 is perhaps the most notorious. Then an individual called Navinder Singh Sarao, operating from his parents' modest London home, triggered a trillion dollar crash lasting 36 minutes, causing a 9% fall in the US stock market. With limited financial resources he was able to draw on commercially available software to place *"$200 million worth of bets that the market would fall"* which he *"replaced or modified 19,000 times"* according to the US Commodity Futures Trading Commission (CFTC) report. This same report described the incident as: *"one of the most turbulent periods in the history of financial markets"*. With their policing of electronic trading described as: *"using bicycles trying to catch Ferraris"* regulators have since taken note and spoofing today has effectively been outlawed.

But it is one thing to identify competitive advantage; quite another to make money from exploiting opportunity through skillful execution. And to succeed you also need luck. Unfortunately Leeson had neither. When he took a trading position in Osaka the offsetting carried out in Singapore had a habit of being executed at a worse price, resulting in a trading loss. The real opportunities he was seeing were not being converted into trading profits. His competitive edge over the Singapore locals in terms of customer flow, access to Osaka and capital resources that allowed him to run bigger positions for longer was not proving to be a winning formula. Nevertheless, with so much potentially running in his favour, and seeing other banks that were trading in both markets making handsome returns, he was convinced that all that was needed was for his luck to turn. What Leeson failed to comprehend was that the banks who shared these advantages were doing other forms of disruptive trading to facilitate complex but very profitable OTC derivatives. The most influential of these options were 'barrier options' which had a trigger price that brought them into or out of existence. Their 'knock in' and 'knockout' features resulted in severe market distortions as their 'delta hedging' trades close to barrier prices were regularly catching Leeson off balance.

Leeson's task for Barings was to build a strong derivative business as an agent for their clients through skillful trading in the market, not to take risks with the bank's money. His competitors traded on behalf of their clients but also with their firm's money. Traders making good money with their bank were very highly paid, as Leeson knew only too well from his time at Morgan Stanley. As every trader aspires for the 'Lord of the Jungle' status that goes with trading with the firm's money, Nick was keen as mustard to acquire that status.

It was frustrating for Leeson that his trading for clients was not reaping the competitive advantage that it should and so, in his desire to be seen as skillful and ultimately entrusted with the firm's money to trade, he started down a road to create the illusion of trading excellence.

Trading hero through 88888 accounting fraud

Under Barings Futures Singapore's management structure in 1995, Leeson doubled as both the manager of the trading floor for Barings' trading on the Simex and head of settlement operations. In the latter role, he was charged with ensuring accurate accounting for the unit. The two roles should have been separated as a single individual carrying out both undermines all of the safeguards built into the accounting and internal control processes. It gave Leeson the freedom to operate without supervision or management control either from Singapore or London, and allowed him to create a very simple accounting fraud to convert market losses into accounting gains.

He did this through an error account that he chose to number 88888, '8' being a lucky Chinese number. The system he created generally booked losing trades to the 88888 account and profitable trades to the Singapore Arbitrage account. By only submitting entries from the Singapore Arb book to management in London he essentially created a *"heads I win and show you my winnings or tails I lose but don't tell you"* formula. To management in London this simple deception allowed Leeson to appear to have the Midas touch. Within the London office he became known internally as a *"turbo-charged arbitrageur".*

Leeson's simple accounting fraud for turning losses into gains

The accounting fraud to turn losses into gains was simple. The way Nick described it to me was as follows:

"I'd tell our Osaka trader to buy 100 contracts of Nikkei 225 futures contracts in Osaka at, say 18,500, and book it to our Japanese Arb book. On Simex I might then sell 200 offsetting contracts (the Simex futures contract was half the size of an Osaka contract) for, say 18,400, so the arb had cost me 100 index points. As a loss-making trade I would book the 18,400 sale on the Simex floor to the 88888 account and, back at the office, create a book profit by entering the Simex sale at, say 18,550, on the Arb book.

That way a loss of 100 points was reported to London as a 50 point accounting profit, even though they were paying out the 100 point loss in cash margin.

We booked profitable trades straight to the Arb books without involving 88888."

But this simple mechanism for creating accounting victory in the face of trading defeat was one that any trainee accountant would easily spot. Nothing reconciles between the fictitious accounts being posted to Barings in London and the accounts for the real trades recorded at the Simex clearing house. This difference should have been self-evident to Barings in London as the cash they were posting to make margin payments was determined by the true profit and loss account, held at Simex. Had a simple check been carried out at any point the fraud would have uncovered. But no one made any checks, not once in three years, allowing the fraud to build into catastrophe.

Internally Leeson's reputation was soaring ever higher. He appeared to have become Barings most valuable individual, accounting for over 20% of the bank's profits. As an investment client we, as did many other investment firms, noted that Barings seemed able to execute our orders at better prices than any of their rivals, and therefore placed more and more business with Baring Futures. This price competitiveness also helped the Singapore market to build volume and market share, as it served to be another reason for trading Nikkei 225 futures there rather than in Osaka.

Back in London the story was that Leeson was making money from low risk arbitraging, profiting from small price differences between Nikkei 225 futures contracts listed in Osaka and those on Simex. Such arbitrage sought to buy futures contracts on one market and simultaneously sell them on another at a higher price. Since everyone tries to take advantage of a price difference on a publicly traded futures contract, the margins on arbitrage trading tend to be wafer thin. Consequently, the volumes traded by arbitrageurs are generally very large if they are to gain any meaningful profit. Arbitrage of this nature is not very risky even if the values are large. However, instead of buying on one market and immediately selling on another market for a small profit, the strategy agreed with senior management, Leeson was also trading futures to bet on which way the market would move.

Whilst delighted that Barings was bringing futures business to Simex, the Singapore authorities could also see from the margin payments that Barings were losing a lot of money. They could not gauge whether or not there were offsetting profits for Barings from the Osaka contract but it was reasonable to assume there might be as they were aware that his brief was to one of executing client business and arbitrage between Singapore and Osaka. Simex had no concerns relating to the 88888 account as it always showed a nil cash balance when the exchange conducted its month end reconciliation check. They were not to know that the nil balance had initially been met by transferring cash from client commission accounts or later, when commission raiding would no longer suffice, through cash raised from a dangerous option strategy.

But there was enough to worry Simex who time and again informed Barings that they believed something was amiss. Each time Barings reassured them that they had a good handle on what Leeson was doing when, in truth, they still carried out no checks at all. That was why, when the fraud unfolded in disaster, there was fury in Singapore with London and with British banking regulators who had access to Barings internal accounts because, had they followed up on Singapore's warnings, they would have seen that the numbers did not stack up.

With cash not reconciling at the clearing house and losses mounting, a device to *"flatten cash"* on a large scale was called for. It was then that a new strategy came into play that kept the fraud going longer and allowed Leeson to raise the gambling stakes to a much higher level, 'the option straddle'.

An options trick to cover the missing cash

Traded options on the Nikkei 225 index were offered on the Simex exchange early in 1993. Had they not been available, the next part of the tale would not have unfolded. Selling options pays cash premium immediately to the writer of the contract and Leeson, seeing this as a quick and efficient way to cover cash losses in the 88888 account, started dealing in them immediately. He chose the 'straddle' as that was the option strategy paid the most cash, trading in the nearest maturities of 1-3 months to turn a quick profit.

The 'Straddle' option strategy

The straddle option strategy has a pay-off profile which resembles a mountain peak. When writing straddles for cash, as Leeson did, equal numbers of call and put option contracts are sold at the same exercise price, typically close to the prevailing market level to maximise the premium received.

Straddle buyers and sellers seek to make money by correctly

---

predicting how much the price of the asset will move over the life of the option. A buyer of a straddle expects prices to move a great deal, but is uncertain in which direction. If confident on direction the buyer would simply buy a call or put option, not both. The call option appreciates if the price rises and the put option appreciates if the price falls. An example of when investors adopt this strategy is while an exploration company is drilling for oil where the outcome will be either a successful discovery that transforms the share value, or the costly disappointment of a dry hole.

The seller (or writer) of the straddle takes the opposite view and believes that the market in the asset has become overexcited and that the price will move very little in either direction, a bet on price stability. The pay-off for the writer of the straddle is the difference between the amount of premium paid by the option purchasers and the exercise price of the option contracts at expiry. If the market price on expiry is the same as the exercise price the writer of the straddle keeps the entire premium; to the extent that the price moves in either direction the seller pays the difference between the exercise price and the prevailing market price. With big price moves come big payouts to the buyers and correspondingly heavy losses to the sellers.

Leeson entered into these straddle positions simply to raise cash to cover the deficit in the 88888 account. He had no particular information or conviction that the Japanese stock market would move little, but that was his hope. During his time at Barings, Leeson had watched the Japanese stock market more than halve from a Nikkei 225 peak of almost 39,000 in 1989 to around 19,000 in March 1992. At month end he would calculate the number of straddle contracts he needed to sell to raise cash in the form of option premium that would offset the 88888 account cash deficit. Leeson then sold precisely that number of contracts. It was a simple approach that paid no regard to the value ascribed by option pricing models. When I expressed surprise that his decision making on position size had not been mentioned in any of the formal reports that followed the bank's collapse, he replied: *"No one asked".*

The only way Leeson could cover his losses in full was if the market level on expiry of the option contracts was exactly the same as their exercise price. Any other outcome would result in loss and necessitate another straddle to be written the following month. On one occasion in 1993 he was very fortunate as the Nikkei 225 Index on expiry of his straddle struck at 19,000 stood at 18,995, almost extinguishing the entire $20 million loss he had then run up. However, instead of sensibly heaving a huge sigh of relief and bringing the fraud to a halt, he carried on betting, as he still put his past trading losses down to bad luck. His motivation was not dissimilar to the Damon Runyon character Bookie Bob who, when asked why he kept betting on the horses in spite of suffering losses, responded: *"If you don't make a bet how do you know it's your lucky day?"*

But as corrective actions go, the straddle is about as risky a strategy as you can choose, especially when you cannot trade out of it. Any sharp move up or down hurts because one or other of the options gains in intrinsic value. Making things worse a sharp movement gives even greater time value to both options as volatility is perceived to have increased, a *"double whammy".* It is even more dangerous if you are unable to trade out of the position or guard against the most painful outcomes. Unfortunately Leeson was subject to all these risks. By accounting for 80-95% of all market positions (known as open interest) and by physically standing on the floor when executing the trades, Leeson could not have been more exposed and visible. When opening or closing his positions the market 'could see him coming' and move prices against him. As he described it: *"If the bid/ask on the screen was 15-17 points and I asked for a price quote to buy to close, it was immediately moved against us to 18-21 points".* And his competitors also knew when he was coming. When he came to the market on the last day of the month to open new straddle positions, they quoted very low premiums.

What confused market professionals was that these straddle sales were done with no apparent regard for price, and generally very poor value on option pricing models. Leeson just seemed to take whatever price was on offer. As time went on he received less and less cash for the same risk. By early 1995 the cash he was receiving was a mere 10% of the amount he had received when he opened his first straddle positions in 1993. And that risk was movement. For banks who offer such options their delta begins at zero but this delta moves rapidly up once the market moves. Known as 'gamma risk' it is a risk that worries a true hedger, but in Barings case no attempt was made whatsoever to hedge gamma. This was not the behaviour of the turbo charged risk free arbitrageur which Barings painted Leeson to be but the polar opposite, that of a turbo charged risk taker.

London dozes but keeps sending Leeson cash

With an eight-hour time difference the Barings management in London were usually asleep whilst Leeson was trading in Singapore. Although he had been reporting large trading profits in their accounting books, this apparent success was not being matched by cash inflows. On the contrary cash was pouring out. The explanation Leeson gave was that this money he was for 'initial margin', the good faith deposit clearing houses require in order to support the futures exposure. The bigger the positions Barings held on the arbitrage book, the greater the margin requirement. Whilst there was some truth in this assertion as his positions were growing, it was unrealised losses that were really draining cash that was being paid to Simex as 'variation margin'. However a great deal of capital held at Simex as initial margin was not for the futures contracts he was authorised to trade, but instead to support unauthorised option straddle positions in the 88888 account. Barings only verified the amount of initial margin with Simex, without checking the nature of the positions this capital was supporting. Had they done so the 88888 account and the option positions they knew nothing about would quickly have been unearthed. As Leeson put it to me, drawing on an analogy from a Sherlock Holmes story: *"the dog would have barked"*.

A puzzle for many is how Nick Leeson, who failed to pass any public mathematics examination and did not avail himself of even the most rudimentary option valuation tool, was able to put on such large and risky option positions on behalf of the bank. There is even bemusement over how he was then able to pour good money after bad, drawing on more and more bank and depositors' cash to support the losses from his disastrous stock market gambles. In Barings' case there was a modest battle going on between a Singapore trader and a London accountant with little knowledge of futures in another time zone. It is a fight the accountant never wins unless backed from the top. Unfortunately the business leader in this case was on a relentless drive to make money, keen to ensure that their trading superstar did not suffer from any internal accounting or treasury bureaucracy that interfered with money making.

The cash movements that should have rendered the collapse of Barings impossible

With most investments you pay the full amount upfront. No further cash or other physical movements take place until the investment is sold. You track the value of your investment through periodic accounting statements or, more frequently, by observing the price in the financial press through or a data provider. However, if you wish, you may choose to be blissfully unaware of unrealised investment gains and losses.

The same cannot be said for holders of futures contracts. Each day the unrealised gain or loss triggers a cash movement of the value of the gain or loss between the investor and the clearing house. This movement is called 'variation margin' and cannot be ignored as each day a cash movement has to be instructed and implemented. When Leeson's positions were at their greatest a one percent market move triggered a cash movement in excess

---

of $100 million.

This physical cash movement from the futures margining system ought to be the best loss management warning system imaginable. That is why fraudulent trading in futures ought to be very hard to accomplish, and the managers who fail to spot such activity much more culpable.

Bet on stability undone by Kobe Earthquake

By the end of 1994 the game was up and Leeson knew it. Although Barings thought he had made a £102 million profit that year, the truth was that he had lost close to £200 million. Barings still had £350 million of capital so, had the fraud been uncovered then, collapse might have been averted.

Early in January 1995 Leeson took out another straddle bet. He again had no particular conviction that the Japanese equity market would move very little, but the trade was forced on him by his need for cash to balance the books. As Leeson himself put it: *"I wasn't running running the position anymore; the position was running me."* And there was nothing more for him to lose, as the money he was betting was Barings' not his. He also knew this straddle was his last roll of the dice.

At the time the Japanese equity market, as measured by the Nikkei 225 Index, stood around 20,000. The bet was already going wrong when the market slipped below 19,500 under modest selling pressure and adverse economic news. But then a natural catastrophe with severe financial fallout occurred. Just before 6am on Tuesday 17th January 1995 the Great Hanshin earthquake, measuring 7.2 on the Richter scale, struck Kobe, an industrial city in the Japanese heartland, 600 kilometres southwest of Tokyo. Although the tremors only lasted 20 seconds its effects were devastating. Over 6,000 people were killed and, other than the Great Kantō earthquake in 1923 which claimed 140,000 lives, it was Japan's worst earthquake in the 20th century.

Over $100 billion in damage was caused and 200,000 buildings destroyed. Its epicentre on the northern end of Awaji Island was just 20 kilometres from the city of Kobe.

For Leeson the Kobe earthquake ended his charade as Asian financial markets went into a tailspin. The Nikkei 225 index dropped almost immediately under 18,000, leaving his straddle seriously underwater. And it was not just the fall in the market level which was damaging. Investors were willing to pay a higher option premium, particularly on the put option, as uncertainty had increased markedly. With his straddles losing money, Leeson needed buyers to come into the Japanese stock market and the Nikkei 225 Index to recover back to 20,000.

He managed to buy himself enough time to overcome the end January book balancing hurdle by entering into accounting fraud overdrive, claiming to the London office that he was owed £50 million by a client who had purchased a large OTC option contract. He then forged confirmations, payment instructions and instructed a number of cash movements at the custodian in order to create the impression that the £50 million from the fictitious client had actually been received.

With no appetite from other investors to bid up the market, Leeson decided to take on the task himself. In a manner reminiscent of King Canute, the English king who sat in a chair on the beach in a vain attempt to push back the sea, Leeson bought more and more Nikkei 225 futures, trying desperately to turn the tide of selling on the Japanese stock market.

After making a little headway, the market resumed its downward path and Leeson's losses rose higher and higher, his exposure to the Japanese stock market increasing to $14 billion. Alongside this stock market exposure he also accumulated a $20 billion interest rate exposure through Japanese Government Bond (JGB) futures contracts. These positions were also heavily loss-making as interest rates spiked upward.

By late February the Nikkei 225 Index had retreated to 17,000 and Barings faced losses that no amount of chicanery could hide. There was also no means for obtaining the amount of cash required to meet Simex margin payments. Resigned to his fate, Leeson left a note on his desk on 23 February 1995 saying simply *"I'm sorry"* before leaving Singapore with his wife. After a short period on the run he was arrested in Frankfurt, extradited to Singapore, tried and imprisoned.

Did Barings have to fail?

Barings Bank collapsed under losses ultimately put at £827 million (US$1.4 billion). Their loss at the end of their last trading day was much less, around £340 million. The number rose alarmingly once the market knew the full extent of the derivative positions that had to be liquidated, marking their prices to make a killing from the bank's demise. An abiding question is did Barings have to fail? Could the rout have been stopped or even reversed? There is no doubt that the bank could have survived had the fraud been spotted before the end of January 1995. But could the bank have survived after its final trading day on Thursday 23rd February 1995?

There are many who view the Barings' legacy as one of regulatory weakness compounded by inept judgement in crisis. The true positions were all known to Simex as well as the capital deployed as margin. Throughout the entire weekend hullabaloo, cooperation between Singapore and London was hampered with fevered efforts at the Bank of England to rescue Barings. Their losses were known as all their positions were exchange traded; none were private OTC positions. As a member of the Bank of England Derivatives Joint Standing Committee I was privy to some of these efforts. Those willing to save the bank ranged from the Sultan of Brunei to major international investment banks. Had they taken on the positions the market would likely have turned. However a combination of human failings and a lack of understanding of futures markets meant a rescue could not be mounted. On Monday 27th February the market sharks circled and the losses spiralled to £880 million through a forced liquidation. Not understanding actually how much capital was still intact as initial margin and held by Simex made decision taking on the financial firepower to be deployed for a rescue uncertain. In the short time window available, there was much more guesswork and foggy thinking than might be supposed. Calm knowledgeable leadership was in short supply. When I visited Asia shortly afterwards and met with exchange officials, there was a palpable sense of shock at the perceived mishandling of the crisis.

Decisions made in financial crises are sometimes characterised as having similarities to those taken in times of war. Judgements with enormous import have to be made rapidly. In the military the individuals making these decisions are known and trained with the knowledge, demeanour and experience to make the right choices at just such a moment. In financial markets it is not the same. Typically there is no one with clear responsibility for handling the crisis and no protocol for managing the process. Those that lead the effort may be poorly equipped for the task and hold no real authority beyond persuasion. You need good luck to have the right person taking the helm; even more to have the right support.

Rogue trading lessons

After the collapse of Barings the Board of Banking Supervision of the Bank of England launched an investigation led by the Chancellor of the Exchequer. Their report published in July 1995 was so bland that its conclusions and recommendations were greeted with derision when debated in the House of Lords. It did not address why the warnings from Singapore went unheeded, nor the manner in which the attempted rescue and wind down of market positions was conducted. The Singapore authorities carried out a separate investigation as the rogue trading had taken place in their jurisdiction. Their report was to highlight many weaknesses in Barings supervision and basic risk controls.

A keener analysis than the Bank of England report was the summary made by Christopher Sharples, then Chairman of Securities and Futures Authority (SFA) the regulatory entity responsible for policing investment banks: *"Mr Leeson pulled the trigger, but the bank gave him the gun, the bank gave him the ammunition, cash. When he wanted more ammunition they gave him as much as they could give him... until they ran out; and then the bank was bust."*

Or perhaps the most telling remark was that of Peter Norris, Chief Executive of Baring Securities, in answer to the question in a BBC interview: *"Is it right that senior management in Barings didn't understand derivatives at all?"* His response: *"I think that is completely true."*

Afterwards banking regulators introduced myriad sets of rules and risk management controls for banks engaging in derivatives business to prevent recurrence. Over time their rules grew in sophistication as the magnitude and complexity of the derivatives business increased. Most people thought that this kind of 'rogue trader' fraud would never happen again but had to change their tune when Jérôme Kerviel bet the French bank Société Générale twelve years later and nearly brought it down. Singapore was also to suffer from another big rogue trading incident in London, this time through their substantial share holding in the Swiss bank, UBS. Singapore's disappointment was heightened but perhaps not entirely surprised; London had let them down before.

The Dutch bank ING purchased Barings Bank in 1995 for the nominal sum of £1 and assumed all of Barings' liabilities, forming the subsidiary ING Barings. Given their buccaneering derivative history it was entirely appropriate that the Dutch should be the purchaser. But it would have been a more fitting end had ING's Dutch rival ABN Amro been the buyer as, by then, they owned Hope and Co., Barings' partner during the golden years.

As for Nick Leeson he was eventually sentenced to six and a half years in prison in Singapore but was released early in 1999 on health grounds. His book 'Rogue Trader' was an instant best seller and was made into a film shortly afterwards, his name becoming synonymous with the title. When asked to speak on matters relating to rogue trading he is fond of remarking: *"I've heard of people writing a cheque that their bank bounced, but I was the first to write a cheque that bounced the bank."*

The Nikkei 225 index on which Leeson had made his straddle bets was not to return to the 20,000 level until 2017. Still conscious of his position Nick chose Twitter to comment *"Not far off my break-even point. If only they'd waited!!"*

25. 'Mr. Copper' and Sumitomo - A mighty fall… or was it? - London & New York 1996

"I believe this is one of the most serious worldwide manipulations of a commodities market encountered in the history of the Comission."

Geoffrey Aronow,
Director of Enforcement, CFTC

Sumitomo Corporation's $2.6 billion loss from trading copper derivatives in 1996 dwarfed the $1.4 billion that had brought about the collapse of Barings the year before. But the loss was more surprising than Barings because it showed that experience, reputation and very deep pockets do not obviate the need for monitoring the trading behaviour of big market participants. Variation margin amounts paid, being the daily cash payments that participants with unrealised losses pay to those with unrealised profits, should not just be monitored to ensure credit worthiness, but also for the insights they can provide on market manipulation.

And like earlier market manipulations that had surrounded wheat, silver, tin and share prices, Sumitomo's efforts appeared to have been designed to push the price of copper up.

Loose credit controls on London Metal Exchange

The London Metal Exchange (LME) is the world's biggest and most liquid base metals market. In the mid-1990s the exchange traded over one billion tonnes of metal contracts with a value of around $2,500 billion. LME was truly an international exchange, with more than 95% of their business coming from outside Britain, and storing the metal they traded in 380 authorised LME warehouses in 42 countries. This global endorsement of the LME was truly astonishing, with the ultimate testament to its reputation being that the price freely established on the London market floor known as the LME 'Fix' had become the price benchmark for every other commercial metal transaction conducted around the world.

Part of the reason for this success was the way the market had structured its relationship with customers and designed its futures contracts. The LME had always placed the needs of metal producers at the forefront of their thinking, and evolvied their market offering accordingly. To this end, a number of their practices differed from those of most other derivative exchanges, of which the most significant was the way that they operated their credit controls to deal with daily market movements. In most markets responsibility to meet unrealised losses, by paying cash in the form of variation margin, rests with the owners of the futures contracts. The broker simply acts as an administration agent, passing money from their customers to and from the clearing house. In the case of the LME it was the clearing broker, not the customers, who was legally obliged to meet these payments to the clearing house, even though the positions taken were not theirs. This was because the LME clearing broker acted as the principal facing the market and not as an agent for clients, the more typical model for derivative exchanges.

This practice suited the metal producers or users who paid or received cash when metals were physically delivered on maturity of the futures contract. It also enabled the brokers to forge deeper relationships with customers by funding their margin payments. But the practice created additional risk for the brokers if customers failed to pay up. Just such an incident had taken place in 1985 when LME members had lost some $600 million and the LME came close to collapse when 22 countries refused to pay up after their tin market price support scheme failed. You may be confident of the creditworthiness of sovereign nations but it is not much use if they refuse to pay and there is no legal redress to make them do so. You need to have their cash, not that of their clearing members, when customer countries are losing money.

No one knows copper like Sumitomo

The House of Sumitomo was founded in the early 1600s by a former Buddhist priest called Masatomo Sumitomo. The firm became synonymous with copper from its earliest days, with Sumitomo appointed the official copper trader to the Tokugawa Shogunate, Japan's ruling family at the time, in much the same way Saburaemon Yodoya had become the official rice trader when the first futures market was established. Sumitomo had gained this status first by establishing a copper smelting process that extracted silver for coinage, a status reinforced through ownership of the Besshi Copper mine on the southern Japanese island of Shikoku, which was reckoned to be the world's largest copper exporter.

As Japan opened up to the West in the mid-1800s Sumitomo involved itself in copper rolling and steel manufacture. By the early 1900s the family firm had risen to become Japan's third most powerful financial conglomerate or *'zaibatsu'*. These politically influential zaibatsus were the backbone of Japan's military-industrial strength during the 1930s and throughout the Second World War. Family control of the business was absolute from the outset, with the head of the Sumitomo family, a direct descendant from the founder, owning 90% of Sumitomo's shares in 1937.

After the Japanese defeat in 1945 the Allies dismantled the zaibatsu and the Sumitomo family's influence diminished. Sumitomo was reconstituted as a group of affiliated companies, which included Sumitomo Corporation and Sumitomo Bank. Sumitomo Corporation was where the core copper business resided, supplementing this business with a wide range of other goods. By the mid 1990's they were one of Japan's four leading trading houses, a truly global business operating in over 90 countries, with annual revenues of $150 billion and $50 billion in assets.

In 1995 there was no stronger, experienced or more respected player in the copper market than Sumitomo.

Yasuo Hamanaka's Fraudulent Corner

It therefore came as a huge shock in June 1996 when Sumitomo announced that their Chief Copper Trader, Yasua Hamanaka, had lost $2.6 billion principally from trading copper futures and options on the London Metal Exchange (LME).

Earlier that year, regulators had already investigated what appeared to be a *"squeeze"* in the copper market; that is an attempt to force up the price by restricting supply. The main protagonist was Sumitomo, since it controlled a large proportion of the copper supply. Hamanaka himself was known as *"Mr. Five Percent"* as he was said to control 5% of the copper market trade. Nevertheless the price had still declined from about $2,800 per tonne at the beginning of the year to $2,000 by June. Over this period Hamanaka built up long positions believing the copper price would increase, and tried to prop these positions up with further purchases as the price slipped.

However, his activities had come to the attention of hedge funds and Herbert Black, a canny Canadian scrap metal merchant, smelt an opportunity to make money from the false market which Hamanaka had created.

Two aspects of the copper market attracted hedge fund attention. First in mid-1995, copper futures on the LME began to trade below the cash or 'spot' price of copper, a condition known as 'backwardation'. The futures price should trade above the spot price, this more normal condition known as 'contango', since the owner of the future has committed no money whereas the purchaser of physical copper has committed the full amount. To the hedge funds this backwardation implied that the price of copper should fall further as it would be rational for owners of copper bars in LME's warehouses to sell their copper and replace it with futures contracts for the same underlying value. That way, the owner of physical copper would gain from purchasing the copper at a lower price when taking delivery of the futures contract. In addition, since no money was committed to owning and storing physical copper there was an additional gain from interest on the funds raised and the absence of storage costs. There was therefore a risk free gain to be had for holders of physical copper. Why wasn't an experienced player like Sumitomo taking advantage of this obvious opportunity?

The answer was that Sumitomo was the source of this market anomaly and the only rational explanation was that they wished to drive the copper price higher by restricting physical supply.

A second unusual signal for the hedge funds came from another exchange where copper and their derivatives were traded, New York's Commodities Exchange (Comex). Although copper was trading at a higher price on Comex than on the LME, it appeared that most sellers continued to be drawn to the LME where they received a lower price. It did not make sense unless they did not want their activity made public as, unlike the Comex where the size of open positions had to be declared in 'open interest' numbers, on LME the size of participant holdings could be kept secret. Scarcity of supply was driving the copper price higher and someone was secretly hoarding copper and refusing to sell on Comex. Why?

Comex operated a different system from the LME, requiring customer cash in variation margin to cover unrealised losses and greater disclosure of large positions. These measures had been put in place after the Hunt's 'corner' of the silver market in 1980, making market manipulation more difficult.

The hedge funds had little initial success in pushing the copper price down by selling copper futures. Hamanaka kept buying against them and Sumitomo's awesome firepower prevailed. When the futures contract expired in December 2005 the price of copper had moved up and the hedge funds lost money to Sumitomo. They renewed their efforts early in 1996 but again were rebutted. The battle for supremacy was reflected in rapid price movements, the volatility of which drove option prices to record highs. Still Hamanaka fought them off, squeezing the market even higher in an effort to overpower and frighten the hedge funds.

His strategy worked until May 1996 when a strike at a Chilean copper mine that had been constraining supply ended. The copper price started to fall as supply increased.

In the meantime, Comex were increasingly concerned that copper trading was gravitating to LME in order to facilitate a corner and that their copper business was being damaged by the process. They complained to their regulator the Commodity Futures Trading Commission (CFTC) who, in conjunction with their UK equivalent the Securities and Investment Board (SIB), launched an investigation early in 1996. It was in the course of this investigation that Sumitomo said that they discovered Hamanaka's misdemeanours which led to their public announcement on 13th June of the copper losses. News of Hamanaka's departure had reached the market earlier on 5th June and the copper price had fallen sharply as a result.

Why did it happen and how did it go undetected for so long? Was Hamanaka like Leeson, another example of someone with too much autonomy, left unsupervised to trade as he wished, and free to conceal losses by falsely accounting his own trades; and for over 10 years? Sumitomo sued a number of brokers for aiding and abetting his trading activities, extracting significant out of court settlements in some cases. One briefly came to court but was quickly settled before much evidence or information from cross examination could be publicly disclosed.

At face value the answer would appear to be an unequivocal yes. Hamanaka confessed to that effect and was jailed for eight years so doing. But Sumitomo was no Barings. Even if Hamanaka did control trading, settlement and accounting, allowing him to cook the books like Leeson, Sumitomo were, unlike Barings, very experienced derivative market users.

Perhaps...

Perhaps there was more to it than that.

Perhaps there was a sound commercial reason for Hamanaka to trade consistently 'long' in order to drive up the copper price. After all, a high copper price served to increase Sumitomo's revenues from copper production and distribution.

Perhaps the trading losses he ran up over his 10-year tenure were more than offset from higher revenues from other parts of Sumitomo's copper business chain.

Perhaps there was a long-standing market operation in place to keep the copper price up. There had been another very well publicised LME market operation by Sumitomo back in 1991, allegedly involving a small brokerage firm called Winchester Commodities, which was designed to restrict copper supply and push up the copper price.

Perhaps they learnt from the Hunts' silver escapade and executed a quieter and more sophisticated strategy under the radar.

Perhaps Sumitomo did not expect to make money from derivative market trading and were unconcerned by Hamanaka's losses prior to 1996.

Perhaps there was a false market that needed smart and committed hedge funds to break it up.

Perhaps, if you look at their copper business as a whole, Sumitomo did not lose $2.6 billion at all.

We will probably never know.

26. LTCM pushes financial economics over the edge - Greenwich 1998

"Even when the experts all agree they may well be mistaken"

Bertrand Russell (1872-1970)

In 1994 John Meriwether, by then a bond market trading legend on Wall Street, brought together a team of gifted arbitrage traders to work with Myron Scholes and Robert Merton, two of the gods of financial economics, to create a hedge fund called Long-Term Capital Management (LTCM).

Meriwether had built his reputation as a bond trader in the 1980s at the investment bank Salomon Brothers. Salomon had been first to embrace proprietary or 'prop' trading as a core business in its own right, backing their market judgment with the firm's own money instead of relying solely on commissions from trading on behalf of their clients. Other big investment banks like Lehman and Goldman Sachs had followed suit and a new breed of smart internal gamblers had come into being. Meriwether was in the vanguard of prop traders, devising arbitrage trading strategies from the new ideas and pricing models coming from financial economics that few others then understood.

Although a quiet individual with an intensely private disposition, Meriwether was to achieve early and unwanted public notoriety for making big bets in a detached and calm, almost serene manner. He featured in a book called *Liar's Poker* written by Michael Lewis, a former Salomon employee, which was published in 1989. The book drew its title from a game of chance where the players have to guess whether the serial numbers that the holder claims to be on a US Dollar bill are true or false. Success required coolness and 'bluffing' skills, with the game said to have been played most afternoons by a circle of the firm's senior New York traders. Meriwether was the acknowledged master and Lewis tells the story of a particular day in 1986 when John Gutfreund, the firm's ebullient CEO, whose advice to his traders was to: *"wake up every morning ready to bite the ass of a bear"*, threw down a challenge to those playing Liar's Poker: *"One hand, a million dollars, no tears."* Meriwether was said to have picked up the gauntlet with his customary calm with the response: *"No John if we're going to play for those kind of numbers I'd rather play for real money. Ten million dollars. No tears."* With the rejoinder: *"You're crazy"* Gutfreund walked off.

Meriwether's proprietary trading team was so successful that their trading activities came to dictate the firm's business strategy. It soon became clear that Salomon needed the services of Meriwether more than he needed the resources of the firm, a situation which came to a head much sooner than either had expected when a bond trading scandal, perpetrated by an individual reporting to Meriwether, embroiled the firm. False bids were made on behalf of investment clients, including the investment firm I then worked for, at one of the quarterly US Treasury auctions for government debt. The bids were really for Salomon's own trading book so that they could obtain a greater allocation of bonds than their permitted quota. When this came to light in 1991, the firm was fined $290 million by the US Securities and Exchange Commission (SEC), then the biggest fine ever levied against a bank. With the fate of the entire firm hanging in the balance their largest investor, Warren Buffett, cut a deal with the US Treasury to step in as Chairman, and oversee a reform of the firm's culture, strengthening the balance sheet through the injection $700 million in additional capital. Gutfreund and Meriwether were both forced out whilst Buffett quickly made clear to those that remained what he would and would not tolerate: *"Lose money for the firm and I will be understanding, lose a shred of reputation for the firm and I will be ruthless."*

It was not a role Buffett wanted, nor one he much enjoyed, describing the experience in his annual letter to investors as: *"far from fun."* However in typically smart fashion, the $700 million he invested in Salomon was in the form of convertible preferred shares. These shares not only paid a handsome 9% dividend each year with an associated tax credit, but were also convertible at any time of Buffett's choosing into Salomon shares at the depressed $38 share price then prevailing. This arrangement gave him full participation in the sharp share price recovery that followed his rescue, and was to culminate in a very profitable outcome when Travelers acquired Salomon in 1997 at a $78 share price.

Leaving Salomon gave Meriwether the opportunity to take his arbitrage ideas and business experience to the next level, and to do so whilst unencumbered by the trappings and regulatory oversight of a large investment bank. It was the genesis of the hedge fund he launched three years later, Long-Term Capital Management.

Feeding off scraps with leverage becomes a big money spinner

Starting with $1 billion of capital, LTCM sought to profit from many of the trading strategies Meriwether's team had developed at Salomon Brothers. Their initial focus was arbitrage of fixed income securities that had become mispriced through market inefficiencies arising from liquidity and time effects. A typical and much favoured strategy was to extract the relative value between two similar securities through what was known as a 'convergence trade'. LTCM would use their mathematical models to calculate and compare the theoretical and market prices of similar long dated government bonds, buying those that appeared cheap and simultaneously selling others to an equivalent value that were relatively expensive.

The price difference between the two bonds was largely explained by trading liquidity. Freshly issued 'on the run' US Treasury bonds enjoyed a price premium over their less liquid 'off the run' equivalents. Although the difference in price between a US Treasury bond that matures in 30 years and one that matures in 29 years and nine months is small in valuation terms, a larger discrepancy often came about because the 'on the run' bond could be traded in greater volumes and on tighter dealing terms than the 'off the run' bond. By buying the cheaper less liquid bond and simultaneously selling 'short' an equal amount of the more expensive bond,

LTCM neutralised the interest rate risk embedded in each bond, and profited when the price difference between the two bonds narrowed. A particularly attractive feature of this strategy was that judging when the price discrepancy would narrow was predictable and happened quickly. A newly issued 30 year US Treasury bond would lose its 'on the run' status, and hence liquidity premium, as soon as the next 30 year bond was issued three months later, leaving LTCM to reap the convergence gain.

Although low risk, the price discrepancies in convergence trades were usually very small. The only way to generate decent returns was by taking large positions that were leveraged by borrowing. LTCM was able to lock in attractive borrowing terms from the Wall Street banks by drawing on their experience and connections, making good profits from low risk arbitrage strategies. Their LTCM strategy, as Myron Scholes described it, was akin to a giant vacuum cleaner: *"sucking up nickels from all over the world."*

Most of Wall Street's finest believed in LTCM and many were investors in the fund. With a trader of Meriwether's stature and proven track record at the helm, there was little fear in the market place that raw academic thinking would cause those traders to overlook anything of importance from the real world of trading, as had befallen the portfolio insurance strategy in 1987.

Glory days brings in the copycats

The fund was a spectacular success from the outset, generating a 20% net profit in 1994, followed by returns of over 40% in each of the next two years. By November 1997, having grown their initial $1 billion of investment capital to $7.5 billion, LTCM handed back $2.7 billion to their investors on the grounds that it was *"excess capital"* they did not need, and would simply serve to dilute future returns.

1997 was a bumper year for LTCM and a truly wonderful one for Merton and Scholes. In addition to basking in the glory of LTCM's performance, they had also received their Nobel Memorial Prize for Economic Science along with the citation for the now deceased Fischer Black.

Their performance was very public and, to many, LTCM was a winning formula built on genius. Everyone wanted to know how LTCM were achieving such returns. Some banks even created trading desks whose sole purpose was to service LTCM and mimic their *"Midas Touch"* by entering into the same trades themselves. These banks also marketed these strategies to other investors, some of whom set aside funds specifically to copy LTCM. The weight of money entering into LTCM trades became of such magnitude that they were *"squeezing the juice out"* of the profitability of many of LTCM's core trades. Trades that had once shown a 0.19% return from convergence were now offering 0.06%, less than a third of earlier profits. Counteracting this effect was the additional leverage LTCM now had from returning capital to investors, through which they were able to squeeze absolute returns from their core strategies even though the convergence terms had become tighter. But leverage alone was not enough and, as the crowding of their core strategies intensified, LTCM's hunger for fresh pastures of arbitrage opportunity intensified.

The extent to which the fund had leveraged to turn small arbitrage opportunities into sizable returns was extraordinary. By early 1998, with less than $5 billion in capital, LTCM owned a $130 billion portfolio of assets together with $1.25 trillion of notional exposure through derivatives. To place these numbers into perspective, the notional value of their derivatives portfolio alone was equivalent to the entire annual budget of the US Government. Much has been made of these numbers although, with their portfolio comprising offsetting long and short positions, the real risk was a great deal lower than the headline figures implied, only being properly evaluated through assessment of their net risk exposure.

With all of this forensic scrutiny from others, a lot of effort went into keeping LTCM's investment activity shrouded in mystery. They had to disclose their leverage, off balance sheet exposure and other financial information to provide complete credit transparency to the banks and trading counterparties who were funding their borrowings. However, to maintain the veil of secrecy around their investment activity, LTCM were careful not to show their full hand to any one of them. Only those within LTCM knew all the cards the firm was holding.

LTCM heads into uncharted waters to avoid the crowd

As LTCM's investment capital grew in value, they felt increasing pressure to put their money to work; otherwise they could not maintain the level of returns they were targeting. With good ideas for bond arbitrage crowded and in short supply, LTCM headed into new territory, embarking on more aggressive relative value trading strategies where the outcomes were much harder to predict. Most of these trading strategies were 'market neutral' in that they were not predicated on interest rates or stock prices going up or down. However, unlike the early convergence trades, it was tough to judge how long they would need to hold their positions before convergence would turn a profit.

One of the new arbitrage ideas was a very large position in two classes of Royal Dutch Shell shares. Created by the merger of the Netherlands' Royal Dutch Petroleum with the UK's Shell Transport & Trading, this oil company was one of the largest in the world. The company retained stock market listings in The Netherlands as Royal Dutch and in the UK as Shell Transport and Trading, generating a number of pricing anomalies. One effect was currency driven as Royal Dutch shares were denominated in Dutch Guilders whilst those of Shell were denominated in British Pounds. Another difference arose from the local investment criteria by which their shareholders judged and valued the company, of which the dividends each share generated relative to other shares in their local stock market were of significant importance. As a consequence the same assets were valued differently by the two stock markets, and ostensibly presented a classic arbitrage opportunity.

In the summer of 1997, when the price of Royal Dutch shares traded between an 8% and 10% premium to that of Shell shares, LTCM took a $2.3 billion position, half of which were 'long' Shell shares that were judged to be cheap, the other half 'short' the relatively expensive Royal Dutch shares. As with their US Treasury bond trades LTCM was expecting the share prices of Royal Dutch and Shell to converge as their assets were the same. However with no timing or event pressure to bring this about, unlike the case with the regular and predictable 'on the run' issuance of US Treasury Bonds, there was no telling when this convergence would take place. By putting on their position, the weight of LTCM money initially moved the position their way. However this initial 'market impact' convergence gain was of no real benefit as reversing the position was likely to have the opposite effect, giving rise to a divergence loss. Indeed, by establishing the position carefully and minimising the market impact of the convergence trade, the big worry was always that a rapid forced closure would cause a much greater divergence loss on exit.

LTCM also took large positions in merger arbitrage territory, principally making bets on whether mergers would be successfully completed or not. This was a surprising strategy as success with this style of investment comes from information advantage, not the mathematics of mispricing where LTCM's real skills and competitive advantage lay.

Banking that volatility will pay heed to history

Another strategy; that of selling long term options on the S&P 500 index, made LTCM a major provider of protection against US stock market volatility. This protection was much in demand at the time, attracting high premiums from companies seeking to insure their pension funds from capital losses and retail investors fearful of a falling stock market. For pension funds it was the same worry that had made portfolio insurance so popular ten years before.

The arbitrage case made for this strategy was that the price of stock index options implied a future stock market volatility of 20%, yet the volatility then being experienced was closer to the long term mean of 15%. The expectation was that the market price of volatility would revert to the mean but, as with the Royal Dutch Shell arbitrage, there was no telling when this convergence would take place. With the benefit of hindsight, they would have been wise to have taken heed of the George Soros maxim: *"When you sell options, you get paid for assuming risk. That can be a profitable business, but it does not mix well with the risks inherent in a leveraged portfolio."*

This idea, which they considered to be *"volatility convergence arbitrage"*, carried a significant risk that had not been properly thought through. The many buyers of protection and an absence of sellers explained why the terms for selling protection had become so attractive. However, by effectively becoming the *"Bank of Volatility"* with themselves as the sole lenders and without any other significant sellers of volatility apart from themselves, the effect of LTCM ceasing to write this risk or, worse still, being forced to exit these option positions, was unquantifiable but likely to be very painful. They were later to find out how dangerous this oversight could be, when they were crystallising massive losses at prices implying an unthinkable stock market volatility of 38%.

Through leveraging their traditional strategies more, and taking on new styles of arbitrage with greater uncertainty of outcome, LTCM was taking on more risk than ever before. Making matters worse was that this risk was being amplified to even dizzier heights by the copycats who were replicating their strategies. With everyone facing the same way as LTCM there were potentially catastrophic consequences if they all chose to extricate themselves from their common positions at the same time.

Flight to liquidity has LTCM facing the wrong way

The key to LTCM's early money making had been to buy illiquid assets and sell more liquid ones trading at a premium price. The strategy had worked brilliantly whilst there was a liquidity premium to be captured and convergence had swiftly followed. The Achilles heel of this approach was if the liquidity premium widened instead of narrowing; divergence instead of convergence. Under such circumstances LTCM's leverage would increase rapidly as mark-to-market losses ate into their investment capital. Such circumstances might even create a liquidity crisis within LTCM itself, as they suffered losses and had no capital available to exploit the more attractive arbitrage terms that divergence would have opened up. In 1998 that is just what happened.

In the spring of 1998 the liquidity premium began to rise. Although LTCM was experiencing modest losses in their existing portfolio, they were initially encouraged by the wider pricing disparity that was opening up for new convergence arbitrage trades. It seemed that if they kept cool and waited for the tide to turn, LTCM would reap chunkier arbitrage returns as divergence in liquidity premiums reverted to convergence. Unfortunately the tide kept coming in and, such was their leverage, 6% of the fund value was lost in May with a further 10% in June, $461 million in all. Having just handed $2.7 billion back to investors, these losses hurt as the margin payments and collateral calls depleted their remaining investment capital.

In July 1998 the shift towards liquid assets received a further boost when Travelers, who now owned their alma mater Salomon, closed their fixed income arbitrage business after suffering heavy losses. Travelers was thought to be the 'biggest LTCM copycat', and the closure of their positions increased the divergence, causing the value of LTCM positions to fall still further. Making it worse, investors around the world were now selling foreign bonds and, in a 'flight to safety', were buying the most liquid US Treasury bonds. Under the weight of this heavy buying the premium for 'on the run' bonds kept rising. LTCM was now losing money not just on US Treasury bond positions, but on convergence trades all over the world. By the end of August their losses had swelled by another $1.85 billion, leaving the fund nursing a loss of over 50% of its value in just eight months. With losses mounting and a struggle to reduce the size of their positions, LTCM was left with just $2.3 billion of investment capital to support $130 billion of physical assets and a derivatives exposure in excess of $1 trillion.

When extraordinary financial market ructions took place in August 1998, following Russia's devaluation of the rouble and default on their debt, another severe weakness in their investment edifice became exposed; their risk models could not explain the scale of the losses LTCM was suffering. Built on data from more stable times when simultaneous shocks to many markets were unknown, they were finding that the expected benefits from diversification across the globe amongst many different asset classes was not in evidence. Their risk models could not explain the loss they had suffered in July except in anything other than extreme remote events.

Damage from inadvertent bet on credit

The Russian default also exposed a somewhat inadvertent bet of considerable magnitude on credit. This risk had come about through purchases of interest rate swap contracts as part of a convergence trade designed to take advantage of heavily overpriced long dated government bonds. With substantial liabilities decades in the future, pension funds and insurance companies had become almost forced buyers of long dated bonds on risk and regulatory grounds to match their financial commitments to their beneficiaries. In short supply, the price of long dated bonds had been bid up to levels where they were viewed as being substantially overvalued compared to equivalent bonds of shorter maturity. The natural convergence trade was for LTCM to sell the expensive long dated bonds and buy the cheaper short dated bonds. The nature of the trade was similar to that of the liquidity convergence trades from new issuance of US Treasury Bonds, although the timing of yield convergence was longer and less predictable. Where the inadvertent credit risk emerged was in taking the trade one step further. Instead of hedging through purchases of short dated bonds, LTCM bought interest rate swaps with the same cash flow characteristics, as these were cheaper to buy and hence served to sweeten the convergence terms even more. However, this final step was to prove fatal as, instead of carrying the risk of default by the US Government or another strong government issuer through purchasing bonds, they were now exposed through the swap contracts to the credit risk of their banking counterparty defaulting. In market parlance LTCM was *"long the credit spread"* between government and bank default risk. With no offsetting transaction to shield this credit risk and banks suffering from their loans to Russia and other weak borrowers, this credit spread widened as investors demanded a much higher rate of interest from banks to compensate for the increase in their default risk. What had started as a strategy to sweeten a convergence arbitrage had turned into an unhedged money loser on credit.

Market exodus from LTCM arbitrage positions

With the value of their fund falling, the leverage on their positions rose rapidly and, with their risk models unable to make sense of the situation, alarm set in. They had little choice other than to reduce their positions quickly to contain the risk and leverage, even though it meant driving prices against themselves and incurring heavier losses. Making it worse was that the copycats had also taken flight and were selling the same positions as LTCM aggressively. Now desperate, LTCM sought an urgent injection of capital from investors but none was forthcoming. By the end of the third week of September LTCM's capital had tumbled to just $400 million, and 90% of the fund's value had been lost over the course of the year. Their physical assets exceeded $100 billion leaving the fund with a gross leverage ratio over 250-to-1. Even after netting off long and short positions the leverage ratio stood at over 50-to-1: an adverse portfolio move of just 2% was likely to render the fund insolvent.

Forced to liquidate whatever positions it could, the fund crystallised heavy losses. The position in Royal Dutch Shell where they had expected the 8% Royal Dutch premium to converge closer to Shell, had instead blown out to 22%, costing the fund nearly $200 million. Other equity pairs trades of this nature, that their mathematical models had assessed to be low risk, also cost them dear.

And now the Wall Street hyenas were circling their giant prey. No longer friendly business partners, they were instead moving in for the kill. Through their copycat activity and other means, they proved to be remarkably well informed about LTCM's positions. Not helping either was that they could not 'camouflage' their trading activity amongst that of other client investment activity in the way the LTCM principals had been able to do at Salomon Brothers. Too big to be nimble, LTCM was left with little room for manoeuvre. Having made a lot of money being the liquidity provider to the market, they now desperately needed someone else to provide them with the same service. But there was none. Instead there was evidence that their banking counterparties were trading aggressively against them, some even suggesting that plans had been drawn up to force them into default so they could buy the LTCM portfolio at a knockdown price.

LTCM had historically borrowed and entered into derivative trades on generous terms and dealers regarded them as 'special', not least as their trading activity was a significant source of business. In good times these terms were extremely advantageous, allowing LTCM to borrow $100 to buy the same value of US Treasuries without paying any deposit at all, where most customers would be expected to suffer a 'haircut' of perhaps $10, meaning they had to provide $110 worth of collateral for a $100 loan. But now their lenders were forcing them to reduce their positions by refusing to provide the funding to 'roll' maturing positions. From being the liquidity provider which the market turned to, LTCM was now finding its own liquidity being called into question.

Collapse and Rescue

On Sunday 20th September 1998, the US Federal Reserve was appraised of LTCM's predicament when Peter Fisher, who would later become a colleague at BlackRock, was asked to go to LTCM's offices where he studied their investment books. Fisher ran the Fed's trading desk and was responsible for their $450 billion portfolio of government securities. The principal concern of the Fed was to determine the likely impact of LTCM's predicament on the broader financial system. It was not their role to save LTCM from default, nor to save their banking counterparties from financial loss. Their sole interest was 'systemic risk'.

There were a number of potential sources of systemic risk that bothered the Fed. Their *"oversized equity volatility position"* was a real worry as many pension funds and other conservative investors relied on these contracts to protect their share portfolios from loss. If this protection was to disappear with no means of replacing this protection elsewhere, uncontrolled selling of the US stock market, such as had happened in the 1987 portfolio insurance debacle, might ensue.

Another worry was that a failure of LTCM would mean that all their OTC derivative counterparties would lose the positions they had established with LTCM, leaving them *"naked"* to risks they thought they had covered. These counterparties would be holding one side of a contract for which the other side no longer existed. There would then be a rush as these counterparties sought to re-establish these positions elsewhere, potentially overwhelming the market as in a run on a bank.

The loss of OTC derivative positions would add further fuel to the fire of stock market selling from their equity volatility customers, as securities that LTCM had posted to counterparties as collateral were liquidated.

But there was something else in the mix that particularly worried the Fed, a crisis catalyst. This *"hair trigger"* to systemic risk disaster was an obscure clause in the legal documentation for OTC derivatives and securities financing relating to *"cross default"*. The cross default clause turned a payment default between LTCM and any one of their many counterparties into a general default with every other counterparty. This meant that were LTCM to fail to meet their contractual obligations to a single counterparty, every other counterparty would treat them as being in default, and prompt an immediate liquidation of all of the LTCM collateral held by banks and other parties.

There was one major lender in this position, Chase Manhattan, the bank John D. Rockefeller had established to look after Standard Oil's money. Chase was to purchase JP Morgan in 2000 and change its name to that of the JP Morgan banking powerhouse it is today.

LTCM had $900 million revolving credit facility from a syndicate of banks led by Chase with terms that made the banks anxious to terminate. Were that to hold a sniff of default then the cross default clauses would come into effect with potentially disastrous consequences. As Fisher described it to me: *"The problem that motivated me was the risk of a default on their line of credit with Chase, triggering cross-defaults on all their repo agreements which would legally require their counterparties to seize and sell all of LTCM's collateral, effectively, all of their assets into the market. This fire sale would have put enormous pressure on the system."*

With LTCM unable to raise more money themselves and running out of road, Fisher's saw a buyout by Warren Buffett as the best outcome: *"I thought most of what we were doing from Monday (21st September) to Wednesday was keeping things warm for Buffett, because the odds of his being successful were so much higher than the remote odds that the bankers could come together with a consortium capital injection."*

AIG, Goldman Sachs and Warren Buffett came up with a proposal to buy out the fund's partners for $250 million, inject $3.8 billion, and to operate LTCM within Goldman's own trading division. Buffett's interest was to buy the LTCM portfolio at a distressed price and publicly show it to be held in strong hands. This action alone would spark a substantial recovery in value as those betting on a forced liquidation on weak terms would be wrong-footed and close their bets. Buffett would then sell off the portfolio on much better terms, reaping a handsome profit. It was the same strategy that the Sultan of Brunei, in conjunction with Goldman, had proposed to rescue Barings over the weekend before their demise in 1995.

However the $250 million offer felt stunningly low to LTCM's partners, not least because the fund had been worth $4.7 billion at the start of the year. Furthermore the offer letter was not phrased in a manner that the two parties alone could agree and, with Meriwether given less than an hour to respond, the deal lapsed.

With an external rescue off the table the Federal Reserve was left with the choice of allowing LTCM to fail or to organise a bailout. Faced with the risk of contagion across the financial system, the Fed called in the heads of Wall Street's biggest investment banks to discuss LTCM's predicament on the evening of Tuesday 22nd September 1998. With the firm teetering on the brink of collapse, the Fed outlined their fear that the failure of LTCM could cause a chain reaction across global markets, causing catastrophic losses throughout the financial system. Against this background, it was agreed that a consortium of 14 Wall Street banks, who were also LTCM's major creditors, would immediately provide a $3.6 billion capital injection.

In return for this capital the participating banks received a 90% share in the fund and a promise that a supervisory board would be established. Connie Voldstad, one of the innovators in the early days of swap markets and who had been a member of the Bank of England's derivatives committee with me, was drafted across the Atlantic to join the oversight committee to lead the rescue and wind LTCM down. He knew from first-hand experience when Barings collapsed, how poor judgement can quickly turn crisis into disaster.

LTCM investors received a 10% stake, still worth about $400 million, but this money was completely consumed by their debts. The partners once had $1.9 billion of their own money invested in

LTCM, all of which had been wiped out.

Their collapse was as public as their success. The Washington Post described it as *"one of the biggest financial missteps ever to hit Wall Street"* whilst the Financial Times led with the headline *"the fund that thought it was too smart to fail"*. For Business Week the story was *"… rocket science exploded on the launch pad"*.

For the academics that 'déjà vu' feeling

For Mark Rubinstein who had been at the centre of the portfolio insurance debacle ten years earlier through the firm he co-founded, Leland, O'Brien Rubinstein (LOR), the resemblance was uncanny. In both cases, the potential difficulties for stability of the economy were enormous and the US Federal Reserve had felt it necessary to call investment bankers or corporations together to save the day. In addition, the cause also was wholly unexpected; an extremely rare event from a statistical perspective which actually came to pass. Rubinstein compared the debacle to his own with portfolio insurance: *"It was the same thing with LTCM. LTCM thought that all of its individual investments made sense. They were hedges, for the most part, and they were diversified internationally across different kinds of instruments. It was difficult for the firm to see how all its investments could go down together. And yet that's more or less what happened. The fund didn't have the diversification it thought it had."*

Warren Buffett's comments to his Berkshire Hathaway shareholders were perhaps the most insightful, not least as he knew the LTCM principals very well from his time at Salomon, and held them in high esteem. He took wry pleasure from LTCM coming to him for help whilst holding a short position in Berkshire Hathaway shares that would cost them $150 million. *"To make the money they didn't have and they didn't need, they risked what they did have and did need - that's foolish, that's just plain foolish. If you risk something that is important to you for something that is unimportant to you, it just does not make any sense. I don't care whether the odds are 100 to 1 that you succeed, or 1,000 to 1 that you succeed. If you hand me a gun with a thousand chambers or a million chambers, and there is a bullet in one chamber and you said 'put it to your temple and pull it' I'm not going to pull it. You can name any sum you want. It doesn't do anything for me on the upside, and I think the downside is fairly clear. I'm not interested in that kind of a game, and yet people do it financially without thinking about it very much".*

Aftermath or 'After Maths'

After the bailout, LTCM continued operations until 2000 when all the positions had been liquidated and the consortium of banks that financed the bailout had been paid back. Personal reputations of several of banking's finest were badly damaged, including that the Chairman of Union Bank of Switzerland (UBS) who resigned after the bank suffered a $780 million loss from their LTCM investment. The theories of Merton and Scholes were also to take a public beating.

Had the Fed not intervened, there are many who believe that an LTCM failure would have caused a stock market meltdown. Their view is that the oversized LTCM bet on equity market volatility and the forced liquidation of the assets they had posted as collateral, would have resulted in an uncontrollable stock market fire sale. Many years later the Fed was forced to step in again to prevent another oversized bet, this time on home loans by the insurance giant AIG, from doing the same. However, the final irony may be that Long-Term Capital Management did not have the long-term capital to survive a short-term crisis.

27. Enron and the virtual company experiment - Houston, Texas 2001

"Real generosity toward the future lies in giving all to the present"

Albert Camus (The Rebel 1951)

When guilty verdicts were handed down in May 2006 against Kenneth Lay and Jeffrey Skilling, both former Enron chief executives, it brought to a close the biggest fraud case in American corporate history. Lay was to die from a heart attack before sentencing, whilst Skilling was sentenced to twenty-four years in prison. The fraud had resulted in the collapse of America's seventh largest company, one of the world's leading energy companies with interests in many other industries. Enron had claimed revenues of over $100 billion in 2000, its final year of operation, and a stock market value of $68 billion. The collapse cost all 22,000 employees their jobs and much of their pensions. It was also to take down Arthur Andersen, one of the big five global accounting firms, who had been responsible for auditing Enron's financial statements. The fraud prompted an entire review of the way companies around the world were governed, with new laws enacted in the United States to prevent reoccurrence. With the focus of the investigation and press commentary on the accounting fraud, the economic story of a bold experiment by an energy giant to use derivatives to create a virtual company became overlooked. Yet this attempt may be Enron's enduring legacy.

The Genesis of Enron

When Lay and Skilling set to work, Enron was a real company in every sense. The company was the largest distributor of natural gas in the United States, owning a 37,000 mile long pipeline network stretching the length and breadth of the country. The company's genesis was the 1985 takeover of Houston Natural Gas by Internorth, the biggest natural gas pipeline company in the United States. Although Lay was Chief Executive of the junior partner, Houston Natural Gas, he quickly assumed control of the combined entity, moving Internorth's headquarters away from Omaha, Nebraska to his home town of Houston, Texas. The recommendation to relocate to Houston had been made by Jeff Skilling, then a McKinsey management consultant. It was a contentious decision in Omaha and their most prominent citizen, the investment titan Warren Buffett, wanted it reversed. As with many things in his business life Buffett was ultimately to have his way, playing a long game to achieve the outcome he sought.

By purchasing Houston Natural Gas for cash, Internorth had turned from being a company with little debt and strong cash generation into one saddled with a heavy debt load and poor cash flow. Oddly enough, weakening the company in this way had been a key objective behind the Houston Natural Gas acquisition. At the time Internorth was under attack by Irwin Jacobs, a corporate raider, who had built up a hostile 16.5% stake. Raiders of his ilk drew on the easy availability of bank financing to launch hostile takeover bids of publicly owned companies, using the target company's own cash flow to service their borrowings. The need by raiders to access reliable cash flow from their victims rendered the financially weak immune or *"shark proof"* from the attentions of opportunistic corporate raiders.

Lay went further, taking on even more debt to buy Jacob's share stake in the company. The main concern of management when under threat from corporate raiders was losing their jobs. If they succumbed to takeover they would be fired. Threatening management in this way was very popular and effective at the time.

Managers like Lay would pay a premium to the prevailing share price to rid their share register of unwelcome suitors. Under normal circumstances a corporate raider would expect to receive a discount to the prevailing share price when selling a large stake. By threatening management with the loss of their jobs it was a *"win win"* situation for the corporate raiders as they either gained control of the whole company or were thwarted and sold their shares to the company at a profit. This tactic, which was essentially corporate blackmail, became known as *"greenmail"* as it placed cash dollars (*"greenbacks"*) into the hands of the raiders whatever the outcome.

Greenmail was then so prevalent that managers created business and financial impediments to protect themselves from takeover by unwelcome predators. Special termination payments known as *"golden parachutes"* were introduced to cushion management from the financial suffering of being fired. In addition *"poison pills"* that damaged the company itself were released when the company fell into unwelcome hands. Once this tide of corporate raiding receded such defences were slowly reversed, not least as they served to protect poor management from being replaced by the shareholders who owned the company. In the years to come Enron was never able either to reduce this indebtedness or to improve cash generation. It was a weakness that would ultimately lead to Enron's demise.

Good money had been paid to brand consultants to come up with Enteron as a *"strong new name"* for the merged company. However, with stationery, advertising, legal contracts and all the accoutrements of corporate presence fresh and gleaming on desks and offices, a comment in the Wall Street Journal that Enteron was the Greek term for intestine or the digestive tract led to a rethink. The company name was hastily shortened to Enron. It was unfortunate that they did not also change their brand logo too as this 'Crooked E' moniker came to symbolise corporate dishonesty as the scandal unfolded.

Friends in high places

When Skilling joined Enron from McKinsey in 1990 the US natural gas industry was facing a simple but fundamental difficulty; the interaction between buyers and sellers was no longer working. Until 1989 the industry had been regulated by a government entity which set the price that producers, pipeline companies, and local utilities paid for natural gas. Through a series of changes in state and federal laws, the industry had progressively become deregulated, leaving the natural gas price to be determined by the vagaries of the market.

Lay had lobbied hard for the deregulation of energy markets, cultivating strong political influence to help bring this about, the most important of which was the Texan Bush family. US President George Bush Senior had encouraged the deregulation process and supported legislation through Congress through which Enron obtained taxpayer subsidies for their investments. Lay enjoyed a particularly warm relationship with his son George W. Bush, then Governor of Texas, furthering his political ambitions by lending him an Enron corporate jet and making substantial contributions to his Presidential campaign. By the time *"George W"* had become President this relationship had earned Lay the affectionate sobriquet of *"Kenny Boy"*.

Natural Gas market becomes dysfunctional after deregulation

When deregulation came into effect Lay saw it as Enron's mission to aggressively exploit the new opportunities that market forces presented, at the expense of their more staid rivals. Everyone in the gas chain from producer to consumer was struggling to contend with the new environment, the main difficulty being the volatility of the market price of natural gas. Whilst there was a predictable core demand for gas, its price and volume fluctuations at the margin were substantial and unpredictable. And it was this marginal demand and supply that now determined the daily market or 'spot' price. A sudden cold spell in the northeast could cause the spot price to rise overnight, hurting consumers. By contrast a period of warm weather could depress demand and prices, resulting in gas producers losing money. Making matters worse was that over 75% of the spot market trading took place over a frantic few days of deal making at the end of each month.

For a gas industry with long lead times for exploration and production, as well as for capital investment in pipelines and power plants, this state of affairs was dysfunctional. Even with an industry-wide glut of natural gas, the biggest industrial users could not be sure that they would be supplied with the volume of natural gas they needed from one month to the next. Pipeline companies like Enron were unable to guarantee a long-term supply to their customers as they also had no means of securing a steady supply of gas at a profitable price. Deregulation appeared to mean that everyone in the supply chain was now exposed to the vagaries of price and volume risks they had not faced before. It was turning many industrial users away from natural gas to oil and coal, on the grounds that natural gas was no longer a reliable energy source.

Making it worse for pipeline companies like Enron was the style of contract demanded by natural gas producers. Known as *"Take or Pay"* contracts they required the pipeline company to pay for the amount of gas they had contracted to purchase, whether or not they took the gas. As the only way for producers to sell their natural gas was through the local pipeline network, Take or Pay contracts were essential. If not the pipeline companies could exert enormous pricing power on producers by threatening to leave them with no revenue by sourcing cheaper gas elsewhere.

Whilst these contracts made sure gas producers were not left at the mercy of their distributors, they also meant that pipeline companies like Enron were left to carry the burden of low gas demand from consumers. When demand was weak their revenues suffered from lower sales without an offsetting fall in their natural gas costs.

Skilling's Gas Bank

Skilling's idea was to create what he called the *"Gas Bank"*. It was nothing less than the first serious effort to diminish the level of risk now faced by everyone in the natural gas supply chain. The basic idea was that producers would contract to sell their gas to Enron whilst gas consumers would contract to buy their gas from Enron. Enron would act in the same way that banks intermediate between borrowers and lenders, earning a margin or 'spread' between the price they paid producers and the price they charged consumers. For both sellers and buyers of natural gas, the uncertainty of the spot market would be replaced by the contractual certainty of the Gas Bank. In truth Enron was performing much the same role as the regulator had before, although claiming they were better at keeping price and demand in tune with market reality than a government controlled regulator.

As long as Enron had a balanced book of matching purchase and sales of natural gas contracts secured at prices which gave the firm a decent profit margin, the vagaries of the spot market price would have minimal impact on the natural gas supply chain. To achieve this Enron needed a mechanism to deal with order imbalances between supply and demand, in much the same way as a bank needs access to other funding sources to deal with imbalances between borrowers and depositors. Furthermore, just as banks hedge the interest rate risk of funding money imbalances with interest rate derivatives, Enron needed a hedging mechanism to lay off the price risk from natural gas order imbalances. As no market in natural gas derivatives existed, Enron created one. Later on they went even further and developed a weather derivatives market to deal with the effect that temperature had on the volume of gas consumed.

But they could do more than just hedge. Like an investment bank, they could make money from the flow of information they could glean from customers of their pipeline business. Being the biggest player and operating in every link in the chain, Enron knew and saw more than anyone else. It was a throwback to the coffee house era of the 1600s, when share trading without access to privileged information was regarded as unprofessional and risky. Their business model was similar to that of Edward Lloyd which turned the trading and information flows exchanged in his coffee house into the Lloyd's Insurance Market. They were also turning back the clock on insider trading as the rules on disclosure for financial markets were largely not applicable. With gas competing with other fuels and energy forms, Enron developed their trading in derivatives across their core businesses, first gas and oil, and then anything energy related. The combination of information and a dominant position in opaque markets that they controlled was a heady mix for profit. Enron Gas Bank was much more than a bank for the energy trade; it was the marketplace too.

And it worked. When combined with their trading in natural gas futures and other energy derivative contracts, Enron became in effect an energy bank with a real sustainable competitive edge over their rivals. In the early years when pricing conditions were particularly favourable, Enron raked in the profits.

The magic of mark-to-market accounting

Enron no longer saw themselves as a conventional industrial company but as a bank operating within a free energy market. They therefore claimed that their accounting treatment should be changed to that of a bank, where profitability is assessed on a *"mark-to-market"* basis.

With conventional accounting realised gains or losses over the financial year are booked to the profit and loss account. With mark-to-market accounting expected future gains or losses are also attributed to the current financial year accounts. The way in which future gains and losses are assessed is by comparing the current market price for selling the investment with the original acquisition cost. Mark-to-market accounting makes a lot of sense for shares or other investments that can be freely bought and sold, at transparent market prices that everyone can see. The approach is less robust when the investment is not traded regularly and the market price is difficult to assess. Using simple and widely accepted financial techniques to discount future cash flows does not do the trick as an alternative, since the assumptions and the price a buyer will pay are often very different from such *"mark-to-model"* values. With complex models, or where the assets are illiquid with no equivalent market price, mark-to-market prices become very hard to validate and open to manipulation. On occasions the value attributed is closer to fiction than fact, and regarded as *"marked-to-myth"*.

Lay and Skilling knew that if Enron was stuck with the conventional accounting approach for a commercial business, their lack of cash and heavy debt load would confine them to a slow moving strategy as they progressively built up cash and paid down debt. But this was not the pace that Lay and Skilling had in mind. Mark-to-market accounting would sidestep this problem and allow them to advance more rapidly. That was why approval of mark-to-market accounting by the US Securities and Exchange Commission (SEC) in 1992 was a cause for great celebration at Enron.

But there were two snags. The first was that bringing future earnings forward meant that efforts today only bore fruit for one year, producing nothing afterwards. With no recurring revenues Enron would have to start afresh each year and find new projects and sources of earnings. The second snag was that these new projects needed a great deal of cash up-front, yet Enron had very little. Mark-to-market accounting did nothing to their real cash. And so began a mighty deception to hide their shortage of cash and heavy debt load, whilst marking-to-myth the value of the projects and businesses they undertook.

Who needs a real business when you can create a virtual replica

Enron's business model for the natural gas industry seemed applicable to other energy industries. They tested it out on other forms of energy and found the formula worked reasonably well. In

Skilling's view, perhaps wearing his management consultant hat, this was a recipe that could be deployed across industries outside the energy sector that were not riven with regulation around insider trading like financial markets.

In Skilling's view Enron's future lay in an *"asset light"* strategy, driven by brainpower not physical infrastructure. Physical assets were an initial foundation stone for accessing trading relationships and gathering an information 'edge' over competitors. Their gas pipeline system had performed this role in the natural gas market and a dominant market position had been won. Once you had established relationships across the supply chain and garnered price control through trading exposure in the underlying asset through derivative contracts, all of the capital and resources tied up by owning and managing the physical assets became superfluous and could be released.

The Skilling formula was to buy the physical infrastructure needed to crack the code and to build a new trading business that secured fast and comprehensive information flow. Once established they would sell the physical assets, leaving Enron with a virtual business where economic exposure was held and hedged almost entirely through derivatives. For a debt laden company like Enron this business model meant that their lack of capital and weak cash flow would not be an impediment to growth.

With this in mind Enron began to apply their energy market formula to other businesses. In the process they pioneered derivative trading in new markets, including weather and fibre optics. By creating and dominating these new markets before competitors and regulators knew what was going on, the money continued to flood in. Buoyed by success, Enron was loved by investors and its share price soared. The virtual business concept needed little capital and meant that Enron could run a much bigger business than would have been possible had they physically owned the underlying core businesses.

In the electricity industry they purchased Portland General and began trading in electricity derivatives. Subsequently Skilling bought paper mills and traded pulp and paper. For their final push Enron built a billion dollar fibre network and launched broadband trading.

The brilliance of the idea and apparent implementation success resulted in Enron being voted *"America's most innovative company"* by the influential Forbes magazine for six consecutive years. Giving an early sign that hubris might be setting in, the lobby wall of their Houston headquarters which described the company's mission as: *"From the world's leading energy company to… the world's leading company"*.

'Asset light' strategy proves to be heavy on capital and cash

But there was a paradox in implementing this asset light strategy that was to become Enron's fatal flaw. A great deal of capital was initially required to purchase the physical assets from which they could gain the market information that would give them trading edge over competitors. The first act in establishing a successful virtual business was to purchase a physical business. And the physical assets did not come cheap as it was no good going in gently to *"test the water"* by purchasing a small player. If you wanted to become the focal point for industry information, you had to target the biggest players. For a company weighed down by debt and short of cash flow, Enron was not best placed to spend vast sums of money on businesses and projects where the revenue and cash flow fruits were some way off. But that is what they did, and dealing with the consequences was to dominate their subsequent behaviour.

Enron's strategy for funding entry into new industries was to match the cost of purchasing physical assets in the new industry with the sale of assets in industries where their virtual business was already up and running. It was with this in mind that they sought to sell Enron Oil and Gas, their gas exploration and production business, in 1995. As one follower of the company commented: *"they didn't feel they needed the gas wells and the people. If they wanted to go long (buy) gas, they could just do it through the trading floor".* Without the physical assets Enron felt they could be nimbler since they were not shouldering the cumbersome management burden of running the underlying business.

But the cash raised from selling physical assets in established Enron businesses did not come close to meeting those for funding new enterprises. Enron was hiring too many people and spending a great deal of money trying to make their new businesses grow. Furthermore the bulk of the value they were ostensibly creating which was shown in their mark-to-market accounting statements, was unrealised and generating no cash. The faster they rolled out their virtual business plan, the more cash they needed. As a consequence Enron had to come up with bigger and bigger profitable projects every year to maintain the illusion of earnings growth which, in turn, worsened still further their cash position.

Their two aims when establishing an Enron to see off corporate raiders, weak cash flow and a heavy debt load, were now magnified many times over and presented a new challenge; how to find real cash and how to conceal their mounting debt. The attempt to resolve these failings in their business model was the genesis of a massive financial fraud that first papered over the cracks and ultimately brought Enron crashing down.

A cash cow called securitisation

Debt and lack of cash would have undone Enron much sooner, but for securitisation, a new technique for raising capital that Skilling had learned about whilst a management consultant at McKinsey. Securitisation allows loans or other assets to be pooled together and then sold to investors in the form of securities. These securities can then be bought and sold in the market, just like stocks and shares. For instance a credit card company, instead of tying up its own capital by keeping credit card loans on its balance sheet, could bundle them together and sell them to investors. Investors, not the credit card company, would then have capital tied up in the loans, and receive the payments from the credit card holders. Investors would also carry the risk of non payment by credit card holders. Meantime the credit card company could use the cash proceeds from the securitisation transaction to lend more money. One of Skilling's consulting colleagues had tellingly commented in 1987 that: *"securitisation's potential… is great because it removes capital and balance sheets as constraints on growth"* adding that *"most financial services companies would be greatly aided by securitising their loan portfolios."*

Securitisation, in principle, provided genuine economic benefits when used to transfer risk and release capital. The practice was usefully applied to a variety of loans from mortgages, credit card receivables and auto loans. By opening the door to a broader base of capital providers, investors could gain access to a broader range of asset classes, with their trading in capital markets removing an illiquidity constraint on bank balance sheets.

For Enron, securitisation was an even more powerful tool, almost the magic lamp of a genie that made debt disappear whilst provided real cash in hand. Future returns on projects could be sold for cash today, leaving investors waiting for future cash flow, not Enron. Furthermore the same mechanism could take debt from new projects off the Enron balance sheet, by placing borrowings alongside the future cash flow in a standalone trust that was owned by investors, not Enron.

But securitisation was not quite as magical as Enron hoped. Investors were only interested in securitised assets that they understood and that could be modelled with reasonable reliability. Most tellingly investors preferred assets that generated immediate cash flow. The assets Enron wanted to securitise came from unusual projects that generated little near term cash flow. Wedded to securitisation, but finding there was little investor appetite for the myriad of assets they wished to offload, Enron ended up selling their securitisation deals to the only people who would buy them, the banks who were structuring them. And the banks would only do so if the small print in the legal documentation saddled Enron with the debt and risk if things went wrong.

Most of the Enron securitisation deals were of this nature. Known as *"boomerangs"* they acted just like the Australian hunting weapon that is shaped to return to its thrower if the target is missed. Desperate to hide debt and generate cash, Enron securitised just about everything that was not *"nailed down"*; fuel supply contracts, shares of common stock, partnership interests and even uncertain future profits expected from many of their international assets. The latter included power plants in Puerto Rico, Turkey and Italy, on which, between 1997 and 2000, they had booked profits of $366 million.

Securitisation, at least the way Enron did it, provided a great short-term cash flow boost. But, as with most Enron deals, the cash was really more debt and a ticking time bomb at that, since most of these borrowings were not supported by assets of equivalent value. As an international Enron executive described one of these securitisation deals: *"It was a purported sale, but it looked and smelled like a financing… not least as the money was coming from banks not investors"*.

Structured finance builds an accounting house of cards

Whilst securitisation generated both cash and earnings, it was not enough on its own to solve Enron's cash flow and debt shortcomings. To overcome these issues they turned to structured finance, an obscure field of finance that can achieve outcomes that transfer risk and other obligations through all manner of complex legal and corporate entities.

For Enron, the most important cash generating device was known as a *"prepay"* and was later to be described by Enron's bankruptcy examiner as the company's *"quarter-to-quarter cash flow lifeblood"*. A typical example would be for Enron to enter into an agreement to deliver natural gas or oil over a period to an ostensibly independent offshore entity for an upfront cash payment. This cash was lent to the offshore entity by a bank who, through a separate contract with Enron, would agree to deliver the same natural gas or oil to Enron for a series of payments over the life of the contract. If one put the transactions together there was no natural gas or oil moving at all. There was only an upfront payment from the bank to Enron in return for a series of payments by Enron to the bank. To all intents and purposes it was a loan that had been structured so that it did not appear as such.

Enron entered into $8.6 billion of these transactions that the bankruptcy examiner described as: *"in substance debt"* but were instead accounted for as trading liabilities. And the banks structuring these deals were placing clauses in the documentation to protect themselves if Enron overreached itself. Some loans became immediately repayable if the Enron share price fell below a certain level. Others were triggered if Enron's credit rating was downgraded.

So adept was Enron's Chief Financial Officer Andrew Fastow and his team at coming up with ways of raising cash and hiding debt that one of their banking counterparties accorded them the highest martial arts status of *"black belts"* in structured finance.

Fraud the last refuge as cash runs out and edifice tumbles

Through the aggressive use of securitisation, structured finance and other accounting devices, Fastow and his team kept the company afloat. Even though the edifice was crumbling, the firm's reputation continued to rise. Enron was lauded for the way they had transformed the manner in which gas and electricity flowed across the United States. Their global reputation was burnished by bankrolling audacious projects in developing countries. Amongst these was a state of the art power plant at Dabhol in India, a steel mill on the coast of Thailand, and a pipeline slicing through endangered Brazilian rainforest. It was in this vein that the Nobel Laureate and

South African President Nelson Mandela came to Houston in 1999 to receive the Enron Prize.

The purpose of all the structured finance deals that Fastow and his team cooked up was to mitigate their debt and cash flow difficulties. These deals kept fresh debt off the books, camouflaged existing debt, and allowed Enron to book decent earnings with some semblance of a healthy operating cash flow. It enabled Enron to borrow the billions of dollars needed to stay in the game. Making Enron's transactions so bewildering was their sheer number and the way they mutated to strip out additional accounting benefits. One vehicle would act as a building block for another, so that unravelling one transaction meant half-a-dozen others had to be closed off. As Steven Cooper, the CEO appointed to wind down Enron after its bankruptcy, described the flow chart that plotted the resulting tangle: *"It looks like some deranged artist went to work one night."*

There was fraud too. Although most of Enron's Special Purpose Entities (SPEs) technically included the 3% of third party money that was assumed to provide an 'arm's length' market value, their independence was undermined by Enron giving implicit, and sometimes even explicit, guarantees that it would cover any losses suffered by investors and lenders. Furthermore, by tossing derivatives called total return swaps into the mix, Enron guaranteed the investor a debt-like return whilst leaving themselves with the actual return on the asset or business. On occasion they even added a cheeky twist by marking-to-market the estimated value that it expected to receive from the asset. Put another way, Enron had 'sold' something and booked earnings and cash flow from the 'sale'. But the asset was not truly gone. They had a big slug of additional debt to be repaid and the asset could still bite them if its value fell. The court-appointed bankruptcy examiner later concluded that much of Enron's liquidity was the *"result, in effect, of loans to Enron for which Enron retained the ultimate liability"*. In other words Enron was lending money to itself.

Enron was not just efficient in creating the illusion of cash and corporate earnings through their structuring and domicile. They used similar techniques to avoid paying tax by locating nearly nine hundred subsidiaries in tax havens. In spite of its size Enron paid no tax at all for four of the last five years of operation.

End of the charade

With so many balls in the air it became impossible to manage the huge mess that the charade had become. Skilling resigned and Fastow departed leaving their public relations machine to cook up the pretence that all was still well. But it was quickly seen through as myriad other pointers to disaster emerged. In November 2001 Enron restated its earnings for 2000 to disclose $586m of losses and barely a week later it admitted to a $690m bank loan due a fortnight later that could not be repaid. The game was up.

It took more than three years to bring Skilling and Lay to justice. 22,000 Enron employees lost their jobs along with 85,000 employees from their auditors Arthur Andersen after they were convicted for obstruction of justice for shredding over three tons of Enron documents.

Although Enron was then the biggest bankruptcy in US history, it was soon to be eclipsed in magnitude by the collapse of WorldCom the following year. 2002 was also to witness an even worse example of hubris and executive extravagance when Tyco unravelled. Yet even now, after more recent large bankruptcies like that of Lehman in 2008, it is Enron that still commands the most attention. Enron destroyed the faith of the American people in the stock market and sparked the draconian Sarbanes-Oxley Act passed in 2002 and the related stiff regulation that now infuses every part of US business.

A book referencing Lay and Skilling in the title as *The Smartest Guys in the Room*, telling the story of the rise and fall of Enron, was successfully turned into a film with the same title. It is a tale even the most fertile imagination could not conjure up, not least the closing scene featuring a sombre former US President George Bush attending the funeral of a disgraced Kenneth Lay. Perhaps that is why a play written several years later entitled simply *Enron* held packed London theatre audiences in thrall as the greed, ambition and arrogance was acted out on stage. It played less well when taken to New York.

But in the real world of commerce, a different game was playing out. Off stage that wily old investment warrior, Warren Buffett, was quietly picking over the bones of the bankrupt Enron. Through his investment vehicle Berkshire Hathaway he bought Northern Natural, the pipeline business that carried Texan gas north into America's industrial heartland. In all the corporate chicanery this real business had almost become forgotten. By adding America's largest natural gas distributor to his stable of companies Buffett took control of the most valuable asset in the original Enron. He also did something he had wanted to do all along; bring the corporate headquarters back to his own home town of Omaha, Nebraska. The Houston nightmare was finally over.

28. Banks turn into money making machines

"A bank is a place that will lend you money if you can prove that you don't need it"

Bob Hope (1903-2003)

Enron was not the only player in the virtual business. The people they relied upon to make the model work, the banks, were themselves already well down the virtual road. They were moving away from relationships with customers they knew and met in the flesh, to a much cheaper model with little personal interaction. Whilst decreasing the cost of servicing clients, this lack of customer knowledge was increasing their business risk, as loan evaluation was carried out remotely by electronic discourse and solely on the numbers. It was a road that would lead the banks away from their core economic role as credit evaluators and distributors of money across the economy, and into profit engines of unimaginable power and influence.

To the outside world this shift in emphasis by those in the money business was harder to spot and comprehend than when commercial businesses like Enron headed this way. As the banks headed into virtual space their progress went almost unnoticed.

'Old Style' banking model

It was a far cry from their origins and traditions. Banking had been a business that made money by lending money to borrowers at a higher rate of interest than the rate they paid to their depositors. The business risk they carried was that their borrowers would fail to repay their loans, or that depositors would cease to trust them and withdraw their money. Knowing and connecting personally with their customers was then a critical component of their business model. For depositors, placing money in a bank is no different from handing over your purse or wallet to someone for safekeeping. If a bank's trustworthiness is in doubt, or depositors perceive that their money is at risk, they will move their money elsewhere, leaving the bank with nothing to lend and their business gone. That is why the image cultivated by bankers for centuries had been one of austere and prudent individuals, not swashbuckling entrepreneurs. It was also why their retail branch managers sought to be seen as pillars of respectability and good standing in their local community.

The mainstay of banking over the years had been to lend the money of individuals to business. The advent of individuals as substantial borrowers is relatively recent, first becoming prevalent in the 1960s. The seeds of the subsequent consumer credit boom were sown by the creation and mass issuance of credit cards and other forms of consumer debt. At the same time banks progressively withdrew from direct customer contact as first computers and then the internet were seen as the means to cut servicing costs. The resulting loss of customer knowledge would later prove to be a very expensive weakness.

Successful banks were those that correctly assessed the ability of their customers to repay loans, so that defaults from bad loans were minimal and the interest charged to borrowers was commensurate with their repayment risk. Banks used to spend a lot of time and resource assessing the ability of their customers to repay their loans. It kept their depositors confident that their money was safe. And banks of this nature had a genuine economic purpose as they were financing businesses and employment as well as enabling their customers to buy the homes, cars or other goods that they needed. The banks had a core role in the economic infrastructure which no one else fulfilled in any meaningful way.

To help guard against loss, particularly from large loans, banks often took an ownership right or 'charge' over their customers' assets. In the case of homes this charge took the form of a mortgage over the borrower's property. If the terms of the loan were not met the bank could take possession and sell the house to recover their loan, condemning those who failed to meet their interest and capital repayments to homelessness, the modern equivalent of King

Hammurabi's slavery.

With the banks holding such an important role in the functioning of the economy, governments and their agents put additional safeguards in place to secure the health and strength of the banking system. The most important of these measures was the amount of capital banks had to set aside as a buffer against losses from bad loans. The more a bank lent out, the more capital they had to hold. Banking supervisors regularly inspected the banks and held statutory powers giving them full legal access to examine loan books, risk management systems and the capital held. If any or all of these criteria were judged to be inadequate, the supervisor could close the bank down. It was a very transparent state of affairs designed to be safe and prudent.

And it was not a particularly onerous business model. If a bank had strong expertise and reputation for assessing credit risk and good customers borrowing and lending their money the business could even be 'relaxing' in the manner of the '3-6-3' banking maxim: *"Take money in at 3%, lend it out at 6%, and be on the golf course by 3pm."*

Capital markets make inroads into lending business

The banks' progression into virtual banking was not entirely of their choosing. Their largest business customers had progressively been deserting them in favour of capital markets during the 1980s, as companies increasingly borrowed money direct from investors by issuing corporate bonds instead of taking out bank loans. Until then borrowing direct from investors was a relatively small part of corporate borrowing, although countries had been engaging investors direct since the 1600s through the issue of securities on government debt. Corporate bond issuance had transferred lucrative business from commercial banks to their capital market cousins, the investment banks who, as their name suggests, made it their business to have the strongest possible ties to companies and investors. This trend was never to reverse and nowadays most large corporate loans are sourced directly from investors.

Investment banks earned their keep by intermediating between investors with money to lend directly to companies seeking capital to develop their businesses. Investment banks were not allowed and did not particularly want any direct interaction with retail depositors and all the associated infrastructure of bank branches. In this way they avoided all the costs and regulatory controls that came with depositors. Instead they focussed all their firepower on companies; and big business in particular. The commercial banks had begun to follow suit either through acquisition or by building up their investment banking capabilities in securities distribution and trading. In the United States, the world's biggest capital market, banks had been prohibited from mixing of deposit taking with securities distribution and trading by the Glass-Steagall Banking Act of 1933. This law had progressively been relaxed in the 1980s and 1990s, encouraged by the Hayek induced mood in favour of unfettered free markets. After much lobbying by the big commercial banks, the Glass-Steagall Act was partially repealed in 1999, ending the affiliation restrictions, and enabling holding companies to own investment and commercial banks.

Glass-Steagall had been passed in the wake of the Wall Street Crash of 1929 to outlaw conflicts of interest between the securities and banking businesses. The riskier securities business was separated from commercial banking so that the cash of depositors could not be used or put at risk by speculating on stock markets. Banking regulators had noted that there had not been sufficient capital and controls for the securities activities of banks. Depositors had felt that their money was not safe, and caused 'runs' on bank deposits as customers rushed to withdraw their money. When this happened the government was often forced to intervene, using taxpayer money to shore up a banking system devoid of trust and robust capital strength.

In a sense Glass-Steagall was an early manifestation of the notion that was later to be referred to as: *"too big to fail"* in the financial crisis of 2008, and was the legislative consequence of the mayhem and bank runs of the 1929 financial crisis. The Glass-Steagall Act broke up banks like the titan JP Morgan into the deposit taking core that continued to bear the name of its founder John Pierpont Morgan (1837-1913), and an investment banking offshoot named Morgan Stanley that was founded by his grandson Henry Morgan with Harold Stanley. An international offshoot called Morgan Grenfell, not subject to Glass-Steagall, was also established in London. The latter firm was later to be purchased by Deutsche Bank in 1990.

Bank business model turned on its head

The banking model that was now emerging was one designed to capitalise on the twin financial trends of deregulation and globalisation. The winning banking formula was judged to be one of access to as big a pool of capital as possible, and the ability to carry out every form of corporate banking and securities trading activity all over the world. Their biggest clients were becoming increasingly global in their outlook and reach and expected their banks to service them wherever they operated. It also enabled the banks to do their business in the lowest tax and most lightly regulated jurisdictions for their clients and increasingly for themselves. As a result unusual exotic locations became 'offshore tax havens' to the financial industry.

Deregulation also allowed banks to trade for themselves instead of acting solely as agents for external investors. Through their principal or proprietary books their *"customer comes first"* principle was eroded as their most important client became themselves. And for the most aggressive banks, their clients did not just become *"second fiddle"*; they unwittingly were to find themselves allies and victims of the banks that they had assumed were their paid agents and acting in their interests. Customer trading flows were used by bank 'prop' desks to inform their own decision making and to hide or disguise their own trading by mixing it in with customer business. One major investment bank even described their customer business as *"camouflage"* as it gave their proprietary trading desk competitive advantage over hedge funds which did not have this means of disguise.

As investors and regulators became aware of these conflicts of interest the banks, through powerful and persistent political lobbying, held them at bay by claiming they kept activities that could compete or compromise customer business separate through internal barriers created by them called *"Chinese Walls"*. But it was the banks with the weakest walls that were the most profitable and dragged the industry as a whole to the lowest common denominator in the race for profits. For many a Chinese wall was more a concept than reality as these walls were typically virtual not physical. As one banker put it: *"We make sure there are no Chinese policing them".*

JP Morgan is seen by many to be the first of the major banks to spot this change to the banking model and to act upon it. In the early 1980s the bank had earned most of its money by making commercial loans. By 1993 lending was no longer the principal profit driver with over 75% of their revenues now coming from investment banking fees and trading profits. It was a shift in their banking model that investment analysts put down to: *"the new forms of finance"* with derivatives the most important of these new forms. In 1994, when Sir Dennis Weatherstone, their Chairman and Chief Executive, retired Fortune quoted one of his senior colleagues describing derivatives as: *"the basic business of banking".*

It would have disappointed Sir Sigmund Warburg who back in 1946 set out with Henry Grunfeld to create a firm of *"merchant adventurers who have to act with a high degree of punch and panache".* The SG Warburg bank which they created ensured that even their boldest endeavours were never at conflict with the interests of their clients. For the new breed of giant universal banks such principles were now a recipe for failure at the hands of less scrupulous competitors. The new mood accepted that, to some extent, a successful bank had to be in competition and at conflict with its clients. It created a 'race to the bottom' of principled decision making. Fortunately

Sigmund Warburg, who died in 1982, was not alive to see his own firm SG Warburg fail in its efforts to go down the universal bank route, ultimately falling into the hands of what was to become Switzerland's answer to the universal bank model, Union Bank of Switzerland (UBS) in 1995. It may have been more than sheer coincidence that UBS decided to retire the Warburg name from its roster of brand names in 2003 just before a series of events, which are covered later, that suggest that the Warburg principles fell away at the same time.

Customer deposits become a capital markets engine

Commercial banks now began to see their access to depositors as a key competitive tool for taking on their established investment banking cousins. Instead of relying on strong links to investors to provide the capital to complete deals with corporate borrowers, a new concept known as the *"bought deal"* emerged where banks could draw on the capital they held from customer deposits to guarantee a corporate customer the funds that they were seeking. In a bought deal the bank would commit to underwrite the entire corporate debt issue, putting the bank at risk if investors did not subscribe for the deal on the terms agreed with their corporate client. They charged fat fees for so doing, often taking for themselves 3% of the funds being raised. As for their depositors, they were not aware of the fact that it was their money that was being put at risk to provide the commercial banks with competitive advantage in securities markets.

The investment banks were quick to spot this change in the market dynamic as, on their home territory of mergers and acquisitions, they found they were losing business to the commercial banks. The investment banks realised that they had to sharpen up their access to capital, cash in particular, if they were to hold on to and advance their securities franchise. Somehow they had to be able to guarantee funding to acquisitive corporate customers without first having to seek funding support from investors in the form of deal underwriting. If not, the commercial banks would be seen to consummate deals more quickly and with greater certainty than investment banks, thereby stealing their most lucrative source of revenues from under their noses. It was this era of fierce competitive fighting for leadership in mergers and acquisitions that enabled a generation of corporate raiders with little capital of their own to come to the fore. It was also the reason why individuals like Irwin Jacobs were able to persuade frightened management in cash rich targeted companies like Internorth to buy Houston Natural Gas and to create the structurally debt laden Enron.

Seeking retail depositors was not a path the investment banks wished to follow but was the one the commercial banks took. They grew bigger and bigger in their relentless pursuit of financial firepower through an acquisition spree of commercial banks. Commercial banks also bought investment banks for their deal making skills and corporate relationships. Citibank went a step further by merging with the insurance giant Travelers Group in 1998 to become the world's biggest financial services company, with a war chest of capital greater than anyone else. Indeed it was this tussle for supremacy and scale that was the origin of the banks becoming so big that taxpayers had to come to their rescue with massive injections of capital when they were in danger of collapse in 2008.

Oddly enough regulators were encouraging the banks in this quest for size as their experience with failing US savings and loans companies in the 1980s had led them to associate size with safety.

Commercial Paper and Repo - the secret sauce of capital for investment banks

The investment banks took a different path to gain the cash firepower for the bought deal. In a frenzy of takeovers and mergers in the late 1980s many investment banks tied up with commercial banks to gain access to capital and stay competitive. Others fought fiercely to maintain their independence and worked assiduously to develop an alternative source of capital by developing a vibrant business to business market in short term debt securities called Commercial Paper (CP). Once established these banks then worked hard to cultivate a strong presence and reputation for their own names within the commercial paper market.

The banks were aided in this task by the growing appetite from investors to hold their cash in money market funds instead of bank deposits, a shift that gave investment banks funding from retail investors through commercial paper on a scale and on similar terms to the commercial banks, but without the heavy cost of running a branch network. This source of funds was to become so vibrant and easy to tap that the idea of leveraging their activities to ever dizzier heights took hold, leading one commentator to refer to the practice as *"the heroin of unsecured funding"*.

Commercial paper (CP) the overdraft facility of big business

Commercial paper is simply a tradable short term loan. These loans can be made for one day ("overnight") or run for as long as nine months. They are money market securities and typically issued by banks and large companies to cover their short term funding needs. As commercial paper is unsecured and only backed by a promise to repay on the maturity date, only the strongest banks and companies can access cash at reasonable prices by going down this route.

Maintaining good standing with credit rating agencies, like Standard & Poors or Moodys, is very important for commercial paper issuers. Otherwise unsecured funding becomes prohibitively expensive and only secured short term funding supported by collateral is available.

But commercial paper could not meet all the capital needs of banks. Investors would not lend unlimited amounts of money to investment banks on an unsecured basis nor on interest rate terms that were as attractive as those from retail depositors that their commercial banking competitors enjoyed. Investors needed to be offered some form of security. The secured funding mechanism which investment banks built up when leveraging their business, and which was to become their prime source of financing, was the repurchase agreement or 'repo'. With repo agreements the borrower passes collateral in the form of other securities to the lender in much the same way as a bank lending to a home owner only hands over cash when they have acquired conditional title through a mortgage agreement. The professionals understood the risk and demanded collateral.

As derivatives usage and securitisation within banks increased, their senior management and strategists began to realise that their business models and much of their existing *"raison d'etre"* had been rendered obsolete. They no longer needed to raise capital from depositors, nor to carry the risks from interest rate and foreign exchange movements that they could hedge using derivatives. Whilst no one would lend them unlimited funds on an unsecured basis, banks could borrow with ease if secured by assets as collateral. For banks with large inventories of securities to finance for their trading operations, their standing in the commercial paper market was important; but the real alchemy was repo.

The leverage magic of repo

A repurchase agreement, or 'repo', is a loan collateralised by securities. For a bank wishing to borrow $100 million from investors for one week, the transaction would be for the bank to sell US Treasury bonds they owned with a contractual agreement to repurchase them a week later. The repurchase price would be set to provide a market rate of interest to the lender.

When entering into a repo the borrower provides security by putting up more collateral than the value of the loan. For a $100 million loan the collateral posted might be $103 million in bonds. This additional collateral, known as the haircut, protects the lender from an unexpected drop in the collateral value of the bonds.

> The bonds are returned to the bank the following week through the repurchase transaction, repaying the loan in full with interest.
>
> With the $100 million in cash borrowed through repos the bank could choose to buy a further $100 million of US Treasury bonds. These bonds could be used as collateral for borrowing another $97 million through repo which could then be spent on the purchase of another $97 million of US Treasury bonds. In this way the bank could accumulate $300 million worth of US Treasury bonds from an original holding of $103 million, thereby leveraging their capital by nearly 3 times.
>
> The repo sequence does not have to stop at this stage and often goes through many more iterations. In this way the bank can finance securities and other assets far in excess of its own capital, often reaching leverage ratios 20 or 30 times their own capital.

It was now so easy for banks to borrow and there was almost no fear of their defaulting. And for those that wanted security, the banks could post part of their vast inventory of securities as collateral. It felt like a truly level playing field and the banks lent money to one another across the financial spectrum at virtually the same rate of interest. This rate at which they lent to one another was needed as a reference for a number of purposes, most notably the floating rate component in derivative transactions. In the London market the major banks were asked to submit the interest rate at which they reckoned they could borrow money from one another, whether or not they were actually doing so. This rate, established by poll, was known as the London Interbank Offer Rate, or LIBOR for short. Many years later in 2012, and in a different and less equal world for bank borrowing, this obscure and hitherto little known reference price became the source of its own scandal, resulting in massive fines for the banks who manipulated the polls for their own ends.

As the role of capital markets increased, and the relationship with retail depositors became more remote, the ties between commercial banks and their customers became less important. The number of client facing bank employees was cut and much the commercial judgement that came from direct customer knowledge left with them. Repo was now the prime source of short term funding for the banks with collateral replacing customer relationships in the pecking order of importance.

Investment banks, who had led the trend, were now accessing retail depositors indirectly as investors in money market funds which bought their commercial paper. The big corporate guns and major financial institutions tended only to lend to one another when holding collateral from the borrower as security.

Money making machine of global banking

With Glass-Steagall de facto repealed, the US banks were free to engage in any mix of business they wished. They could raise almost unlimited amounts of capital with ease, conducting their business and that of their clients in whatever tax or regulatory jurisdiction they chose; typically where taxation and regulatory oversight was low, preferably close to zero. They also shed much of the risk they did not want through derivative transactions whilst circumventing regulatory capital requirements by moving loans to offshore jurisdictions, or into structures that required little or none. These were heady days for the banks.

Globalisation of business, in conjunction with a substantial and liquid market in derivatives, enabled companies to borrow from whichever country where investors would lend to them cheapest. Through instruments like cross currency swaps, these loans could be switched into whatever currency they wished to borrow in. Through derivatives the bulk of the market risk they would otherwise have had to carry could be shed; exposure to adverse movements in exchange rates, interest rates and the stock market. Momentum was also building to shed the only major risk that remained, the credit risk on their loans to customers.

As if that was not enough, they topped off the new banking model with icing in the form of the chicanery of structured finance, parcelling up risk into chunks that suited the appetite of different investors. This device, almost a form of alchemy, made the sum of the parts worth much more than the whole.

They wasted little time *"making hay whilst the Sun shone"* by leveraging up their balance sheets by taking on vast inventories of loans and securities. They also had another trick up their sleeve, beyond commercial paper and repo, to leverage up their profit engine, which was securitisation. Just as they had facilitated this practice for Enron through offshore structures, they were also doing similar transactions for themselves, removing loans and other assets from their balance sheets to circumvent the capital constraints that they otherwise faced from regulators. Some of these practices were later prohibited as part of a regulatory clampdown on shadow banking. These structures then came onto the balance sheet of the banks, requiring them to set aside capital to cover the risk they were taking.

With more financial power than their traditional customers were demanding, the banks sought out new ways for their corporate customers to use this capital. Cash constrained companies with big ambitions like Enron were their ideal customers, with their insatiable appetite for innovative securitisation deals to buy up business lines and future revenue streams for cash. Without this easy money Enron could not have made their cashless journey to disaster through the myriad of offshore structures that they initiated in partnership with the banks.

But even with companies like Enron, there was not enough demand from corporates to make full use of the supply of easy capital. As a result a new beneficiary of this greater lending capacity was brought into the frame, the man in the street. Their needs in consumer credit and financing for large items like cars were part of this, but the biggest of all was home loans.

It was the business of home loans that was to provide the scale of demand that would turn the banks into a runaway train of risk and leverage, which was only brought to a halt on the buffers of the collapse of the most aggressive of the major players, Lehman Brothers. The Lehman demise in 2008 was to lead to the reinstatement of much of the Glass-Steagall Act in 2010 in the form of the *"Volcker Rule"*. This rule reintroduced the separation of deposit taking and securities trading and was named after its proposer, Paul Volcker, Chair of President Obama's Economic Recovery Advisory Board and a former Chairman of the US Federal Reserve.

But the banks were still left with the risk that their clients would default. If they could pass on that risk exposure then the constraints around lending would fall away and they would have an unencumbered business model that could transform them into giant money making machines. And a solution to that challenge was already in sight, one designed to cater for the fallout from a massive natural disaster, credit derivatives. In the short term it was to sow the seeds for more money making but ultimately to lead the banks on a journey to hubris and financial disaster.

29. Credit derivatives supertanker runs aground on the banks

"Credit is a system whereby a person who cannot pay gets another person who cannot pay to guarantee that he can pay"

Charles Dickens (1812-1870)

At the start of the new millennium it seemed to many that the extraordinary pace of innovation and growth in financial derivative markets had passed its peak. In less than twenty years these markets had gone from a standing start to surpass the size of the world's share and bond markets on which they were based. A period for reflection and consolidation seemed long overdue, not least because it was hard to conceive of any development of significance that could drive these markets to even greater heights.

But this notion was quickly to be dispelled as the mightiest derivative innovation of all took hold, credit derivatives. In less than six years the growth of these instruments would surpass that of all of their predecessors, their $70 trillion notional value eclipsing the $50 trillion reached by equity markets and $60 trillion by bond markets since their advent in the 1600s. The impact of credit derivatives was such that, when they first ran aground in 2007, world financial markets were thrown into a state of paralysis. Moreover the banks who had spawned credit derivatives became their most conspicuous victims.

Credit Default Swaps - Financial innovation from environment disaster

In light of what was to come, it was perhaps telling that the event that initiated credit derivatives was an out-of-control supertanker that ran amok, causing what some claim to be the most devastating man made environmental disaster in history. The financial spillage that came from credit derivatives some twenty years later was also to wreak massive devastation, finally bringing to a halt the unimpeded advance of financial derivatives.

Just after 9pm on 23rd March 1989, one of the largest supertankers in the world, Exxon Valdez, fully laden with crude oil from Alaska's Prudhoe Bay oil field, embarked from the Valdez oil terminal for Long Beach, California. The ship's captain was drunk before he boarded, retiring from the bridge a couple of hours after setting sail to sleep off the effects. An hour later, and shortly after midnight, the ship ran aground on Bligh Reef in Prince William Sound, spilling its cargo of crude oil into the sea.

The effect was catastrophic. Over 10 million gallons of crude oil spilt and spread over the surface of 11,000 square miles of ocean, polluting some 1,500 miles of coastline, decimating the fish and wildlife populations as well as the livelihood of countless people in the surrounding area for decades to come.

It took five years for the American legal system to bring Exxon, the owner of the supertanker and world's largest oil company, to account. The Court awarded $287 million of actual damages claimed by the 32,000 plaintiffs who had suffered. They also determined an additional $5 billion in punitive damages, equivalent to Exxon's annual profits at the time. Exxon's plea in mitigation; that they had already spent over $4 billion cleaning up the oil spill, fell on deaf ears.

Exxon immediately appealed the judgment but, with no certainty that they would succeed or when payment might be demanded, had to arrange for funds to be immediately available. They therefore approached their principal bankers, Barclays and JP Morgan, requesting a $4.8 billion credit line, a facility that would commit these banks to make this money available any time it was called for.

Whilst JP Morgan was keen to meet the needs of such an important client, the economic case for providing such a credit line was poor. The credit line would make JP Morgan little money whilst using up valuable bank capital that could be deployed much more profitably elsewhere. But to turn down Exxon's request made no commercial sense as it would jeopardise the strong relationship that the two firms had built up over many decades. Rejecting their request for a credit line might open the door to competitors seeking to gain a foothold into more lucrative future banking opportunities from Exxon.

Exxon Valdez highlights the inefficiencies of credit lines

This dilemma was not new. The banks, and JP Morgan in particular, had been confronted by this conundrum again and again with their biggest and longest standing clients. What was needed was a way to retain the overall client relationship by taking the entire loan onto their books, but without carrying the full burden of loss if the customer defaulted. If a mechanism could be found to transfer some or all of the credit risk, the bank could then make the case to banking regulators that the loss from a customer default was much reduced and less capital needed to be set aside to cover this risk.

The idea that JP Morgan came up with was the Credit Default Swap, or 'CDS' contract. As had been the case when Salomon brokered the first interest rate swap between IBM and the World Bank, the trick was to find a party for whom the risk exchange made sense. The party JP Morgan chose to approach was the European Bank of Reconstruction and Development (EBRD) with the suggestion that the EBRD assume some of the credit risk of the Exxon deal whilst JP Morgan retained ownership of the legal and financial obligations to Exxon relating to the credit facility.

It made sense for the EBRD to do this as they had plenty of money to lend. However, owing to a charter that only permitted them to lend to borrowers of high credit standing, they were left with limited scope to make profitable loans. As a result the EBRD was keen to find ways to increase the return on their investments without breaching their credit quality constraint.

Under the terms of the CDS contract, JP Morgan paid the EBRD an annual fee for assuming much of the default risk from the Exxon credit line, leaving EBRD on the hook to compensate JP Morgan for the bulk of any loss on the loan. EBRD liked the idea because they judged that the chance of Exxon defaulting was slim, whilst the fees JP Morgan paid them augmented the return on their investment portfolio. In this way, as with all derivative concepts, the risk exposure was transferred to EBRD whilst legal ownership of the risk remained with JP Morgan.

For EBRD the CDS contract provided a steady and higher stream of income that they could add to the revenue they received from the highly rated bonds or loans they already held. As the EBRD director responsible for the transaction commented at the time: *"It seemed like a win-win situation".*

From these beginnings the credit default swap emerged as an insurance-like contract where the buyer of default protection makes a series of quarterly or annual payments over the life of the swap to the 'seller' who assumes the default risk. In return, the buyer of the protection receives a substantial payoff from the seller if the borrower fails to repay their debt. Over time the CDS contract evolved so that a broader range of credit events could trigger payments. Many were triggered by less demanding credit events than corporate default, such as a company undergoing a restructuring, seeking bankruptcy protection from creditors, or even just a ratings downgrade from one of the major credit rating agencies.

The Exxon transaction had demonstrated that the exposure of banks to default by a large customer could be passed on without loss of relationship or control. Other banks were quick to follow suit. To start with they used CDS contracts in the same way as JP Morgan, to reduce credit risk exposure to their biggest customers, enabling them to make much bigger loans than they would previously have contemplated. Those taking this risk shared the default risk with the bank and gained comfort from the fact that the initiating bank carried the same risk as they did, and had done careful due diligence on the borrower's ability to repay the loan.

CDS contracts made the traditional syndication method for

handling big loans look arcane by comparison. With syndication the lead bank would spread the risk of default by inviting other banks to take a share of the loan. With credit default swaps, the lead bank could commit to making the entire loan to the company once satisfied that they could pass on a chunk of the default risk, effectively separating the constraint of capital provision from default risk.

For EBRD it was also the route to gain the return on an asset without having to put up any capital; in effect the CDS contract enabled them to gear up their loan book. A lending mechanism with no direct connection to the borrower had been born.

Banking freedom is complete and new business model takes hold

The Exxon/EBRD transaction paved the way for a handful of sophisticated investors to participate in JP Morgan's loan portfolio without all the paraphernalia of loan or security issuance documentation. These investors were more interested in participating in a diversified portfolios of loans, not having all their 'eggs' tied up in single names. Like EBRD their investments were coloured by their risk appetite and credit constraints, which the banks catered for initially by offering portfolios of companies from their loan book that carried the appropriate level of risk. But it was not always easy to find a good spread of the right names in the amounts needed to make up the portfolio.

To circumvent this difficulty, the banks came up with the idea of augmenting the portfolio with the risk from companies that, whilst overall, did not meet the requisite credit criteria, but could be included if sliced into risk tranches. The tranches broke the overall default risk from the portfolio into layers; the lowest layer taking the first loss and the highest only suffering a loss once all of the layers below had been exhausted. Investors like EBRD with a low risk tolerance could participate in the safest layer whilst those seeking greater returns could elect to invest in the higher risk tranches. This risk splitting, whilst having a legitimate genesis, was the first step along a path that would lead structured finance towards Collaterised Debt Obligations (CDO), a form of financial instrument that would have a toxic denouement.

Securitisation and Structured Finance

Securitisation is a process that takes all manner of cash flows and bundles them up into securities that can be bought and sold by investors. Many types of cash flow have been packaged up into such securities, ranging from home loan payments ('mortgages') to those for car purchase, repaying credit card debt and business loans.

This securitisation of cash flows was taken a stage further by BlackRock founder Larry Fink who broke these securities down into smaller pieces or 'tranches', structuring the risk in such a way as to match the risk appetite of particular categories of investors.

Tranching creates different classes of securities, typically with different credit ratings, from the same pool of assets. The cash flow from the underlying asset pool is then split and meted out to the security in each layer, with those carrying the greatest default risk receiving the highest proportion of the cash flow, whilst those carrying little risk receive a lower proportion. A key goal of the tranching process is to create at least one class of securities whose rating is higher than the average rating of the underlying collateral pool, creating rated securities from a pool of unrated assets.

In the next iteration of this market, loans from other banks and corporate debt securities were included in the mix by the issuing banks. Within the market and amongst banking regulators, this extension of the supply of credit was welcomed, being seen as an innovative way to expand lending capacity within the economy. By shedding the constraint of limited capital within the banking sector, funding from the whole of capital markets could be brought to bear. It was this expansion of available funds that was to fuel an unprecedented credit boom, the ramifications of which went well beyond the thinking of the initiators of credit default swaps.

Credit rating agencies give investors confidence to dip their toes in

But there was one major drawback; persuading mainstream investors to take on all of this credit risk. Up until then banks were the specialists evaluating the financial strength of companies. Investors had neither the experience nor and people to do the job. Moreover there was no telling how long they would take, nor if they even had the appetite, to build up such a skill set. Luckily there were other forces at work concerning investors that were in the banks' favour, one of which was an increased confidence and reliance on quantitative approaches for evaluating all manner of risk. Cheap computing power allied broad agreement on methodology had changed market perception, the most important manifestation of which was RiskMetrics, a toolbox for risk developed by JP Morgan, which they cleverly decided to freely distribute to the entire market.

In 1992 I attended the first RiskMetrics presentation in London. The meeting was held in the main assembly hall of what had been the City of London School, before the school was moved nearby alongside the River Thames and former classrooms formed part of JP Morgan's European headquarters. The surprise with RiskMetrics was not in the modelling approach, but the enthusiasm with which senior management of the major financial institutions embraced a single number, known as 'Value at Risk' or 'VaR'. Although the developers of RiskMetrics went to great lengths in their presentation to explain the context and uncertainty surrounding this number and how it should be interpreted, the VaR number quickly became a term quoted with abandon around the luncheon tables of senior bankers. The attraction of VaR was that this single number described how much capital was at risk across a bank with many thousands of investment positions all over the world. For a senior banking executive to be able to say to colleagues or regulators that the market risk the bank running was unlikely to give rise to more than

$1 million loss on a particular day under adverse circumstances, implied a strong level of knowledge and control. The statistical confidence attached to the number and reliance on historic returns and correlation data was conveniently forgotten.

A handful of specialist companies also made it their business to provide investors with the *"ABC"* of default risk calculation. The three key credit rating agencies carrying out this role were Standard & Poors, Moody's and Fitch. It was to them that the banks turned to help them persuade investors to take on the credit risk. If the ratings agencies could translate default risk into an alphabet from A to D that investors would trust, then banks could change their business model from loan origination backed by their own capital to originate and distribute loans with the banks free from default risk.

Warning Sounds from Motown - Papering over the cracks

Documenting CDS contracts to deal with events that constituted default was tricky. The first sign that something might be awry came in October 2005 when Delphi, the largest US auto parts manufacturer, filed for bankruptcy. It was the biggest bankruptcy filing in the US auto industry's history, sending shock waves not just through Detroit and Washington, but Wall Street as well.

Delphi had been the auto parts division of General Motors (GM) until spun off to shareholders in 1999 as a separate company. In 2005 GM was still Delphi's biggest customer, accounting for over half their revenues. Although Delphi's collapse made a huge dent in GM's car manufacturing capabilities, they were in no position to intervene. GM was facing severe difficulties of its own, having already posted a loss of $4.1 billion in the first nine months of that year, and was embarking on a cost cutting drive to save $7 billion from its $41 billion annual expenditure budget.

It was a sad comedown for the company founded by William Durant in 1908 which, under Alfred Sloan's leadership, had become the world's biggest car manufacturer and most profitable company. GM had been the world's number one car manufacturer for seventy-five years and would remain so for another two years, before being overtaken by Japan's Toyota in 2007. However the firm's profitability had long been in terminal decline and would culminate in the humiliation of bankruptcy and a bailout by the US Government in 2009.

The revered *"Mr. General"* as GM was known, had held over 43% market share in the US through brand names which included Buick, Cadillac, Chevrolet, Opel and Vauxhall. Like its long standing US rival Ford, the business was headquartered in Detroit, a city whose economy was so dominated by the motor business that it was known as *"Motown"*. Even when Detroit's name became better known around the world through music stars of the 1960s that included Michael Jackson, Diana Ross, Stevie Wonder and Lionel Richie, the motor industry connection stuck, and the style of music they created was dubbed the 'Motown Sound'.

Financial economics a mixed blessing

The new financial economics was viewed as a mixed blessing by GM management. On the plus side their access to borrowing was assisted by the easy credit afforded through credit derivatives. Moreover, when hedging financial risk with OTC derivative contracts, they did not have to put up any capital. On a more negative side note accounting for corporate pension liabilities shifted to a 'market adjusted' basis, leaving the company vulnerable to short term fluctuations in interest rates.

This latter effect was of a sizeable concern, since GM's pension commitments alone were adding $1,800 to the cost of every car they made, increasing their effective manufacturing cost by almost 20%. For a company already struggling to compete with the lower production costs of foreign car manufacturers, these pension liabilities were competitively crippling them, particularly as the pension costs of their rivals were minimal. As if this was not enough, they also had to contend with contractual commitments, made from the 1960s, to provide free health care for all their employees.

When this benefit was given, the cost was expected to be much lower as the inflation in health costs that occured over the decades that followed had then been unthinkable. For the unions representing the car workers the more expensive this health care commitment became, the less willing they became to compromise. The company was being choked by this intransigence just as surely as the jobs that depended on the business were being placed in jeopardy.

On Wall Street it was the deteriorating credit market background that made Delphi's default such a significant event. Delphi's filing for bankruptcy protection triggered frantic activity of a different sort, as there were a host of untested effects associated with default in CDS contracts that had been ignored or brushed aside. In the heady rush of surging market growth in a benign credit environment there was uncertainty as to how some contracts would settle and be paid out when bond issuers defaulted. Delphi was seen as a good test for these effects. There was also something of a mess with the legal paperwork supporting these contracts as the generation of legal documentation lagged well behind the pace at which deals were being initiated and sold.

But the most pressing issue was that the $20 billion value of CDS contracts tied to Delphi bonds was greater than the $2 billion value of the Delphi bonds that were outstanding. Since the credit derivatives contracts were paid out against delivery of Delphi bond certificates there was a danger that $18 billion of the CDS contracts would be rendered worthless. This shortage of physical bonds caused panic amongst the owners of CDS contracts, forcing them to buy up worthless Delphi bonds in order to realise their CDS gains. The ensuing 'short squeeze' drove Delphi bond prices up 24% when rationally they should have been marked sharply down close to zero. The absurdity of the situation led the banks to declare a moratorium on Delphi bond and CDS trading. After discussion amongst market practitioners it was decided that an auction process be set in motion to agree a fair price for Delphi bonds at which all CDS contracts would be settled in cash without handing over bonds. This hastily arranged cash settlement approach stopped the mad scramble to purchase worthless bonds.

The ad-hoc nature of the solution served as a reminder that, despite its huge size, the credit derivatives market had little experience of shocks. The same issue had occurred a month earlier when Northwest, a US airline, filed for bankruptcy. On that occasion a group of investment banks had determined the settlement price for Northwest CDS contracts through speedily setting up an online auction. That precedent had helped the market to resolve the Delphi situation, even though the legal basis for resolving the matter in this way was far from robust.

The Delphi bankruptcy also opened up another avenue of concern in the CDS market as Delphi was a popular name as a 'reference entity' in thousands of credit derivative transactions. Over a third of 'synthetic CDOs' rated by credit rating agency Standard & Poors, and worth billions of dollars, included exposure to Delphi debt. Delphi's default triggered payments under these CDOs. An odd feature was that none of these contracts were directly tied to Delphi bonds, as synthetic CDOs are not backed by an actual portfolio of loans, taking their value instead by reference to such a loan portfolio.

The Delphi situation also drew attention to a way in which CDS contracts were being deployed, which was very different from conventional insurance. As a put option on default you did not have to sustain a loss in order to claim on the CDS contract. By buying a CDS contract on a company without owning any of its debt, you could simply make a bet that the company would default. With synthetic CDOs in particular you could have more money riding on a default than the value of the defaulting loans. These 'naked' CDS positions created, for the first time, an economic incentive to force a company into bankruptcy, rather than to rescue the company and its employees. This style of investment was first to haunt the market and then cause mayhem in the global financial crisis that erupted three years later when Greece erroneously judged itself to be a victim of a 'naked' CDS attack to drive them into bankruptcy.

Although the Delphi episode had almost brought the market to a standstill, the reaction by regulators and commentators, once the initial panic was over, was relatively relaxed. Academic opinion was to judge these events: *"just the right sized shock"* that the market needed and: *"how markets and institutions evolve - you want something that exposes vulnerabilities but is not entirely destructive".* This sanguine mood was echoed by Tim Geithner, head of the New York Federal Reserve, when he remarked that the: *"growth in volume and complexity of new instruments… has advanced, as it typically does, ahead of improvements in the trade processing infrastructure and risk management and control practices".*

Other than prompt a high-profile campaign to clear up the paperwork backlog and develop more common standards for legal documentation, nothing was done. It was a benign approach; simply papering over the cracks.

With hindsight one wonders why their reaction was so muted as clear warning bell had sounded on what was to come. Perhaps it was because a bigger prize was at stake. There was excitement at the unprecedented availability of cheap credit that had been released by the extension of credit risk beyond the banking system, and into a more widely dispersed group of providers across the financial system. Securitisation, structured credit and credit derivatives were part of a new paradigm. It was to become a regulatory blind spot with the subsequent headlong growth attracting more fascination than alarm.

And so it was that the events surrounding the Delphi default were not seen as evidence that the banks might not properly understand the ramifications of their financial engineering. Instead the credit risk of companies and even sovereign states passed quietly and almost unquestioned from the big commercial banks to investors around the world.

Investors take credit risk and then loans from the banks

It did not take long for investors effectively to become bankers by taking the credit risk that the banks offloaded in the form of their loan books into capital markets. As the process took hold investors hired teams of credit specialists from the banks to evaluate the loans they were buying. With the advantage of long lending experience and intimate knowledge of the loans they were packaging into securities, it was inevitable that the investors to whom the banks were selling their loans would initially suffer as the *"new boys on the block"* with the weaker hand. By playing up the expertise of the credit rating agencies some investors were persuaded that there was a referee of sufficient quality for the contest to be conducted on a reasonably level playing field. However, with the banks paying the credit rating agencies to opine on the quality of their loan instruments, it was perhaps wishful thinking.

With few traditional investment managers initially involved, the banks supported some of their own people to become investors in credit, providing capital and the full infrastructure support they needed through investment management outsourcing units they set up and called 'prime broking'. On the whole these former bankers were amongst the smartest investors, not least because they understood credit and their role in making the new bank model work.

At the other end of the spectrum, less able investors were seduced into investing in credit risks, financial instruments and structures they knew little about. They were to prove ready victims and with many *"losing their shirts"* when the market turned against them.

Subprime and the mortgage muddle

Once the transfer of credit risk on corporate loans to investors through securitisation and structured finance was well established, the door was open to offering consumer loans on a similar basis. The banks passed these loans on with impunity, principally in the form of home mortgages. Bearing little of the risk, the banks packaged up bigger and bigger portfolios of home loans with less and less fuss about the borrowers and their credit quality. It was a path that would take them into the mire of subprime mortgages.

'Subprime' was a euphemism for borrowers who were very unlikely to be able to repay their loans, placing almost total reliance on the money being repaid by the property retaining its value, a massive bet that property prices would not fall. The market also came to operate in an opaque fashion with mathematical models relied upon for pricing. There were too many securities and too few comparable secondary market transactions against which to benchmark prices. Furthermore there were very few who understood the loan content of the security packages being offered. As a result the quality of the loans fell without most investors realising what was happening. Some bespoke 'over the counter' instruments were constructed in such a way that they contained a great deal of 'under the counter' risk. And the chicanery became worse as risks that the banks were unable to offload were shifted into offshore constructs that made them appear to be owned by others. By so doing the banks were able to avoid setting capital aside, even though the small print showed that the issuing banks still carried the risk.

BP suffers from CDS backlash with Macondo oil spill

The Exxon Valdez litigation was finally settled 14 years after the spill in 2008, with the punitive damages cut from $5 billion to $507 million by the US Supreme Court. It remains one of most devastating human initiated environmental disasters ever caused at sea, although massively topped by the $65 billion in restitution expense when BP's Macondo well blew in the Gulf of Mexico in 2010.

When capital was required as security to meet the claims arising out of the BP disaster, the chicanery of a bank credit line backed by a CDS contract was ruled out by the US Government. It was not the time to propose clever alternatives. After all that had gone before, the mood was to keep it simple and stick to basics. BP was therefore initially instructed to put $20 billion of cash into a fund, and for the money to remain there until all the costs and claims relating to the oil spill had been paid.

30. Insurers are drawn into the party

"Derivatives are financial weapons of mass destruction"

Warren Buffett (born 1930 in Omaha, Nebraska)

For insurance companies, Credit Default Swaps (CDS) represented competition from the banks in their core business. Those buying these contracts regarded them as insurance against corporate default in everything but name, even though the contracts were not labelled or regulated as such. And it was galling for the insurers to find that an important chunk of their credit insurance business was bypassing them and being taken by the banks. To insurers CDS contracts symbolised a new world in which the banks were *"eating their lunch"*.

But credit was not the only insurance business under attack, nor was it the most worrying. The insurance industry as a whole was in a state of crisis. Their credibility and financial strength were at a low ebb, making them vulnerable to attack in many of their core business lines. Making matters worse was that their entire business model was being challenged by some of their biggest customers.

Their credibility had been called into question in the early 1990s after the near collapse of the Lloyds of London insurance market from natural catastrophe losses and fraud. The natural catastrophe claims had come from a series of North Atlantic hurricanes that had struck the Eastern seaboard of the United States. At the same time fraud cases brought by investors against Lloyds businesses were choking the law courts and had brought public disgrace not dissimilar to that which the banks were to experience after the financial crisis of 2008. On top of this the insurance market was also becoming embroiled in a seemingly never ending stream of health related claims arising from buildings that incorporated asbestos into their structures.

Close to default, a rescue was mounted for the Lloyds insurance market, the centrepiece of which was a financial lifeboat called

Equitas. Its purpose was to raise the necessary capital to assume the market's past liabilities, thereby keeping Lloyds solvent and able to continue writing new insurance business. Set up in 1996, I had the privilege to lead the team from Mercury Asset Management that was tasked with gathering and investing these assets on behalf of Equitas to cover these past liabilities. Warren Buffett was later to purchase Equitas in 2006 through his investment vehicle Berkshire Hathaway, taking on all of its liabilities, finally bringing the threat of Lloyds default to an end, as well as providing closure from future liabilities to the individual *"Names"* who had underwritten the risk.

Weaknesses identified in the insurance business model

A major strategic worry for the insurance industry was that some of their most important corporate clients were looking for insurance to take a different form. The oil company BP had openly challenged the insurance model, seeking an insurance product offering more akin to a financial contract. Their concern struck at two fundamental tenets of insurance; the financial strength and integrity of an insurance contract and the contractual nuisance associated with indemnity.

Financial strength was a big issue as their biggest customers were financially stronger than the insurers who ostensibly were protecting them. In the event of a major disaster it was more likely that the insurer providing the protection would collapse than the company suffering the loss. This effectively rendered insurance policies against major risks worthless. The near bankruptcy of Lloyds of London had brought this shortcoming into sharp relief and many companies took risks they had previously insured with Lloyds onto their own shoulders by self-insuring.

Concept of indemnity called into question

Big companies also viewed the concept of indemnity as archaic and inconvenient. The idea of indemnity is that you pay an insurance premium in return for which you receive a contract covering potential losses suffered by the policy holder. With home insurance for example, a policy holder can claim for losses suffered from fire or any other form of damage. The amount paid out is determined by reference to the cost of putting the property back into the condition it was before the fire or other damage took place. As many who have suffered loss and made claims on insurance policies will attest, the process of identifying and proving loss, as well as loss evaluation can be slow and often cumbersome with the money not paid out for some time. For those more used to financial markets, an insurance policy feels like a put option of uncertain pay out wrapped up in a tortuous and convoluted settlement process.

The requirement to provide proof of an identifiable loss made little sense to big companies. They were used to buying protection in financial markets that paid out quickly in easily calculable amounts, irrespective of identifiable loss. With foreign exchange they might enter into a forward contract to protect them against loss from the currency risk of an overseas purchase. The payout would be determined simply by the change in the foreign exchange rate. Were the same transaction to be one of insurance, indemnity would come into play and any payout become associated with a subjective calculation of actual loss suffered. If the transaction for which you needed a currency hedge had not gone ahead it was possible that the financial contract would pay out whilst the insurance policy might not.

For their biggest customers derivative contracts were preferable to insurance for other reasons too. Apart from being simpler and cleaner in terms of certainty of pay out and the better credit standing from collateral posting, they were tradable too. Capital markets were more transparent and had much more money to deploy than insurance markets. The case for capital markets' involvement in insurance was strong from a customer and national good standpoint.

The banks had already spotted the capital markets opportunity in insurance, having changed their business model radically such that corporate and personal loans were now funded through securitisation, and not their own capital. The insurers faced a conundrum but could see their own weakness. In times of few claims they had too much capital and received low returns. When claims were high their capital was depleted and they looked weak as counterparties just when insurance premium rates for new business were attractive. It was a cyclical boom or bust business model as Lloyds of London had found to its cost. A business model with less permanent capital and more transient capital was called for, one where capital arrived in times of shortage and left to seek returns elsewhere when not needed. This was a capital market model with transient capital provided by investors where banks and insurers acted as intermediaries, packaging and distributing securities between the corporates and investors.

At the height of this debate I attended a presentation made by BP to insurers, investors and banks which cited an oil refinery that had suffered severe fire damage to explain why insurance as a risk management tool was not attractive for their business. The insurers had put a lot of time and effort into estimating the cost of rebuilding the refinery but the amount was of little practical relevance as refinery developments and business conditions meant that rebuilding a replacement refinery of that size or even in that location made no commercial sense. Indemnity and the insurance process for calculation and payment for loss represented a poor business model. How much better would it be to enter into a contract that pays out immediately when the event occurs for a known amount that both BP and the insurer had already agreed upon.

The point being made by BP was that history and legal constructs had embedded indemnity into insurance and that these same principles were in danger of shutting insurers out of the market for their biggest customers in favour of financial constructs.

It was a hard message for insurers to absorb, not least as indemnity had become a central tenet of insurance law for very good reasons. When fire insurance was introduced to protect against loss of property following the Great Fire of London in 1666 and life insurance introduced for loss of life after the Great Plague in the previous year, the idea of paying on the basis of realised losses made complete sense. Their enshrinement into law had come about to prevent abuse, and deter those of murderous intent. In the early days of life insurance, policies were on occasion taken out on the lives of people who would then be murdered so that a third-party policy holder could claim for the insured sum. With indemnity this could not happen as the scoundrels owning these life insurance policies could not claim that they had personally suffered loss.

In a sense, it was a return to a debate that had taken place four hundred years earlier with the Dutch adopting commercial protection through put options whilst the British had travelled the alternative path of insurance. What had brought about the downfall of put options in the Dutch tulip mania of the 1600s had been the inadequacy of their legal status and credit support. But these shortcomings were now in the past as the capital markets of the 1900s had brought in binding legal documentation and the credit support of collateral.

Insurance had evolved as an awkward put option, which the policyholder purchased that could not be sold or priced by anyone other than the insurer who had originally written the policy. Its credit support was opaque and, through the indemnity concept, left an additional obstacle, the 'burden of proof' of liability as well as proof of actual loss firmly on the shoulders of the policyholder. For insurers' customers insurance was a slow and unequal battle that the big companies were turning away from.

Earthquake brings Wall Street challenge to insurers

The emerging tussle between insurers and banks came to a head after the Northridge Earthquake struck San Francisco to catastrophic effect in 1994, and the US Federal Government had to step in and provide emergency relief to cover the damage. Many homeowners had insufficient protection whilst those who did were to find their insurer lacking the funds to cover their loss. So that the Government did not have to step in again, the California Earthquake Authority (CEA) was set up so every California homeowner had earthquake insurance cover. When Morgan Stanley, one of Wall Street's finest, was appointed to structure the risk so that it would be carried by capital markets around the world and not by insurers, the banks thought their big breakthrough into insurance had finally arrived. Both insurers and the banks regarded this transaction as the bellwether deal that would finally end the insurance exclusivity role first established in Edward Lloyd's coffee house. Henceforth the spoils would be shared with the descendants of the coffee houses that had nurtured stock markets, Jonathan's in London and Tontine in New York.

Towards the end of 1996 the terms of the CEA earthquake insurance contract were set and the placement of the security by the banks was underway with investors around the world. There was shock when the wily Warren Buffett stole the deal by undercutting the capital market price with an insurance underwriting contract from National Indemnity, one of his insurance companies. Wall Street cried foul to the California insurance regulator, making the case that the security offering should go ahead for the broader national good as the capital market alternative was critical if the American people were to be securely protected against the perils of future natural catastrophes of windstorms, floods and earthquakes. If this transaction did not go ahead, gaining access to capital markets for insurance risk would be severely restricted. But it was to no avail.

The deal was stolen from under Wall Street's nose and, although some banks continued to pursue the capital markets route through issuance of insurance securities for a time, the major effort fizzled out and Wall Street returned to their traditional role in insurance markets, focusing on raising capital for insurance companies. There was plenty of banking business of this nature to do, not least in spawning a major new insurance industry in Bermuda to fill the space left vacant by Lloyds of London after its near collapse. Some banks also created investment vehicles for insurance and carried out investment transactions alongside the insurers; but the major battle was lost.

Buffett's watchfulness of capital market intrusion into insurance markets was close and concerned. At Mercury Asset Management (now part of BlackRock) I was responsible for setting up a pilot investment fund. to develop and test the new concepts and structures that combined our investment and capital markets expertise with the wide ranging insurance underwriting skills of the world's biggest reinsurer, Germany's Munich Re. Buffett's key lieutenant who ran National Indemnity, Ajit Jain, and had led the CEA counterattack on Morgan Stanley, paid us regular visits in 1996 to discuss market developments and investment ideas. As it quickly became apparent that his visits were simply fishing expeditions we ended the dialogue. When we carried out the first capital markets transaction in insurance involving natural catastrophe risk from AIG and brokered by Benfield's Matthew Harding (who at the time was also bankrolling London's Chelsea Football Club to prominence), Jain appeared to become alarmed, offering to buy the fund and all its investments.

By now insurers and their insurers, the reinsurers, realised that their capital, though substantial, was tiny compared to capital markets. Seeing themselves as capital constrained in the eyes of their biggest customers for major natural catastrophes, they formed capital market groups and began to behave like banks to source, package, and distribute insurance risk.

Warren Buffett's curious relationship with derivatives

Much has been written about Warren Buffett. An investment titan by any measure, he has grown a $1 investment in Berkshire Hathaway, the entity he invests through, in 1964 to over $10,000 by 2017, along the way becoming one of the richest people on the planet. That achievement alone would mark him as a man of considerable talent and influence. However there is another quality for which he is held in high esteem; wise honest plain speaking about investment. Buffett expresses his opinions in folksy style at Berkshire Hathaway's annual gathering in his home town of Omaha, Nebraska, known as *"Investors Woodstock"*. These 'nuggets' are savoured by investors from all over the world, myself included.

Buffett's investment methods and views on different businesses are well documented. Insurance is a business he likes a great deal whilst the airline industry was one he used not to. Derivatives are thought to be financial instruments he finds abhorrent, principally based on a much-publicised comment in his 2002 newsletter to Berkshire Hathaway shareholders. There Buffett described derivatives as *"financial weapons of mass destruction"*. It was a remark that resonated strongly as military *"weapons of mass destruction"* were being much debated at the time in the context of Iraq's missile capability. The possibility of chemical weapons being deployed against the West by their President Saddam Hussein was cited as a major factor for the invasion of Iraq in 2003.

What some missed was that the prompt for Buffett's comment was the scandal and losses that had come to light around that time following Berkshire Hathaway's $22 billion acquisition of General Re, one of the world's largest reinsurance companies, in 1998. They already suffered $1.6 billion of losses when a 'black hole' was found in the accounts of their derivatives subsidiary General Re Financial Products. The entire acquisition was called into question when their Chairman, CEO and other executives were investigated and convicted of fraud for creating and hiding a transaction which inflated the reserves of another giant of the insurance business, American International Group (AIG). Finding it impossible to sell the business, Buffett closed it down.

On learning that it would take years to unwind some of the complex and long term deals General Re Financial Products had entered into, he made another of his memorable utterances: *"The reinsurance and derivatives businesses are similar: Like Hell, both are easy to enter and almost impossible to exit"*. Indeed his mood and commentary seemed to be like that of most investment managers, closely linked to how their investments were performing; upbeat when going well and irascible when not.

However, the odd thing is that, instead of avoiding derivatives, Buffett has always been well wired into their development. He has taken advantage of situations like Salomon, described earlier, when derivatives have given him the opportunity to make a great deal of money through deals structured on very favourable terms to himself or directly at times by making very big bets using these instruments.

My own view is that all of Buffett's negative comments on derivatives were simply irritation at the incompetence of senior management and a desire to prevent capital markets encroaching on his insurance business. His public pronouncements, whilst born out of frustration with the General Re Financial Products debacle, also suited his own business purposes. Whilst publicly speaking out against the instruments that facilitated capital market involvement in the insurance market, he was privately seeking more and more of this business for himself. In a sense the General Re debacle gave him a platform to talk his own book.

Aside from his public utterances, his record with derivatives cast him more as a fan than an opponent. For a man who ostensibly dislikes derivatives, he kept very close to them and made some of his most spectacular bets through these instruments. Buffett chaired and invested in the biggest and most aggressive derivatives bank, Salomon Brothers. One of his insurance entities National Indemnity was legendary for taking huge derivative bets on stock market levels, volatility and natural catastrophes. Perhaps he just wanted to keep the biggest gains from derivative opportunities for himself.

He had mixed views on the entry of investors into insurance as it was one of the mainstays of his investment vehicle Berkshire Hathaway and a business he had nurtured and built up over the years. He loved the insurance business for many reasons, not least the capital float they derive from receiving insurance premiums up front with claims coming later; and potential for additional delays and returns built in from waging the kind of war of attrition with policy holders that the Florentine merchant Francesco di Marco complained of in a letter to his wife in the 1300s.

All of this insurance being traded in financial markets had not gone unnoticed. All of the major insurers and reinsurers set about developing their capital markets capabilities where they perceived there was opportunity and felt they had competitive advantage. Whereas Warren Buffett went for big plays through National Indemnity Swiss Re created a capital markets group in the style of an investment bank. Zurich Insurance pushed hard with a wide ranging agenda through their subsidiary Centre Re which proved to be overambitious. Munich Re, the world's largest reinsurer, entered into a variety of initiatives, including the pilot fund they ran with us at Mercury Asset Management. The major insurance brokers also followed suit, often hiring teams of investment bankers to spearhead their entry into capital markets.

And this in turn led to a surprising turn of events. Having seen the banks off from the insurance business, the insurers turned around and started to take on the banks in financial markets. And one in particular was to take the lead in grappling with the financial markets opportunity, the largest insurance company in the world, American International Group, known best by the acronym, AIG.

31. A giant lobsterpot called AIG

"Bankers keep bringing lobster pots into my office, investment structures that are easy to climb into but tough to crawl out of. I remind them that I am an investor not a lobster"

Andrew Dalton (1949-2011)
Vice Chairman of MAM & Co-Founder of DSP

After his success in stealing the reinsurance contract for the California Earthquake Authority (CEA) from under the noses of the Wall Street banks, Warren Buffett came to be seen as the standard bearer warning the banks that they encroached on insurance turf at their peril. Less prominent was another insurer with a bold strategy that had been hatched much earlier. Their strategy was not simply to defend their insurance business from outsiders, but to take on the banks on their home turf of capital markets. The insurance company was AIG and their arm for carrying out this task was AIG Financial Products (AIGFP).

From Chinese roots to star of capitalism

The genesis of American International Group (AIG) was an insurance business set up in China in 1919 by an American called Cornelius Starr. Over time the company successfully expanded its reach and influence such that, by the time the reins were handed over to Maurice 'Hank' Greenberg in 1968, the firm had grown into a global insurance titan.

Under the restless Greenberg the company thrived, growing profits for 25 years at 15% per annum, an extraordinary achievement unmatched by almost any other public company. Ever ambitious and innovative, Greenberg personally encouraged and oversaw the business, taking on unusual and difficult to evaluate insurance risks, from aircraft hijacking to satellite launches and concert tours by rock stars. Few of their rivals had the will, capability or diversity to compete for such business, leaving AIG to reap handsome profits from their daring. The firm's success and financial strength was a source of immense personal pride to Greenberg, with the 15% annual profits growth track record becoming almost an article of faith. Later, this profit outcome was to assume such importance that, when the numbers were no longer truly there, the firm attempted to hold on to the story at the expense of proper accounting.

In the late 1980s, as the distinction between capital and insurance markets was beginning to blur through the advent of securitisation and credit derivatives, Greenberg began to explore ways by which AIG might step into Wall Street's capital market domain. This interest was not born of a particular wish to attack the banks, rather to diversify the business away from the vagaries of the insurance cycle. AIG had already reaped the benefits of scale from product and geographical diversification, such that further acquisitions within the insurance industry would serve only to increase their business risk. As Greenberg expressed it at the time: *"We're so big we're never going to swim against the tide. We are the tide."*

There was a strong strategic case for insurers to enter the domain of banks. Insurance companies could offer long term investment products in illiquid assets on much better terms than the banks. Regulators did not require insurers to set aside as much capital as banks to cover such risks as their contracts with policy holders were much longer term. With banks liquidity was of paramount importance so that depositors could withdraw their funds at short notice. Adding to the long-term attraction was the fact was that customers and the market regarded AIG, with its AAA credit rating, as one of the strongest companies on Earth.

Another aspect that intrigued Greenberg was the way derivatives and structured finance could be used to shift risk and economic exposure across national borders, to whichever jurisdiction offered the most favourable regulatory and tax treatment. It seemed that AIG's size, global reach and financial strength were built for these free market times. All that was needed was a plan and the wherewithal to profit from their natural advantage.

Building the 'all purpose' risk machine

Greenberg saw AIG's future in managing risk in the broadest sense, not confined simply to those traditionally carried by insurers. At the time risk management was in a state of flux as the slow and laborious manual calculation methods of the past were being superseded by faster and ever more powerful computers. It had become possible to carry out detailed numerical analysis at a granular level and then to revise the entire computation with a handful of keystrokes. Such speed and accuracy was unthinkable with manual calculation, when the only tools available to speed the process were mechanical calculators and slide rules.

The introduction of the IBM (International Business Machines) personal computer in 1981 kick-started a revolution in calculation capability with the introduction of the software of spreadsheets. A second generation of IBM computers launched in 1985 that, through the new *"Windows"* software of Microsoft, was able to run several programmes simultaneously, accelerated the process exponentially. The influence of Windows was such that Microsoft gained a virtual stranglehold with over 90% of the operating system software for the personal computer market. It was to leave Apple, their main rival and previous market leader through their Mac DOS software, to struggle and to fall from grace.

Meanwhile the major providers of financial market data, Bloomberg and Reuters, were in the throes of creating platforms to transmit live market prices directly into spreadsheet calculations, heralding the new and dramatic experience of real time computation.

This raw computational power gave banks and investment managers a new opportunity to tackle the complexity of risk management. When I joined Mercury Asset Management (MAM), the investment arm of the bank SG Warburg, in 1987 I was not only given a remit to lead their derivatives effort, but also charged with introducing quantitative risk management capabilities into the portfolio management process. Such was the perceived investment management opportunity that a new firm, BlackRock, was founded in 1988 with risk management as the central plank of their offering. BlackRock was to become the world's biggest asset manager in little more than twenty years, and along the way became my employer, through the 2006 acquisition of what was once Warburg's asset management business.

AIGFP formed as capital market engine

Greenberg felt that this was the moment for AIG to enter the capital markets business. To this end he hired a team of derivative specialists from the investment bank Drexel Burnham Lambert in 1987, not long, as it turned out, before Drexel collapsed from excesses in their junk bond business. The leader of this derivatives team was Howard Sosin, an unusual individual with a doctorate in the heavily mathematical derivative pricing theory. Sosin had come to financial markets from Bell Laboratories, the facility originally founded by Alexander Graham Bell, the inventor of the telephone. Bell Labs was then the most prestigious technology research facility in the world and credited with making many ground breaking discoveries, including radio astronomy, the transistor, lasers and a number of computer operating systems and languages. Along the way individuals at Bell Labs had been awarded eight Nobel prizes.

Sosin's concept was to offer customised derivative products to large corporate clients that hedged their financial risks. AIG would charge a premium price for this service, removing as much market risk from themselves as was economically possible through hedging. Their central idea was to *"squeeze the arbitrage juice"*.

After setting up a subsidiary, AIG Financial Products (AIGFP), to undertake this business, they began by offering long dated interest rate swaps. These derivatives principally provided their clients with protection against the vagaries of changes in short term interest rates. AIGFP's trading philosophy was only to engage in arbitrage and to take as little risk as possible. Sosin had no interest and did not believe in using the firm's capital to make proprietary bets on the direction of the market. Whilst common practice within investment banks, Sosin's view was that form of trading was a *'mug's game'.*

The beating heart of AIGFP was the sophisticated computer risk model they developed which evaluated their entire portfolio of positions 'holistically' as a single entity. It was quite unlike the asset risk models of most banks. Banks tended to manage risk categories separately, typically ending up with a patchwork quilt of hedging books covering each form of risk exposures. Although built to handle interest rate swaps, their model and approach was also applicable to many other thorny money problems. By combining all market, accounting and transaction details in a single place, they were able to bring a robust pricing discipline to evaluate the increasingly complex trades that their clients were contemplating. With none of the walls and 'fiefdoms' that banks created, there were no barriers to dialogue and innovation. In essence AIGFP was a smart risk management business that used financial derivatives to extract profits from financial, tax and regulatory arbitrage opportunities. Greenberg liked the concept and their competitive edge over the banks, not least as it met with his oft repeated wish: *"All I want from life is an unfair advantage".*

One aspect of AIGFP's competitive advantage was that long term illiquid positions sat much more comfortably with them than they did with banks. Their size and financial strength allowed them to hold a large book of positions whilst carrying little residual risk once those from currency, interest rate and stock markets had been hedged with derivative contracts. Often no additional hedging was needed when a new position was taken as the risk was small relative to that of the overall book, or cancelled out entirely by an offsetting position they already held. Unlike many banks which were often forced for regulatory or internal reasons to break their risk book into multiple self-contained business packages, AIG did not have to follow suit. AIGFP could therefore amalgamate all their financial exposure into one large risk bucket.

AIGFP passes under the regulatory radar

The capital requirements of insurers like AIG were not subject to the same burdensome reserve requirements as banks, nor did they face much questioning or particular interest from regulators. As AIGFP did not deal with the public, the firm was not subject to the many rules and constraints of investment managers or banks. Nor did they produce sales or marketing literature that needed vetting. AIGFP were not even heavy traders in public markets, so there was no significant paper trail. They were simply carrying out private deals with a handful of sophisticated companies, banks and investors with the commitments they entered into being backed by the substantial strength of their AAA long-term credit rating. Although AIGFP was technically monitored by the US Office for Thrift Supervision (OTS) as part of their brief for the firm as a whole, the focus of the OTS was on the core insurance businesses. With neither concern nor expertise in cutting-edge financial products, AIGFP had virtually no regulatory oversight.

Clash over remuneration calculation

The division was a big success from the start. No one else was as adept as AIGFP at milking the gains to be had from structuring deals with efficient financial hedges to take maximum advantage of tax and regulatory regime differences. But, whilst the business thrived, tension was building between Greenberg and Sosin over remuneration. Under the terms of their contract, the AIGFP team was paid 38% of the future profits embedded into their deals up-front. Greenberg was becoming uncomfortable with this arrangement, as the numbers were large and being calculated on a system created and run by the people receiving the money. With many of the deals taking thirty years or more to play out, AIG and its shareholders would be left on the hook for any future profit discrepancies or anything else that might go wrong. Sosin's claim that the positions were 'marked-to-market' was fiction as there was no way of knowing with certainty what the future profits would be, and rarely a market price that could be used as a reliable reference point. In truth the profits being booked were 'marked-to-model' and, given the conflict of interest and AIGFP's control of the model, 'marked to remunerate' was probably a better description.

Greenberg's worries about mark-to-market accounting were surfacing elsewhere around that time. Enron, a firm that would become a major source of AIGFP business, was starting down the same route of booking future profits to the present. It was a journey that would carry Enron to giddy heights on fictitious profits, before falling back to earth with an almighty bump when they ran out of cash and the firm collapsed.

After a bitter arbitration battle over how much money AIGFP had really made for the firm, Sosin parted company in 1993 with a paycheck of nearly $200 million from his five-year tenure. After he left, Greenberg set up a covert group, which operated from a nearby office in Connecticut. Without the knowledge of AIGFP, this team of auditors and financial engineers built a parallel computer system to track their trades and independently assess the value of the mark-to-market profits AIGFP were booking.

AIGFP were now flourishing through a chameleon like ability to put on whatever face and colour best solved the regulatory or tax constraints of their diverse client base. Their $140 million profits of 1995 had more than doubled to $323 million by 1998 as they pushed further into structured investments, hedge fund deals and guaranteed investment contracts (GICs) for public sector municipalities. The GIC deals had AIGFP acting somewhat like a bank in that they were borrowing surplus cash from state and local governments to fund lucrative deals for themselves, whilst only paying a slightly higher rate of interest to their municipality clients.

These golden years, when the skillful circumvention of tax, accounting and regulatory hurdles was not cast as unacceptable evasion, took a turn for the worse after Enron collapsed in 2001. Enron's systematic abuse of derivatives as part of its fraudulent corporate accounting led to certain forms of derivatives becoming the focus of regulatory scrutiny and falling into disrepute. Structured deals for corporations had been a large part of AIGFP's business and, as Sosin's successor Tom Savage was to put it: *"The response to Enron really reduced the toolbox for Financial Products. It wasn't at all clear to me where future profits were going to come from."*

Bistro that serves risk-free profits

It was when AIGFP were looking to plug their revenue gap in 1998 that JP Morgan approached them with a 'structured' deal carrying the unwieldy title *"Broad Index Secured Trust Offering"* but the catchy acronym *"Bistro"*. Little did they know that it was this transaction that would spawn a $12,000 billion structured credit market of CDOS that, ten years later, would become the focal point of a financial crisis that would bring Western banks to their knees. This crisis would result in AIG itself only surviving by being placed on life support through a $189 billion capital injection from US taxpayers.

The idea behind Bistro was not new. Instead of selling a corporate loan to investors in the form of a single security which paid interest in return for carrying the default risk of the company, Bistro packaged together a portfolio of such loans from a diverse group of companies. As the chance of all the companies defaulting on their loans was less than any one of them going under, the risk of loss was lower than for a single company.

> ### Collateralised Debt Obligation (CDO)
>
> A CDO is a structured financial product that packages a pool of loans together into securities for sale to investors. Investors who buy these securities receive the cash flow from the loans within the pool by way of interest and capital repayments. The loans of the debt pool are held as 'collateral' on behalf of the holders of these securities by a third party. The 'structured' component of the CDO arises as more than one class of security is issued on the

assets in the debt pool, each carrying a different entitlement to the cash that is generated.

In a typical CDO, the loan pool is split into three separate securities, each carrying a 'tranche' of the default risk, the risk layers being not unlike tiers on a wedding cake. Cash flow from the loan portfolio is paid to investors in a prescribed sequence. The top 'senior' tranche collects its cash entitlement first, then the middle or 'mezzanine' tranche, with the bottom 'equity' tranche the last in line. If the cash collected by the CDO is insufficient to pay all investors, it is those in the lower layers that first suffer losses.

With the lowest equity tranche shielding those higher up from loan defaults, investors in their equity tranche are allocated a larger proportion of the expected cash flow as compensation for the greater risk they carry. By similar dint the mezzanine layer receives a higher proportion than the top 'senior' layer, which loses nothing at all unless the capital in lower tiers has been completely exhausted.

In the late 1980s, when CDOs first came to prominence, their assets were solely corporate loans. By the early 2000s retail loans in the form of automobile, credit card, student education and home loans were introduced into CDO pools. Investors had become sufficiently comfortable with these structures to accept any loans within the debt pools provided their cash flow was reasonably predictable. For banks this expansion was welcomed as securitising loans into capital markets meant that capital that they were holding against consumer loans could be released and used to make money elsewhere.

It was the introduction of lower quality 'subprime' home loans around 2003 that turned the CDO from a niche market into the mainstream. CDO issuance soared from $30 billion in 2003 to $225 billion in 2006 whereas the quality of the loan pools fell precipitately. Whilst adding fuel to the fire of the US housing boom they were also creating a class of security so toxic that CDOs became dubbed *"Chernobyl Death Obligations"*, a reference to an explosion in 1986 at a Ukraine nuclear reactor which caused radioactive material to be released into the atmosphere with catastrophic consequences.

When the US housing bubble burst in 2007, CDO prices were amongst the hardest hit. Losses running into hundreds of billions were suffered by some of the biggest financial institutions, leading to bankruptcy or, for systemically risk critical firms, bail out through government intervention with taxpayers' money.

The shielding from the lower tiers of Bistro meant that the risk of loss in the top tier was very small indeed, so low that the credit rating agencies assessed the default probability of these securities to be less than the long term AAA rating they accorded to the strongest companies in the world. JP Morgan cleverly highlighted this feature by branding top tier securities *"super senior"*, creating the perception of even greater strength to risk averse investors.

But JP Morgan wanted to go further still, to make the 'super senior' tranche almost completely risk free. If they could persuade AIG to provide insurance cover against the remote risk of loss on super senior securities through writing credit default swap (CDS) contracts, JP Morgan could make the case to banking regulators that the bank carried no risk of loss, and therefore need not set aside any capital to cover defaults in the loan pool. The risk to AIG was assessed to be so small that AIGFP was offered a tiny fee for taking this risk, just 0.02% per annum of the potential loss they were underwriting. However 0.02%, when multiplied by many billions of dollars, added up to an appreciable income stream and a high return on capital, since AIG did not have to set aside much capital to cover the risk.

But AIG had stepped away from the central plank of their business model, to offset as much risk as possible through hedging and to eschew outright market bets. They were now taking a massive bet on credit markets, a stance they justified by believing that the risk in writing these CDS contracts was negligible. In AIGFP's view all they were doing was reaping arbitrage gains from regulatory capital differences between banks and insurance companies.

'Super Senior' and the fatal correlation flaw

However, the reliance that the financial engineers placed in their own risk modelling of CDOs, particularly the 'super senior' layer, was misplaced. As Paul Volcker was later succinctly to opine: *"They (financial engineers) build models to give them more confidence to make bigger bets on the back of the illusion they've created about the future; stupid."*

The smarts at JP Morgan already knew this and felt that the numbers coming from the risk modelling for deals like Bistro could not be trusted. The thorniest topic for debate revolved around 'correlation', the extent to which defaults in a portfolio of loans might be interconnected. Predicting correlation cannot be achieved from simply 'crunching' the numbers. You have to understand the businesses and competitive interaction within their industries to gain a good handle. As the default of the motor industry component supplier Delphi had demonstrated, companies can be brought down when a major customer from the same industry, General Motors in this case, struggles. By contrast, in the retail business, the failure of a major retailer might benefit others in the same industry by reducing competition or be detrimental to all retailers if there is a common cause, for example a drop off in consumer spending. As correlation can work in either direction, the assessment of default risk for a portfolio of companies can be fiendishly complex to model mathematically. And even if you are able to determine a sensible correlation number, (0 if completely independent, 1 if they move together), there are other important variables to take into account.

The most important shortcoming is that correlation numbers are calculated by modelling past data and rest on the assumption that the same relationship between the two companies will persist into the future. Yet the future is never the same as the past. Another concern relates the stability of correlation. The number does not stand still, moving closer to 1 in times of crisis. Because of these weaknesses Paul Volcker was scathing about the reliance placed on correlation analysis, describing the confidence placed on such computations: *"plain daft"*.

For the Bistro deal these correlation deficiencies were not particularly worrying as markets were stable and corporate defaults rare in the initial pool of companies that JP Morgan had selected. Although less than 1% of the loan pool was expected to default in any one year JP Morgan had set aside $700 million of regulatory capital for the Bistro deal, enough to cover defaults by 10% of the loan pool.

Retail loans markedly increase CDO risk

The CDO structure, when allied to the simple rating framework of the credit rating agencies, proved to be an effective way to persuade investors to buy the loan portfolios. For the banks who packaged and distributed these securities, the large scale participation by investors provided a profit bonanza. Investment banks now saw any future income stream as a candidate for securitisation, bundling together portfolios of all manner of consumer loans, including those from credit cards, student education and home mortgages.

Almost without drawing breath, a securitisation construct designed to transfer corporate credit risk from banks to investors was now being deployed to shift consumer credit risk away from the banks. Just as the banks had passed what little risk remained with them from securitised corporate loans onto AIGFP through CDS contracts, they were now able to repeat the trick with securitised consumer loans.

By the end of 2004 the banks found themselves struggling to sate the appetite which investors now had for all forms of securitised loans. With such a profitable revenue stream the banks turned to a loan market with much more dangerous characteristics, home loans to borrowers of poor credit quality. Categorised as 'subprime', this friendly euphemism really implied that these borrowers would fail to pass the normal creditworthiness tests of the banks and were usually forced to borrow from less reputable sources, loan sharks and the like. With investors and not the banks on the hook if the home borrowers defaulted, the banks slackened the credit reins sufficiently to include a category of very high risk home borrowers with little prospect of repaying loans, nicknamed 'Ninjas' (*"No income, no job or assets"*).

AIGFP was now selling CDS contracts on AAA rated subprime bonds for little more than the 0.12% a year they had charged for corporate loans. When modelling the default risk on consumer loans, they applied broadly the same diversification logic as they had for corporate loans. The belief that there was a diversification benefit came from the historical data used to calculate correlation risk. As there was no past experience of a nationwide housing price slump, their models assigned a probability of zero to such an occurrence. When AIGFP was questioned by an analyst on the risk and stability of their huge portfolio of credit derivatives, their head, Joseph Cassano, had responded with calm and confidence that: *"It is hard for us, without being flippant, to even see a scenario within any kind of realm of reason that would see us losing $1 in any of those transactions."* To AIGP the swap contracts were like catastrophe insurance; payments for events that would never happen.

With their sanguine analysis of subprime mortgages and consumer loans, the banks ratcheted up the subprime mortgage content within the portfolios AIGFP was insuring from 2% to 95% in a matter of months. In a flash AIGFP had taken a $50 billion exposure to subprime mortgage bonds, becoming the world's biggest holder of subprime mortgage risk. Making matters even worse was that the insurance arm of AIG had also invested heavily in the same toxic securities that AIGFP was insuring.

AIFGP had slipped from being the 'back stop' insurer of relatively secure company loans into being the ultimate backstop for high risk personal loans. *"The problem,"* as one AIGFP risk manager expressed it: *"was that something else came along that we thought was the same thing as what we'd been doing."*

Downgrades and Collateral Calls

When the US housing market turned down, AIG's exposure to US subprime mortgages came home to roost. At first they were relatively immune to the markdowns in value, as their strong credit rating meant counterparties did not require them to post collateral against unrealised losses. However many of their CDS contracts had 'credit rating triggers' that required them to post collateral if their credit standing was lowered.

When the banks started writing down their holdings of super senior risk in the autumn of 2007, AIG refused to follow suit. Their argument was that swings in credit default reference indices like the ABX, which was used as a *"mark-to-market"* proxy, bore no relation to economic reality and AIG, as an insurance company and not a trading house, could take a long-term view and had the resilience to ride out what they saw as *"a short-term bump in the road"*. Unlike banks, the collateral terms of their CDS contracts with counterparties reflected this approach as there was almost no requirement for them to post collateral on mark-to-market losses, unless their credit quality fell below AAA.

However the banks were now calling for collateral, citing the plummeting value of some of the subprime assets underlying securities that AIGFP had insured. Early in 2008 AIG was forced to admit that its auditors, PwC, had discovered a *"material weakness"* in their accounts. The problem was that when AIG insured super-senior CDO debt, they had not set aside sufficient reserves to follow through on the associated collateral commitment.

AIG was not prepared for the avalanche of claims from counterparties they were now receiving. When AIG announced some $43 billion of write-downs of super-senior assets, they joined the banks in frantically trying to plug their weakened balance check through the issuance of fresh shares.

By the middle of September 2008 AIG faced a new, even more deadly threat. The largest credit ratings agencies warned that they were considering removing the insurance group's AA tag due to their subprime woes. Such a decision threatened to create a new squeeze, since it would trigger a contractual requirement for AIG to post even more collateral on CDS positions. On top of this, the rapidly crumbling real estate market was causing the ratings agencies to downgrade the securities inside CDOs, including the 'super senior' layers that investors had been led to believe were watertight. These downgrades made AIG more vulnerable as they had insured super-senior layers through CDS contracts.

As more and more collateral was called for, AIG was running out of cash. Their systems and mentality were ill equipped to handle their difficulties as they had never expected their AAA credit rating to be threatened and therefore to be pressed to post collateral. As their long-term credit rating had now fallen from AA territory into A, they found themselves trapped in the lobster pot of illiquid subprime mortgage exposure with no means of escape.

And the illiquidity of securitised investments had come as something of a surprise. It had widely been assumed that the process of *"slicing and dicing"* credit would create a more 'complete' free market financial system. But instead credit products had become so complex and bespoke, that most never traded at all and could only be valued by models.

The Financial Crisis Inquiry Commission (FCIC), which was set up by the US Government and reported in 2011, concluded that: *"AIG failed and was rescued by the government primarily because its enormous sales of credit default swaps were made without putting up the initial collateral, setting aside capital reserves, or hedging its exposure - a profound failure in corporate governance, particularly its risk management practices. AIG's failure was possible because of the sweeping deregulation of over-the-counter (OTC) derivatives, including credit default swaps, which effectively eliminated federal and state regulation of these products, including capital and margin requirements that would have lessened the likelihood of AIG's failure".*

Rescue by US Taxpayer

When the denouement came to AIG, the major banks hovered on the brink of collapse too. Lehman was allowed to fail even though its linkages to others in the financial system could not be properly charted. Unlike Lehman, AIG was judged too big to fail, and not allowed to collapse into bankruptcy. the US taxpayer first put up $82 billion and then, when it quickly became apparent that more money was needed, stumped up $185 billion, the largest financial rescue of a company in history.

At the height of the crisis I was invited to AIGFP's London office in Mayfair to discuss their predicament and to advise how best to wind down securities and financial instruments whose value then exceeded US$3 trillion. The bulk of the most toxic exposure resided with the London office where, together with another BlackRock colleague, Pete Sanderson, we were embedded for several months from October 2008. It was an office atmosphere like no other. Individuals who had been seen as super smart and paid handsomely, were to be seen going back and forth across the Atlantic to face questioning and potential prosecution by the US Department Of Justice (DOJ). The families of AIGFP employees were vilified and threatened. Protection by sophisticated security firms had to be arranged as some employees faced death threats from within and outside the office. There were regular visits from those representing the interests of US taxpayers. Some regulators, with only a smattering of knowledge and oversight responsibility, chose to visit, more from curiosity than to question. It was no surprise that many of the AIGFP employees were deeply depressed, regarding their careers and some even their lives to be in shreds. In such a frozen atmosphere there was a complete absence of the buzz and banter that is typical of a trading floor.

In such a crisis environment it is easy to become submerged in a myriad of issues and end up, in spite of the urgency, achieving nothing. We therefore elected to identify the most critical tasks and focus our entire effort on their solution. The first task we focussed on was the reestablishment of lost trading links with the most important counterparties. Next we worked to close down a large and particularly risky book of business, one which was very difficult to insulate against loss and which infected the hedging strategy of almost all of the other 24 risk books.

The shock of the largest insurance company in the world, which for much of its life had been one of only a handful given the strongest AAA financial credit rating, with 88 million customers and 166,000 employees in 130 countries, being brought down by less than 20 people in their derivatives subsidiary, left many incredulous. Their $3 trillion book almost entirely made up of derivatives contracts was at its epicentre. As Hank Paulson, US Treasury Secretary at the time, commented in his memoir: *"AIG's incompetence was stunning."*

In spite of this, the AIG story is not about mathematics and financial formulae, or even poor trading decisions. It is a parable about people who thought they were super smart, that they could outwit competitors and market forces alike, and who behaved as though they were uniquely positioned to sidestep the disasters that had destroyed so many financial dreams before them. The collapse of AIG was a failure of culture, values, governance and, above all, leadership with the rot starting at the very top.

In the end the US Government made a $22 billion profit from their incursion, once the Maiden Lane vehicles that held the illiquid assets, named after the street in New York where AIG has its headquarters, were finally liquidated in 2012. It was an outcome that had seemed very unlikely in 2008.

Greenberg continued to fight for the company that was once his own fiefdom for many years afterwards, even suing US taxpayers for $25 billion on the grounds that the US Government rescue had stripped huge value from shareholders.

32. Hedge Funds revolutionise investment management

"Do not seek to follow in the footsteps of the men of old; seek what they sought"

Matsuo Basho, "The Rustic Gate" (Late 17th Century)

As derivatives swept through the banking system, the world of investment management stood on the side-lines, puzzled bystanders observing a financial hurricane. Justification for this curious detachment, even abstinence, came from clutching at an increasingly tenuous straw that derivatives had little to do with investment or that they carried unacceptable risks for the prudent investor.

Their case was reinforced by Warren Buffett, doyen of investment managers and second richest man in the world after his friend Bill Gates, the founder of Microsoft. Buffett had famously dubbed derivatives: *"financial weapons of mass destruction"* in his 2002 newsletter to Berkshire Hathaway shareholders. As discussed earlier this comment was as much to deter competitors from entering his core insurance businesses as it was from frustration at finding a 'black hole' of losses in the derivative subsidiary of the reinsurer he had acquired, General Re.

Although Alan Greenspan, Chairman of the US Federal Reserve, had countered in testimony to the US Congress that: *"derivatives have been an extraordinarily useful vehicle to transfer risk from those who shouldn't be taking it to those who are willing to and are capable of doing so"* and that: *"the financial system as a whole has become more resilient"*, his comments were largely ignored. As a consequence very few investment managers ventured into derivatives and, if they did, it was only to dip their toes in briefly in order to change economic exposure quickly and cheaply through the greater liquidity and lower dealing costs in futures markets. Some also purchased put options to protect their portfolios against capital loss.

'Old School' investment managers resistant to change

With hindsight it might seem odd that investment managers made so little use of them. It was almost as though the tools were too powerful, the opportunities and choice too great. Derivatives were to change the central tenet of investment from 'will the price rise?' to 'what will the price do?' and with it the corollary of more ways to be wrong and lose money.

You also had to be something of an evangelist to use derivatives. Investment systems were designed to purchase and sell securities which required no operational management after settlement beyond periodic valuation. Investment managers were not equipped to cater either for the daily monitoring and physical movements associated with margin and collateral that modern derivative markets required to confirm credit quality, or for the attendant 'lifecycle' events of exercise and expiry. The treatment of derivatives by regulators and tax authorities was also out of step with market developments. They did not understand the fundamental changes that these instruments had wrought and based their rules and judgements on derivatives using precedents from investment in securities. But with no pressure for change from the investment management industry, there was no urgency for the authorities to act.

For many traditional investment managers derivative scandals were seen as justification for doing nothing. At times such disasters were almost celebrated, suggesting there was wisdom in steering clients away from derivative opportunities on the grounds that they were averting an apocalypse. In truth senior management struggled to grasp the threats and opportunities that derivatives presented to their business. Furthermore, with investment management already a very profitable business with gross margins of over forty per cent, there was no hurry to change a winning formula.

As a consequence many failed to heed the message from the market place to their cost and their view that standing aside and insisting that investment should continue to be confined to traditional asset ownership was becoming increasingly fragile. The central plank for restricting investment only in assets that went up in price remained tenable as long as the associated belief that holding equities or bonds for the long term could be shown to be the most effective way to make money. For this they drew on past data that rarely stretched back even as far back as a hundred years. But, as the data was studied more and more carefully, the evidence became less and less convincing.

Return maximisation was the central credo for investment. Risk was something that caused short term price fluctuations but could largely be ignored. Actuaries had drawn on this belief to 'smooth' the returns on the pension funds which they advised, encouraging the bulk of pension fund money to be invested in shares, the riskiest financial assets of all. The flimsy basis for these beliefs is best illustrated by the investment commentary in actuarial textbooks. I was shown a book by an actuary for our life insurance business with long experience. He had kept his reference textbooks for actuarial students in the 1960s, a time when shares generally yielded more than bonds. The explanation given in the actuarial textbook was that *"shares yield more than bonds because they are riskier"*. When bonds began to yield more than shares in the 1970s most actuaries and investors initially treated this phenomenon as an unsustainable aberration. However once the trend failed to reverse and became the norm, actuarial textbooks altered their explanation. Opening a more recent actuarial textbook the same life actuary turned to the equivalent section which read that *"shares yield less than bonds as they provide capital appreciation whilst bonds do not"*, this effect being described as the *"reverse yield gap"*. Perhaps in time we will revert to the original yield gap but I doubt if the kind of explanations given in the past will be revived.

Exodus of investment talent to hedge funds

The notion that investment might imply making money from reading markets correctly, irrespective of direction, frightened investment managers more than their clients. The clients assumed that making money came from correctly reading markets, and investing accordingly was what they thought they paid their investment managers to do.

The edifice finally crumbled and the battle lost by the traditionalists when the brightest and the best from the major investment management firms voted with their feet and left to set up on their own. With the constraints of their former bosses removed, and often their best clients going with them, they formed boutique businesses that became known as hedge funds. It was a re-run of how many of today's giant specialist fund managers like Fidelity came into being in the 1950s, at that time seeking to escape from the torpor of the major banking houses who then managed the bulk of the money for pension funds. The new investment vehicles were called hedge funds because they did not simply buy and own investments that they thought would rise in value. They also reduced their stockmarket risk by taking short positions when they thought a share price would fall.

The departure and rapid success of the initial pioneers sparked an exodus of talent from traditional investment management firms. Free from the constraints and cost base of the investment houses they had left behind, hedge funds set their performance based remuneration at a very high level, which was soon to catapult the most successful proponents into the elite of the rich and famous. Their popularity reversed a downward spiral in investment management fees, bringing into being a far more lucrative fee structure than had existed before. Fees soon ranged around what became known as the '2 + 20' structure, a 2% annual fee determined by the value of the assets they managed with an additional performance fee of 20% of the gains in fund value. These fees were more than ten times those that they had typically been able to levy on large clients at the traditional investment management firms they had left behind and led Bill Gross, then Chief Investment Officer of investment manager PIMCO, famously to describe hedge funds as: *"a remuneration strategy (for the manager) not an investment strategy (for the investor)".*

Hedge fund managers set up their funds in obscure foreign countries to circumvent the regulatory and tax constraints that might curtail profitability or render their investment strategies impossible. Although hedge fund managers mainly based themselves in the major financial capitals of London and New York, the power of mobile electronic communications was now such that location was no longer an investment constraint. Investment managers on remote tropical islands were at no disadvantage to those physically close to financial markets. The days of investment management being built around gleaning inside information in coffee shops was long gone, to be replaced by the new appendages of Bloomberg and Blackberry, each of which had brought about an access and communication revolution of their own.

Bold thinking creates a new universe of investment opportunity

Many of the early hedge funds adopted 'long/short' strategies, buying shares they believed would rise in price and selling those that they thought would fall. It was not a difficult psychological departure for them to do so as the routine of their investment processes identified both. Instead of simply buying those that they liked they could now make money from those their research suggested would fall by selling their shares 'short'. Long/Short investing increased an investment manager's ability to make money from their skills.

And hedge funds opened up other attractive opportunities. If, for example, you bought shares you favoured to the same value as those you sold, the latter expected to fall, the investment risk associated with the rise and fall of stock markets, known as 'beta', was eliminated altogether. The risk that remained was solely the investment skills of the hedge fund manager, known as 'alpha'. This outcome meant that, for the first time, an investment manager's skill could be captured without general market risks outside their control. With market risk typically much higher than stock selection risk, the overall portfolio risk was markedly reduced. And investors were willing to pay handsomely for those who were real money makers, by allowing leverage of manager skill to replace the general market risk they had previously been forced to carry.

As their familiarity with derivatives increased, the hedge funds managers developed new investment processes to capture different investment ideas for making money. Instead of focussing solely on direction (whether share prices would go up or down) they began to focus on magnitude (how far share prices might move) and timing (when they would move). Others managers profited by judgements on movement or 'volatility' (how much shares prices might move or even making money by anticipating they would not move at all) or how the price of different shares or assets would move relative to one another, known as 'correlation'. They also broke down the risk of securities into their constituent parts, keeping only the risks they wished to carry whilst eliminating those they did not. By embracing, rather than resisting derivatives, hedge funds came to alter the notion of what constituted investment, changing the concept forever.

Their creativity knew no bounds and, now that the investment banks had the mathematical tools to offer a wide array of products, hedge funds could capture all manner of investment ideas and themes. Traditional 'long only' managers appeared to be dinosaurs by comparison.

With the investment systems of traditional managers proving inadequate and the new hedge fund managers having no desire to own infrastructure, the banks created platforms for everything the hedge fund managers needed to ply their trade. The banks called their comprehensive offering *"prime brokerage"*, providing them with rich pickings from trading commissions, lending money for leverage as well as the shares to sell that enabled hedge funds to short securities. Their services also encompassed custody and valuation, in other words provision of the entire infrastructure a talented manager needed to invest in whatever manner he or she wished, even if they desired to carry out their trading from the beach of a remote tropical island. As hedge funds traded much more frequently than traditional managers, the banks queued up to help them grow, even raising money for them through a service known as capital introduction.

Banks also saw hedge funds as the means to test and distribute the risks of high margin innovative investment products they had created. Overall the hedge funds proved to be such an all-round bonanza that some banks even supported talented employees to leave and set up hedge funds on the grounds that their alma mater could harvest richer pickings from their talents by acting as prime broker.

Of the major financial centres it was London that benefited the most from the development of hedge funds, not least as UK regulation, particularly around leverage, was more 'light touch' than alternatives like New York.

Big Managers embrace new world

The success of hedge funds was not just down to talented managers using the full array of financial tools to maximise returns for their investors. There was also dissatisfaction amongst investors with the way traditional managers were measuring themselves.

Up until the late 1980s investors and their managers had sensibly measured investment performance, mainly by evaluating the amount of money their portfolios had gained or lost, their 'absolute' return. In the early 1990s, with the introduction of index funds that could track the major stock market indices, active managers came to be measured by how much value they added from being different from the stock market as a whole, leaving the judgement on stock market participation to their clients, deeming it to be outside their control. Whilst sensible for assessing the stock picking skills of managers, it left the investor responsible for the biggest influence on making or losing money, the types of assets they held and their allocation of money between them. Risk and return for the investment manager became that of making money relative to an agreed benchmark although, for the investor, investment performance was still principally about making or losing money.

With index portfolio management, the aim is simply to track a particular stock market index. In a sense the investment strategy becomes driven by the measurement yardstick with keeping trading costs as low as possible the critical task. However by the turn of the century, active investment managers had also become caught up in a phobia about benchmarks such that their investment strategy was driven more by their measurement yardstick than by their investment views. As with passive investment management the benchmark had become the strategy instead of a measurement yardstick.

A tipping point was reached in 2000 when equity markets fell sharply following the bursting of the stock market bubble in technology company shares. Investors voted with their feet and turned to investment managers who were deemed to be 'outcome orientated' in that they sought to make money in absolute terms or relative to liabilities that pension funds were committed to meeting. By now hedge funds were well established and perfectly placed to meet the tide of investor money which now headed towards money makers from skill, the alpha producers, or to those offering cheap ways into asset classes, the beta providers.

The uneasy equilibrium between traditional investment managers and hedge funds was also to break as the most successful hedge funds had become a credible alternative in size and philosophy to traditional investment management firms. Under fee pressure and internal criticism, hedge fund manager practices were finally introduced into the mainstream. Encouraging this thinking further was that the financial economics of Fischer Black and his genre was now filtering into accounting and actuarial practice and the investment strategies of pension funds. The attachment to stock market indices as performance measurement benchmarks of the

1990s now appeared to be a strange twenty-year interlude as the philosophical return to basics meant losing money was always seen as underperformance.

Recognising their folly, some of the top executives in major investment management firms who historically had opposed derivatives now changed tack, and took to embracing derivatives. By so doing they were able to retain star managers likely to cross the divide and join hedge funds, whilst also empowering new talent with the skills and tools to provide the investment solutions their clients were asking for. In the same wash the practice of siding with regulators and others to curtail derivative activity ceased and been replaced by an energetic tide for reform.

Hedge funds were the conduit that brought derivatives into investment management and their appetite for opportunity and innovation shows no sign of abating. As banks have retreated from large swathes of business to focus on retail depositors and strong corporate borrowers, hedge funds have stepped in to fill the commercial void. The importance of their role in lending first came to the fore in the 1990s when Mexico defaulted on their debt. Whereas the losses from Latin American government defaults in the 1980s had been borne entirely by a few big banks, it was investors in dozens of hedge funds and mutual funds that suffered when Mexico defaulted. It was this event more than any other that demonstrated to regulators and the market that credit risk had migrated from the banks into capital markets.

33. Lehman failure exposes creaking market infrastructure

"The key to risk management is never putting yourself in a position where you cannot live to fight another day"

Dick Fuld, Chief Executive Officer, Lehman Brothers

25 Bank Street is a tall office tower in the Canary Wharf financial district of London's Docklands. The history of this building tells much about the events that have shaped and, at times shocked, the financial world in the new millennium.

When construction began in 2001 the building was earmarked to be the European headquarters for Enron. After Enron collapsed in November that year Lehman Brothers took on the lease, also choosing to make the building their European headquarters. When Lehman became the first occupier of the building in 2004 the firm was a top tier global investment bank and prized as a financially strong tenant. This strength was enhanced to almost 'watertight' status as the lease payments had the additional security of being underwritten by AIG, the world's biggest insurer with the finest AAA long-term credit rating. However, as an illustration of the scale and speed of how financial circumstances can change, just four years later, Lehman had gone bust and AIG was on the life support of a $189 billion financial rescue by the US taxpayer. Two years later JP Morgan, the biggest winner from the financial crisis of 2008, purchased the building and made it their European headquarters. 25 Bank Street has seen it all.

No rescue for Lehman

Much has been written about how Lehman went bankrupt and why the bank was allowed to fail. It was a certainly a massive jolt for the whole financial club as it had seemed unthinkable that a rescue would not be mounted for such an important player in global investment markets. After all the US Government had stepped in earlier that year to keep Bear Stearns, a less prominent firm, alive with taxpayer support for an emergency takeover by JP Morgan.

Dick Fuld, Lehman's CEO, had believed that he had not fallen foul of his adage and would manage to *"live to fight another day"*, confident that the US Government would have little choice other than to step in and shore the firm up. The risk to banking counterparties from Lehman's $7 trillion exposure to credit default swaps, and the turmoil that would ensue amongst investors who had money tied up with them through their prime brokerage services, was thought to be too great to be countenanced. Armageddon in global financial markets would surely follow a Lehman collapse.

But mounting a rescue for Lehman was a much tougher proposition than Bear Stearns had been. Their borrowings of $660 billion had the bank leveraged to the hilt, holding just $1 of their own capital for every $30 of assets they owned. Furthermore the assets they had leveraged were either risky, through derivatives and their broker dealer business, or illiquid through investment in property and private equity. This lethal cocktail of extreme leverage and illiquid assets relied on funding through short-term borrowing arrangements, and repurchase agreements ('repos') in particular. When the weaknesses in the quality of their portfolio of assets used as repo security came to light, this source of funding melted away. At the same time other sources of short term funding had become restricted or closed off altogether when the financial crisis struck.

Their international orientation also stood against a US taxpayer rescue, unlike Bear Stearns whose difficulties were principally domestic and linked to the US housing market. Much of their business, particularly in derivatives, lay outside US jurisdiction and the associated liabilities were mainly to non-US counterparties. It made the notion of a US taxpayer bank bailout to support foreign creditors politically unpalatable. There was also a rising tide of public feeling that rash banks like Bear Stearns should be punished, not saved, from their financial misdemeanours. Part of this argument ran along the lines that if big banks were rendered *"too big to fail"*, their management would adopt riskier commercial behaviour, secure in the knowledge that it would be taxpayers and not the firm that would suffer the 'moral hazard' should their aggression fail to pay off.

There was also little appetite from fellow banks to help Lehman. The firm had a poor collegiate record, refusing ten years earlier to put up the amount of money the other big US banks had put up to rescue LTCM. This refusal had grated somewhat as LTCM had been rescued to prevent a broader systemic meltdown in financial markets, with Lehman fingered as the most likely 'next domino' to fall over. So collapse Lehman did, causing collateral damage to derivatives markets that would reverberate for years to come. Along with those of AIG, the failings of Lehman were to become the cornerstone for a wholesale change in derivative market infrastructure and regulation. The collapse of Lehman's prime brokerage business was also to trigger an extraordinary corporate cameo that we discuss later, where Porsche came close to taking control of the automotive giant VW.

In derivative markets the fall of Lehman shone a light on the robustness of the processes and legal framework around counterparty default. Once again clearing houses, who were dealing with the exchange traded derivatives component of Lehman's business, came good. In Europe, for example, LCH Clearnet assumed control of all Lehman's positions, transferring client positions to other clearing members, and liquidating the bank's own positions without loss. A similar exercise was carried out in the United States by the firm I worked for on behalf of the Depository Trust and Clearing Corporation (DTCC). OTC derivatives fared less well where Lehman itself, and not a clearing house, was the counterparty. It was the unravelling of these positions that was to expose a number of practices that had crept into OTC derivative processes and supporting legal documentation across the industry, acting as a 'wake up' call to the unwary on dangers that had crept into the small print, and been overlooked. These weaknesses were particularly evident in the contractual arrangements between clients and counterparties, particularly around the operational processes dealing with the segregation of client assets and the handling of collateral.

Spotlight turned on hidden risks within Prime Brokerage

The main territory where these shortcomings came to light was in prime brokerage. Prime brokers, as their name suggests, were offering hedge funds more or less the entire suite of investment management services in return for becoming their principal brokerage partner. The prime broker would gain the lion's share of a hedge fund's business by providing custody for their cash and assets, handling all aspects of accounting and portfolio reporting, as well as trading on their behalf. Whilst the prime broker left the hedge fund manager free to trade with other brokers, all of their transactions flowed through the prime broker's master account. Where the prime broker made their real money was in providing the financing through which hedge funds could leverage their portfolios and also the stock borrowing that facilitated 'short' positions.

When going 'long' or 'short' shares, a popular investment approach was to do so by entering into Contracts for Difference or 'CFDs'. With these instruments, instead of buying and then later selling shares, the hedge fund had only to pay cash to the value of any losses when closing off the position. Gains and losses were paid in cash through their master account with the prime broker. Since the hedge fund did not have to pay the full value of the shares to which they were exposed, as they did purchasing physical shares, CFDs were great instruments for leveraging hedge fund portfolios.

However it was when one turned the spotlight on such practices, the detail of which were typically set out in paragraphs towards the end of long and turgid prime broker legal agreements, that the risks to the unwary became apparent.

CFD purchase would typically be initiated by the hedge fund purchasing physical shares in the market. The hedge fund would be charged for the shares in full through the prime broker account. However ownership rights to the shares would reside with the prime broker through a practice known as rehypothecation. This allowed the prime broker to use the shares to earn additional revenues for themselves by lending their customers' shares to other investors. In effect the hedge fund had paid for an asset they did not hold title to. The European arm of Lehman Brothers was particularly fond of using client collateral in this way. The practice seemed to be harmless until Lehman went bust, leaving hundreds of hedge funds facing a long struggle and the burden of proof to claw back assets that they had paid for but were not held in their name.

If there was one healthy outcome from the turmoil following the collapse of Lehman, it was that investors paid more attention to the conditions and terms of custody on how their assets were being held and used.

34. Rule changes after the storm

"In times of change learners inherit the earth; while the learned find themselves beautifully equipped to deal with a world that no longer exists"

Eric Hoffer (1898-1983)

In November 2008, when Queen Elizabeth II of the United Kingdom was opening a new academic building at the London School of Economics (LSE), she was baffled by how the financial crisis could have taken so many economists by surprise. She spoke for many when asking: *"Why did nobody notice it?"* Her husband Prince Philip, Duke of Edinburgh, was characteristically more blunt when later visiting the Bank of England, admonishing them: *"Don't do it again!"*

After the Lehman collapse and the taxpayer bailouts of the banks and AIG, public anger erupted across the world at the economic cost of the freewheeling shenanigans of the financial elite. Bankers and derivatives were seen as the main culprits, prompting Governments and financial regulators to set about reforming both.

Victory for exchange traded derivatives

Derivatives had been understood to be valuable instruments for lowering risk within the financial system, as well as improving price discovery and risk management. But unregulated derivatives seemed to have had the opposite effect, concentrating not dispersing risk whilst reducing price transparency. Making matters worse was that their most recent innovation, credit derivatives, had been accompanied by so many rules and convoluted legal small print effects that the nature of the contract had become hard to comprehend. In particular the language describing what constituted default became a minefield for argument that even PhDs of finance struggled to explain.

With derivatives the central concern was the OTC market. It was too big, too complex, too interconnected and yet largely unregulated and hidden from view. If the banks were too big to fail, it was in part because derivatives made them too interconnected for any major player to be allowed to fall. Regulators concluded that the infrastructure surrounding OTC derivatives was fundamentally unsafe, whilst that of their exchange traded derivative cousins was open and robust. The solution that was lit upon was to force OTC derivatives to become as close to exchange traded as was possible and for them to be governed by a similar market infrastructure. In the United States two senators, Chris Dodd and Barney Frank, championed the proposal through the US Congress, passing into law in 2010 as the Dodd-Frank Wall Street Reform and Consumer Protection Act. In Europe similar legislation was passed in 2012 under the banner of the European Market Infrastructure Regulation (EMIR).

Part of the reason for taking the exchange traded approach was that there was not felt to be enough time for any root and branch re-think of derivative market infrastructure. There was also pride amongst exchanges that their infrastructure had withstood the market turmoil and come through unscathed. It seemed to exchanges that the financial crisis had presented them with a 'once in a lifetime' opportunity to take control of the OTC marketplace, a prize that had eluded them for more than 30 years.

Supporting the case for exchanges as a safer option for market infrastructure needed little advocacy in the US as none of their clearing houses had ever failed. Outside the US regulators and lawmakers were less sanguine as their history on clearing house safety painted a different picture.

Banks resist reform of OTC derivatives

When the legislative process was in full swing during 2009, I was invited by Senators Dodd and Frank to speak at a private meeting of the committee they chaired. They asked me to comment on a variety of conflicting submissions and concerns that had been put to them, as well as to point to lessons from the history of these markets. Armies of lobbyists, predominately mobilised by the banks, had been fighting hard, putting up stern resistance to any reform of OTC derivatives markets. The principal objective of the banks was to keep this massive profit engine intact and no stone was left unturned in their efforts to ensure the legislative process was conducted at a snail's pace.

Some opined that public fury would soon abate and the appetite for reform would then recede as new political priorities took precedence. But those opposing reform had misjudged the mood of the people. Their argument, that legislation carried adverse unintended consequences, that the legislators should stand aside and leave such complex and difficult reforms to the market, fell on deaf ears.

There were obvious weaknesses that had to be addressed, of which transparency and the risk of systemic default were the most pressing. Because OTC derivative positions were private and only known to the two parties to the transaction, no one knew the extent the major banks and insurers like AIG had become interconnected. When trying to assess the impact of allowing Lehman or AIG to fail, too much of the analysis on systemic risk had been guesswork. Had Lehman's OTC positions been held within the market infrastructure of exchange traded derivatives, those dealing with the financial crisis of 2008 would have had all of this information at their fingertips and been able to make much better informed decisions. As it was there was no data to fine tune decision making and those in charge had been forced to take the blunt *"blunderbuss"* path of a worst case assessment and mount a wholesale rescue.

To outsiders the resistance of the banks to openness was surprising as they were supposed to be the champions of free and transparent markets. As the Financial Times journalist Gillian Tett put it: *"One of the founding principles of free market theory is the idea that markets work best when there is a free flow of information. Yet, some of those bankers who have been promoting free market rhetoric in recent years have also been preventing the widespread dissemination of detailed data on, say, credit derivatives prices."*

As a consequence forcing OTC derivatives trading onto a market infrastructure that mirrored that of exchange traded derivatives was to become the cornerstone of the derivative reforms passed into law under the US Dodd-Frank Act. For the exchanges this was manna from heaven as the biggest and some of the most lucrative OTC derivative contracts, interest rate swaps in particular, were mandated to reside in their laps. It was fortunate that this law came into force in 2010 as weaknesses in the exchange traded model became exposed the following year when MF Global, a major clearer of exchange traded derivatives, ran into difficulty from poor trading bets on European government bonds. To keep themselves afloat they had raided the futures margin deposits of their customers in much the same way as Barings had 15 years before.

Little enthusiasm or incentive to implement reforms

The speed at which the shift to the new exchange traded world came into being relied on the support of the banks. They were the clearing members who intermediated between investors and the market infrastructure of exchanges and clearing houses. Being forced to invest resource and capital to introduce an unprofitable regime they did not want was never a recipe for cooperation. To enforce change the regulatory authorities joined the public ranks of *"banker bashing"* to cajole them into action. Matters came to a head in 2013 when the European Commission charged thirteen banks and two other organisatons, ISDA and Markit, with collusion in preventing the emergence of trading credit default swaps (CDS) on exchanges, alleging they were seeking to protect the profits from their OTC business. It was even suggested that ISDA and Markit, on the advice of the banks sitting on their internal committees, had included explicit restrictions in licences that made it impossible for exchanges to enter the CDS business.

Life is tough for regulators and others whose job it is to police derivatives markets. They have always struggled to keep up as the markets, instruments, players, and techniques have progressed quickly, sometimes at lightning speed. The old adage of *"closing the stable door after the horse has bolted"* does not provide even rudimentary protection. Derivative instruments in imaginative hands are so adept in their evolution that they can morph into something so different that one is no longer policing the financial equivalent of a horse, nor is the enclosure a stable.

Like oarsmen, regulators tend to look backwards when seeking to progress forwards. From time to time they glance ahead to make sure there is no imminent danger of a collision, but not for long so not to be: *"put off their stroke"*. Credit rating agencies are often described as being: *"a day late and a dollar short"* as their ratings downgrades generally come after markets have already reacted to poor news and loss in value has already been crystallised. Regulators are sometimes thought of as much more pedestrian: *"years late and millions of dollars spent"*.

The issues regulators should be focusing on

When one muses as to what might have happened had there not been a knee jerk reaction to the financial crisis of 2008, but instead a root and branch review to make derivative markets fit for purpose in the 21st Century, a very different policy response comes to mind. The market structure and regulatory framework that accompanied the advent of financial derivatives in the 1970s needs to be reformed to cater for weaknesses that the subsequent forty years have exposed as well as to cater for new instruments and market developments, of which electronic trading and processing is perhaps the most significant. Another priority is to reshape the sanctions and control of the entities that have been the source of both heavy losses and been threats financial market stability, as there has been too much repetition of errors and misdemeanours.

Of these, uncontrolled leverage in support of a mistaken investment view had caused massive disruption on many occasions, with Barings perhaps the poster child of the genre. Poor understanding of the nature and risk of investments has also been a recurrent theme from the earliest days of OTC derivatives. There have been far too many cases, both in the public domain, and under the private radar, where customers have been conned or simply foolish, entering into transactions they did not properly understand. On occasion their banking counterparties have been partly to blame by glossing over or failing to explain how sensitive these positions were to certain risks.

Other issues that have surfaced concern the safety of the money that customers have put up to protect the integrity of the market. Keeping this money safe is of paramount importance, yet surprisingly, regulators at times place the security of the market and its clearing houses above the protection of customers. They should perhaps try and connect the dots with those who created clearing houses in the first place, in Japan in the 1700s and Britain in the 1800s, and remember that protecting customer money is the primary reason for their existence.

Making sure that customers have the money to meet their obligations is another recurring theme with the posting of sufficient collateral in the form of margin critical to ensuring market integrity. Nothing is more important than keeping this money safe and making sure it is correctly documented so the owners know where it is, what it is worth, how easy it is to sell, and that it cannot be taken or used by others. With derivatives there are no share certificates of ownership, just pieces of paper, nowadays mainly in electronic form, that tell you who has contractual exposure to whom and what the terms and conditions attaching to this exposure are. The rest of risk relates to all the usual frailties of human nature.

Credit control has encouraged the use of the battle hardened clearing houses. Their role also helps solve the administration and standardisation issues of OTC players, particularly in swap markets. More instruments should be pushed this way and, since most of the major clearers have substantial firm positions, margin money from clients should be ring fenced from that of the firm by segregation. By so doing the muddle between firm and client money cannot exist.

A key aspect that is now being recognised and picked up is how to mobilise the best people to handle a particular crisis. The financial world does not have formally appointed decision makers in the same way that sovereign states do through their political leaders, or the military engaged through a clearly defined chain of command. In a national crisis, leadership and decisions become vested in officials or practitioners who assume the mantle and gather around them a team of individuals they know and feel have the relevant knowledge. An interesting game in the aftermath of a financial crisis is to look at who took charge and made the key decisions and who, from their knowledge and experience, would have been best equipped to take charge. The two rarely coincide. On occasion fortune smiles and some individuals with great experience, knowledge and address books step up to the plate. But there have been some howlers too, when individuals in high authority with neither the relevant knowledge nor experience, have assumed the mantle. As time is always short, mistakes cannot be rectified nor a poor decision maker exposed and replaced in time.

Rules and procedures can be drafted on process and powers to handle a major financial crisis, but these can only be written to cope with an identified cause. Yet no crisis is ever the same as the last and the critical issue that has to be tackled is only properly observed and understood by a few. That is why there is an increased focus on clearing houses having default managers and an understanding of who should quickly be drafted in to deal with emergencies.

The financial crisis of 2008 seems a long time ago, yet the vessel of regulatory change intended to address the issues that arose is still moving. Many consider that the boat has steered off course and advocate that those pulling the oars should glance ahead before proceeding further.

35. Risk management systems bypassed with awesome ease - Paris 2008

"You lose any notion of the sums when you are involved in this sort of job. It's dematerialised. You get a bit carried way."

Jérôme Kerviel (2008)

Whilst the financial world was embroiled in the credit crisis, trying to unravel a tangle of financial instruments of almost unfathomable complexity, a Leeson-like tidal wave was about to engulf Société Générale, France's second largest bank. It came in the form of an announcement that the bank had lost €4.9 billion ($7.2 billion) in trading futures, the simplest of all derivatives, on account of the fraudulent trading activity of a single junior trader, thirty-one year old Jérôme Kerviel.

It seemed unthinkable. *"SocGen"* was no Barings. They had just been voted *"Equity Derivatives House of the Year"* by Risk Magazine and many surveys amongst their peer group and market professionals placed SocGen at the top of the equity derivatives tree, comfortably ahead of their giant US investment banking rivals. They were even tackling the US banks in their own back yard, boldly using the 'Superbowl' climax to the American football season to erect a giant derivatives trading floor in New York, where their investment clients could test out a wide array of trading strategies to make money from the football game that they could deploy afterwards in financial markets. It was SocGen's showcase for demonstrating their mastery of the more complex instruments that many of their rivals struggled to evaluate. Their innovative investment solutions were cleverly conceived and appeared well grounded within a sophisticated risk management system and a deep bench of talented individuals. For SocGen to spawn the biggest rogue trader in financial history was not credible.

The announcement came on Thursday 24th January 2008, a few days before a gala dinner in London when the Risk Magazine award was to be presented. The bank's statement suggested that the entire fraud had been perpetrated in just eleven days that month, and that there had been no prior warning.

Keeping the losses secret causes ructions

SocGen's press release said the bank had first become aware of the fraud the previous Friday but chose not to alert the authorities until the following Wednesday so that they could liquidate the position in secret. Cognisant of how a £300 million loss at Barings had risen to over £800 million through unwinding under the spotlight of publicity with the market knowing what they were doing, the SocGen executives thought they were being financially astute.

Friday's alarm had come from a combination of a very large variation margin cash call against loss making exchange traded futures positions, and a check on the validity of a large offsetting OTC market position that had been booked to Deutsche Bank as the counterparty. Deutsche had no knowledge of the position and nor had their trader, a former SocGen employee, on whose trading book the position was alleged to be held. Under intense questioning on Saturday morning, it was established that the Deutsche trader was telling the truth and that the perpetrator was a junior trader at SocGen called Jérôme Kerviel. Over the weekend SocGen's senior management learnt the full extent of Kerviel's activities, and this enabled them to start unwinding his futures positions early on Monday morning.

Unfortunately there was an unintended consequence from this secrecy. The US Federal Reserve (Fed), noting abrupt and unexplained falls in Japanese and European equity markets during Monday when US markets were closed for the Martin Luther King public holiday, became worried that their own market would suffer a similar fate. The Fed therefore took the preventative measure of cutting US short term interest rates by 0.75% before their stock market opened on Tuesday morning. When the Fed learned on Thursday that it was not an economic event, but a French rogue trader with positions in European markets that posed no threat to the US stock market, they were unhappy to have been kept in the dark. The French President, Nicolas Sarkozy, knew nothing either, and was angry that SocGen's senior management had not notified the authorities sooner. Sarkozy's mood was not helped by commentary in the press suggesting that his eye was more on his lover Carla Bruni, the supermodel and singer whom he later married, than on affairs of state.

Betting more than the bank through stock index futures

SocGen's account of how the losses had accrued told a simple story. Kerviel had bought futures contracts on three European stock market indices, the UK's FTSE-100 Index, Germany's DAX-30 Index and the broader European Eurostoxx-50 Index. He had built up this 'long' position very rapidly, amassing a €50 billion bet that European stock markets would rise. Kerviel had concealed the riskiness of the bet by entering into fictitious offsetting OTC derivative contracts on the same indices which, when netted off against their exposure through futures positions, made it appear to SocGen risk managers that he had not made a bet on the market at all.

Kerviel's biggest position was on the Eurostoxx-50 contract traded on the Eurex exchange. This €30 billion bet dwarfed the €18 billion on the DAX-30 and the €2 billion on the FTSE-100. He had been losing money as European stock markets had fallen and, in much the same way as Leeson had increased his positions on the Japanese stock market, Kerviel had increased his positions as he followed the gambler's trap that the French had invented in the 1700s known as a 'Martingale' of 'doubling up' to recover his losses. Much as Japan's Kobe earthquake had put paid to Leeson and Barings Bank twenty years before, the 5% drop in European markets on 18th January sunk Kerviel and exposed the fraud.

But how had he managed to do this? With a €50 billion position bigger than the €32 billion market capitalisation of the entire bank, Kerviel had not just 'bet the bank'; he had gone even further. How could one supposedly 'junior' trader out of 120,000 SocGen employees, have circumvented their much vaunted risk management systems and brought a bank, that had its origins in Napoleonic times and had survived two World Wars, to its knees in less than a fortnight?

The explanation that SocGen initially gave was that Kerviel, prior to joining their arbitrage department as a trader in 2005, had worked in the risk management department that controlled traders and: *"used this knowledge to avoid these controls or make them inoperable"*. They added that: *"In order to ensure that these fictitious operations were not immediately identified, the trader (Kerviel) used his years of experience in processing and controlling market operations successively to circumvent all the controls which allow the bank to check the characteristics of the operations carried out by its traders, and consequently their real existence".*

The methods Kerviel had used to cover his tracks and avoid SocGen's controls were listed as: *"instruments with no cash movements or margin call which did not require immediate confirmation"* which in layman speak were OTC derivative contracts. There had also been: *"misappropriation of IT access codes belonging to operators in order to cancel certain operations"* to enable him to book or cancel entries in different trader books. This was how he had been able to place the fictitious trade with Deutsche Bank that had alerted management on another SocGen trader's book. In addition he had been *"falsifying documents"* and spreading the fraud widely: *"ensuring that the fictitious operations involved different financial instruments to increase his chances of not being controlled".*

When SocGen's finance director came to see us shortly afterwards as part of a road show to explain these losses and to seek BlackRock's support for an emergency rights issue to raise €5.5 billion of new capital, he described it as: *"an elaborate strategy to avoid and confuse our risk management processes"* and that: *"he had been too clever to stop quickly enough".* He admitted that their initial public statement that the fraud had taken place over eleven days was false. Kerviel had evaded detection on significant market positions for almost a year, choosing very specific operations with no cash movements or margin calls and which did not require *"immediate confirmation"* and by constantly switching between different types of instrument.

Eery parallels with Barings

When questioned why €2.5 billion cash margin calls on a €50 billion futures position had not triggered alarms we were told they were: *"not of a different order of magnitude from volumes expected for a big investment bank"*. At the time SocGen had the biggest European equity derivatives book in the market and, as a consequence, large daily cash movements were not of themselves unusual. To those listening it felt as though SocGen's derivative management was no better than Barings had been.

However Kerviel's fraud was clever, much more sophisticated than that of Leeson. His experience of the bank's risk management and control processes was considerable and he was able to prevent a risk management alarm going off by posting offsetting OTC option positions onto the books of the same traders that he had allocated his futures trades to. And the traders to whom he assigned these trades were kept in the dark by Kerviel moving positions from one to another, meeting queries from them and SocGen risk controllers with the claim that they were *"booking errors being reversed out"*. In addition to evasion of controls on cash movements, he traded out of the fictitious OTC positions just before settlement dates on OTC positions when flags would have been raised by risk managers as money was about to be exchanged with trading counterparties.

Most puzzling was that Kerviel was not supposed to be taking risky bets on market movements at all, let alone be betting the bank in this way. His job, and the fraud was uncannily similar to that of Nick Leeson, was described as 'arbitrage' to take advantage of 'small discrepancies between equity derivatives and cash equity prices'. Every position he took in actual shares and futures contracts was supposed to be equal and opposite in size.

There was one serious blind spot in SocGen's risk management processes that saved Kerviel from early detection. Like most banks SocGen assessed its traders' risk on a 'net' basis, without paying much heed to their 'gross' exposure. Kerviel had no defined gross exposure limit and, in any event, it was not visible as SocGen amalgamated all the firm's trades together. That is why his €50 billion exposure did not set off any alarm bells. By creating a fictitious portfolio of trades that appeared to balance those he was really making, his net exposure stayed within set ranges and he remained below the radar.

Unanswered questions from Kerviel's trial

After the story broke, Warren Buffett, in his annual letter to shareholders in Berkshire Hathaway, the $220 billion conglomerate he had assembled over 43 years of savvy investing, reprimanded the banks for: *"inventing new ways to lose money when the old ways seemed to work just fine."*

SocGen's chief executive and other senior executives were brought down by the scandal. At Kerviel's trial of June 2010 their chief executive confessed that he: *"did not attend enough to the risk of fraud"*. Kerviel claimed in court that his superiors were aware of his activities, backed by evidence that their compliance officers were aware of 75 instances where he had breached his brief. It seemed that senior management executives were aware of Kerviel's conduct but chose not to call him to account.

Kerviel was found guilty on charges of forgery, breach of trust and unauthorised computer use. He was sentenced to three years in prison later that year and ordered to repay the entire €4.9 billion to SocGen. This sum was later reduced to €1 million on appeal with the judge and tide of public opinion taking the view that Kerviel was more a victim of an unhealthy systemic culture than a criminal fraudster.

To this day his $7 billion losses top the rogue trading tree by a substantial margin. However, in sharp contrast to others like Leeson and later Adoboli who were vilified by the press in the UK, Kerviel was portrayed as a naïve victim of France's banking elite, the son of a seaside hairdresser and a metalwork teacher who was enticed by a corrupt system and pushed to break the rules. A 2016 film entitled *L'Outsider* cast him in that light and the civil courts awarded him more than €400,000 in compensation for unfair dismissal. The Court was also to press for SocGen's award of damages against him to be quashed because of their lax management controls. In these cases the most telling comments came when the judge, in his summing up, said the bank: "*cannot pretend it was not aware of Jérôme Kerviel's fake operations*" and the state assistant prosecutor in the damages case comment was that SocGen was responsible for the: "*voluntary slackening of the rules with a view toward short-term gain.*"

But, to those reflecting on the case, something did not add up. Why had Kerviel done it? The usual hunt for a personal bank account or other hidden assets showed that he had 'no hand in the till' and derived no personal financial gain. How could such positions build up at such an alarming speed without the alarm going off?

Noting that the roster of rogue traders was growing and learning that some, like Kerviel, had made good profits before losing on a grand scale, some were wondering if senior management within certain banks were creating a culture and privately condoning ambitious traders who roamed outside their brief and limits to prove their money making credentials. Some suggested that the career 'fast tracking' of individuals from France's elite schools and universities meant that those, like Kerviel, who had a less illustrious education, felt he had to do something spectacular in order to progress within the bank. As the Financial Times (FT) was to put it: "*What would have happened if Jérôme Kerviel had stopped while he was ahead?*" Lord Myners, in a subsequent letter to the FT, succinctly asked the telling question: "*Why do banks announce only losses, and never profits, as a result of unauthorised trading?*" Perhaps the open way in which Chicago's exchange floors had promoted trading talent had been supplanted by something less transparent when trading shifted to bank trading floors. In any event the Myners' question remains unanswered.

36. Option trading in the fast lane - Porsche goes into overdrive - Stuttgart 2008

"My CFO can make money even when we're not selling cars"

Wendelin Wiedeking, Porsche Chief Executive

In September 2008, with the focus of attention on Lehman's default and the rescue of insurance giant AIG, a remarkable cameo act slipped almost unnoticed under the media radar. The principal actor was the car manufacturer Porsche; and the irony of the tale was that the bankers and hedge fund customers who most coveted Porsche's 911 sports cars were the unwitting victims.

The stage had been set some three years earlier in June 2005 when Porsche announced their intention to increase a long standing 5% shareholding in Volkswagen (VW) to 20%, ostensibly to provide VW with protection against an unwelcome takeover. The idea was that a 20% Porsche stake, when combined with a similar sized shareholding held by VW's home state of Lower Saxony, would make it almost impossible for anyone to mount a hostile takeover.

It made sense for Porsche to insulate VW in this way as it also protected their own business interests when many of the world's major car manufacturers were combining with one another through cross border mergers. Close personal and commercial ties had bound Porsche and VW together ever since the two companies were founded in the 1930s and over the years they had jointly developed many cars and technologies together. At the time, they were working together to produce their second generation 4x4 vehicle, the Porsche Cayenne and VW Touareg.

VW owed its existence to Porsche because Adolf Hitler, shortly after becoming German Chancellor in 1933, had instructed Porsche founder, Ferdinand Porsche, to design and build a basic 'volks wagen' (*"people's car"*) capable of transporting two adults and three children at 100 km/hour. Porsche designed the car that became affectionately known all over the world as the Beetle and initially headed VW himself. Twenty-one million of these iconic cars were produced between 1938 and 2003 and the Beetle remains the longest running and biggest selling car model ever made.

The first Porsche sports car contained many components made for the VW Beetle, a pattern that has persisted ever since, allowing Porsche to forge a business model closer to that of a car designer than a manufacturer.

Porsche's foreign exchange challenge

The way Porsche built their VW share stake showed their management team to be every bit as adept at financial engineering as they were renowned for their engineering prowess in building cars. They had already demonstrated their derivatives expertise through their skillful management of foreign exchange risk. Porsche had almost all of their manufacturing costs denominated in Euros yet, by 2003, over 50% of their global sales revenues came from selling cars in non-Euro currencies, mainly the US Dollar. Their profits had therefore become very sensitive to movements in the Euro/US Dollar exchange rate. A strong US Dollar relative to the Euro resulted in healthy profit margins whilst a weak US Dollar was damaging and could lead to significant losses. It therefore made good sense for Porsche to protect themselves by hedging their foreign exchange risk.

The simplest approach they could adopt was to enter into forward foreign exchange contracts where they committed to sell their future US dollar revenues forward in exchange for Euros purchased at an exchange rate agreed in advance. In this way they could insulate the business from adverse foreign exchange rate movements by matching their Euro costs with Euro denominated revenue exposure. However this hedging technique could only furnish Porsche with short-term protection, a year ahead at best. The weakness of forward contracts was not just their poor liquidity for periods greater than a year; they could also turn into risky speculative currency bets if US car sales turned out to be less buoyant than expected and Porsche had sold more US dollars forward than they actually received from selling cars.

Forecasting car sales is hard, even for one year. Predictions further into the future are more unreliable, as is the case with many other industries. That is why few businesses feel safe hedging their currency risk for longer than the year ahead. However, this approach has its own shortcomings. Taking out new forward contracts each year would provide little protection against a longer term decline in the US Dollar as the hedge for the next year's revenues would be set at the exchange rate prevailing at the start of the following year. For a business like Porsche, with long term embedded Euro costs, something different was needed to tackle uncertainty of sales revenues and to protect them against a long term weakness in the US Dollar.

The strategy that many of the major volume car manufacturers like Toyota, VW and Mercedes had adopted to deal with longer term US Dollar risk was to build local manufacturing plants in the United States. In that way a good proportion of their sales revenues was matched by manufacturing costs in the same currency. But that strategy did not sit well with Porsche. Their car volumes were too small to justify the expense and management resources to manufacture abroad. Furthermore much of their brand cachet came from the quality and reputation associated with their German manufacturing heritage. As their business strategy could not circumvent the foreign exchange issue in the way other car manufacturers could, the solution they arrived at was wholly financial, involving a variety of hedging techniques based around a cocktail of currency options, of which compound options were to become the most prominent.

Magical profit machine called compound options

Compound options might sound innocuous but they lie at the exotic sports car end of the currency option spectrum. They are not simply options to buy or sell a currency at a future date but options to buy or sell the currency options themselves; in other words, options on options.

The world of compound options

With compound options you acquire the right to buy other options at terms agreed in advance. Cheaper than more conventional options, they provide the scope for making big bets with little money. However, before you can exchange the asset you wish to buy or sell there are two premiums to pay and two options to exercise; making the total premium payable greater than that of the premium on a single option.

Compound options come in different forms as they can be call or put options on call or put options. For example a caput is a call option on a put option; in Porsche's case with currency options they held call options on US Dollar put options which some later termed 'Kaputt' options after the German word that means 'destroyed' or 'broken' as this is precisely how the writers of these options felt afterwards.

The flexibility of these options is that when 'in-the-money' you can choose to take your profit at a moment in time that particularly suits your interests; in Porsche's case they chose to do so close to their accounting year end.

As a long term strategy this hedging was prescient as the US Dollar almost halved in value against the Euro in less than eight years, falling from a peak of US$1 buying €1.21 in 2000 to only €0.62 in 2008. Hedging by any method would have been helpful but, in Porsche's case, they had been much smarter. Such was the fall in the US Dollar that Porsche were able to crystallise their US Dollar revenues through compound options at a better exchange rate than had prevailed at any time during the year in which they were exercised. Porsche had executed a very sophisticated programme that lasted longer and was to turn the US dollar decline into a three-year corporate profit engine. Porsche's compound options not only protected their US Dollar revenue for the next three years, but did so at whatever time was most advantageous for the company.

Although Porsche said little about the scale and success of these activities it was clear to analysts looking under the hood of their financial statements that the money involved was enormous. In the 2003 financial year, when the company reported profits of €163 million, it was estimated that Porsche had lost over €300 million from making cars but gained around €500 million from currency hedging their US dollar exposure.

In 2004 the profits from currency options came in even higher, accounting for around €800 million of Porsche's €1.05 billion profits. As they were only reporting gains they had crystallised from maturing and closed positions, Porsche had more profits tucked away in the glove box in the form of their remaining currency hedges that were set to mature in 2005 and 2006. With their latest 4x4 Cayenne model coming into production and about to become a source of revenue instead of being a development cost drain, the near term profit outlook for Porsche was looking very rosy indeed.

Buoyed by the success of this currency hedging their CEO complimented his CFO's money making talents at the 2003 Frankfurt Motor Show with the comment: *"My CFO can make money even when we're not selling cars".* It was a remark he would come to regret as it served to reinforce a growing belief amongst investors that the company was behaving more like a hedge fund than a car manufacturer. It would lead to the company being labelled a 'hedge fund' in investment circles, a yoke that would come to haunt Porsche as the VW stake building story unfolded.

VW stake building as a profit engine

When it came to building their VW stake, Porsche again did their homework with meticulous attention to detail. They were savvy enough to know that if they simply announced that they were proposing to increase their VW stake by 15%, they would simply drive up the purchase price against themselves as they competed with others in the market to buy VW shares. But, just as Robert Holmes à Court had used options to capitalise on his stake building in publishing and natural resource companies, Porsche followed the same path when building their VW stake.

Stock market rules meant that Porsche was unable to buy very many VW shares before being forced to publicly declare their intentions. It was these rules, allied to the knowledge and experience gained through their foreign exchange dealings, which led them to consider VW share options. One aspect they immediately noted was that the declaration rules around certain option contracts were much less onerous than those for shares. Through option contracts Porsche could purchase as many VW shares 'synthetically' as they wished by simultaneous purchase of call options and sale of put options on VW stock around the prevailing €45 market price. It was economically an identical transaction to buying the shares except that it would go unnoticed by the market, as there was no requirement to report private OTC derivative contracts to the market. They also had the call option contracts drafted as Contracts for Difference (CFDs) that on maturity settle in cash at the difference between the exercise price and the prevailing market price, and not through delivery of shares. Had the contracts been settled as shares they would have had to declare the additional shares stake they had acquired. Another precaution to make sure no one knew what they were doing, was to focus their trading activity through a single trusted stockbroking firm outside the mainstream of investment banks.

When Porsche announced their decision to increase their VW stake to 20% the VW share price jumped 5%, substantially increasing the value of their existing share stake as well as the option positions they had quietly accumulated. By making this announcement six weeks before their 31st July financial year end, these market gains served to boost their 2005 reported earnings.

In 2006, with Porsche now holding the 20% stake in VW shares they had said they wanted to buy, the market assumed their stake building was over and, with no buying pressure to propel the price higher, VW's share price drifted back to around €50. It was at this time that the huge earnings fillip Porsche had enjoyed from their compound options on foreign exchange was coming to an end and they were keen to find something to replace the earnings hole they had left behind. Porsche had downplayed the significance of the earnings boost from foreign exchange in prior years, preferring to have investment analysts ascribe a stronger trading performance to their car manufacturing. Success can be addictive and a derivative drug was taking hold. It was in this mood that they decided to carry out another stake building exercise, this time taking their VW shareholding up to 25%.

This move was again to prove very profitable. Porsche had acquired the additional shares that took their VW stake from 5% to 20% at around €45 and now paid close to €50 to take it up to 25%. When VW's share price then doubled to over €100 in 2007, Porsche could no longer hide that they were making much more money from their VW stake and option positions than from building cars. When asked why call options played such a prominent role in their stake building they claimed that this lessened the price risk they carried on their VW share purchases. This was technically correct as, were there to be a massive decline in the VW share price, they only stood to lose the call option premium they had paid and not the entire share price fall. However this explanation masked a deeper sophistication.

Porsche's financial market exploits were attracting plaudits and criticism in equal measure. But no one could question the flawless execution of their Finance Director, Holger Haerter, his skills being worthy of the original master of the genre, Robert Holmes à Court.

But now many financial commentators were openly suggesting that the company had turned from being a sports car maker into a hedge fund. They had a point as, although the accounting numbers for the financial year ending in July 2008 were not presented to show it, Porsche had made €6.83bn from VW options, €1bn from the rising value of its VW stake, and €1bn from selling cars. This was a source of considerable irritation within the company, particularly as Germany had as strong a distaste for hedge funds as they had respect for engineering excellence. A leading German politician had reflected the public mood when describing hedge funds and private-equity firms as: *"irresponsible locust swarns who measure success in quarterly intervals, suck off substance and let companies die once they have eaten their bones…"* The German Chancellor, Angela Merkel, when president of the G8 group of industrialised countries in 2007, had placed hedge funds at the top of the list of threats to financial stability. This discomfort came to the surface when an investor on a financial analyst call asked: *"Is not Porsche a hedge fund?"* to which the Porsche spokesman responded with the thinly disguised rebuke: *"We make money from hedging and building cars. The difference is that hedge funds don't make cars the last time I looked."*

Porsche raises the stakes by becoming predator

But now Porsche had reached a form of crossroads. They could no longer argue that a further increase in their VW stake was to defend VW from an unwelcome takeover. Their 25% stake, when augmented by Lower Saxony's 20%, effectively ruled out that possibility. A further 5% would render the exercise mathematically impossible. If Porsche bought any more shares in VW the market would no longer view their intentions as defence but instead the polar opposite; an audacious strategy by Porsche to take control of VW. With VW jockeying with General Motors and Toyota to become the biggest selling car manufacturer in the world such a strategy from a minnow like Porsche seemed fanciful, even wild, akin to a Porsche 'David' taking over the VW 'Goliath.'

But Porsche could not afford to stand still. They had borrowed money to buy their VW stake and relied on these shares, as Robert Maxwell had with Maxwell Communications Company, to be of sufficient value to act as collateral for their debts. They now had to choose between standing still, raising their VW stake further, or to go into reverse and reduce their VW shareholding. The latter was regarded as a non-starter as, with such a large stake, they would almost certainly turn their VW investment from a profit generator into a loss maker. Staying still was not attractive either as once it was thought Porsche were no longer buyers, the VW share would lose its support and be open to attack from short selling hedge funds. It had become a high stakes game of poker where Porsche had to choose either to raise or fold.

And the dilemma facing Porsche management had its own fascination. The idea of these two companies coming together had captured the public imagination, as well as that of investors and the motor industry. With their close historic linkages and descendants of Ferdinand Porsche running both companies, there was no shortage of story material for the media to exploit.

Hedge funds drawn in and ease VW stake building

The publicity and the activity in VW shares were now to attract a new predator into the ring, hedge funds, whose managers were paradoxically amongst their most enthusiastic customers. For them there was a 'relative value' opportunity between the high stock market value of VW shares relative to those of its major competitors.

One measure of stock market valuation is the amount you have to invest in a company's shares to buy €1 of annual earnings. This relationship of share price to earnings is known as the 'p/e ratio'. In September 2008, with the VW share price standing at €207, investors had to pay €17.1 for each €1 of earnings, a 17.1 p/e. With rivals Toyota trading at 8.7, Daimler (Mercedes) at 9.5, and Porsche itself at 2.3, VW had become, in stock market terms, by far the most expensive car manufacturer in the world.

The hedge funds sought to profit from the ratings of car manufacturers coming closer together by entering into 'pairs trades' where, for example, purchases of shares in Toyota were matched by sales of an equivalent value in the relatively expensive VW shares. Making this trade particularly compelling was that the hedge funds believed that Porsche's buying of VW shares had come to an end. They thought Porsche was now trapped in a lobster pot of their own making and lacked the firepower to continue their stake building. It seemed to the hedge funds that the VW share price had been left vulnerable to attack, with Porsche's dilemma presenting a golden opportunity for financial profit.

Porsche's management could see what was happening and the catastrophic damage that would be wreaked on their earnings and reputation if they stood still. They knew they were at a tipping point and had to choose between certain defeat or an extraordinarily bold move; to acquire all of VW and relieve the debt laden Porsche by gaining access to VW's cash pile.

And they held an ace up their sleeve that their hedge fund adversaries knew nothing about; a card of such power that if judiciously deployed could deliver a knockout blow to Porsche's adversaries.

Porsche sets a bear trap

By September 2008 Porsche had built up a 35% stake in VW shares. By now hedge funds and other investors were actively betting that the share price would fall by taking 'short' positions. Their short bets were established by selling VW shares, stock futures and contracts for difference (CFDs) or through purchasing VW put options. One way or another all of these approaches involved borrowing from a holder of VW shares and then selling these shares into the market. Since borrowing shares from other shareholders is the only means by which stock can be shorted, that is why investment analysts track the amount of stock borrowed as a means of measuring the extent to which investors are betting on a share price decline.

Short Selling - How to sell shares you do not own

When you enter into an agreement to sell shares (or indeed any other goods) the buyer will only pay when the shares are delivered. As short sellers do not own any shares they have to find some to deliver. The way they do this is by borrowing the shares from an owner of the shares which they then deliver to the buyer.

The shareholder who lends the shares receives a fee from the borrower for facilitating the transaction. The shareholder can claim their shares back at any time for any reason but will typically only do so when they themselves wish to sell the shares.

The aim of the short seller is to buy the shares back at a lower price, profiting by the difference, and then returning the borrowed shares to the original owner.

The Lehman Turbocharger

When Lehman declared bankruptcy on Monday 15th September 2008 stock markets around the world fell on the news. The German market also dropped except that the share price of VW, their largest company, was conspicuous in running sharply upward against the tide, cushioning the overall market decline. Opening at €207 on Monday morning the VW share price rose to €304 on Thursday, a 47% increase in just four days. The share price continued on an upward albeit volatile path over the next few weeks, reaching €398 on 16th October.

At first market commentary to explain the rise in the VW share price was relatively benign. Lehman had been the biggest facilitator of the short positions in VW shares for hedge funds by borrowing shares they could sell as part of their prime brokerage services. Those who had lent their VW shares to Lehman were now demanding their return, forcing the short sellers to buy the shares back in the market. With a queue of forced buyers and the owners of stock unwilling to lend or sell shares, the price had only one way to go, and that was up. The feeling was that once the shorts had bought the stock they needed to neutralise their exposure, things would return to normal.

This initial 'short squeeze' was made worse by the limited number of VW shares available to purchase. Porsche now owned 35% of the company and Lower Saxony 20%. Index funds who held VW shares benignly at their weighting within the stock market index might lend their shares but would not sell, as their passive tracking strategy paid no heed to whether or not the shares were cheap or expensive. They held the shares in order to track the index and, in the case of VW, it was their most important holding as it represented over 25% of the Germany's stock market as measured by their DAX Index. Share price volatility was explained by the bears wrestling hard but to no avail through the short squeeze, which was why VW's share price had climbed to €398 by mid-October. VW had almost doubled in a period when the DAX index had fallen by a quarter. Most DAX shares had fallen much further with the index itself propped up by its high flying biggest constituent, VW. By then the short squeeze appeared to be over and things appeared to have returned to normal when the VW share price then fell back, returning to almost whence it had come, reaching €211 on Friday 24th October.

Shock and awe as knock in options kick in

But then the afterburners kicked in. On Sunday 26th October Porsche stunned the market by announcing that, not only had they made share purchases to increase their VW stake to 42.6%, this was being augmented by an additional 31.5% stake purchase through derivative contracts, bringing their holding up to 74.1%. The latter part of this announcement came as a complete surprise and had a 'shock and awe' effect on financial markets. It transpired that Porsche had secretly bought OTC 'knock in' call options from banks, some of which were exercisable into VW shares at a share price of €150, the remainder at €200. The knock in feature meant that the option to purchase VW shares had not existed until the VW share price had reached €250.

Knock in options come from a family known as barrier options; that is to say they only come into being if the agreed share price barrier is reached. Their polar opposite barrier option 'cousin', the 'knock out' option, operates the other way round, being a 'live' exercisable option to start with that ceases to exist if the barrier share price is reached. The knock in options meant that, until the VW share price reached €250, the banks writing these options had no certain liability to hedge. However once the shares reached €250 they had an enormous liability to manage.

The maths was breathtaking. 12% of VW's shares had been borrowed by short sellers who, in the fall from €398 to Friday's €211, had recouped some of their losses they had suffered following the Lehman collapse. To close off their positions these investors, principally hedge funds, needed to buy 12% of VW shares and return the shares to the shareholders who had lent them. But now Porsche controlled 74% of VW and, with Lower Saxony confirming it would not sell any of its 20% stake, there was only 6% of VW shares left that were potentially available for purchase in the market. With 12% to buy and only 6% available to sell, the short sellers faced an insoluble mathematical task.

On Monday morning the VW shares opened at €520 and the mad scramble that ensued to buy the few shares that were available took the VW share price to €1,005 during Tuesday's trading session. At this share price VW was not just Germany's largest company, it was also the most valuable company in the world by market capitalisation, even eclipsing the oil giant Exxon Mobil. One investment analyst described the move as: *"probably the biggest short squeeze in history… a short squeeze to infinity."*

For the investors, caught wrong-footed from betting that the share price would fall, this upward move was disastrous. And it was not just hedge funds that suffered. Others, including a much-respected German industrialist, were to commit suicide over their personal losses.

Denouement - Porsche reverses into VW

With such extraordinary share price gyrations going on in their largest company Germany's financial regulator, BaFin, launched a probe into Porsche's stake building. In the meantime the stock market was left in the dark over Porsche's intentions and next move. But now Porsche was coming under intense financial pressure to complete a VW takeover quickly. They had borrowed €11.4 billion from the banks to fund their VW stake, €7 billion of which was borrowed in their most recent stake building. Borrowing conditions were tough as the financial crisis had left banks very short of capital. They could only sustain Porsche borrowing of this magnitude if confident that Porsche would be able to repay them from VW's cash pile.

It was Porsche that was now running out of road. Lower Saxony had turned against Porsche and their 20% VW stake gave them a legal right to veto an unwelcome takeover. This right was enshrined in the Volkswagen Law which was passed in 1960 when the company was privatised. Desperate to complete the takeover, Porsche took Lower Saxony to court to nullify the veto but lost the case. With access to VW's cash denied it was Porsche who were now in dire straits, verging on bankruptcy through their debt load. Lacking the financial firepower to continue, and after jostling to stay in the game, Porsche was forced to surrender to its intended victim, succumbing to a takeover by VW. Instead of owning VW, Porsche would join a stable of twelve brands that spanned truckmakers Scania and MAN, luxury marques Bugatti, Bentley and Lamborghini, carmakers Skoda, Audi and motorcycle maker Ducati. The tables had been turned and the predator had become the prey.

Once the dust settled from their extraordinary market operations, all kinds of legal wheels began to turn and it was no fun at all for Porsche's senior management. Hedge funds, especially when outsmarted, can be sore losers. Their $24 billion in losses said to be the biggest single loss in hedge fund history. Four funds sued

Porsche and their two most senior executives for more than $1bn in one of the largest damages claim battles corporate Germany had ever seen. A lawsuit was also filed in New York accusing them of market manipulation and that they: *"repeatedly misled investors and lied about Porsche's positions and intentions with respect to VW"*. In all, claims with a total value of €5 billion were filed. Ultimately the lawsuits were deemed worthless in 2016 with the judge's reasoning described as: *"judicial execution of the prosecution"*. By the time the VW acquisition of Porsche was finally completed VW itself had become embroiled in its own murky scandal over fitting devices that falsified emissions data.

Porsche had come very close to winning the car giant and, but for Lower Saxony's veto, would have done so. Instead they ended up as one of eleven marques in the VW car and truck empire. With their knock in options Porsche had knocked themselves out.

37. Tarnished country accounts made to shine

"God gave watches to the Swiss and time to the Greeks"

Anon

As companies and other organisations found derivatives a formidable tool for dodging and weaving their way around the tax, accounting and regulatory rules that national governments had painstakingly crafted into legislation, the stage was set for perhaps the most surprising players of all to join the derivatives game, the sovereign states themselves. They came to the party to circumvent international laws and agreements that restricted their political and economic room to manoeuvre, and were guided by the same bankers who they had complained were running rings around their own national rules.

It was a curious moment in time too, coming when governments around the world were becoming increasingly frustrated with the whole business of derivatives. What had been sold to their politicians, treasury departments and regulators as the way to free their markets from protectionism and red tape, turned out to be a quick and easy financial bypass around every tax and regulatory measure nation states had chosen to enact.

All sorts of global initiatives to bring the banks to account were failing as there was always a country willing to offer them a benign and accommodative home, thereby winning business from any rival states who were seeking to tighten up on financial behaviour or loss of tax revenues.

And it was easier for states to skip around undesirable international rules and regulations than it was for companies to circumvent the law. International entities struggled to police and discipline sovereign states as fines or other forms of punishment tended to founder; and politics entered the equation, often overturning a binding legal agreement. There was also something of the spirit of *"If you can't beat them, join them"* that drew countries into playing the derivatives game.

Accounting tricks to join the Euro

"I'm not worried about the deficit. It's big enough to take care of itself."

US President Ronald Reagan (1911-2004) -
Gridiron Club annual dinner (1984)

In the early 1990s rules were drawn up for the amount of debt and relative size of budget deficit that European countries were permitted if they wished to replace their national currency with the Euro, a new pan European currency. The purpose of these rules was to rein in fiscal profligacy amongst aspiring Eurozone entrants, whilst giving considerable local autonomy over the means by which each country met these stringent targets.

The rules were first proposed in the Maastricht Treaty of 1992 and became enshrined into European law in 1996 under the Stability and Growth Pact (SGP). The rules concerning debt specified that the total national debt should not exceed 60% of Gross Domestic Product (GDP) and that the annual budget deficit should not be more than 3% of GDP. The deficit limit was considered the more important of the two targets and countries that breached the 3% maximum were to be subject to heavy fines, up to 0.5% of annual GDP. These fines were to be paid into the coffers of the European Commission in Brussels under the terms of the Excessive Deficit Programme (EDP).

To meet these terms for entry, and then to maintain this borrowing discipline after adopting the Euro, proved to be a considerable challenge. For some of the southern European countries these targets appeared to be out of reach. Yet such was the political imperative for European economic and monetary union that informal support was given to a number of creative accounting initiatives that served to ease the economic burden of meeting the SGP targets.

Italy plays the first creative accounting card

It was important for the European currency project that Italy joined the initial Euro launch at the beginning of 1999. However the SGP rules appeared to present an insurmountable obstacle. Italy's overall debt in 1997 stood at 110% of GDP, and to lower an annual budget deficit from 7.7% in 1995 to the 3% maximum by 1998 seemed well nigh impossible. To give Italy a fighting chance of complying with their SGP borrowing targets, their sovereign debt management team was given the latitude to augment real economic measures with more artful accounting and financial tricks.

Derivative contracts figured in both the real and artificial measures taken in 1996 once the SGP rules came into force. Through these transactions and other measures Italy was able to improve their reported financial standing, cutting the publicly reported budget deficit to just 2.7% in 1998, the decisive year for Euro membership approval. How Italy had achieved this was regarded less a miracle and more something of an economic mystery as, over the same period, their tax receipts had increased only marginally whilst government spending as a proportion of GDP was much the same. Nevertheless the budget deficit numbers they presented were accepted and Italy was able to join the Euro launch.

The window dressing that brought the public accounts into line included much more than derivatives. The task itself was not particularly onerous since GDP, the denominator for both of the key ratios, was itself a movable feast. As Enrico Giovannini, Professor of economic statistics at University of Rome and a former President of Istat, Italy's statistical body, quipped: *"Non-statisticians often suggest that measuring happiness and well-being is a tricky task. But have you ever tried to measure GDP?"* By way of illustration, when Italy started to take account of their *"off the books"* shadow economy in 1987, their GDP grew 18% overnight. This action took the size of their economy past that of countries like the UK, making Italy the Western world's fourth largest economy. More recently, in 2014, when Istat decided to include drug trafficking, prostitution, and alcohol and tobacco smuggling in their economic output numbers, Italy's GDP increased again. Not only did such changes make the SGP limits less onerous, they were also beneficial in money terms as Italy was allocated more money from the EU coffers as a consequence.

Entering into derivative contracts was not in itself unusual. Such transactions are part of the normal routine of government financing as they source funds from investors around the world by issuing bonds in foreign currencies, typically US Dollars, Japanese Yen or Swiss Francs. With their daily bills in Euros and repayments of the borrowed money in foreign currencies, European government treasury departments enter into cross currency swaps for much the same reason as IBM and the World Bank did when carrying out the first cross currency swap transaction in 1981. Governments also routinely enter into interest rate swap contracts to protect themselves from higher borrowing costs.

Loans created through unusual cross currency swaps

Under normal circumstances cross currency swap contracts are simply agreements to swap cash flows in different currencies, thereby alleviating currency risk. However in the case of Italy, and later as we shall see with Greece, these contracts also served to provide loans that did not show up in the public accounts.

With a normal 'vanilla' cross currency swap, the exchange rate usually referenced is the prevailing market 'spot' or forward rate between the two currencies. This results in principal amounts of the same value being exchanged on contract maturity. Furthermore the market value of the swap contract at inception is typically nil.

This was not so for the cross currency swaps carried out by Italy's debt management agency. Instead of choosing the prevailing 'spot' or forward exchange rate for denominating the underlying amounts or 'notionals' of the two currencies being exchanged, different 'off-market' exchange rates were selected. With different notional amounts the cross currency swap had an immediate market value, which was compensated through an upfront cash payment.

The common theme of these artful cross currency swap transactions was for Italy to obtain an upfront cash payment from the counterparty. This cash could then be deployed either to reduce the budget deficit for the year in question, or to repay existing public debt. Both uses were helpful in meeting the SGP targets. Economically, the upfront cash component of these transactions, all carried out with the major international banks, was no different from loans. However, by embedding these payments inside cross currency swaps, they were treated as *"off balance sheet currency transactions"* and not counted as loans on either their public accounts or for SGP measurement purposes.

In return for this upfront cash Italy had to pay a higher stream of interest payments during the lifetime of the swap. These interest payments were often deferred until the swap matured and paid out in the form of a large 'balloon' cash payment comprising the initial upfront cash loan and all of the interest payments. These 'off market zero-coupon cross currency' swap contracts provided the means for implementing a classic *"kick the can down the road"* strategy for postponing debt repayment.

Much of the detail surrounding the cross currency swap transactions remain vague as neither Italy nor the banks publicly disclosed or were willing to comment on these deals. Some feeling for the scale of Italy's derivatives dealing can be gleaned from the observation that €160 billion, 10% of the country's government bond market, was hedged using interest rate swaps. Over time however more information has come to light as these contracts matured or were 'rolled over' into new positions. It was then that losses were crystallised and the cost of these transactions became subject to fierce criticism.

Greece follows suit

Greece made no attempt to join the Euro in the first wave. They had reasoned that the scale of their budget deficit, public debt load and domestic inflation rendered the SGP conditions well out of reach. They therefore opted to give themselves more time, and targeted a 2001 date for joining the Euro. In the intervening period Greece made good economic progress as inflation fell along with the budget deficit. Their SGP credentials were further boosted by a rise in GDP, in part driven by public sector reforms. However they were still some way off the SGP targets for joining the Euro with public debt stubbornly remaining above 100% of GDP, well over the 60% limit. Their borrowing costs also failed another SGP test, as they were suffering the highest rate of interest in the Eurozone. To bring their public accounts into line Greece therefore followed Italy's lead and headed into creative accounting territory.

With further to travel than Italy to bring the numbers into line, a more substantial effort was called for by Greece. The Greece statistical agency, who compiled the numbers on GDP, public debt, budget deficit as well as others relevant to SGP tolerances, was quick to step up to the plate with imaginative ideas. So adept did the head of this government agency prove to be at coming up with ideas to meet the Euro conditions, that he became known as *"The Magician"*. As the Greece economist for one of the big global banks commented: *"We always saw the head of the statistical agency of Greece… He first made inflation disappear. He then made the deficit disappear."*

One such trick Greece deployed was to make the losses of the state railway disappear altogether. The railway lost over €1 billion each year and had more employees than passengers, prompting the suggestion by a former minister that they save money by paying for their passengers to travel by taxi instead. Their losses vanished altogether for SGP accounting purposes when the railway company issued shares to the government in what was designated a *"financial transaction"*.

In other securitisation transactions, which was described by one commentator as *"a garage sale on a national scale"*, Greece officials essentially mortgaged the country's airports and highways to raise much-needed money. Some of the Greek deals were named after figures in Greek mythology. Greece received an upfront cash payment in 2001 to reduce the public debt through a transaction called Aeolos, after the god of the winds. This payment came from selling future income from landing fees at the country's airports. Another securitisation deal called Ariadne sold off the revenue from the national lottery for an upfront cash payment.

They also copied Italy by entering into cross currency swap contracts linked to Greece's outstanding yen and dollar debt to bring their national debt ratios within their SGP target. They made no attempt to hide this activity; quite the opposite. The Greek finance ministry's public debt division even made a public statement in November 2001 regarding their debt management strategy in which they pledged to reduce debt servicing costs by means that included *"the extensive use of derivatives"*.

The scale of this creative accounting by Greece became evident after a new government took office in 2004. When senior civil servants in the Department of Economy and Finance were asked how the 1.5% budget deficit publicly announced by the previous government a month or so earlier compared with the true figure, the new deputy minister was told the true figure was 8.3% of GDP, well above the 3% Maastricht Treaty limit.

France and Germany set tone by ignoring the rules

Italy and Greece were not alone in flouting the Euro rules in the Maastricht Treaty. Nor did they act without the knowledge and approval of the European Union. Der Spiegel, a German magazine, obtained official documents from 1998 that demonstrated that Helmut Kohl, then the German Chancellor, had decided for political reasons to ignore warnings from his experts that Italy was believed to be *"dressing up"* its accounts and would not meet the Maastricht treaty criteria for entry. Italian officials, including their former finance minister Giulio Tremonti, have also confirmed that the European Union was aware and approved of Italy's use of derivatives in the build up to Euro entry.

But the ones who really torpedoed the Stability and Growth Pact (SGP) were France and Germany. In 2003 they both exceeded their budget deficit limits, Germany from the reunification cost of West and East Germany, France from weaknesses in spending discipline. With their budget deficits exceeding the 3% of GDP limit, the European Commission had the powers and was legally obliged to fine them for these infringements. However the European Union finance ministers overruled the Commission by voting not to enforce the SGP rules. The European Union is often criticised for the power wielded by the unelected and allegedly unaccountable European Commission. The message that this decision sent to every other country in the Eurozone was that of a more relaxed enforcement of the SGP, not a great signal for the stability and financial discipline underpinning the single currency.

On what would turn out to be a pivotal moment, the European Commission had run up against something much more powerful than the SGP, the combined will of the democratically elected governments. As Romano Prodi, the President of the European Commission between 1999 and 2004 and himself a former Prime Minister of Italy, told the BBC, *"Clearly I had not enough power. I tried and they [the finance ministers] told me to shut up."*

Germany recognised the likely effect on other countries. Deitrich von Kyaw, Permanent Representative to the European Union, admitted that Germany *"really sinned"* although *"not a real sin"* as they had simply *"flexibilised the schedules."* However he did concede that *"But when a big country does that, how can you afterwards impose on smaller countries, including Greece, to obey the rules?"*

Tacit approval given to creative accounting

The behaviour of France and Germany had rendered the Stability and Growth Pact as good as dead. It could be argued that had happened earlier in 2000 when European finance ministers had fiercely debated whether or not derivative deals used for creative accounting should be disclosed and it was agreed they should not. The political imperative of European monetary and currency union could not be placed in jeopardy by local difficulties with budget deficits and overall indebtedness. Punishing offenders and excluding those who failed to achieve the SGP targets were put to one side whilst creative accounting was quietly blessed to keep as much as possible hidden from view.

Attempts to evaluate the extent to which public accounts had been dressed up have been rebuffed at every turn. When Bloomberg News went to the European Union General Court in 2012 to uphold a freedom of information request for files held by the European Central Bank (ECB) describing how Greece used derivatives to hide its debt, the Luxembourg based court rejected the case on the grounds that disclosure of the files *"would have undermined the protection of the public interest so far as concerns the economic policy of the European Union and Greece".*

This tacit approval to fudge the accounts was baked into SGP evaluation methods. The way in which the European Commission and the European Statistical Office (Eurostat) calculates debt for SGP accounting purposes is set out in ESA95, a 243-page manual on government deficit and debt accounting, which was published in 2002. The drafting of the section on derivatives was the subject of fierce arguments between the government statisticians and the debt managers of certain Eurozone countries. The statisticians wanted derivative related cash flows treated as financial transactions. As such would have had no influence on budget deficit or borrowing costs. However the debt managers opposed this approach, insisting on having the freedom to use derivative contracts to adjust deficit ratios. The debt managers won the day and was the reason why cross currency swaps became an effective tool for window dressing the national accounts.

Some measure of the relaxed manner with which creative accounting was viewed came to light when a new Greek government took office in 2004. Whilst there were doubts concerning the accounting numbers there was: *"pressure, but not the sort of thing that is breathing down your neck. Everyone who could read the numbers could see that the numbers are off.....even if you allow for constructive accounting."*

Window dressing to join Euro comes home to roost

As long as this window dressing activity was kept away from public scrutiny, the charade could continue. However, once the lid was lifted and the nature, extent and cost of the creative accounting associated with derivative transactions were exposed, the mood began to change.

The first concerns were expressed in 2001 when Gustavo Piga, an Italian economics professor, in collaboration with the Council on Foreign Relations and the International Securities Market Association (ISMA), published a paper accusing European Union countries of 'window dressing' their accounts. The paper specifically referenced a cross currency derivatives contract taken out by Italy in 1996 and caused a storm, not least the comment: *"Derivatives are a very useful instrument... They just become bad if they're used to window-dress accounts."*

However the nature and extent of Italy's involvement remained hidden from public view and was merely a subject of conjecture and rumour within the derivative fraternity until 2012 when a confidential report by the Rome Treasury came into the hands of the Italian press and the Financial Times. This document appeared to have been commissioned to understand and determine how best to restructure derivative transactions entered into in the late 1990s. Unfortunately these transactions were maturing at the height of the European sovereign debt crisis and were proving very costly to restructure in spite of the efforts of Mario Draghi, head of the European Central Bank, implementing a variety of measures to lower EU government borrowing costs. Draghi had formerly been Director-General of the Italian Treasury when Italy joined the Euro, and hence had an intimate knowledge of these transactions and the financial predicament Italy was in.

The Italian treasury report highlighted €8 billion of losses crystallised in the first half of 2012 from eight derivatives contracts with a total notional value of €31.7 billion taken out with foreign banks in the late 1990s. With Italy's state auditors expressing concerns at the size of the losses, the finance police were asked to intervene.

As public concern mounted, those policing the SGP rules rowed back from their previous accommodating stance. Eurostat, the European Union's statistics agency, no longer accepted the exclusion of loans from derivative and securitisation transactions, commenting: *"in a number of instances, the observed securitisation operations seem to have been purportedly designed to achieve a given accounting result, irrespective of the economic merit of the operation."*

Unusual derivative contracts expensive to construct

In 2009 irregularities in the public accounts of Greece also came into the public domain, in particular a $1 billion loan taken out in 2002 that was reckoned to have cost $200 million. The transaction illustrated how unusual loans of this nature are very expensive to construct as well as showing that the charges made by the banks not as egregious they might seem.

From the perspective of the lending bank a long-dated illiquid loan was being extended to Greece. The risks the bank faced by advancing such a loan came from a number of sources, where default by Greece, liquidity, interest rate and currency are the most significant. To hedge the default risk of a $1 billion 20 year loan to Greece, the bank entered into credit default swaps (CDS) with investors. The credit risk embedded in the CDS is evaluated by reference to the difference or 'spread' between a relatively risk free European government bond issued by a country like Germany, and that of Greece. In 2002 the spread on long-dated Greek government bonds was 0.3%, or 30 basis points. This meant that Greece had to pay 0.3% per annum in interest more than Germany to compensate investors for Greece's greater risk of default. For a $1 billion 20 year loan, covering the default risk cost $60 million.

The liquidity charge arose as the loan to Greece was illiquid. Unlike publicly traded Greek government bonds, investors could not expect to sell out of this loan if circumstances changed. A charge was therefore levied to compensate for being 'stuck' with the loan until maturity, or being forced to accept a discount in order to sell the loan to someone else. A 3-5% discount is not uncommon in such circumstances, amounting to a $30-50 million charge on the $1 billion loan.

Additional charges come from hedging interest rate risk and, since the loan was structured in the form of an unusual cross currency swap, currency risk too. Greece could have borrowed the $1 billion by issuing public debt for $60 million, making the cost of disguising the loan $140 million. Cooking the books for the prize of joining the Euro had not come cheap.

38. The rogue trader rides again - London 2011

"He was just a gamble or two away from destroying Switzerland's largest bank"

Prosecution counsel at trial of Kweku Adoboli (2012)

When the story of Jérôme Kerviel, the rogue trader at French bank Société Générale, emerged in 2008 a junior back office clerk at UBS, Switzerland's largest bank, received an email from a good friend. The friend pointed to *"interesting parallels"* with the life of the UBS clerk and added: *"Please don't let me read about you in the papers in the same fashion. It would destroy my faith in human nature forever."* The back office clerk to whom she sent the email was twenty-eight year old Kweku Adoboli and her concern was to prove prescient.

Nine months later, having progressed from back office support to become a trader on the exchange traded funds desk, Adoboli embarked on a path uncannily similar to that taken by Leeson and Kerviel, making bets on the direction of stock markets using stock index futures contracts. Like them he hid his risk taking under the pretence that he was offsetting his futures positions with equal and opposite positions elsewhere. Adoboli's bets on the direction of stock markets initially lost money but then his luck turned and he began to make money. Given what was to come, it would have been better if Adoboli's early losing streak had continued, as his gambling activities would have been exposed sooner with the losses and reputational damage containable. As it was, carried along on a wave of rising confidence, self-esteem and remuneration, he built up his trading activities until unmasked on 14th September 2011 having lost $2.3 billion, the largest unauthorised trading loss in British banking history. Even more shocking was that he been sitting on a much bigger loss of $11.8 billion the previous month on 8th August. No one had spotted this and, had they done so, Adoboli would almost certainly have brought down the entire bank, eclipsing the losses of Leeson ($1.3 billion) and Kerviel ($7 billion loss) in the pantheon of rogue traders.

Like Leeson and perhaps Kerviel too, Adoboli had wanted to be a star trader, although in his case he had neither the flamboyant floor presence of Leeson nor the forensic accounting guile of Kerviel to hide his fraudulent trading. Instead he concealed his unauthorised trading by following the well-trodden rogue trader path of inventing fictitious offsetting transactions, hiding losses, and buying time by extending settlement dates.

Exchange Traded Funds camouflage stock market bets

To be a rogue trader you need a business reason to be using the bank's money to make stock market bets. Leeson's bets with Nikkei 225 stock index futures in Singapore were supposed to be offsetting equal and opposite client positions on Japan's Osaka Stock Exchange. Kerviel was ostensibly hedging the bank's overall exposure to European stock markets. In Adoboli's case access to the bank's money was given to allow him to hedge the firm's risk from originating European stock market positions in Exchange Traded Funds (ETFs).

The role of the ETF desk on which Adoboli worked was to facilitate purchases and sales of European ETFs for UBS clients. If a client gave an order to invest €10,000 in a DAX ETF, Adoboli and his colleagues would buy the German DAX 30 Index shares in the correct proportions to the same value and use these to create a single DAX ETF share investment for the client. A further component to the mix was currency trading as ETFs can be denominated in different currencies to allow investors to buy into the performance of foreign stock markets without carrying the related currency risk.

Exchange traded Funds (ETFs)

ETFs are portfolios of shares that are traded on stock exchanges as single shares in much the same way as any company share.

Investment in portfolios of shares through ETFs had become more and more popular after their advent around 2000 as a

---

means of gaining investment exposure to a portfolio of shares through a single share purchase. The most popular European ETF was that on Deutscher Aktien Index (DAX), a stock market index comprising Germany's thirty largest companies. Instead of having to buy the thirty constituent shares in the correct proportions an investor could achieve the same portfolio outcome in a much cheaper and less cumbersome fashion by buying shares in a single security, the DAX ETF.

Dealing in the shares within ETFs are principally carried out by the major banks, and not the fund provider, of which the firm I worked for, BlackRock, through their iShare offering, was by far the biggest. Banks like UBS were authorised by the fund provider to buy shares on behalf of the ETF for delivery into the ETF portfolio, with cash and ETF shares exchanged in return.

Like company shares ETFs are priced throughout the trading day, their movements tracking those of the underlying shares within the portfolio. In this way they differ from mutual funds which are priced less frequently, typically once each day.

With ETF business growing rapidly, the amount of trading and hedging UBS carried out through its 'Delta One' desk as a consequence had become substantial, even though they were not one of the major players in ETF origination known as Authorised Participants (APs). The term 'Delta One' provided cachet to these relatively straightforward trading activities. It meant that the positions that they held moved one-for-one in tandem with the investments they related to. More complex effects from gearing or optionality, which result in accentuated or nonlinear movements, were not part of their remit. Those on Delta One desks preferred to be thought of as analogous to the US elite military Delta Force than the airline with the nickname *"Don't expect luggage to arrive"*

Adoboli's deception came from pretending real stock market bets through stock index futures were connected to equal and opposite positions in ETFs. Banks tend to look at market risk on a net basis, so when a bet that the market will rise is offset by an equal and opposite position that it will fall, the market risk is judged to be nil. The reason why those controlling risk within the bank did not realise that some ETF trades were fictitious trades arose from shortcomings in the way the share trades between the banks for ETFs were being settled and reconciled.

Extending settlement dates for fictitious trades

When share trades are agreed, the two parties to the transaction normally confirm the price, number of shares, and settlement date details straight away with the exchange of cash for shares taking place shortly afterwards. Those charged with checking that trades are real and correct review the written or electronic confirmation from the counterparty to the trade which they then reconcile with the booking from their own trader. The confirmation process should highlight fictitious trades straight away. If not the physical exchange of cash for shares on the settlement date a day or so afterwards would certainly identify a false trade as the transaction would fail because either cash or shares failed to be delivered.

Rogue traders tend to centre their deception around the confirmation process as it only involves falsifying documentation, not the trickier and much more carefully policed processes surrounding the physical movement of cash and securities on the settlement date. Faking correspondence is a well-trodden path amongst rogue traders; both Leeson and Kerviel travelled that way when carrying out their deceptions. All you have to do is pretend that the counterparty to the transaction has confirmed the trade and nothing more will be asked until settlement. That is why keeping trading separate and independent from confirmation is a key control in preventing false trade entries in the accounting books. To allow someone to trade who has intimate knowledge of the downstream processes of confirmation and settlement and give them access to the accounting books is an open invitation to rogue trading.

Once you have falsified confirmations to make a fictitious trade look real the next trick is to postpone discovery by keeping the settlement process at bay. Adoboli achieved this in two ways. First he confused the true picture by cancelling or amending positions, claiming he was correcting errors. The second method was to set a long settlement date. The scale of this activity came to light during Adoboli's trial when it was revealed that on 11th August 2011 he had hidden $1 billion of losses on Germany's DAX stock index overnight in a suspense account by claiming they were misbookings.

Smoothing profits and losses of real trades with an 'umbrella' account

Successfully trading ETFs should make good steady money, but not in the amounts or with the swings between gains and losses that go hand in glove with stock market bets. To 'smooth' the volatility of his trading Adoboli, with a nod towards Nick Leeson's 88888 account, set up an special 'umbrella' account into which he could book some of his futures trades. Its purpose was to *"smooth volatility"* so his trading appeared less risky and *"paint a picture of consistent performance"* so that no alarm bells would ring with senior management.

His stock market bets in 2009 and 2010 paid off handsomely. The ETF desk was posting good profits and his remuneration was rising in step. Gaining confidence Adoboli made even bigger bets in 2011 and was $80 million in profit by mid-year. Conscious of the danger that he might be unmasked for making much more money than could be ascribed to an ETF trading business, he hid $40 million of these gains by posting them into the umbrella account. By so doing these profits were not shown in the management accounting books for the ETF business, allowing Adoboli to earmark this money either to cover any future losses, or to drip feed the gains back into the ETF desk's accounts to inflate their profits and bonus payments.

With $40 million in the umbrella account Adoboli felt he had the firepower both to increase the size of his bets and to feed his

ETF business account so that his career and remuneration would continue in an upward trajectory.

The betting spiral that dragged Adoboli down

As with Leeson and Kerviel, the deception began after he had suffered an unfortunate loss. In October 2008, he bought ETF shares from a client which fell in price before he had hedged the market risk with an offsetting sale of stock index futures. Faced with an unrealised loss of $400,000 Adoboli elected to hide the loss rather than tell his manager, deciding to hold on and *"run the position"* in the hope that the price would recover.

In evidence eerily reminiscent of Nick Leeson's explanation for setting up Baring's 88888 account, Adoboli testified that he established the 'umbrella' account to hide this large initial loss.

The bets he took were on the direction of European stock markets, principally in stock markets like Germany's DAX index on which he traded ETFs. The real bets he made were in stock index futures, the fictitious offsetting transactions were in ETFs. Disguising the fictitious ETF trades was easy for him to accomplish as both of his previous roles had been on the ETF desk, first as back office support and then as desk assistant. He knew everything about the bank's booking and control processes, even being involved in their development.

In testimony to court Adoboli explained how he racked up the $2.3 billion of losses during 2011 in three distinct phases of trading, all during a period of severe market turbulence. On this occasion the road to ruin was not a surprise shock like the Kobe Earthquake that finally sunk Leeson, but a volatile market journey during a Eurozone debt crisis that was punctuated by political surprises.

In the first period between 23rd and 30th June 2011, he sold futures on European stock index futures, betting that their stock markets would fall as the Eurozone crisis worsened. He masked these positions by creating a fictitious long position in ETFs in the same stock markets. Unfortunately the market rose instead and his losses mounted until, after reaching $147 million on 30th June, he changed direction and *"flipped his trades"*, buying futures contracts instead. He was now betting that stock markets would rise, which they duly did, providing an opportunity to close out his bet in mid July for a small loss. But he missed his chance as the market then plummeted down. Within a matter of weeks, he had lost $1.5 billion against a desk limit of $50 million. Then, taking on the mantle of a drunken gambler, Adoboli bet more and more of the bank's money. As he put it: *"I absolutely lost control. I was no longer in control of the trades we were doing… I kept buying into the dip"*. Now in a manner more and more reminiscent of Nick Leeson, he increased his position again and again.

When questioned in court about why he had *"flipped"* his bet from being short on 30th June to long the following day his explanation was that of a gambler's hard luck story: *"I broke, I just broke… I should have held on".*

His losses peaked at an astonishing $11.8 billion on 8th August, at a time when the fictitious ETF trades on the books of the bank made it appear that he was down a much more modest $2.3 million. By now Adoboli had become so muddled in his head and with his own false book keeping that he could no longer keep track of his market exposure or how much money he was losing. As he put it *"I did not know just how large the position was. I didn't know, I'd become desensitised to just how big the trades were."* This was hardly surprising as by now he was booking over 100 fictitious ETF trades a day and doing a similar number of real futures transactions in the market.

In the third and final phase of this trading Armageddon, Adoboli reversed his bet once more, taking an even bigger short position between 11th August and 13th September. To conceal this action he increased his fictitious ETF position with extended settlement dates to an amount that could only make sense if UBS dominated the entire European ETF market. The market went his way enough to recover the bulk of his losses from the 8th August low point, but not enough to eradicate them.

By now, the stories he was concocting to explain reconciliation *"breaks"* in the bank's accounting books were becoming less and less credible and he knew it. The books were regularly failing to balance amounts over $3 billion and, having booked over 10,000 fictitious ETF trades in three months, Adoboli could no longer paint a credible story or amend bookings to cover his tracks. On 14th September realising, as the prosecution counsel put, it that his *"pyramid of fraud had collapsed"*, he left work at lunchtime and sent an email from home confessing that the ETF trades were *"not real trades at all"* and that his explanations had been *"just lies".* He was arrested in the early hours of the following morning after being grilled by UBS executives and lawyers.

A remarkable feature of Adoboli's behaviour in the final days was his apparent ebullience. On recorded calls to our ETF desk, I listened to him seeking information about the market size and trading liquidity of certain ETF securities. His voice intonation and mood were remarkably positive, effusively expressing gratitude for information provided in enthusiastic and flowery language. I have no knowledge of psychiatry so cannot say whether or not this kind of behaviour is common with those in crisis under extreme stress. But it was certainly surprising to listen to these tapes afterwards, knowing the circumstances and his predicament.

UBS were left to close $8.7 billion in open market positions and to try and make sense of over 10,000 ETF trades Adoboli had booked, the vast majority of which were fictitious, giving a loss of $2.3 billion.

At Adoboli's trial the prosecution counsel was to say: *"He was just a gamble or two away from destroying Switzerland's largest bank."* In truth, he probably achieved that when he was down $11.8 billion on 8th August with the bank only saved by failing to spot the fraud until the loss was a more manageable $2.3 billion.

The missing rogue trader controls

In the aftermath, questions were raised over why rogue trader controls brought in during 2008 following Jérôme Kerviel's activities had not highlighted Adoboli's activities early on. The truth was that there was no evidence that they had been implemented.

All the tell-tale signs from previous rogue trader scandals were clearly observable. There were accounting adjustments to fictitious trades and a litany of alleged booking errors that had been altered. As with Leeson, there was a hidden account where the real profit and loss action was taking place, set up by a trader from the back office with intimate knowledge of the processes and controls. This account had concealed the winning and losing trading bets he was not supposed to be making. It almost felt as though UBS had cloned SocGen's Kerviel rather than guarded against him.

The bank admitted they had fallen short. In court they were to agree that: *"If a trade had been fictitious, when operations ring the counterparty to confirm the trade, they would see the trade didn't exist".* The long-dated settlement control that should have come into play when a settlement date had been extended by 14 days or more after the date on which the trade was confirmed had not been *"functioning properly"* when Adoboli carried out his lethal trading. Their balance sheet verification process, a monthly check intended to ensure reported profit and loss matched with actual assets: *"was carried out,"* but *"it was the speed and precision with which it was operated that we needed to improve".*

As for the umbrella account to conceal his market trading, it was seen to be almost a copycat version of Leeson's 88888 Account. Its existence and role was not even particularly well hidden. Overall the deception had only been kept alive at the Swiss bank for more than three years by sloppy management and a catalogue of inventive lies.

The real shocker was the amount of cash that the bank had paid out every day in variation margin to cover unrealised losses of Adoboli's futures positions. At its peak, almost $12 billion in cash had been paid out without ringing alarm bells, even though such sums stood out as huge in the context of the entire firm and all of their clients. It was the same warning signal that Barings had ignored until the money ran out altogether. UBS had very nearly followed suit.

A perfect storm of reputational damage for UBS

The discovery could not have come at a worse time for UBS as the bank was already faltering in its attempts to rebuild its investment banking franchise. The bank had nearly collapsed in the financial crisis of 2008 when having to write off $50 billion in sour mortgage loans. They had also been fined $780 million and nearly lost their US banking licence for helping wealthy US clients to evade taxes. As if that was not enough their 150th anniversary celebration in 2012 was to be overshadowed by being embroiled in the LIBOR manipulation scandal for which they were ultimately to be fined $1 billion.

But it was not just the time but also the place. The Board and senior UBS executives were meeting in Singapore on the eve of their Formula One Grand Prix night race when the Adoboli news broke. UBS were major sponsors of Formula One and Singapore's sovereign wealth fund had become the biggest shareholder in UBS in 2007 after investing $10 billion to shore up the bank's capital following subprime losses of the same value. This investment had subsequently performed poorly and, given its magnitude, was already something of an embarrassment.

To Singapore it felt as though they were experiencing Barings and Leeson all over again. A rogue trader betting with stock index futures and poor UK banking supervision had caused them to suffer reputational embarrassment and financial loss at their highest profile international event. Even more galling was that the loss appeared to be almost a carbon copy of Leeson's fraud. Had the UK banking authorities paid heed to the issues that had led to the collapse of Barings, Adoboli could not have wreaked this havoc on UBS.

The scandal that ensued was to claim the bank's entire top

management team who were either fired or fell on their swords. This was followed by an immediate shrinkage of 500 jobs and a 60% cut in the bonus pool. The bank then retreated from fixed income trading with another 10,000 redundancies.

Their UK regulator, the Financial Services Authority (FSA) levied a £29.7 million fine on UBS for *"significant control breakdowns"*. They also criticised the bank for ineffective computer risk controls and the *"poorly executed and ineffective supervision"* that enabled Adoboli to breach risk limits and to book fictitious trades time and again.

Kweku Adoboli was convicted of fraud in 2012 and sentenced to seven years in prison for perpetrating Britain's biggest bank fraud. UBS was left fighting to restore a battered reputation. It was another sobering reminder of how rogue bankers are motivated by huge potential bonuses to take dangerous risks. But in the court of life how should one judge the rogue trader who goes to the casino and loses his employer's money? Who is to blame: the gambler, the careless employer or the casino? I go with the answer given by a former head of a major investment bank: *"All three"*.

The mystery of rogue trading

For those working outside the financial industry, the amount of money lost by rogue traders appears extraordinary. Even more puzzling is how seemingly innocuous junior employees, far from the heady heights of senior management, turn out to be the perpetrators of enormous damage to their employers. Furthermore the nature of the fraud by Adoboli, as with Leeson, Kerviel and others before him, are not particularly sophisticated, nor was it new. With robust management controls recurrence ought to be well nigh impossible.

However there is something in the nature and culture of banking that routinely breeds this behaviour. Only the big numbers at the tip of the iceberg reach the public domain, and the silence in response to the question: *"Why do we not hear of rogue trading profits?"* tells its own story.

The answer is twofold. First, in a desire to identify and retain their most skillful traders, those with trading roles can receive life-changing financial rewards in a handful of years. That possibility creates a form of pressure to succeed by taking bigger and bigger risks, particularly when observing the change in lifestyle of successful peers. This peer pressure is seen as driving trading individuals to their misdemeanours, and frequently the favoured line of defence of rogue traders when they land up in court.

Then there is the failure in management controls. Simple checks are absent or carried out with minimal care or little understanding. In spite of all the brilliant modelling and analytical tools that are available, risk is seen as losing money whilst return is making profits. Losing money requires immediate attention and resources are quickly brought to bear, typically through an operational risk team that seeks to assess and then eradicate the cause.

By contrast profit generation is welcomed and not subject to great scrutiny. If someone is ostensibly making a lot of money, people prefer to view them and their activities in a positive light. Stories suggesting gains are being generated by a unique idea or a new industry opportunity that the firm is exploiting more cleverly than the competition are lauded rather than analysed. Sceptics who pour cold water on success are either regarded as jealous or not bright enough to grasp the idea. The risk team is less inclined or encouraged to investigate on the grounds; *"if it ain't broke don't fix it"*. More damning still is that, in trading territory, the gods of banking are often found wanting. Their route to the top is more likely to have come from successful careers in mergers and acquisitions, far from the madding crowds of markets. There are some who fear that the largest banks are *"too big to fail"* but perhaps it is that they are simply *"too big to manage"*.

39. Feeding frenzy on a London Whale - London 2012

"It's a tempest in a teapot driven by sour grapes hedge funds…"

**Internal email by senior JP Morgan executive
to top management**

Jamie Dimon, Chairman and CEO of JP Morgan, was the last of Wall Street's big beasts to retain his swagger after the 2008 financial crisis. He had watched his rivals go down with the wreckage of their failed banks, or retreat wounded from the limelight. This left him alone on the stage leading the largest and most profitable US bank, cast as the smart cat who had scooped the financial cream. So it came as a big surprise in 2012 to see the ship he had steered so adeptly through the financial storm capsizing in the waters they had been first to chart and were thought to know better than anyone else, credit derivatives.

Curiously it was the magnitude of their success in the financial crisis that had taken them down this path in the first place. Before the crisis investors had spread their cash deposits roughly equally between a group of trusted major banks, a practice that helped all of these banks to fund their short term liquidity needs. There had been differences in borrowing rates to take account of variations in credit quality and the need for capital but, with a market assumption that no major bank was likely to fail, these differences had been small. All of this changed in the aftermath of the Lehman default. Borrowing costs of banks soared as the availability of funding fell away, in part as investors were prohibited from depositing cash with the weaker ones on risk and regulatory grounds.

The latter was becoming a 'Catch-22' situation as many investors had regulatory constraints imposed on them that only allowed them to place deposits with banks accorded high credit ratings. As weaker banks had their credit ratings cut, so their ability to borrow was curtailed, causing the credit rating agencies to lower their ratings still further. It was the loss of confidence spiral well articulated by the old banking maxim *"A bank is no more when trust in its credit worthiness is gone"*.

Headache as well as opportunity from cash pouring in

JP Morgan now basked in the sunshine of trust and respect. As the big winner they hoovered up the cash deposits from their rivals who had lost their customers' trust. With so much money they could overwhelm struggling competitors who no longer had easy sources of short-term capital to tap. JP Morgan was now the lord of the jungle. But having money pouring in was not as rosy as it seemed. Demand to borrow these funds by their biggest corporate customers was low as they too were accumulating cash. Making matters worse was that their corporate treasurers were also placing their excess funds with JP Morgan. With few good quality customers to lend the money to and short term interest rates held close to zero by the US Federal Reserve in an effort to stimulate economic growth, JP Morgan found themselves sitting on a massive war chest of cash assets that they were struggling to deploy and could earn little money from. Instead of generating profits from this cash these deposits were having the opposite effect, diluting the return on their assets and to their shareholders.

Almost all of these deposits flowed into their central treasury for investment known as the Chief Investment Office (CIO). The portfolio expanded more than tenfold during 2011 from $4 billion to $51 billion. By early 2012 the amount the cash the CIO had to deploy had swollen to a staggering $375 billion.

The usual role of a bank's treasury department is to hedge credit exposures on their loan book to provide some protection against potential client defaults. Treasury also provided internal funding for the bank's other businesses, including the racier trading desks of the investment bank where their proprietary and market bets were typically placed. When their cash deposits were in excess of these needs they would generally invest the balance in low risk securities and other similar financial instruments. But now these excess funds were so enormous that their traditional approach to cash management had become overwhelmed and almost rendered redundant. Somewhere in the mix of difficult hedging conditions for their loan book, low returns on cash and the huge financial firepower from their excess deposits the CIO unit morphed from a treasury function with some trading around the edges, into a market beast of seemingly unstoppable power. The CIO came to acquire a wide ranging brief to mix treasury with proprietary trading and an enormous appetite for risk. Sometimes it happens that when you have too much money you lose control. For JP Morgan it was to prove costly to their reputation and pocket.

Hedging strategy altered as cost of default protection soars

Between 2007 and much of 2011, the CIO had used the conventional treasury method of buying credit default swap (CDS) contracts on companies to whom they had lent money to provide their loan book with some protection against customer default. This approach had worked well over that period with the bank making $2.5 billion from their credit hedging activities as economic conditions had weakened. Towards the end of 2011 the price of CDS contracts on individual companies was becoming prohibitively expensive and continuing to hedge the loan book in this way was being called into question.

Europe was the main culprit where there seemed to be no end in sight for the Eurozone crisis. The financial standing of their banks was a constant concern with several only being kept alive through taxpayer bailouts, money that most of their countries governments could ill afford, as some were themselves teetering on the brink of default. In their haste to put the banks on a sounder footing, new rules to beef up bank solvency ratios were introduced, placing much tougher capital hurdles for doing business.

To allow both the banks and sovereign nations to fund cheaply whilst weak from a credit standpoint, governments and their central banks came up a crafty ruse, to make savers carry the cost.

By setting interest rates close to zero, with some central banks even daring to go into negative territory, depositors found themselves in the unprecedented position of having to pay the banks to hold their money. Savers were now the unwitting saviours keeping their countries and banks afloat through the hidden tax of foregone interest as well as funding government borrowing with cheap loans. To win support for this stance the central banks embarked on a decent public relations campaign, claiming that the measure was financially prudent and a sensible means for stimulating economic growth. Keynes might have approved but Hayek most certainly would not.

Optimism leads to offsetting bet on credit

Whilst the market was pricing in a very high charge for protection against default risk, the picture JP Morgan was seeing, particularly in the US economy, was very different. The business of their corporate clients was recovering well and it seemed to the bank that the prospect of widespread default was receding. For this reason the CIO looked to change tack on their approach to hedging the bank's overall credit exposure and the way they deployed excess cash.

The strategy they came up with sought to both protect their loan book and to deal with the high market cost of credit protection. The essence of this strategy was to continue buying protection against default of their major borrowers through single name CDS contracts but alleviate the expense by selling CDS contracts for around the same value on a basket of companies, most of whom they had not lent money to.

It was a sensible way to offset the general 'expensiveness' or 'richness' of the credit protection they were buying against customer default. They refined this approach by entering into CDS contracts relating to segments or 'tranches' of the default risk on these baskets of companies. These tranched contracts limited the amount of default risk the CIO was taking in much the same way as insurance companies reduce their risk by making policy holders to bear an initial 'excess' amount before insurance cover kicks in.

Tranching credit default swaps (CDS)

CDS contracts are traded on a wide range of corporate credit indices. The company names that make up the CDS portfolio for a particular index are typically of very similar credit standing to one another. The most prominent index within the CIO portfolio was the IG.9 Markit CDX North America Index, the 'IG' reflecting the 'investment grade' credit standing of the constituent company debt. This index comprised 125 equally weighted CDS contracts of companies across six industry sectors.

The seller of a CDS tranche contract does not suffer the full potential loss arising from company defaults within the index portfolio because the default risk is divided into discrete risk 'tranches' through which investors only carry a predetermined portion of the loss suffered by the index portfolio. Each tranche carries a layer of losses, defined by 'attachment' and 'detachment' points, with the value of losses determined by their position or 'seniority' in the hierarchy of the capital structure. A credit tranche is analogous to a risk 'layer' in insurance and in option terminology is described as a 'written call spread.'

In a typical tranched CDS index the lowest 0-3 tranche, known as the equity tranche, absorbs the first 3% of losses of index defaults. The next 3-7 'mezzanine' tranche absorbs the next 4% of losses, being fully insulated against the first 3% of losses by the equity tranche. Further losses are absorbed by higher ranking tranches, with the 7-10 and 10-15 'senior' tranches, and the 15-30 'super-senior' tranche.

Mismatched hedging risk brings inadvertent bets

The new strategy worked best when there were a few defaults by companies on which they had purchased CDS contracts, and no more than a handful of losses on the IG.9 contracts they had sold.

This wager seemed destined to lose money in 2011 until November when AMR Corporation, the parent company of American Airlines, filed for bankruptcy, triggering a $453 million gain on the CDS contract the CIO held. This transaction was later to be referenced in an investigation by the US Senate when arguing that the CIO strategy was gambling and not hedging since JP Morgan was unable to link the AMR gain to *any loan or credit loss suffered elsewhere in the bank.*

In one sense this general approach was hedging and, in another, outright speculation. The companies on which the CIO was buying CDS contracts were 'high yield'. These companies paid generous interest coupons to investors on their debt securities as compensation for their probability of default. By contrast companies in the IG.9 index were 'investment grade', paying debt holders a lower rate of interest as their default risk was deemed to be less. In a true hedge you mitigate a risk you have in one direction with a position in the other direction that offsets some or all of the economic exposure. Offsetting high yield debt exposure with investment grade exposure is akin to hedging apples by selling pears, both 'fruits' of the economy but very different in nature. Furthermore the argument that their high yield CDS contracts were hedges against the JP Morgan loan book did not stack up as they were purchasing them on companies like AMR where the bank had no credit exposure at all. Hence all one can say in support the hedging argument was that the IG.9 position was a vague hedge against the US credit market as a whole and a genuine hedge against the high market cost for credit protection.

Where strategies of this nature can unravel is when the vagueness and complexity of attempts to hedge risk creates inadvertent bets. It is a derivative hole into which many have fallen. What starts as a well understood hedging proposition when the initial position is put on, in this case to deal with the expensive coat of credit protection, soon becomes muddied by subsequent market movements and hedge mathematics. As the market moves one can find oneself countering profit and loss effects whilst, at the same time, attending to an overall position which is being driven hither and thither by technical hedging conflicts between different risk factors. After only three or four iterations of market movement and hedge adjustments it is often difficult to pinpoint what market move one would hope will happen next and the entire hedging programme morphs into confusion.

Bullish outlook turns hedge into bet

In December 2011 the European Central Bank (ECB), under newly appointed President Mario Draghi, unleashed a tidal wave of liquidity into the corporate debt market, triggering what one analyst described as: *"the mother of all credit rallies."* Draghi backed up the ECB action with strong words: *"… the ECB is ready to do whatever it takes to preserve the euro… and believe me, it will be enough."*

With the likelihood of corporate default lower, the price of high yield CDS contracts fell. Losses on this leg of the CIO credit book were countered to some extent by gains on the investment grade positions taken by selling the IG.9 CDS contracts. Instead of unwinding the losing high yield positions and booking a loss, the CIO decided to ramp up their winning IG.9 positions massively. They increased the value of outstanding IG.9 CDS contracts in the market as a whole by 50% in little more than a month, and took their net credit exposure up from $55 billion at year end 2011 to $89 billion by mid February 2012.

They did attempt to hedge some of this 'long' credit position in the IG.9 by buying single name CDS contracts in investment grade companies, but there was neither the liquidity nor did the CIO seem to have the appetite to keep the two legs balanced. As a consequence, instead of hedging the credit risk of the bank, the CIO had turned to betting on credit, a fundamental change in the nature of their credit operations. Downturns in the credit market would now give rise to losses on the loan book with further losses from a credit hedging portfolio that was supposed to provide loan loss mitigation. As one investor to put it: *"The CFO described the (CIO) trades as part of a hedging policy, but this was wrong by 180 degrees."*

Their bullish position in the IG.9 Index initially worked well during the first quarter of 2012 when stocks surged and economic data suggested economic recovery was gaining traction. However they were still losing money overall as their IG.9 hedges were not keeping pace with the rally in high yield bonds they were wagering against.

More pain was to come when the credit environment worsened early in April when the price of the IG.9 index CDS protection they had sold rose by an alarming 40% in just 10 days. The overall mark-to-market losses they suffered on this move made no sense on their risk models; the expected correlation effects were not there. To those who had been expressing concern for several months that something was wrong with their evaluation of the risk this portfolio was taking, this move was the final straw.

VaR limit increased and risk model changed as losses build

Modelling the market risk carried by the CIO should have been the 'bread and butter' of JP Morgan's skillset. After all they had created RiskMetrics, the key risk tool that had become the market standard for the financial industry, introducing 'Value at Risk' or VaR into the financial market lexicon. They understood the shortcomings of the VaR number only too well, particularly where it related to credit. This awareness had been one of the main reasons why JP Morgan had so adeptly sidestepped much of the damage suffered by other major banks in the 2008 financial crisis. And they knew that the villain of the piece in 2008, correlation, was as untrustworthy as ever.

At the time the efficacy of the models used to evaluate default risk was being called into question and the subject of keen debate across the finance industry and in academia. Default is something of a 'cliff edge' risk. One moment you feel completely safe and the next you are plummeting into default. It makes hedging extremely difficult as the nature and quantum of the hedging is complex, yet trading decisions have to be taken very quickly.

Adding to the CIO modelling risk uncertainty was poor trading liquidity. Much of the $483 billion of gross notional value the CIO portfolio held early in 2012 comprised giant positions in esoteric structured derivatives. Their IG.9 CDS holding alone was $81 billion, yet only $1-2 billion typically traded each day in these contracts. It was a monster 'lobster pot' of illiquidity last in evidence during 2008 when AIG had hit the buffers with 'super senior' CDS contracts.

The CIO was also out of control internally. They had breached their VaR limits on 300 separate days and losses were now mounting at an alarming rate. Even though the portfolio risk was well above their internal VaR limits, there was little the CIO could do to extricate themselves. Closing positions in such illiquid positions would simply serve to accelerate losses which already were causing pain. To deal with the situation senior management approved a temporary increase in the VaR limit and, more controversially, allowed the VaR model itself to be modified.

The combination of the revised VaR model and increased limit allowed the CIO credit hedging book to swell from a net notional value of $55 billion in mid January 2012 to $89 billion in late February. In spite of the increase in size, the new VaR model suggested the portfolio risk in February was less than in January, even though the number from another risk evaluation tool the bank used, the Comprehensive Risk Measure (CRM), suggested the risk had doubled. The CRM also came with a number, $6.3 billion, which the portfolio could lose over the next 12 months, not far off the final $6.2 billion outcome. However the CIO elected to ignore the CRM number in favour of the revised VaR number.

It turned out there had been an error in the spreadsheet that was used to calculate the revised VaR number, a mistake that underestimated volatility risk by almost 50%, thereby understating both mark-to-model risk and unrealised losses. It was this catalogue of missteps that later led Jamie Dimon to later describe the CIO credit portfolio as: *"flawed, complex, poorly reviewed, poorly executed and poorly monitored."*

Hedge funds held at bay as CIO creates lobster pot of illiquidity

Why the CIO chose to flex its muscles in the IG.9 Index during January and February instead of taking a hit and cutting their losing position in high yield CDS contracts instead seems strange to many. Increasing the size of an illiquid portfolio that is losing money is either brave or foolhardy. Perhaps the decision by the CIO to deploy 'shock and awe' firepower was coloured by a preoccupation with finding ways to capitalise, rather than suffer, from the billions of dollars flowing into their cash pile every day. But the consequence of 'upping the ante' was that they were becoming trapped in a giant lobster pot of illiquidity.

Their massive selling of IG.9 CDS had created a very cheap way for buyers of investment grade credit protection to gain market exposure. A price discount of some 30% relative of equivalent credit positions had been opened up which alert hedge fund managers were quick to spot. For them buying these contracts provided a very cheap way to bet on credit deterioration or rich arbitrage pickings from buying IG.9 CDS and selling an equivalent portfolio of much more expensive investment grade companies.

Whilst the CIO was building their $81 billion position in the IG.9 the hedge funds on the other side of the trade were puzzled as to why the discount would not narrow. To their chagrin the expected gains from arbitrage closing were stubbornly failing to materialise as the IG.9 price would not budge. Had the buyers known of firepower then ranged against them they might not have tried to narrow the discount and instead heeded the African adage which translates from Swahili: *"If you are holding the hind leg of an elephant when it has a mind to run, it's best to let it run".*

In normal circumstances an ongoing seller welcomes rising prices as they receive more money for the goods and services they are selling. However what was unusual with the IG.9 was that the CIO had an incentive to keep the price down as a higher price would inflict heavy mark-to-market losses on their existing position.

It was the persistence of the discount and their failure to move the price that alerted the hedge funds to the strength of their antagonist. Market talk began to circulate that a "whale" was ranged against them in the IG.9 Index. Since it was already clear that brute financial force on their part would not win the day, the hedge funds turned to another weapon in their armoury that they had used to good effect in the past to gain ascendancy; publicity.

Unmasked in public for showing too much muscle

To bring the market position into public view articles and other commentary were began to appear in the financial media, including Bloomberg and the Wall Street Journal. There were briefings, typically from anonymous fund managers, complaining that credit markets were being distorted by the behaviour of JP Morgan. To colour the story for maximum impact they brought Bruno Iksil, the French-born trader who headed the CIO credit desk in London into the limelight, branding him *"The London Whale"* or *"Voldemort"*, the powerful villain from the Harry Potter books..

As the story gained traction in April and was even provoking regulatory interest, the bank elected to downplay the activity as well as their losses, even though the latter were by then over $1 billion. Jamie Dimon, appreciating how important it was to keep the hedge funds on the back foot by wielding the threat of unlimited financial firepower, publicly dismissed the hullabaloo as a *"complete tempest in a teapot"*.

Hedge fund sharks devour the floundering whale

With financial lobster pots there are two ways to make bumper profits and two routes to disaster. The most common profitable choice is to carry on building positions until the game is won and the opposition capitulates. That was always the aim of commodity market manipulators like Old Hutch in the days of Chicago 'corners' in the 1860s. When building positions you first gain control of then take it in the direction you want, brushing aside those standing in your way. The other profitable route is more subtle, exiting in secret to a new player desire. The road to ruin is either 'stay and hold' or 'cut and run.' Porsche knew this when building their VW share stake but lost out in the end when the German courts prevented them from taking the winning acquisition step.

For JP Morgan neither of the profitable routes was now open, particularly for their IG.9 holding. They were in the same position as the Hunts had been with silver in the 1970s, with the only means of exit through those that they had pinned down by their firepower, the hedge funds. After a few lame attempts to show they could still fight, the CIO gave up any pretence of defence, allowing the hedge funds to close in and feed at will on the carcass of their defunct hedging strategy. With nowhere to hide the hedge funds had a field day, turning 2012 into a bonanza year for those running credit strategies. Much of the $6.2 billion loss JP Morgan ultimately suffered could be seen showing up in coffers of hedge fund accounts. Just as Barings losses went from £340 million to £880 million when their positions were known and defence non existent, so JPM's $2 billion in the first quarter of 2012 was followed by a further $3.8 billion in the second quarter as they cut the net notional size of their positions by 75% to $39.5 billion. By the end of the third quarter when the credit book had been run down to a containable size, their total losses from the London Whale saga had reached $6.2 billion.

Rubbish tip of regulatory data exposed

The investigations into the London Whale brought to light weaknesses amongst those who were charged with policing financial markets, the regulators. Part of their remit was to identify and monitor risks to the financial system and, where appropriate, to take preventative action.

Those dealing with the 2008 financial crisis had been hampered by a lack of market data on the interconnectivity of banks and other financial institutions, particularly those relating to bilateral swap contracts. That was why, in the aftermath of the crisis, global policymakers mandated that all OTC derivatives trades be reported to information warehouses. It was thought that regulators and other interested parties could then properly scrutinise trading activity, and would have done so before if they had had this data.

But implementing this laudable aim to bring greater transparency brought something else to the surface, a weakness the industry was well aware of but regulators were loathe to admit; that there was confusion and disharmony amongst regulators over what they were trying to achieve and hence the information that needed to be disclosed.

When the rules around OTC derivative disclosure first came into effect in the United States during 2013 all of the data relating to the historic trades carried out by the CIO during the London Whale period became available. However when the CFTC, the main US derivatives regulator, began their investigation they confessed they could not pick out JP Morgan's trading calamity from the chaotic data they had at their disposal.

The central problem was that regulators had overloaded themselves with far too much data, most of which they struggled to understand. In the lead up to the provision of data on OTC derivative trading there had been considerable frustration within the industry on the onerous burden being placed on participants and the inconsistency of the requirements of different regulatory regimes. On one occasion I asked a leading regulator what information they would be seeking from the data so that the relevant data could be presented in the clearest possible way. *"We would like all the data you have"* was the response. As for how the data would be used: *"I don't know; we have no one earmarked to look at it."*

With so little guidance the task of making sense of it all fell to the data warehouses, of which the US Depository Trust & Clearing Corporation (DTCC) was the most important. Their Chief Executive, Michael Bodson, confirmed that all of the data on the London Whale had been reported but: *"It just was not easy to read".*

The DTCC is a remarkable organisation, handling almost unimaginable quantities of data. They sit between vast swaths of equity, corporate bond and US government securities trades, managing the transfer and settlement of several thousand trillion dollars of assets every year. Their reach and data repositories extend all over the world, and covers over 80% of global swap transactions.

Handling all of this data was a colossal job, with 100,000 entities sending around a billion messages to the DTCC every month. It was hardly surprising that they struggled to cope, and as Bodson admitted: *"We just got overwhelmed. Our technology was not up to snuff. We should take the criticism that was appropriate but it was such a mammoth task."*

When Europe introduced their own reporting rules in 2014, Bodson pointed to a similar story of market confusion emerging, with part of the responsibility resting with the regulatory watchdogs: *"There is a naivety from some regulators. They felt pressure to get rules done but ..... I don't think they understood what they were asking for."*

Without a global standard on how trade data should be reported, what purpose it is being gathered for, or even the basics of common file formats and trade identifiers, the pile of almost unusable data provided at great cost continues to pile up.

Lawyers and regulators go easy on Iksil

The nature and scale of JP Morgan's trading losses caused a storm in Washington and prompted an investigation by US Senate as well as by a number of regulators. All of their reports were damning, and not helped by email correspondence that emerged showing the bank had not been joined up internally. It seemed that the CIO were convinced that their positions were not just under under external attack by hedge funds but also internally by proprietary traders within the investment bank.

When the law enforcement agencies took over the baton, pressing charges against the perpetrators, Preet Bharara, US Attorney for Southern District of New York, expressed shock that: *"Not just one bank… but one trader at one bank… can do catastrophic harm, in practically the blink of an eye."*

When Iksil's case eventually reached the courts and became subject to regulatory scrutiny the outcome was unexpected. Unlike Leeson, Kerviel and Adoboli he was not censured or charged with any criminal or regulatory misdemeanour. Instead the law enforcement agencies simply asked Iksil to testify as a witness against others in JP Morgan who were alleged to have *"concealed massive losses".* One example that was used in the SEC evidence was an instruction by Iksil's supervisor to mark a loss of $9.5 million to the portfolio when the true figure was over $500 million. The Department of Justice (DOJ) also sought to bring charges against a junior trader who had unwillingly marked fake prices and ran a spreadsheet that showed the prices marked in JP Morgan's books alongside the true market prices.

Not obtaining a guilty plea from such a key player as Iksil was regarded as *"extraordinarily unusual"* by one prosecutor and a break from court precedent. The most cited case was the 1992 case brought against the John Gotti, boss of the Gambino mafia crime family. Under a deal with the government, Sammy 'The Bull' Gravano, even though the star witness in gaining a conviction against Gotti, still had to plead guilty to 19 murders and serve five years in prison.

The decision to not charge Mr Iksil or force him to plead guilty reinforced the contention that prosecutors believed he had not acted as a rogue trader, but with the knowledge and support of senior management. Preet Bharara, appeared to confirm this view when saying the Iksil deal was *"rare"* and adding: *"I don't think you could call him blameless"* but he *"did sound the alarm more than once".*

The UK's Financial Conduct Authority was one of four regulators to close its investigation without bringing any charges against Iksil, instead censuring CIO management and JP Morgan. Heavy fines were subsequently levied on the firm by the US Department of Justice (DOJ), SEC, FCA, and CFTC, as were individuals who failed to alert the authorities to the danger and losses from the CIO trading strategy.

Iksil remains bitter to this day for being singled out for notoriety. He tried to set the record straight by writing a open letter to the press setting out his own version of events. He felt he had been the victim of media attention *"for no good reason".* Clearing his name by testifying to the US courts that he was acting under instruction of senior management became the central priority in his life. However, in his anxiety to clear his name Iksil had continued to speak out, even setting up a website called London Whale Marionette to set out his version of events. But by going too public with his utterances, Iksil undermined his credibility as a witness and, to his disappointment, the Department of Justice, dropped the case. The question of bank complicity will never now be openly tested, although the $920 million in fines JP Morgan has had pay out to the regulatory authorities tells its own story.

But to some the real lesson of the London Whale is that giant banks like JP Morgan are not only too big to fail; they may also be too big to manage and too big to regulate.

40. Not slowing down as the benefits shine through

"First they ignore you, then they laugh at you, then they fight you, then you win."

Mahatma Gandhi (1869-1948) attributed

It was Fischer Black who said: *"There are so many ways to use derivatives that I'm almost surprised when someone doesn't use them. Producers and consumers, investors and issuers, hedgers and speculators, governments and financial institutions: almost everyone can use them".*

From the numbers involved it looks like everyone has listened. The CME, the world's largest derivatives exchange that Leo Melamed first led into financial markets in 1972, trades close to US$1 quadrillion (US$1 billion billion) in derivatives contracts annually, a number that exceeds the entire annual production of the world's largest economies. Furthermore there are some who reckon derivatives now account for well over half of all financial market transactions.

Along the way these remarkable instruments have freed up world markets, created new asset classes and changed the nature of banking, investment, even insurance, and all of this in little more than forty years.

In the same way that these instruments introduced certainty to farmers for the price of their produce, so manufacturers today use them to secure price certainty for their raw materials and goods. Businesses have become more resilient against price shocks and risks outside their control, whilst new business models have emerged.

Companies that used to suffer from the vagaries of interest rate and currency movements now routinely address them both through the related derivative instruments. Homebuyers have also benefitted since banks are able to offer their customers fixed rate mortgages by hedging their own interest rate risk.

In investment the same qualities are drawn on for more certainty of income or capital, whether for pensions or other purposes. Without derivatives building for the future would be a much more uncertain process.

Viewed in the context of the scale and speed of endeavour, it is perhaps unsurprising that there have been hiccups along the way. An individual breaks a bank, another runs up positions and losses of almost unimaginable magnitude. Against this background supporters and detractors of derivatives have tended to polarise and hold very strong views. There is little neutral opinion to be found in the derivative narrative and, to some, derivatives will always be: *"the eleven-letter four-letter word"*.

The derivatives game today is as exciting and inventive as it has always been. It may have grown up but it is far from middle aged. Lessons have been learned and the structure and control of these markets have rendered repetition of some past misdemeanours less likely. But there will be further rogue episodes as clever and determined individuals will always find a way, even if their tactics and means of implementation are different.

A very healthy development has been the progressive falling away of the specialist's veil and mystique, as more and more people use derivatives and recognise their value and power. In the market place exchanges keep opening, consolidating and closing. The pace is also quickening as trading becomes more and more in keeping with an electronic and connected infrastructure. Technology has also had a huge influence on derivative growth as operational and valuation complexity can now be dealt with by a touch of a mouse or a dropdown menu. Processes that once were slow and administratively cumbersome now need no human intervention and are carried out swiftly at almost no cost.

Every derivative contract ends up being exercised, maturing or expiring. It was always my hope that I would be able to write the derivative story after the first two events but before the third.

Index